Membership Development

An Action Plan for Results

Susan,
Here's to
Membership Success!

Dana Hines

Best of luck
with all your
fundraising

Pat Rich

Aspen's Nonprofit Management Series

Extraordinary Board Leadership:
The Seven Keys to High-Impact Governance

Doug Eadie

Effective Nonprofit Management:
Essential Lessons for Executive Directors

Robert L. Lewis

Membership Development:
An Action Plan for Results

Patricia Rich
Dana Hines

Nonprofit Mergers: The Power of Successful Partnerships

Dan H. McCormick

Aspen's Nonprofit Management Series

Membership Development

An Action Plan for Results

Patricia Rich, ACFRE
President
Rich Associates
St. Louis, Missouri

Dana Hines
President and CEO
Membership Consultants
St. Louis, Missouri

AN ASPEN PUBLICATION®
Aspen Publishers, Inc.
Gaithersburg, Maryland
2002

Library of Congress Cataloging-in-Publication Data

Rich, Patricia.
Membership development : an action plan for results / Patricia Rich, Dana Hines.
p. cm.
Includes index.
ISBN 0-8342-1971-9
1. Nonprofit organizations—Management. 2. Fundraising. 3. Membership campaigns.
I. Hines, Dana. II. Title.

HD62.6 .R53 2002
658′.048—dc21
2002018474

Orders: (800) 638-8437
Customer Care: (800) 234-1660

Editorial Services: Christie M. Matlock
Library of Congress Catalog Card Number: 2002018474
ISBN: 0-8342-1971-9

Printed in the United States of America

1 2 3 4 5

Dedication

W E DEDICATE THIS BOOK TO EVERY-
one who works in membership in nonprofit
organizations. For many nonprofits, it is
the membership that is the heart and soul of
the organization. Having a strong membership program ensures that the organization
can accomplish its mission. We applaud the
staff and volunteers who strive to make
their programs the best that they can be
and, in turn, serve their communities.

Table of Contents

Foreword

I HAVE BEEN INVOLVED IN MEMBER-ship for many years, and I was thrilled to hear that, finally, there was going to be a book about our work. There has been very little written about membership and really nothing that tells a volunteer or staff person how to actually create, implement, and manage a membership program. I am going to make certain that all of my staff read this, and I'll recommend it to anyone who is at all involved in membership or wants to be.

This "primer" is a major addition to the field and will serve the many kinds of non-profits that have a membership base. It is wonderful to have in one place, at one time, all of the information needed to develop and maintain a membership program. The examples, the reports, the ideas will be as helpful to someone like me, who has many years of experience, as to someone who is new to the field.

I am delighted to be the first to thank the authors for their work. In institutions like mine, where the membership program is the basis for how we interact with the public, this book will be an invaluable tool to help us achieve our goals. We are here to serve the community. *Membership Development: An Action Plan for Results* will help us do that.

Roanne Katcher
Manager of Membership
High Museum of Art
Atlanta, Georgia

Preface

WE HAVE BEEN WORKING WITH ORganizations that have membership programs for much of the past 20 years. Many are museums, gardens, zoos, and other cultural institutions, but there have also been groups dealing with the environment, other public issues, hobbies, sports, volunteers, and health care. What we learned many years ago was that there was not a good resource for people given the responsibility of a membership program. We began holding seminars throughout the country on how to plan, design, implement, and manage these programs. For the seminars we wrote a workbook that forms the basis for this book.

This book is written as a resource for those who work with membership programs, supervise them, or who are considering starting one. The philosophy behind the book is that planning the program will ensure that the organization's needs are met. We believe that a thoughtful plan is the first step in implementing a program that will meet the needs of the institution, the community, and the members. With a plan, activities are cohesive, resources are well used, and goals are met. We believe that the membership program should be integral in achieving the institution's mission. To do that well, we believe that planning is the key.

When we began writing and mentioning to colleagues that our topic was membership, we contended with questions about the church group, the hospital auxiliary, and local volunteer associations. This was in addition to our fundamental work with cultural institutions. This led us to our decision to include information for all types of groups. As we started thinking about the various types of membership programs, it became clear that we needed a way to cope with the variety of groups. We decided to categorize them and developed a chart of types of membership programs. The many types are discussed in Chapter 1. The book has information that will be helpful to all membership programs, no matter their type. That said, however, there is more information in the book for membership programs that are the basis for fundraising for the institution. We do believe that for many nonprofits, the membership program should be an integrated part of the development effort.

The book gives the new membership person a thorough background on what is involved and how membership fits into a larger nonprofit organization or is the basis for the organization itself. The book gives the seasoned membership person new ideas and ways of looking at things. The book gives the organization considering a membership program the information it needs to plan and develop one that is appropriate for the institution. Everyone who is involved with a membership program will find new ideas as well as other relevant information.

Throughout the book we have taken the liberty of making recommendations about a number of practices that are currently in vogue in membership programs. These recommendations are the result of our experience with many different types of membership programs and how they fit into the organization's development and other efforts. Not everyone will agree, but until there is more academic research on this topic, we will stand by the recommendations, based on what we have experienced and the results we have seen. We hope that all membership staff, whether paid or volunteer, at least consider the suggestions. Too often we find practices in place because "we've always done it that way." Change is difficult, but as we all know, doing the things the same way will produce the same results. If different results are desired, then change must occur.

In much of what is involved in membership, there are multiple ways of doing things. The issue is to select the method that works for the specific organization. It is important to review the choices on a regular basis. Our fundamental belief is that the membership program must be very well planned, effectively executed, and continually evaluated. Without these steps, the program will be haphazard and reactive, rather than proactive. It will then not necessarily produce the results that are wanted and needed by the organization.

We believe that a membership program offers an effective way to develop a donor base and constituency for a nonprofit. The result is to grow the member's relationship with the nonprofit while at the same time growing the organization or institution. When the relationships are developed in a thoughtful, attentive, and conscientious manner, the organization will prosper, and its mission will be fulfilled.

Acknowledgments

WE DOUBT THAT ANYONE WRITES A book in a vacuum. We certainly couldn't and didn't. We thank many of our colleagues in the nonprofit sector who have been helpful during this process. They have been helpful in sending materials, providing information, and clarifying our thoughts. This book belongs as much to them as it does to us. It is our fondest hope, however, that this book will belong to everyone involved in membership in the nonprofit sector.

We thank Michael J. Rosen, CFRE, from Philadelphia, who provided the writing for the sections on telemarketing, ethics, and dues processing. A direct response and dues processing consultant with more than 20 years experience, he has been a good friend to us for many years, speaking on these issues at the Membership Consultants seminars, writing on them for other publications, and providing the information in other training situations. We thank Kathryn Rich, who provided all of the computer graphics for the book and did it carefully and cheerfully. It is a special pleasure for a mother to be able to work with her daughter.

Special thanks go to Richard Daley, President/CEO of the Arizona-Sonora Desert Museum, Agnes Garino, membership volunteer, and Ellen Livingston, retired fundraiser. Each read most of the entire book while in process and made the kinds of comments that are so important for clarifying information and making certain that relevant questions and topics are covered.

And thanks, too, to many in the membership and nonprofit world who answered questions and generously provided information during the past year while we were writing and researching. This list is in alphabetical order, mentioning only the affiliation of each; we could think of no other way to do it other than writing a short essay on what each contributed, which would have been yet another book. The colleagues include: Patty Arnold, Missouri Botanical Garden; Lynette Ballard, Unity Health; Lois Bliss, Friends of the Kirkwood Library; Donna Bruner, Missouri Historical Society; Dwight Burlingame, Indiana University, Center on Philanthropy; Barbara Dougherty, the Metropolitan Museum of Art; Beverly Duzik, Desert Botanical Garden; Aarik Eberhardt, Access Fund; Christy Fox, Opera Theatre of Saint Louis; Lisa Goin, Phyllis Noone, and Ginger Allingham, The Heard Museum and Guild; J. Hazen Graves, Faegre & Benson LLP; Sue Greenberg, St. Louis Volunteer Lawyers and Accountants for the Arts; Greg Harris, The National Baseball Hall of Fame and Museum; Cynthia Holter, Saint Louis Zoo; Roanne Katcher, The High Museum of Art; Marcia Kerz, The Oasis Institute, Sharon LeeMaster, The Alford Group; John McClusky, University of Missouri-St. Louis; Joanna Osborn and Walter Sczudlo, Association of Fundraising Professionals; Gerry Padberry and Phyllis Robb, The Art Institute of Chicago; Camille Pons, The Arizona-Sonora Desert Museum; Peter Ruger, Southern Illinois University; Margaret Skidmore, Museum of Fine Arts, Houston; Nancy Thompson, Thompson Consulting; Jim Weidman, the Saint Louis Art Museum; and Gloria White, ret. Washington University. This wonderful group gave us information ranging from legal issues to membership voting to by-laws to volunteer roles to African-American sororities and fraternities. We could not have had as complete a look at membership without the help of every one of them.

We also thank Laura Mayhew Albes, Alisa Gilliam, Misty McMullin, Deborah Nelson, Doris Plummer, Mae Soule, and Geri Stallman from the staff of Membership Consultants for their help on the book. Putting it all together, reports, charts, and graphs would not have been possible without them.

Last but not least, we acknowledge our families, friends, and colleagues, who have put up with our piles, our questions, and our lack of time for them while we were writing. We want all of them to know how much we appreciate their patience and good humor while we were typing away.

CHAPTER 1

The Meaning of Membership

Patricia Rich and Dana Hines

I don't want to belong to any club that will accept me as a member.

—Groucho Marx

FOREVER FORMING ASSOCIATIONS

GROUCHO WAS IN THE MINORITY. Wanting to belong is a very strong trait for most of us. We want to belong to a family, to a group of friends, to associations where we feel comfortable. From our schools to scouts to our church, we often want to join and be a part of a group. As Alexis de Tocqueville wrote in 1840 in *Democracy in America*, "Americans of all ages, all stations of life, and all types of disposition are forever forming associations. There are not only commercial and industrial associations in which all take part, but others of a thousand different types—religious, moral, serious, futile, very general and very limited, immensely large and very minute . . . . Nothing, in my view, more deserves attention than the intellectual and moral associations in America" (Tocqueville 1966, 485–488).

As Tocqueville says, associations come in many different types; in belonging to them we become members.

Just what is membership? Membership is a fluid concept, defined by each individual group. It can mean writing a check, providing volunteer service, professing faith, increasing self-development, advocating for an issue. It can mean one or all of these and more. Tocqueville's observation about "forever forming associations" is, perhaps, even truer today than in the 1830s, when he was visiting America. And as he says, the groups can be "religious, moral, serious, futile, very general and very limited, immensely large and very minute" (Tocqueville 1966, 485). While the landscape of membership programs still resembles Tocqueville's descriptions, the proliferation of groups to which we can belong has grown exponentially. For those who are working in membership programs, this provides ever increasing challenges. This book is a tool to deal with the challenges. It is a primer for anyone who is new to membership programs, interested in beginning one, or involved in changing one. Information is also included for those who work, as paid or volunteer staff, in all of the types of membership programs.

The astonishing growth has been seen in many types of membership programs. Cultural institution programs are expanding in numbers of members and in the services the programs provide. One can now be a member of the Metropolitan Museum of Art through the Internet and never personally enter the galleries. Public issue organizations have grown with their issues. AARP, "dedicated to shaping and enriching the experience of aging" (www.aarp.org), is now America's largest nonreligious membership organization with more than 30 million members. Environmental groups have grown along with public interest in conservation and endangered species. Organizations like the World Wildlife Fund are international. Individuals interested in a rare disease have found each other, exchanged information, and raised funds. Affinity groups are now available from A to Z— from the Azalea Society of America to the Z Car Club. If there is an interest, there is a group. This is just a sample of the explosion in membership programs.

The nature of what people want to belong to has also changed. This poses challenges for membership programs. Robert Putnam, in *Bowling Alone: The Collapse and Revival of American Community*, has chronicled what has happened to membership organizations across the country. Growth is occurring in organizations like AARP, environmental groups, and self-help groups like hobby clubs and book discussion groups. At the same time, he notes the loss of membership in many traditional organizations, such as parent-teacher associations (PTAs), labor unions, fraternal organizations such as the Lions and Elks, and in women's groups like the League of Women Voters and the Federation of Women's Clubs. Numbers of volunteers have also dropped in traditional groups like the Boy Scouts and the Red Cross (Putnam 2000, 48–64).

So what does this mean for membership programs? First, it is important to remember that people still want to belong to associations. Many membership programs are flourishing. Why do some flourish while others lose members? There are certainly external factors over which a membership program has no control. Putnam discusses women entering the workforce; urban sprawl; technology, which includes television, the VCR and, now, computers and the Internet; and, in particular, generational change (Putnam 2000, 277–284). The membership programs that will flourish are those that recognize what is happening in the world and how it affects them as well as those that understand their niche and appeal and how to reach people with similar values and interests.

This book is based on the concept that developing a plan of action for the membership program is the best way to ensure that the membership program will thrive. Developing a plan means that the organization takes a look at both the external and internal environments in which it exists, defines a clear purpose, and develops realistic goals. In doing this, the organization can determine where it wants to go and how to get there. A plan ensures that the program can meet the goals it has set and make wise use of resources in so doing. Planning is the essential step in the program effort, and the plan becomes a valuable tool in implementation.

A crucial point before beginning to plan is understanding the type of membership program involved, the characteristics of members who join, and the reasons why they join. When membership is mentioned, most people name a variety of associations to which they belong. Belonging to a church, a professional organization, a zoo, a country club, and the American Automobile Association (AAA) serves very different purposes. The reasons to join are different, the people who join are different, and the benefits involved are different. Even Tocqueville recognized this wide variety.

CRITERIA FOR TYPES OF PROGRAMS

The types of membership programs shown in Table 1–1 represent a systematic classification developed to make it easy to talk about the variety of programs in existence. The table clarifies the different types of membership programs by considering their characteristics including purpose, reasons to join, and criteria for membership. The membership program's type has a bearing on the program's design and structure. Knowing the type of program makes it easier to define the goals for membership. It is far easier to make choices about benefits, marketing, dues structure, events, and other issues involved in developing a successful program when the goals of the program are clear.

Purpose

Purpose is the primary reason for the membership program. If this reason didn't exist or has changed, the program would have to reinvent itself. All membership programs, in reality, have more than one purpose. It is important, however, to determine which purpose is the most important. If constituency is important, then a plan will concern itself with growth. If volunteer workers are most important, then the planning issue becomes finding members who have the time and interest for the institution, or changing the nature of the volunteer jobs to meet the needs of potential members. The issue is not just increasing numbers of members. In professional associations, the plan will reflect goals that lead to promoting the profession and developing benefits to encourage those in it to join.

Most programs will have multiple goals. Income for many will be an essential one. Income will come from dues and by integrating the membership program into the development efforts. Additional income will come from sales of a variety of products and services. If the programs did not bring in any income, would they exist? Yes and no. For some institutions the membership is a large part of the budget; for others, very small. For some, covering costs is enough; for others, generating large amounts of income is important. This, of course, must be taken into consideration

Table 1-1 Types of Membership Programs for Individuals

Characteristics		Program Type			
	Visitation	Public Issue	Participant	Volunteer	Faith-Based
• **Purpose**	Building a constituency	Building a constituency	Gain active participants	Attract volunteers for the organization	Gain participants and volunteers
• **Reason to Join**	Interest, good value	Support the cause	Self development	Be useful	Serve others in faith context
• **Criteria for Membership**	Interest	Interest	Time to participate	Time to volunteer	Belief in work of the faith
• **Dues Structure**	Graduated	Flat or graduated	Flat	Flat	Flat
Types of Organizations	Cultural institutions	Issue groups, public radio and television	Youth groups, civic groups, self-help groups	Auxiliaries, guilds, friends linked to an organization	Religious congregations and faith-based charities
• **Examples**	Indianapolis Children's Museum; Missouri Botanical Garden (St. Louis)	League of Women Voters; Mothers Against Drunk Driving (MADD); Wisconsin Public Television	Girl Scouts; Boy Scouts; Junior League; Rotary	Heard Museum Guild Organization (Phoenix); Barnes-Jewish St. Peters Hospital Auxiliary (St. Louis)	Knights of Columbus; United Methodist Women

Table 1-1 continued

The Meaning of Membership 5

Characteristics	Loyalty	Affinity	Professional	Social	Brand Loyalty
Purpose	Strengthen relationships	Promote interest in subject area	Promote the profession	Social ties	Retain customers
Reason to Join	Continue relationship	Education	Professional development	Social life and standing	Value
Criteria for Membership	Prior relationship	Interest	Professional requirements	Social relationships	Customer or client
Dues Structure	Flat	Flat	Flat or based on criteria	Flat	Often "free," dependent on being customer or client
Types of Organizations	Alumni associations; fraternities and sororities	Subject related clubs and organizations; book clubs	Professional associations and related groups	Golf, country and eating clubs	Credit card; frequent flyer
Examples	University of Michigan Alumni Association; Delta Sigma Theta; Veterans of Foreign Wars	Local garden club; local investment club; Z Car Club	Association of Fundraising Professionals (AFP); American Medical Association (AMA)	University clubs	American Express; Delta Sky Miles Program; American Automobile Association (AAA)

Program Type

with dues structuring, benefits, staffing, and other program issues.

Reason to Join

Above all, the prospective member must have an interest in the organization's mission and activities. If there is no interest in the mission, there is no reason for the person to join. There will be multiple reasons why people join, and it is important to know as many as possible; however, there is usually one reason that is the driving force. For visitation-based institutions, membership is a good value for the money spent when free or discounted admission is involved; in volunteer organizations, the member wants to make a difference, to be useful, or has friends involved. For some membership programs, such as those in cultural institutions, the reason to join may continue for a lifetime. In others, membership may be linked to another factor, as is the case with many professional organizations, where membership may end when the person retires. In addition, there will be people who join only because they believe in what the organization does—benefits or other incentives are irrelevant. Knowing these reasons becomes essential in order to position and market the program effectively.

Criteria for Membership

These are the criteria imposed by the institution in order for someone to join. Some criteria are strict requirements, as in professional associations where one must be employed in the profession. Participant-based organizations may have a time requirement. Loyalty organizations always have a prior experience that is a prerequisite in order to join. For example, to join an alumni association, one must have attended the school.

Dues Structure

This is a basic issue. Virtually all membership organizations have dues. There are a few that are free (the Z Car Club on the Internet), some ask for a small amount (AARP is $10 per year), and some, especially professional associations, require a large amount. There are some programs with a sliding scale, and this arrangement can occur on both ends of the spectrum. An organization that wants to attract a diverse membership might base its fee on what the person can afford or offer subsidies or scholarships for membership. A professional association that has income level as a criterion for membership would charge more as the person's income increases.

Dues have two main structures: flat dues are the same for everyone; graduated dues have different levels at which people can join. Another important issue relates to how dues are collected. Annual dues are collected once a year for the entire organization; anniversary dues are collected on the anniversary date of the member's enrollment. How dues are structured and collected is one of the first things that needs to be decided when beginning a program.

PROGRAM TYPES

The types of membership programs that are in existence defy easy definition. There are a variety of types and a variety of purposes for membership programs just as there are a variety of nonprofit institutions and organizations. Table 1–1 illustrates the multiplicity of these programs.

The actual name of the program type reflects the defining characteristic for the membership program. For example, "visitation-based" institutions are different from "public issue" organizations, even though both are developing constituencies. Having a place to visit is a defining characteristic that makes visitation-based institutions different from all others. While hospitals are places that can be visited, the membership programs (usually hospital auxiliaries) are not based on visitation, but rather on attracting volunteer workers. Knowing and understanding this defining characteristic is crucial in developing a membership program.

The defining characteristic is the main issue that affects a membership program; however, a program may change over time in any of the categories. Many membership programs could fit into more than one category. For example, a visitation-based institution might also take on public issues, have affinity groups, and use volunteer workers. The defining characteristic and its primary purpose are the first considerations when planning the membership program.

Visitation-Based Programs

A visitation-based program is one that is a part of or related to a museum, zoo, botanical garden, historic house, or other institution that attracts visitors. These institutions are interested in developing a constituency for attendance, contributed and earned income, education, community support, advocacy where appropriate, and volunteers. The membership program is often integrated with the institution's development program. The membership becomes the donor base for fundraising efforts. It also becomes the way the institution relates to its donors. There are no real criteria for membership, though members usually have an interest in the subject matter or events at the institution. Dues tend to be graduated and many join at the "basic" level because it is a good value, offering free or discounted admission.

These institutions tend to be local, although there are "stars" with national and international recognition. Those that are local will have, for the most part, a local membership. Those institutions that are well known are able to have nonresident membership programs as well as a local base. The Metropolitan Museum of Art and The Chicago Art Institute are in this category. With new technology, institutions with specialized collections are able to offer Web memberships with benefits suited to the online audience. The Metropolitan Museum of Art now does this.

The distinguishing characteristic of the visitation-based program is that there is a place to visit and, most often, a major member benefit relates to admission. With a membership, the admission is offered free, at a reduced cost, or for a certain number of visits. There are also visitation-based institutions that are free to the public. When this is the case, the admission benefit is related to special exhibits or theater presentations that have an admission charge; access to increased hours for admission; or free parking. The St. Louis Science Center, for example, has free admission, but tickets to the Omnimax® theater become an admission benefit.

The Smithsonian Institution, comprised of numerous museums, including the National Zoo, has both a local and national membership program, even though all of the museums and the zoo are free to the public. The major benefit is its publication, *Smithsonian Magazine*, which is another way for institutions with free admission to offer a desirable benefit. In addition, many of the separate museums and the zoo each have a membership program, with its own list of benefits.

For visitation-based institutions where there is no fundraising, such as those supported by public funds or an endowment, membership is still a desirable program in order to develop a constituency and find volunteers. There are very few institutions in the United States that currently do no fundraising at all. Of those that are heavily supported by public or endowment funds, many have also found a need to raise private funds as a supplement for operations or for special exhibits and programs. The National Zoo, for example, on its Web site (www.fonz.org), asks members to help "fund new exhibits and improvements to old exhibits."

Public Issue Programs

Organizations that are formed around issues often offer membership programs. The major purpose in this case is to develop a constituency. These programs are centered on one or several related public issues. Groups devoted to a neighborhood issue, the environment, women's issues, senior issues, education, and so forth, are all a part of this category. Members join because they want to make a difference in the local, regional, national, or international community. For those who are active in the organization, there is the added benefit of working with like-minded people. The organization's prerequisite is that a member is interested in the issue, and it is hoped that the member will help work on it. Some of these organizations have enormous political clout because of the number of members and the members' level of activity. AARP and the National Rifle Association (NRA) are organizations that have used their numbers to press their case.

The members may be called upon to help educate the public, the media, legislators, and government officials about the issue and all of its ramifications. For example, Mothers

Against Drunk Driving (MADD) has as its mission "to stop drunk driving, support the victims of this violent crime, and prevent underage drinking" (www.madd.org). There may also be other programs associated with the organization's mission, such as MADD's support services for victims of impaired driving, public awareness campaigns, and a variety of youth programs. These groups can be local, regional, national, or international. Some, like MADD, are national with local chapters.

Many members are happy to write a check to support the work of others because they do not have the time to help on a sustained basis. Putnam's interest in *Bowling Alone* is in the amount of social capital created by organizations. Social capital is—on a very basic level—the connectedness between and among people and the community. For example, the League of Women Voters (the League), a group that is organized on a grass-roots level with face-to-face meetings, discussion, and volunteer service, adds much to social capital, while Greenpeace members need only write the check. It is the public issue groups that do not require social capital that are showing enormous increases in membership, while groups like the League have been losing members during the past three decades (Putnam 2000, 155–156).

While both of these organizations clearly focus on public interest issues, how they approach the issues is very different. In planning for their varied futures, they must take into consideration what is happening in the world around them.

Participant Programs

For some programs, active participation is a condition of membership. These programs want the member's time and efforts. In fact, that is the prerequisite for joining and remaining a member. Scout organizations, for example, expect that their members will be active scouts; otherwise, there is no reason to join. Rotary International looks for members who are "willing to help and participate in projects" (www.rotary.org). Junior Leagues and service leagues also often have a participation requirement. The reason to join these programs is to participate in the organization's projects. This participation may include self-development, a chance to give back to the community, and a way to meet new people and network.

These programs will also develop a constituency, raise funds, and educate their members, but participation is the main purpose of membership and the reason to belong. Dues vary from very little money (e.g., $5 annually) to significantly high dues (e.g., several hundred dollars annually) and are often flat. Many of these groups will also have fundraising activities and expect members to support them.

Volunteer Programs

Much like participant-based programs, volunteer programs expect a level of personal involvement. The difference is that these organizations exist to serve the aims of a larger institution or organization rather than their own. The involvement is in service to the institution to which the organization is attached. The many varieties of volunteer programs are discussed in Chapter 10.

The organization and the volunteer group may work together to decide which projects the group will undertake and which volunteer positions its members will fill. The hospital auxiliary that runs the gift shop, the opera guild that raises funds, and the theater backers who provide actors with meals are all examples of these programs.

Dues are usually modest though many require that the participant first be a member of the institution itself. Time is always a requirement.

Faith-based Programs

More than anything else, people join religious organizations (Putnam 2000, Chapter 4). These are places of worship as well as related organizations. Belief in the work of the faith (not necessarily the faith itself) is the requirement for membership. With their diverse programming, religious organizations offer many choices for their members. Religious organizations provide options over the entire range of membership programs. There are religious programs that are active locally, regionally, nationally, and internationally.

Belonging to a faith-based institution may include dues and other fundraising activities. For some, the concept of tithing is an integral part of the financial obligation; for others, a simple dues commitment; and for yet others, belief is enough. For as long as the American Association of Fund Raising Consultants (AAFRC) has been charting philanthropic donations, giving to faith-based institutions has always been the largest segment, ranging from over 40 percent to more than half of all philanthropic donations.

Virtually every religious institution has a core of workers, those for whom faith is translated into volunteer service. For some of these institutions, this volunteer commitment is a requirement. Some of these institutions also have membership programs within their structure, such as a Jewish temple's sisterhood, a group of women from the congregation, or a men's club that conducts activities of particular interest to the congregation's men. Many of these organizations also take on community issues, providing food pantries, homeless shelters, and programs to alleviate addictions. The Salvation Army is certainly one of the best known for community volunteer work and it is important to remember that it is a faith-based membership organization with many of its activities run by the officers of the Army.

Faith-based institutions also become involved in public policy issues in a variety of ways. Some of the most contentious issues in our society (pro-choice vs. pro-life; prayer in school) are based on belief. There are institutions on all sides of such issues, and they often call on their membership to help make their feelings known.

Loyalty Programs

"Once a member, always a member" might be the motto of these organizations. Alumni groups of all sorts fit into this category. All levels of education now have alumni groups, from elementary school through graduate and professional training. Other loyalty groups include sororities and fraternities, Veterans of Foreign Wars, and any other organization for which the membership requirement is having been a past member or participant. The purpose of these programs is to stay in touch with the members and keep the relationship between the member and the organization vital and strong. With our mobile population, members may live anywhere in the world. Fundraising is one of the reasons to keep effective ties, but the need for a constituency is also important for the times when issues arise. In alumni associations, the alumni program itself often does not include the fundraising campaigns, but the closer the alumni feel toward the school because of alumni association information and activi-

ties, the easier the fundraising calls will be for the development department. Dues for loyalty programs tend to be flat, with other fundraising done in a variety of ways.

The eight African American sororities and fraternities that comprise their national and local Pan-Hellenic councils are a particularly good example of this type of program. The groups were initially undergraduate chapters, but the ties were so strong that graduate chapters of each have been formed. The relationships resemble those of family, and the ties that bind the members to these organizations are deeply rooted in the African American culture and tradition. Once a member, always a member until death, whether actively involved or not.

Affinity Programs

If there is an interest, there is a group. Rather than having an issue as the major focus, these membership programs are formed around a subject. People join these groups to further their interest and education in the subject, whatever it might be. This is an opportunity to meet people with the same interests and to participate in activities with them. Membership appeals to those who have an interest in the subject matter. The groups range from the Azalea Society of America to local ski groups to book clubs to the Z Car Clubs (all about Datsun/Nissan Z-cars) around the world.

The requirement for membership in these groups is an interest and usually a small membership fee to cover the cost of mailings and meetings, and not a lot more. Members come and go depending on their level of interest in the subject. There may be attendant issues that the group becomes involved in, and there may be some fundraising, but it's that interest in the subject that is at the heart of the membership. Some of these organizations are now beginning to "meet" on the Internet, though most continue to meet in person, produce publications, and hold events. There is often no need for other fundraising; events tend to be self-supporting.

Professional Associations

Just as there is a club for every interest group, there is an association for every profession—and then some. The criteria for membership in a professional association are set by each organization. They may include educational criteria as well as actually holding a position in a particular field. Advancing the profession is the foundation for these organizations, but they also have a multitude of other activities. Professional education is usually essential, ethics for the profession are frequently developed, and advocacy for the profession and related issues is often important. Members join for the educational activities, networking within the profession, and, in general, to be a part of how the profession develops. Unions are another type of professional association with differences that may include job-related mandatory membership with the benefit of being represented in bargaining.

There are also groups in this category that are subsets or multidisciplinary. For example, there are major associations such as the American Medical Association, and then subsets that focus on specialization within the field (American Academy of Family Physicians) or on cross-disciplinary interests (American Medical Women's Association). In addition, there are local groups defined by position that would fall into this category, such as a local group of women in business or consultants.

Social Organizations

On a very personal level, many people want to join social groups—golf clubs, luncheon clubs, and other "elite" groups. These groups need members in order to continue, and they provide, for the member, a sense of belonging, status, and prestige, and, often, networking opportunities for social, business, and community involvement. The membership core usually focuses on business relationships (often the luncheon clubs) or on social relationships (the country and golf clubs). Many of the luncheon clubs offer programming of interest to spouses, couples or families, and the social clubs will have similar events.

Typically these organizations have a membership procedure and often require a new member to be sponsored by other members. When these organizations see a drop in membership, they react much as any membership program, by developing acquisition and retention strategies that are appropriate to them. Dues and other financial requirements make some of these memberships the most expensive of the membership programs. Monies given to these organizations are not tax deductible.

Brand Loyalty

The interest in and compelling nature of the concept of membership is also used in the world of commerce. With the idea of membership well accepted among a variety of institutions, the notion has also been used by the for-profit sector, particularly as a marketing device. The American Express card tells its owner that he or she has been a "member since" the card's acquisition date. All of the airline frequent flyer programs call their customers "members." The AAA (American Automobile Association) began as a nonprofit and "represented the interests of motorists and other travelers" (www.aaamissouri.com). It is still a nonprofit, but now perhaps best known for its member services of emergency road service, along with insurance, travel, and financial services, and numerous other related activities, including its sponsorship of school safety patrols.

Many of these groups have events for members, newsletters, Web sites, and a great number of the trappings of a traditional nonprofit membership program. For the most part, the brand loyalty membership programs are free, though open only to clients and customers of the company involved. These programs are, above all, testimony to strength of the notion of membership.

THE ROLE OF INCOME

While building a constituency, promoting professions and interests, finding volunteers and participants, and keeping relationships are the primary purposes of the membership programs, the one issue that all programs grapple with is that of income. For many of the organizations, income is the significant reason to have the membership program. A membership program should be designed to earn income for the organization. An institution should not subsidize a membership program. Of course, there are exceptions. One exception would be organizations like the scouts, where the membership fee is minimal for the children, and various and additional kinds of fundraising support the activities.

For the most part, however, the dues should, at a minimum, fully cover expenses. This is true for many affinity groups for whom out-of-pocket expenditures are really the only funds spent. It is also true for some of the volunteer groups, such as hospital

auxiliaries with very small, token dues and for some arts institution guilds where the member must first be a member of the organization and then pay an extra fee to belong to the guild. For most other organizations, funds come to the institution through dues; using the membership as the donor base for fundraising; offering products; providing food service options; using the membership base as an incentive for sponsorships and advertising; and by members raising money for the institution through events and other fundraisers.

Income is an integral component of membership programs. Deciding the role that it plays in any one program is an important decision before planning or changing the program.

Dues

Membership dues will range from a major portion to a very small part of the institution's budget, depending on the size of the overall budget, the amount of the dues, and the number of members. But in almost all organizations, this funding is important. In addition to its potential size, membership money is important because it is unrestricted, funds that can be used where the need is greatest in the institution. More importantly, with a well-run membership program, renewals bring in money annually. The lifetime giving of a member can be substantial. Because this funding is annual, it is also predictable and, thus, an excellent source of the base of a funding program.

Dues can be large or small, graduated or flat. For most programs, it is important for the dues to cover the cost of the membership along with extra funding for the institution. For some large, regional or national organizations, the important issue is to gather significant numbers of members. For example, a national organization might have dues that are minimal, but the number of members is so large that the program works. Consider AARP with $10 dues and more than 30 million members. The organization might also offer products, sell advertising in a magazine, and have other means for raising funds. Other organizations have dues that begin at a high level, preferring to use the donor club model, focusing on, perhaps, fewer members, but those members give much larger amounts of money. Whichever financial model is used, it needs to reflect what the organization needs and wants. No matter the model, the organization does need, at a minimum, to break even, and, in most cases, bring income into the institution.

Graduated dues are those that offer levels of membership, each level with additional benefits. Graduated dues are important if fundraising is an essential part of the membership program. With graduated dues, an organization can upgrade members, eventually turning some of the members into major donors. Flat dues are often used in organizations that want volunteers and participation. The membership base is then used to solicit additional funds. The purpose in these organizations is the participation.

Development

The membership is the donor base for many institutions with membership programs. This base can be used for numerous other development programs. The possibilities include a second annual gift, special project giving, major and capital gifts, and planned giving. This is discussed in detail in Chapter 3.

Marketing

The membership base becomes the database for direct marketing. The institution can market directly for attendance at new exhibits, education programs, and lectures; for sales in the gift shop; earned income projects; special events; and a variety of other opportunities. Having the database for a direct marketing program is also very appealing to some corporate sponsors who are interested in marketing their products to the organization's members.

Earned Income

Offering products to members is another way to increase income. In institutions with visitation, there is the possibility of gift shops and food service. For all organizations, there is a variety of possibilities ranging from logo merchandise to insurance products to affinity credit cards (credit cards marketed through the organization with the organization's logo) to publications. Not all members will be interested, but if the member base is sufficiently large, enough of the members will have an interest to make the offer worthwhile for both the member and the organization.

It is important for an institution that charges admission to understand that as the membership grows there may be an adverse effect on income from the turnstile. This is due to a frequent visitor becoming a member and no longer paying admission. However, the ongoing renewal, upgrading, other fundraising activities and earned income generated often bring more to the institution than admission alone. In addition, with the membership program, some who join never visit the institution, but join to show support for the work that is being done.

Additional Memberships

The membership is the group to solicit for additional memberships. This is particularly appropriate for institutions with visitation or widespread popular appeal. There are a variety of memberships that can be offered. Gift memberships, especially for the holidays, are popular. Gift memberships at other times during the year can also be made available. For example, these memberships are popular for gift-giving times such as Mother's and Father's Days, Administrative Assistant's Week (formerly Secretary's Day), and Valentine's Day. Depending on the organization, other times might also be suitable.

Corporate Sponsorships

To secure sponsorship funding, a corporation is often interested in an organization's demographic profile. Who visits? Who is a member? The demographic profile is the information about the age, income, residency, and other such traits of the membership. A large membership with a demographic profile that matches the corporation's target audience can be helpful when recruiting sponsors for programs, projects, and exhibits.

THE APPEAL OF MEMBERSHIP

Who Joins?

A joiner is not a joiner is not a joiner. Different kinds of people join different kinds of membership programs for different kinds of reasons. A 1986 study by J. Allen Williams Jr. and Suzanne T. Ortega, "The Multidimensionality of Joining," tackles the question of whether or not "the generally established social and demographic predictors of membership have equal relevance for all types of voluntary associations" (Williams and Ortega 1986, 35). The study focused on five types of organizations: those that are called on our table of types of membership programs faith-based, professional, affinity, issue, and a combination of participant + volunteer (see Table 1–1). (Their terms are "church related, job-related, recreational, fraternal/service, and civic/political" [Williams and Ortega 1986, 37]. They used nine variables to analyze: "education, race, gender, age, marital status, whether the respondent is a household head, number of children under 18 residing at home, size of community and region" (Williams and Ortega 1986, 37).

The results are interesting: only "race and education were found to be significantly related to all five" (Williams and Ortega 1986, 42). "It can be seen that for all organizational types, the higher the level of education, the greater the likelihood of belonging" (Williams and Ortega 1986, 38). The proportion of African Americans joining all five types of groups was higher than the rate of whites. Putnam corroborates this: "...racial differences in associational membership are not large. At least until the 1980's, controlling for educational and income differences, blacks belonged to more associations on average than whites, essentially because they were more likely than comparably situated whites to belong to both religious and ethnic organizations and no less likely to belong to any other type of group" (Putnam 2000, 280). In conclusion Williams and Ortega write, "The findings that only two of the nine independent variables examined here are significantly related to all five types of associations strongly suggests that joining is multidimensional" (Williams and Ortega 1986, 41).

Williams and Ortega did not include membership in museums and other related institutions. A 1994 study of a major art museum, "Membership in Museums: A Study of Customers of Cultural Non-profit Institutions," by C. Bhattacharya, M.A. Glynn, and H. Rao, profiles the museum membership as having a high level of education and income, more female, and predominantly Caucasian. "In general, the demographic characteristics of our sample—educated, upper-middle class professionals—were fairly consistent with those reported in studies of arts consumers" (Bhattacharya, Glynn, and Rao 1994, 413). In fact, work with member surveys by Membership Consultants corroborates this demographic, as do visitor surveys conducted by New Venture Research, a cultural institution/performing arts market research firm.

These studies clearly show one thing: the only variable that tends to cover all membership programs is education. Other than that, the characteristics that define one organization's members and those that define another's can be very different. While characteristics are different across membership types, there are similarities within types. The person who joins one museum may well join another; the person who joins an environmental group may well join another; the person who volunteers at one activity in the community may volunteer at another. This is very important to remember when selecting a target market for potential members. Familiarity does not breed contempt; it breeds more members.

Motivations for Joining

Why do people want to become members? Just as the Williams and Ortega study results "strongly suggest" (Williams and Ortega 1986, 41) that the characteristics of joiners are very different, so are their motivations for joining. There are two sets of benefits

that motivate and appeal to members: tangible and intangible. The tangible ones are those that are physical or real, many of which have a financial implication. The intangible benefits are those feelings that a member gets from belonging to the organization.

Tangible Benefits

The tangible benefits include everything from a membership card to a discount in a shop to free admission to an invitation to a lecture. They include receiving publications, the ability to buy insurance and secure football tickets. They include the mug or tote bag that is offered as an incentive to join. Virtually all membership programs include tangible benefits. But we also know that, in many cases, the tangible benefits do not equal the amount of money paid for the membership.

In fact, the study by Bhattacharya, Glynn, and Rao found that, at least at one major museum, "In describing their visiting behavior, nearly all (90 percent) of the respondents had visited the museum at least once in the last twelve months; however, less than one-fifth (19.2 percent) visited 6 or more times, the approximate point at which the member begins to realize economic gains from the free admission benefit of membership" (Bhattacharya, Glynn, and Rao 1994, 414). While it is not at all scientific to generalize from one study, anecdotal information supports this. There is a small core group of members who will visit frequently; most will not come enough times to realize the economic advantage. Additionally, there are large memberships at visitation-based institutions where there is no admission fee at all.

Intangible Benefits

What are the intangible benefits that motivate people to join? There are many. The basic motivation for many may be the idea of belonging, particularly to those organizations that we believe are doing something meaningful. In beginning psychology, most of us learned about Abraham Maslow's theory of motivation, described in his book, *Motivation and Personality*. He portrays people as having five levels of needs that are fulfilled in a hierarchical order. The first two levels describe the need for basic survival efforts: food, water, safety, and shelter. But the third level has to do with belonging. Belonging is a very strong sense for people, including the needs for acceptance, relationships, and being a part of a group. The last two levels deal with esteem and fulfilling one's potential. Many membership organizations provide the activities and forum for a member to receive respect and admiration, and provide challenges for members to, as Maslow says, "reach their potential" (Maslow 1954, 35–48).

Members, however, rarely describe why they want to combine into associations in these terms. When a member is asked why he or she joined a group, the tangible benefits and those that relate to family, community, personal interests, and supporting a worthwhile organization are the ones that are cited. While members rarely speak in terms like Maslow's, those programs that make members feel like they belong, they are valued, and that their membership makes a difference are the ones that are very successful. A membership brochure from the Chicago Botanical Garden quotes a long-time member as saying, "This is my garden. I have a sense of belonging…"

Reasons People Give for Joining

There are a number of reasons that people give for joining an organization. It is important to know how people feel about joining a

group because when a group can meet significant needs, those needs become the important issues in marketing the program. For example, members of a program may believe that having a membership is a good value, a way to meet new people, a network for business, or an educational opportunity. Those beliefs, in turn, can be used in marketing the program to potential members. How to discover what members of a particular program value is discussed in Chapter 9.

Value

For members, particularly of visitation-based institutions, value is the initial motivation to join. Members who join at the basic levels of these institutions are "value members." These are members who are interested in benefits such as free or discounted admissions, free or reduced parking, and other discounts. As discussed earlier, many of these members do not pass the economic point of paying for their membership with use. These benefits, however, are important because they are the starting point for the member to become involved in the organization.

Pursuing a Personal Interest

All of the membership programs have some basis in a personal interest. Whether it is a hobby, the environment, our faith, or our career, the membership organizations that relate to our interests have appeal. The organization that makes members feel like they belong and provides a way to satisfy these personal interests will be able to hold on to its members. The level of interest will vary among members. The successful organization will have a set of programs and information for those with a casual interest in the subject matter and another for those for who are interested in depth. For gardeners, for example, members of NGC

(National Garden Clubs) may learn the basics of flower arranging and horticulture, may avail themselves of educational opportunities in the schools sponsored by NGC, and are able to meet other gardeners, to exchange ideas.

When the members lose interest, the membership tends to disappear. To keep the interest high, it is incumbent on the membership program to provide programs and information in a format and on an interest level that is appealing. The membership program cannot afford to become stagnant. With visitation-based institutions, this manifests itself in having new programs, new exhibits, new attractions. The museum that is the museum with nothing added will soon lose its appeal. Public issue organizations need to stay on top of the most recent and the most relevant information, legislation, and regulations in their area. The same is true in professional associations.

Making a Difference

Members with this inclination want to provide direct service to another individual, or volunteer for or create support groups that make a difference in others' lives or for society. These members feel good about what they are doing and have a real sense of self-satisfaction. Many types of membership programs offer these opportunities. In a professional association, an experienced member might be a mentor to a new professional; in a faith-based organization, a member may be involved in services for the poor; and in a volunteer organization, a member might give direct service through a hospital auxiliary. Many join public issue groups because they believe that their membership will support work that will make a difference for the issue at hand, such as better government, the environment, or health care. The challenge for these organizations is to make sure that their members know that they are making a difference, whether through volunteer work or support for the cause.

Giving Back

For some, joining a group by making contributions of time and money is a way of giving back to an institution or to the community. Belonging to an arts or cultural organization, because it is important for the community to have these facilities, fulfills this need. This may well be the reason behind longtime memberships in visitation-based organizations, where the members do not join just for the economic value. On a more personal level, a member of a hospital auxiliary may have joined as a way of giving back because a family member received exceptional care when ill.

Many join alumni associations or keep active with their fraternities and sororities because they feel that the education, the relationships, and the networking that they have gained from that prior experience is worth supporting. While contributions to faith-based institutions are always the largest segment of gifts given during a year, gifts to educational institutions are the next largest (Kaplan 2000, 23). People feel very strongly about the important role of education in their lives and want to give back. And, as discussed in the work by Williams and Ortega, as well as by Putnam, education is the one predictor of joining. This accounts for, at least in part, the strength of alumni programs of all kinds.

Pride

Many people want to be associated with what they consider a worthwhile organization. People join civic organizations and cultural institutions to show pride in their community. Rotarians wear their lapel pins as a sign of pride in their organization. Many alumni are proud of the schools they attended and join the alumni association. Members of hobby clubs who are proud of their particular interest or craft are willing to work in their organization to continue the programs. Most of all, members in participant and volunteer organizations who contribute their valuable time are very proud of what they and their organizations do. Pride is one of the factors that encourages their participation and is why they are stalwart supporters.

Being with Similar People

The relationship, faith-based, professional, and social organizations all provide the member with a group with which he or she will be comfortable. With a common bond, whether it is experience, faith, profession, or lifestyle, the members immediately feel a sense of belonging. One of the attractions to join a social organization is the sense of belonging that the organization confers. All of the relationship programs are based on this premise. Veterans' groups provide a place for people who have shared similar experiences. This can be a very strong stimulus for membership. Family and friends have not gone through the same experience and can't discuss it in the same way that another soldier can.

Networking

Although some consider networking to be an overused term, there is no doubt that many membership organizations offer the potential for the members to network. Networking is defined as "the exchange of ideas and information among people who share interests and causes" (NSFRE 1996, 120). It is particularly important in professional associations and in affinity groups for serious hobbyists. In professional asso-

ciations, networking is often cited as a member benefit by the association and a reason for joining by members. Rotary clubs offer "a network of people who can help you become more successful in business" (NSFRE 1996, 120). In both groups, the offer of an organization in which to share information, acquire education, and develop a network of colleagues with the same interest is of great value. Of course, there is some networking in all groups. Many join social clubs, business-related organizations, and similar groups to be in a place where networking may set the stage for working together.

Status and Prestige

Rarely admitted, but certainly an important motivation, is status and prestige. Some organizations confer status and prestige because other important people are involved. This is particularly true for some educational and cultural institutions. It is certainly also true for social clubs (country clubs, luncheon clubs), for those organizations for which a level of accomplishment is a necessary prerequisite (exclusive professional groups), and for those groups for which a certain position is a necessary prerequisite (civic groups based on position in employment). Often endorsements or recommendations are necessary in order to be considered for membership for these organizations. There is also status and prestige in relationship organizations, particularly when the school, sorority, fraternity, or other organization is considered a status organization.

SUMMARY

The meaning of membership is different for each member, for each organization. This can be seen in the multidimensionality of types of programs, the members they attract, and the members' motivations for joining. All of these differences underscore the individuality and unique bases for individual membership programs. There are, however, commonalities among the decisions that need to be made in planning, structuring, and implementing a membership program. The meaning of membership is defined by how the organization or institution develops its program.

REFERENCES

Bhattacharya, C., M. A. Glynn, and H. Rao. 1994. Membership in museums: A study of customers of cultural non-profit institutions. *Conference Proceedings of ARNOVA*, Session H8, October, 413–414.

Kaplan, A. E. (Ed.). 2000. *Giving USA 2000.* Indianapolis, IN: AAFRC Trust for Philanthropy.

Maslow, A. H. 1954, 1970. *Motivation and personality.* New York: Harper & Row.

National Society of Fund Raising Executives. 1996. *The NSFRE fundraising dictionary.* New York: John Wiley & Sons.

Putnam, R. D. 2000. *Bowling alone: The collapse and revival of american community.* New York: Simon & Schuster.

Tocqueville, A. 1966. *Democracy in America.* (G. Lawrence Ed. and Trans.) New York: Harper & Row.

Williams, J. A., Jr., and S. T. Ortega. 1986. The Multidimensionality of joining. *Journal of Voluntary Action Research 15*, no. 4: 35–43.

CHAPTER 2

Planning for Membership

Patricia Rich and Dana Hines

Phil Rizzuto: "Hey, Yogi, I think we're lost."
Yogi Berra: "Ya, but we're making great time."

PLANNING AS THE FOUNDATION

THE BASIS FOR A NONPROFIT ORGA-nization is its mission. The mission statement defines why the nonprofit exists. The organization's plan is its map of activities for fulfilling that mission. Without a plan, the organization may or may not reach its goals—how will it know? And will the goals fulfill the mission? Planning is a systematic way to make certain that the organization's goals are relevant to the mission, and that its various activities will accomplish the goals.

For membership programs that are their own organization and not part of a larger institution, there is a need to develop a plan for the organization with membership as an integral part. For the membership program that is a part of a larger institution, the membership should be designed to fit into the larger overall institutional plan and to help fulfill the organization's mission. The membership program is one of the major outreach programs of an institution and endows the organization with a base of people who can become involved and invested. Even in an institution that does not have a plan, planning for the membership program is still advised and will be helpful to all involved.

Planning is the basic first step in developing a membership program. Peter Drucker, the management guru who is credited with inventing the concept of management (Beatty 1998, 101), says, " . . . for the non-profit organization . . . you need four things. You need a plan. You need marketing. You need people. And you need money" (Drucker 1990, 53). All four are as important for the membership program as they are for the organization as a whole. And the plan is first. The other three are covered later in this book. Why bother to spend the time to plan? As Yogi says, you may be making great time, but may be lost doing it. For Drucker, the plan leads a non-profit into "converting good intentions into results" (Drucker 1990, 53). There are clear organizational reasons to plan.

First, it gives the membership program a way to deal with limited resources. No matter the size of the membership program, there is never enough time, staff, volunteers, or money to do everything. Planning gives a way to allocate all of the resources in a rational manner. The membership program is made up of diverse parts—acquisition, renewal, programming, benefits, and more. Where should the money be spent? How much staff and volunteer time should be spent on each area? Unless there is a cohesive plan, the squeakiest component will get the oil. Having the plan gives staff and volunteers the reason to say "no" to projects that would use resources and take the program in a nonproductive direction.

Second, planning gives everyone involved in the program a unified vision of the future, and the whys and hows of the effort. This becomes the basis for cohesive-

ness in implementing the program; everyone understands what is happening. In the work life of most people who are involved in membership, the tasks that need to be completed can be overwhelming. Juggling the varied duties of a program's facets gives little time for reflection or vision on a daily basis. Having planning as a project that must be done, gives those involved permission to spend time on thinking about the future and what needs to be accomplished. It also gives everyone involved the opportunity to understand the direction of the program, the desired results, and the reasons for myriad tasks. The planning helps everyone to be "on the same page."

Third, the plan is also a communications tool both internally and externally. Planning offers the opportunity to include others in the organization who have an impact on membership in the planning process. When the plan is complete it can be shared with everyone, so they understand the direction of membership. When all parts of the organization plan are complete, it allows everyone to see how his or her piece of the puzzle supports the whole, reduces isolation among those working in the institution, and brings about the feeling of everyone working together. The plan communicates the organization's direction to all of the external audiences for the organization such as volunteers, board members, and other related groups.

Fourth, using the plan as a base, there is a sense of accomplishment for everyone involved as the work is completed. Membership staff need to know that they are making progress, that projects are moving in the right direction. Having measurable steps along the way gives this guidance and that sense of accomplishment felt when a task has been completed. For supervisory personnel, goals and objectives are one way that employee performance can be measured. Was the work in the plan accomplished? Were goals and objectives met? Having a basis on which to consider these questions is important.

Along with completion, the plan provides a method to evaluate the work. If the goal for the membership program is "to have a successful program," everyone will have a different idea of what success looks like. During planning, it is essential to reach agreement on questions like: How many new members equal successful acquisition? During the evaluation time, the question becomes: Did we meet our goal? The same is true for each part of the program. Successful projects can be celebrated and repeated. Those that were not as successful can be changed. As someone once said, repeating things that don't work will bring the same results. Having measures in the plan provide a way to know how successful, or not, the program and its projects are.

Last, but not least, is the message the plan sends to the entire organization that the membership program is well run and thoughtfully managed. If the membership is the entire organization (as in a hospital auxiliary), this is critical. Without members there is no program. For those programs that are losing members, strategies for acquisition and for retention need to be evaluated frequently. This includes all of the parts of the membership program as discussed in Chapter 4. For an objective evaluation, there is no better basis than having a good plan.

For the membership department in a large organization, sending the message about good management is also crucial. The program needs to have respect if it is to attract increased resources, be seen as an important part of community outreach, and understood as a means for furthering the organization's mission. Having a plan and meeting its goals and objectives is one of the ways to do this.

Having a plan is also a message for external constituents. A plan can increase the possibility of finding funding for membership program activities. There are sometimes funders who are willing to help a local membership program, understanding that it is the basis for the organization's fundraising programs. This may happen on the national level as well. Funders are almost always interested in seeing plans before committing funds. In addition, organizations that are working to become accredited in their field may need plans for all of their activities, including membership. The plan is a clear signal that the program is being conducted in a professional manner.

THE PLANNING PROCESS

Strategic, Long-Range, and Operational Planning

When people talk about planning, it is first important to distinguish between the different terms. Do not become distressed over the terms. *Strategic* and *long-range* are terms that are often used interchangeably. The terminology is not as important as what needs to be accomplished.

Long-range planning takes current activities and plans for them into the future. There may be some change in what is done, but actions are predicated on "existing conditions" (National Society of Fund Raising Executives 1996, 105). Long-range planning tends to be more of the same, taken into the future. If the membership program is working well for the organization, with no major issues at hand, putting this framework around planning is appropriate.

Strategic planning takes a deliberate look at the environment and the impact it may have on the program. If the planning group for a membership program understands that business as usual will bring the same results and that isn't what the group wants, then strategic planning is desirable. Strategic planning may result in major changes in direction, in approach, or in desired results. For example, a membership program that has reached a plateau and isn't growing, when growth is desirable, will want to make its planning strategic in nature.

Operational planning is developing the work plan for the year. It is derived from the long-range or the strategic plan. This is the plan that details the objectives and action plans that everyone follows to make certain that the tasks are accomplished. There should be an operational plan every year. This is the plan on which the budget and the work calendar are based.

Management by Objective

There are many planning methods, systems, and strategies. Any method will work as long as it is followed. The method suggested here is easy to use and based on "management by objective" (MBO), which was first described by Peter Drucker (Drucker 1954, Chapter 7). His management concept is that a plan will have objectives by which performance is measured. Objectives flow from the goals. In a nonprofit, all of this derives from and serves the mission of the organization. The issue is to have a way to ensure that good intentions are converted into results. If a different method is used, make certain that there are parts of the plan that are measurable, so that evaluation can take place.

MBO, as we apply it to a membership program, begins with the mission of the organi-zation, followed by the purpose for the program, goals to achieve the purpose, objectives designed to bring about the goals, and action plans that include all the activities to support the objectives. This is graphically presented in Figure 2–1, Management by Objective. The planning process itself involves discussion of the purpose, goals, objectives, and action plans and committing the plan to paper. The document, particularly the objectives and action plans (e.g., operational plan), becomes the basis for the budget and the yearly calendar. It provides the objectives against which the work is measured. In order to develop the plan, it is first necessary to organize for the planning process.

The process presented here is a general outline for actually doing the planning for a membership program. It is important to organize the facets of the planning before beginning, so that the process moves along smoothly and in a timely manner. There are a number of decisions about the planning process that need to be made before starting.

Length of Time

How long should planning take? There is no absolute answer to this question. Because of the time needed to discuss and come to decisions about strategy, strategic planning will take more time than long-range planning. In strategic planning, time is also spent on detailing the strengths, weaknesses, opportunities, and threats (known as a SWOT analysis), that face the program. Long-range planning assumes that conditions stay the same, thus alleviating the need for this step.

For most groups, the length of time is very dependent on the people involved. The amount of time they are able to give to the planning process is often a determinant. While the planning should not be prolonged forever, neither should it be consigned to one two-hour meeting. It is important for the planning leadership to think through the process to develop a reasonable timeline. Having an external deadline (e.g., the budget process) is one way to contain the time spent.

The other major issue in timing is the approval factor. The greater the number of people who must approve the plan, the longer it will take from inception to adoption.

The Forces Driving the Planning

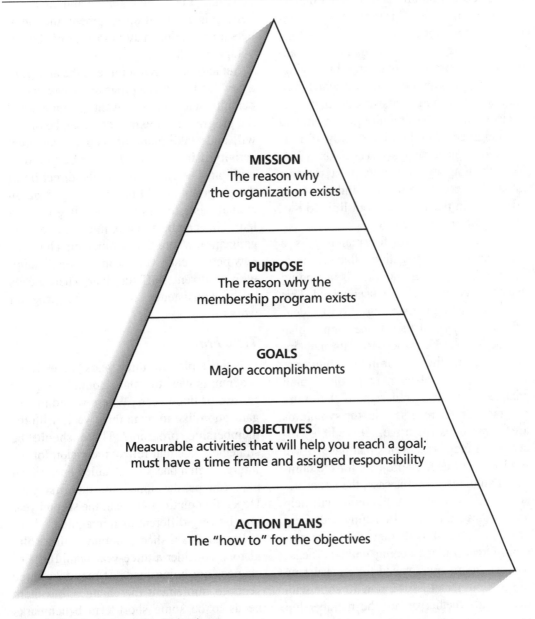

Figure 2–1 Management by Objective

There are several forces that drive planning. A membership program may experience one or more of them. The specific impetus for an operational plan is often the budget process. In fact, many programs use the budget process as the planning tool. Take this year's program, add for inflation, maybe add a program, and, voilà, a budget for the coming year. This is short-term planning and does not encourage a serious look at the program as a whole. Drucker addresses this way of planning by saying, "The budget is the document in which balance decisions find final expression; but the decisions themselves require judgment; and the judgment will be sound only if it is based on sound analysis" (Drucker 1954, 87). Planning by budgeting is a reactive rather than proactive method and has some efficiency in the short run, but little to recommend it in the long run.

A frequent impetus for planning is a symptom—usually negative—that the membership is declining, no one is attending events, or volunteers have disappeared. This calls for a strategic planning effort to identify the causes and then to develop a plan that addresses the issues. Results may include shifts in direction or in how things are done. The new plans may involve small changes or a major redesign of the entire program. On the reverse side, the symptoms are sometimes positive—incredible increases in members, events that have grown too large, not enough projects for the number of volunteers. In this case, the issues become more operational. Planning will help answer these questions. Be happy with these problems even though they do cause turmoil. Organizations coping with the negative symptoms must spend time discussing the environmental issues, how to cope with them, and whether or not the membership program can do anything about them.

In a large organization, the organization's planning may be the driving force. The membership planning, then, is a part of the organization's planning. The challenge for those involved in membership is to make certain that the membership program is a part of the overall plan. If the development department is doing planning and the membership is a part of development, the membership planning may be a part of the development planning.

Yet another driving force is the arrival of a new leader for the program. A new membership manager will want to understand the program as it exists, and then he or she will undertake planning as a management activity if it is a part of his or her job description. The caveat is that the direction of the program should not be changed on an annual basis unless there is a major problem. This can be an issue in a volunteer organization where the membership chair is a new person each year or in an organization with recurrent staff turnover. There needs to be consistency in how the program works.

Time Frame

Is this a plan for three years? Five? If the program is new, the plan should have goals for two or three years. Where would the organization like to be in three years with the membership program? There should be strategic goals that reflect the vision for the future. Then a one-year, detailed operational plan can be developed for the first year. Depending on the first year, the second year may be very different than imagined.

For an established program with a solid history, consider a three-year plan. If major changes are being made, it may take three years to implement the changes, but there needs to be some short-term benchmarks along the way to make certain that the changes are working. If not, contingency plans can be implemented.

PLANNING STEPS

The planning steps are easy to follow and will provide a substantial plan for the membership program (see Exhibit 2–1). This process can be used by a volunteer organization, by a small nonprofit with one staff member, or by a big institution with a large staff in the membership department. If, in reality, one person is going to write the plan, then that one person should still follow the basic process. This should be considered a way to make the work easier in the long run, because once the plan is in place, the direction is clear, and it becomes much easier to stay on track and reach the goals. Otherwise, the membership effort, as Yogi might say, may be making good time, but it may be lost.

1. Select the Planning Leader

Who will design and manage the process? Who will lead the meetings? Who will document the discussion and decisions? Who will write the plan? This can be done in-house or with an outside facilitator. If the decision is to do this in-house, then the responsibility to take the leadership role and keep the process moving must be assigned to a staff person or volunteer. The lead person needs to be a good group facilitator, listener, and writer. The person should also spend some time learning the program if it is not his or her main responsibility. The advantage to using someone in-house is that there is no additional cost. The disadvantage is the time it takes from other duties.

If it is at all possible, the recommendation is to use an outside facilitator. A facilitator is particularly helpful if those involved do not have the time or experience to manage and lead the process, if there may be very conflicting ideas that have to be reconciled by a neutral outsider, or if someone with membership experience will bring an added dimension—and knowledge—to the process. It is particularly important that the facilitator have planning experience. A facilitator can ask the questions that an in-house person might be uncomfortable asking and bring up issues and ideas from his or her experience that might not be available otherwise. Using a facilitator also makes it possible for the staff and volunteers to participate fully, something that may not be possible for the person who is leading the meeting.

The facilitator is the facilitator, listener, and writer. His or her role is to plan the

---

Exhibit 2–1 Planning Steps

1. Select the planning leader	8. Create action plans
2. Gain participation	9. Write the plan
3. Provide information base	10. Prepare the budget
4. Agree on purpose	11. Construct a calendar
5. Develop a SWOT analysis	12. Gain approval
6. Develop goals	13. Work the plan
7. Establish objectives	14. Evaluate

process, manage it, conduct the meetings, and, in the end, put the plan on paper. The facilitator works with the staff and volunteers to help devise a format for the plan and write it. He or she is not a substitute for the participation of those who need to be involved. Facilitators are usually paid, but it is sometimes possible to find someone with the right skills who will do the work on a pro bono basis.

Look for a pro bono facilitator at nonprofit management resource centers (sometimes a part of the local United Way), at organizations like the Junior League that may offer the service, at the business school of a local university, or at a consulting firm that may have a board member as a client. It is important to speak with possible facilitators before hiring one, whether it is for a fee or pro bono. A facilitator whose personality does not fit with those working closest with him or her will not provide a good experience. It is also important to check references to make certain that the facilitator is the right person for the group.

2. Gain Participation

Asking the potential participants to become involved is the first step in gaining participation. With everyone's busy calendars, scheduling the planning meeting is often the most difficult part of the process. Who needs to be involved? Will it be only the membership staff person or volunteer? If the organization has staff, then both staff and volunteers might participate. If membership is a part of the development office, the development director should be included. Also, consider including the support staff. The staff who enter data and answer phone calls often have very good ideas about how and when to structure membership campaigns.

Is there a volunteer component to the program? If so, include the volunteers who are most involved in helping recruit and keep members. Are there board members who would be good additions to the planning group? If the staff is small, the executive director might also be involved. In a larger organization, it is helpful to include other staff who have a role in membership. One of the key values in planning is coordination among departments, and this is the time to do it. For example, if the special events staff work on the membership events, include someone from that area. It may also be helpful to meet with program, education, publications, and other staff whose work has some relationship with the membership program and the members.

Often in a small organization the same person is executive, development, and membership director. While this scenario makes it easy to have all positions in the room at the same time, there is much to be gained from having a larger group. If this is the case, work to find others who might have relevant ideas. If the organization is mainly or totally volunteer driven, then all who are involved in membership and related activities should be included in the planning.

How many is too many? Planning groups have the best discussion when there are 7 to 12 involved. If there are many more than this, it will take much longer to plan. For every person who is added to the group, the time needed expands exponentially. Then why not have just one person? This is certainly the fastest way to plan; however, it also produces the least in terms of results. With more people, more ideas are generated, more creativity stimulated, and, most importantly, more people have "buy-in" and, therefore, a commitment to the final plan. To work the plan takes both personal and financial commitment, so the more people who are involved and who have a stake in the outcome, the better the results.

Potential participants will ask, "How long will this take?" There is never a good time and never enough time to meet or plan. But if it is agreed that planning is important, a group will make time for it. This is one of the benefits of taking time to develop a real plan—everyone is required to consider the facets of the plan and commit thoughts to paper.

There are a number of variables for the length of time it will take. First is the current state of the program—less time for a well-established program, more time for a brand new program. More time is needed for a program experiencing difficulties than one that has few issues to confront. It will take more time with more people, less time with fewer involved. It will take longer if the organizer (e.g., the membership manager) has a multitude of other activities that also take time. Perhaps the most difficult part of planning is making and taking the time to do it; however, once done, the time needed to implement is always shorter.

If it is at all possible, have at least two planning meetings. It may be that the work can be done in one lengthy session (four to six hours), but if there are two sessions, there will be time for the participants to think things through between the meetings. Sometimes an idea that seems brilliant at first glance gathers doubts over time. If there are major issues involved, it may be helpful to have more than two meetings.

In the real world, the time available may be too little. If this is the case, the planning leader needs to suggest ways to shorten the time the group spends together. This might include having the committee react to parts of a plan (perhaps developed by small subcommittees) rather than trying to create them; presenting the background material in written form ahead of time so that no time is taken at the planning meeting going over it; or having several very short meetings, each focused on an issue, so that committee members can fit them into their schedules.

3. Provide Information Base

Everyone involved in the planning should have a base of information from which to discuss the issues. This might include the history of the program, current staffing pattern, statistics on acquisition, renewals and upgrades, and the relationship of the membership program with the fundraising program. Materials can be assembled and sent to planning committee members ahead of time. There should be a review of the materials and the meaning of the information at the beginning of the planning session. Questions for clarification should be answered, but this is not yet the discussion time. The program should also be put into the context of the organization, so that planning participants understand how the program fits into the overall organization and what it means to the organization. The planning leader should not assume that the participants are all well versed in the program.

4. Agree on Purpose

Once the informational foundation is set, the group must agree on the purpose of the program. The discussion should take into consideration how the membership program fits into the organization's mission and goals. The purpose needs to fit the mission of the total organization and role of the department where the program resides. Thus, if membership is part of development, it must fit with that department's overall purpose and goals. The same is true if membership is a part of the marketing department or elsewhere in the organization. While membership marketing is based on benefits, it is also promotes belonging to an organization in which the potential member believes. No matter the benefits, a prospective member must recognize the importance of the institution and its mission. The program must reflect what the institution is trying to accomplish.

If there is more than one purpose for the program, then priorities must be established. For an institution with a long membership history, this may take a few minutes. For a new organization or one that wants or needs to make changes, this will be a long and extremely important discussion. There needs to be a consensus among the planning committee on this issue.

5. Develop a SWOT Analysis

A SWOT analysis is a listing of the Strengths/Weaknesses and Opportunities/ Threats for the membership program. This discussion provides a basis and the information for the issues that need to be addressed. For the SWOT analysis, the facilitator leads the group in a listing of the SWOTs. Then they are discussed to select those that are the most important.

An attribute can be both a strength and a weakness; the issue for the organization is how to manage it. For example, rapid growth in the membership program might be a strength; however, it might also be a weakness because the membership department staff have become overburdened and are not able to service the increased numbers in a timely manner. When the planning group discusses membership growth, membership staffing, then, becomes one of the planning issues in order to determine how to provide the appropriate level of service. The

same is true of opportunities and threats— the opportunity for more members might also be viewed as the threat (or challenge) of not being able to provide the service.

6. Develop Goals

On the most basic level, the two fundamental issues for every membership program are acquisition and renewal. If a program is not acquiring new members, it will die simply by attrition—by not replacing those members who do not renew. Acquisition is necessary even if the organization wants to maintain, and not increase, its membership numbers. Without a renewal program, there is loss of ongoing income and a dependency on acquisition efforts, which can be expensive and are almost always more expensive than renewal efforts. There must be a goal for acquisition and one for renewals in every membership program plan. For each of these goals, as well as for all the others, it is necessary to select a focus (see Exhibit 2–2). For example, in acquisition, the focus might be increasing the number of members, increasing or maintaining the rate of acquisition, or adding or changing the methods for acquisition. The same is true for renewals. The planning group decides what the focus should be.

After the acquisition and renewal, there should be three to five other goals that relate to critical issues, with at least one goal for each critical issue. Those issues come from the institution itself and most likely will have been discussed in some manner during the SWOT discussion. If there is a strategic plan for the institution as whole, the membership program needs to look at these goals with an eye to supporting them. For example, if an institution wants to attract family visitation, the membership program should consider benefits and/or events that appeal to families. If an organization needs political support for an issue, the membership program needs to appeal to the group from whom support is sought. Other goals might address upgrades, events, adding adjunct programs (e.g., Internet membership), technology, or recordkeeping. The focus of these goals and which other goals are selected depends on institutional goals, the status of the current program, budget, and other resource needs, such as staffing and volunteer help. Goals are written as the major ends to be accomplished for the program.

Decide on the three to five issues to be discussed during the planning before beginning the planning process. While these might change during the discussion, they will provide a good starting place. From the issues, goals will be developed; thus, the issues need to be those that should be addressed during the next year. While it is always exciting to

Exhibit 2–2 Selecting a Focus

Goal: Acquisition
Select a Focus:
- Increase number of members
- Increase/maintain rates
- Add/change methods
- Others

Goal: Renewals/Current Members; Lapsed Members
Select a Focus:
- Maintain rates
- Increase all rates
- Increase rate of first year members
- Add/change method
- Other

Goal: Upgrades
Select a Focus:
- Develop a program
- Increase/maintain rates
- Other

Goal: Events
Select a Focus:
- Bring members to the institution
- Encourage nonmembers to join
- Meet interest needs of members
- Raise funds
- Other

Goal: Other
Select a Focus:
- Recordkeeping
- Volunteers
- Publications
- Travel
- Internet membership
- Public relations
- Other

add new activities to the program, make certain that continuing activities are also included. For example, the ongoing direct mail acquisition campaign may be working very well and will be continued in its present state. Additional direct mail may be developed for selected market segments as used in the example in the following section, "Establish Objectives." When developing the calendar and the budget, include continuing activities as well as new ones.

7. Establish Objectives

After goals, objectives are written. The system is called MBO because the objectives provide the basis for managing the program. Objectives are measurable activities that will help you reach the goals. Objectives are written for each goal, and every goal must have at least two objectives. Each must have a time frame, be measurable, and have assigned responsibility. From a practical point of view, the objectives are the work that must be done to accomplish the goals. Saying that it is important to acquire a certain number of members is one thing, figuring out how to do it and what it will cost is quite another. The objectives are really the heart of the plan.

The committee then works on the objectives. How will a particular goal be accomplished? Ideas should be generated, with the group agreeing to two or three of those that seem most realistic. While discussing the goals and objectives, it is imperative that the leader keep the budget in mind. For example, if the committee wants to conduct a direct mail campaign, the leader needs to know whether or not this objective is realistic. It is not time well spent to have the committee concentrate on an activity that may be impossible. Remember that each objective must be measurable, have a time frame, and include assigned responsibility. For the

institution that wants to attract family visitation, one objective might be "to develop a membership brochure that appeals to families by February, with the membership manager responsible." Another might be "to develop a direct mail campaign targeted to families that increases net family membership by 300 members by June, with the membership manager responsible." And yet a third might be "to add three events during the year that appeal to family members by December, with the volunteer committee responsible." It is essential to understand that what is measured is what will happen. The above objectives will produce a membership brochure appealing to families, a direct mail campaign to net 300 family members, and three family-oriented events.

8. Create Action Plans

For each objective, there is an action plan: How will the objective be accomplished? Action plans can then be discussed, if appropriate. If there is membership staff, developing action plans is often assigned to the staff. If volunteer involvement is necessary for the plans to come to fruition, it is helpful to have them involved in the discussion to decide what is possible and to gain their commitment. If the organization is a volunteer one, everyone who needs to participate should be involved in the action plan discussion. The action plans for the first objective, "to develop a membership brochure that appeals to families," might include a focus group of current members representing young families to determine what is appealing to this segment of the membership; a review of current membership materials to determine if they have the appropriate messages; speaking engagements at groups with younger members that include an incentive to attend events designed to appeal to this group; on-site sales during these events to add members might be action plans for other objectives. For this planning, it is helpful to include the staff responsible for marketing, admissions, and/or visitor services. Each of these action steps would have a date and someone responsible.

9. Write the Plan

After each goal and its objectives and action plans are developed and agreed to, the plan must be committed to paper. The planning leader, or the facilitator if one has been a part of the process, writes the plan. Once written, it should be presented to the planning committee to make certain that the plan is recorded as discussed and that everyone agrees. Exhibits 2–3 through 2–7 are examples of the goals, objectives, and action plans part of a written plan. Most often the document will also have an introduction, discussion of the current state of the program, dialogue about the critical issues facing the program, and

---

Exhibit 2–3 Sample Membership Plan: Acquisition, ABC Center, 200X

PURPOSE:
The purpose of the membership program is to develop a constituency for the ABC Center by serving, motivating, and retaining current members and attracting new members on a continuing basis. ABC will generate revenue and support through the membership program.

All activities are the responsibility of the membership manager.

GOAL: Increase the membership through new member acquisition.

OBJECTIVE: 1. Implement a fall direct mail campaign to add 100 new members each year by December 31.

ACTION PLANS:
    a. Develop concept by July 30.
    b. Select lists by August 15.
    c. Produce and mail package by September 30.
    d. Evaluate package by November 30.
       i. cost per dollar raised
       ii. number of members (percent of response)
       iii. evaluation of lists
    e. Redesign package as necessary for next mailing.

OBJECTIVE: 2. Bring in 50 new members from the ABC summer open house event in July.

ACTION PLANS:
    a. Train volunteers.
    b. Decide on location for promotion.
    c. Test location.
    d. Conduct on-site membership acquisition.

OBJECTIVE: 3. Include membership acquisition in public programs, educational events, and publications as appropriate to add 50 new members.

ACTION PLANS:
    a. Provide information and volunteers as necessary.
    b. Train and schedule volunteers and staff.

Exhibit 2–4 Sample Membership Plan: Renewals, ABC Center, 200X

PURPOSE:

The purpose of the membership program is to develop a constituency for the ABC Center by serving, motivating, and retaining current members and attracting new members on a continuing basis. ABC will generate revenue and support through the membership program.

All activities are the responsibility of the membership manager.

GOAL: Increase renewal rate to 75% by a strong renewal program.

OBJECTIVE:
ACTION PLANS:
	1. Implement a regular renewal mailing by January 31.
	  a. 1st renewal letter—two months prior to renewal date.
	  b. 2nd letter—one month prior to renewal date.
	  c. 3rd letter—month during renewal date.
	  d. 4th letter—one month after renewal date.
	  e. Evaluate.

OBJECTIVE:
ACTION PLANS:
	2. Develop a lapsed member campaign by June 30.
	  a. Design campaign by May 31.
	  b. Send lapsed member mailing twice a year, in June and December.
	  c. Evaluate.

OBJECTIVE:
ACTION PLANS:
	3. Implement a telephone renewal campaign by February 28.
	  a. Write a script.
	  b. Develop any necessary materials.
	  c. Train volunteers and staff.
	  d. Implement calling in month after renewal is due, before 4th letter is sent out.
	  e. Evaluate.

---

worksheets that document what will actually be done. (Worksheets are included in Appendix A.)

10. Prepare the Budget

The budget is then developed (see Appendix C for sample budgets). The budget should include all membership activities, not just those that are discussed in the plan. For the plan review, the budget should show the magnitude of expenditures and increases in income. In many cases, additional financial resources are not available. If an acquisition or stronger renewal program looks promising, the institution might take the up-front risk, knowing that there will be net income in the end. With each program component there needs to be a cost and the projected revenue or impact attached to it. Therefore, if an item is funded—or not funded—all involved need to know the ramifications of adding or deleting that item from the membership plan.

With a plan in hand, it is sometimes possible to find outside funding and in-kind donations to help with the program. There are some funders who are willing to fund infrastructure issues such as a membership program. For example, a local corporation might be convinced, on the basis of the revenue projections from the budget, to help

Exhibit 2–5 Sample Membership Plan: Upgrades, ABC Center, 200X

PURPOSE:

The purpose of the membership program is to develop a constituency for the ABC Center by serving, motivating, and retaining current members and attracting new members on a continuing basis. ABC will generate revenue and support through the membership program.

All activities are the responsibility of the membership manager.

GOAL: Upgrade members on a consistent basis, developing them into donors.

OBJECTIVE:	1. Implement upgrade program to increase upgrades to 10% by July 30.
ACTION PLANS:	a. Design upgrade program with incentives by April.
	b. Test incentives in July mailing.
	c. Fold upgrade program into renewal program by July.
	d. Select appropriate incentive by December.
	e. Evaluate in January.
OBJECTIVE:	2. Hold special recognition event for support level members in October.
ACTION PLANS:	a. Develop volunteer committee for event.
	b. Plan event.
	c. Implement.
	d. Evaluate in one year.

---

with acquisitions because it will leverage ongoing operating support for the organization. If it is decided that a telemarketing campaign would be most effective to regain lapsed members, perhaps a real estate office would donate space and phones for an evening, or a telemarketing company might donate a certain number of calls.

For some donors, an event may have appeal. For a new organization or institution, a donor who understands that membership is a way to develop the donor base, which will provide operating income into the future, may be willing to underwrite all or part of the program. The issue is that these fundraising approaches are best made when the plan is complete, and potential funders understand the value of their contribution to the program as a whole.

If additional funding is not possible, then deciding how to shift and reallocate re-

sources will be necessary. It may be more important to the institution to have the family members than to conduct several of the usual member events, thus necessitating changing the focus of some of the current events. Or the organization may be willing to mail fewer pieces in the regular direct mail program in order to be able to mail to the family segment. These are all issues that can be discussed during the planning process.

To determine budget magnitudes, it is necessary to have a good idea of the cost of activities. Reviewing past history and adding for inflation can accomplish much of the estimating process. With new programs, cost estimates will take research. This is also the time to assess staffing issues. If a major drive for new members is planned, are there enough support staff to enter data? Or is it possible to use temporary help? If there is not extra help, what will be the ramifica-

Exhibit 2–6 Sample Membership Plan: Activities, ABC Center, 200X

PURPOSE:

The purpose of the membership program is to develop a constituency for the ABC Center by serving, motivating, and retaining current members and attracting new members on a continuing basis. ABC will generate revenue and support through the membership program.

All activities are the responsibility of the membership manager.

GOAL: Produce membership program of activities and events at ABC.

OBJECTIVE:	1. Implement four members' events each year to attract at least 75 members each.
ACTION PLANS:	a. Develop volunteer committee for each event.
	b. Plan events.
	c. Implement.
	d. Evaluate in one year.
OBJECTIVE:	2. Hold two preview parties for members before two ABC exhibit openings.
ACTION PLANS:	a. Use a volunteer committee if possible.
	b. Design and send invitations.
	c. Implement.
	d. Evaluate.

---

tions? And can the institution live with them? For example, if it will take four weeks to process a membership application instead of two, can anything be done to alleviate the situation—knowing that many people will call asking for their membership cards? In a volunteer organization, it is particularly important to know if there is enough volunteer help to accomplish what is proposed. Budget issues often determine modifications in plans. Modifications are not necessarily a problem, but are better considered before the year starts than to have surprises during the year.

11. Construct a Calendar

The calendar should be attached to show when the work will be accomplished and can be designed in written (Exhibit 2–8) or chart (Exhibit 2–9) format. The calendar should include all the activities of the membership program, not just the new ones in the plan. When developing the calendar, it is important to consider the length of time for many of the projects. A direct mail campaign takes about 12 weeks to reach the mailbox and another 3 to 6 weeks to bring in the income. An event can take several months to plan and implement; very large ones may take a year. It is imperative to remember these timelines when developing the calendar.

Other institutional events must be factored into the calendar. These might include events implemented by other departments or mailings to the membership from other areas. On-site sales should be coordinated with large institutional events and high visitation times. It is also essential to consider the real-life calendar. If the institution attracts children, remember the school calen-

Exhibit 2–7 Sample Membership Plan: Recordkeeping, ABC Center, 200X

PURPOSE:

The purpose of the membership program is to develop a constituency for the ABC Center by serving, motivating, and retaining current members and attracting new members on a continuing basis. ABC will generate revenue and support through the membership program.

All activities are the responsibility of the membership manager.

GOAL: Develop an improved recordkeeping system for ABC.

OBJECTIVE: 1. Assess needs by June 30.
ACTION PLANS: a. Develop a list of management needs.
   b. Develop a list of reports needed.
   c. Interview data entry staff about needs.

OBJECTIVE: 2. Research software for recordkeeping by August 15.
ACTION PLANS: a. Talk to four other comparable organizations in the area.
   b. Research fundraising literature.
   c. Request information.

OBJECTIVE: 3. Make a recommendation to executive director by October 1.
ACTION PLANS: a. Request and receive proposals from three vendors.
   b. See demonstrations of their software.
   c. Make recommendation with budget and timetable.

---

dar. Campaigns can be tied to holidays such as Valentine's Day or Mother's Day. For an environmental group, Earth Day might provide an auspicious time for a mailing. Events should not be scheduled on major religious holidays (check with local religious organizations for dates). It is difficult, if not impossible, to find many volunteers (and sometimes staff) to help during the winter and spring holiday seasons.

12. Gain Approval

The written plan is then submitted to whoever needs to review and approve it. If necessary, rework those items that do not receive approval. Once approved along with the budget, the plan can be worked. Periodically during the year, the plan should be reviewed. Along with reviewing the actual plan, developing a cash flow projection is very helpful, and for many institutions necessary for the acquisition and renewal part of the plan (see Chapter 13). Monthly review of the financial projections is the fastest way to determine if the plan is working. If something is not working as expected, corrections should be made. If the acquisition numbers are not where they should be, perhaps an extra campaign can be added or a planned one augmented. Perhaps research is needed to make certain that the acquisition marketing program is appropriate for the audience. Whatever the case, the periodic measurement against the plan is an important evaluation method. At the end of the year, a complete evaluation should be done in order to prepare for the next year's planning.

When the entire plan, calendar, and financials are reviewed at one time, omissions, conflicts, and unrealistic expectations can be

Exhibit 2–8 Sample Calendar, ABC Center: Written Form

EVERY MONTH
Send out monthly renewal letters.
Call lapsing members.
Work on membership events.
Prepare monthly reports—new members, renewals.
Monitor monthly budget and cash flow.

JANUARY
Monthly activities plus:
Compile end of year reports—new members, renewals.
Review plans based on evaluating programs and on approved budget for year.
Write Annual Report article.
Print membership renewal supplies for the year.

FEBRUARY
Monthly activities plus:
Hold a membership event.
Plan renewal phoning for lapsing members for the year.

MARCH
Monthly activities plus:
Prepare membership cost-benefit analysis for the year.
Implement membership renewal incentive for the year.

APRIL
Monthly activities plus:
Design upgrade program; implement.
Hold membership event.

MAY
Monthly activities plus:
Design lapsed member campaign.

JUNE
Monthly activities plus:
Recruit volunteers for summer event on-site membership acquisition.
Prepare lapsed member mailing.
Assess recordkeeping needs.

QUARTERLY
Write articles for organization newsletter.

JULY
Monthly activities plus:
Train volunteers for summer event.
Hold summer open house event.
Plan direct mail membership solicitation.
Research computer recordkeeping software.
Fold upgrade program into renewal program.

AUGUST
Monthly activities plus:
Finalize fall direct mail membership campaign; acquire lists.

SEPTEMBER
Monthly activities plus:
Hold members' event.
Write report and recommendations on computer software.
Mail fall membership solicitation.

OCTOBER
Monthly activities plus:
Write plans for next year for membership.
Develop projections and budget for next year.
Hold support-level member recognition event.

NOVEMBER
Monthly activities plus:
Evaluate direct mail campaign.
Hold a membership event.

DECEMBER
Monthly activities plus:
Review and update list of honorary members.
Send out staff and honorary membership cards.
Prepare lapsed member mailing.

Exhibit 2–9 Sample Calendar, ABC Center: Chart Form

	January	February	March	April	May	June	July	August	September	October	November	December
Send out monthly renewal letters.*	✓	✓	✓	✓	✓	✓	✓	✓	✓	✓	✓	✓
Call lapsing members.*	✓	✓	✓	✓	✓	✓	✓	✓	✓	✓	✓	✓
Work on membership events.*	✓	✓	✓	✓	✓	✓	✓	✓	✓	✓	✓	✓
Prepare monthly reports—new members, renewals.*	✓	✓	✓	✓	✓	✓	✓	✓	✓	✓	✓	✓
Monitor monthly budget and cash flow.*	✓	✓	✓	✓	✓	✓	✓	✓	✓	✓	✓	✓
Write articles for organization newsletter.†			✓			✓			✓			✓
Compile end of year reports—new members, renewals.	✓											
Review plans based on evaluating programs and on approved budget for year.	✓											
Write Annual Report article.	✓											
Print membership renewal supplies for the year.	✓											
Hold a membership event.		✓		✓					✓		✓	
Plan renewal phoning for lapsing members for the year.		✓										
Prepare membership cost-benefit analysis for the year.			✓									
Implement membership renewal incentive for the year.			✓									
Design upgrade program; implement.				✓								
Design lapsed member campaign.					✓							
Recruit volunteers for summer event on-site membership acquisition.						✓						
Lapsed member mailing.						✓						✓
Assess recordkeeping needs.						✓						
Train volunteers for summer event.							✓					
Hold summer open house event.							✓					
Plan direct mail membership solicitation.							✓					
Research computer recordkeeping software.							✓					
Fold upgrade program into renewal program.							✓					
Finalize fall direct mail membership campaign; acquire lists.								✓				
Write report and recommendations on computer software.								✓				
Mail fall membership solicitation.								✓				
Write plans for next year for membership.									✓			
Develop projections and budget for next year.									✓			
Hold support-level member recognition event.									✓			
Evaluate direct mail campaign.										✓		
Review and update list of honorary members.											✓	
Send out staff and honorary membership cards.											✓	

* Every month
† Quarterly

identified and corrected. All staff and volunteers on whom the plan might have an impact should be included at this point for review. This is particularly important in large organizations, where the effect on a particular department's plan may not always be apparent.

For example, the public relations department may be considering a speakers' bureau, and the membership department's interest in speaking to groups with family members might affect both departments' plans.

13. Work the Plan

Now it is time to get to work. The calendar provides direction on what needs to be done each week; the budget and revenue projections are an evaluation tool to use monthly to make certain that the program is on target. As Drucker says, "plans are only good intentions unless they immediately degenerate into hard work" (www.brainyquote.com).

14. Evaluate

Evaluation is the means by which the organization knows if the plan is working, and, more importantly, if the program is achieving what it set out to do. Evaluation on a regular basis is also the way the membership manager makes certain that the plan is used and not put in a drawer or on the shelf until the next planning process is announced.

The plan contains objectives that are the basis for evaluation. The objectives should be reviewed monthly or quarterly. If major changes are being made and results need to be monitored, such as with a change in acquisition methods, monthly reviews may be useful. If the plan is running smoothly without major issues, quarterly may be enough. The evaluation of the objectives against the plan should be in writing and discussed with whoever is the ultimate supervisor of the membership program. This may be the board in a volunteer or very small organiza-

tion. It may be the development director in a large organization.

Evaluating the plan on a regular basis allows changes to be made in a timely manner. It also allows for readjustments if they need to be made. The acquisition mailing may be mailed later than expected, and this delay may change the cash flow projections and the staffing pattern for data entry, and alter the plans for a renewal mailing. This review gives all involved the chance to understand why and how the plans need to be adjusted as quickly as possible.

A WORD ABOUT FLEXIBILITY

The plan is finished. The budget is approved. The cash flow projection looks good. An opportunity arises that has no relevance to the plan whatsoever. The plan is an objective way to say "no" to a well-meaning, but inappropriate, suggestion. But what if the opportunity does make sense? Never pass up an opportunity that will benefit the institution and truly makes sense for the membership program. When this happens, it is time to see how the opportunity will fit into the plan. It may be necessary to postpone another activity for a few months, or until the next year. Depending on the circumstances, maybe it can be added without a lot of changes to the original plan. Whatever the case, make certain that all involved understand the ramifications. The issue for planning is to maintain the integrity of the program while remaining flexible. Sometimes opportunities really are too good to ignore. The planning process should be willing to embrace them. Good plans are flexible plans.

REFERENCES

Beatty, J. 1998. *The World According to Peter Drucker*. New York: The Free Press.

Drucker, P. F. 1990. *Managing the Nonprofit Organization*. New York: HarperCollins.

Drucker, P. F. 1954. *The Practice of Management*. New York: Harper & Row.

National Society of Fund Raising Executives. 1996. *The NSFRE Fund-Raising Dictionary*. New York: John Wiley & Sons.

SUGGESTED READINGS

Hardy, J. M. 1984. *Managing for impact in nonprofit organizations: Corporate planning techniques and applications*. Erwin, TX: Essex Press.

Allison, M. and J. Kaye. 1997. *Strategic planning for nonprofit organizations*. New York: John Wiley & Sons.

Porter, M. 1985. *Competitive advantage: Creating and sustaining superior performance*. New York: The Free Press.

Steiner, G. 1979. *Strategic planning: What every manager must know*. New York: The Free Press.

Tregoe, B. B. and J. W. Zimmerman. 1980. *Top management strategy: What it is and how to make it work*. New York: Simon & Schuster.

CHAPTER 3

Membership and Fundraising

Patricia Rich and Dana Hines

We make a living by what we get. We make a life by what we give.
—Winston Churchill

MEMBERS GIVE

MEMBERS GIVE—AND THEY GIVE TO more than the membership program. No matter the multitude of purposes for having a membership program, bringing in revenue is almost always an important factor. Depending on the total funding structure of the organization, the membership program may provide either a small part or a substantial portion of the organization's total operating budget. For an organization funded wholly by membership, the financial consideration is obvious. For institutions with various sources of financial support, the financial consideration can be less clear.

Why does a nonprofit decide to have a membership program? Why wouldn't a public issue organization just ask for donations to support the cause? Why don't visitation-based institutions just market for attendance and then ask for annual gifts? Why don't hospitals and museums advertise for volunteers rather than having auxiliaries and guilds? How does a nonprofit make this choice?

MEMBERSHIP OR ANNUAL GIVING?

Many fundraisers equate having a membership program as equivalent to annual giving. Annual giving is defined as "1. an amount given annually. 2. a fund-raising program that generates gift support on an annual basis" (National Society of Fund Raising Executives [NSFRE] 1996, 9). Interestingly, membership is not defined in the *NSFRE Fund-Raising Dictionary*.

There is a difference. While annual giving generates gift support, a membership program is equally as interested in generating a constituency and developing a relationship with the donor. A membership program assumes an equal relationship between the member and the institution. The donor is not just making a gift, but rather there is an implied relationship. That relationship is based on the exchange of money for benefits, both tangible and intangible. At the basic levels, the benefits and the dues have some relationship. People who join an organization because of the economic value they perceive in the membership are known as "value members." In programs with graduated dues, the benefits become increasingly intangible at the higher levels, and the dues are more of a contribution. People who join at the higher levels are known as the "support members" of the organization.

Annual giving is a gift "ask." Membership is a gift ask with a program that encompasses it. Membership is more marketing oriented and more promotional in its appeal. Members have expectations that there will be benefits, member service, activities, communication, and recognition— all of which are designed to increase the interest and involvement in the organization. It is that sense of belonging and of solidify-ing the relationship between the member and the organization that is so important.

WHY MEMBERSHIP

Why should an organization consider a membership program when sending an annual gift solicitation seems so much easier? There are a number of reasons that affect all organizations, and some reasons that depend on the type of organization. For all organizations, there are the benefits of constituency, education, public financial support, corporate marketing support, public relations, cash flow, and dependability, consistency, and predictability. Visitation-based and public issue organizations have the additional benefits of attendance and cause-related support.

Building a Constituency

With the implied relationship that a membership brings, there is the opportunity to build the support group for the organization. Not only will the constituency support the institution financially, but in other ways as well. From time to time, all organizations need public support, even if the organization is not a public interest group. This support may be for a cause. A zoo might enlist the support of its members to help bring the message about an endangered species to those who make decisions about it. The support may also be asked because of an issue that arises. A botanical garden enlisted the support of its members when a new highway building project threatened its grounds.

Education

Most organizations have education as a part of their mission. Having a membership group with which to communicate on an ongoing basis through publications, visitation, events, activities, networking, and classes is significant. The membership group has a basic interest in the subject matter and, by self-selection, is a group ready, willing and interested in learning more about it.

Public Financial Support

The membership may be helpful in seeking and obtaining public funding. For example, a school may be seeking public (e.g., government-related) funding for capital expansion and ask alumni association members to endorse the project. A museum may be seeking direct tax support, and members may be willing to be a part of the campaign to win it. An organization seeking tax credits for donors may be well served to have members give backing to the idea. In all cases involving public support, having a significant membership program is one way to demonstrate that the organization has support in the community.

Corporate Marketing Support

Much like with public financing, corporate marketing support becomes more of a possibility with a substantial membership program. A company that is interested in marketing to a certain group of people is very interested in an organization that has members who meet that market profile. For example, one outdoors-related organization has corporate support from a company that manufactures outdoors sporting goods equipment. It is a mutually beneficial relationship. The membership receives information about the newest products (a service for the members who like to be up-to-date in this area), and the company is reaching potential customers. The organization also sends the membership other information

and educational materials, and calls on the membership to help support environmental issues that affect outdoor programs. In organizations that attract a wider variety of people, such as cultural institutions and museums, it is important to learn who the audiences are. When these institutions can quantify the demographics of their members, the information is there to use with marketing proposals to corporations.

Public Relations

The most effective public relations is always word of mouth. When people are members of an organization, they often will talk about it, share information with others, and, ideally, persuade others to join. Being a member, for most people, is year-round and constant, not a single annual act of giving. This encourages them to talk about the organization. The membership also becomes a marketing tool for the institution. At a visitation-based institution, a new exhibit is marketed to the members, who, in turn, tell their families, friends, and neighbors. Members can be encouraged to bring others to exhibits and special activities. For an issue organization, having the membership spread the word about good work, upcoming events, and important concerns is invaluable. Every membership organization should consider its membership as a means of public relations for the organization and use it as such.

Cash Flow

Organizations with annual giving programs tend to ask for the annual gift at one time during the year. Organizations with significant membership programs are acquiring members all year long. Anniversary dues, which are paid on the anniversary of joining, are the most effective for cash and work flow purposes. Thus renewals take place throughout the year, ensuring cash flow throughout the year. If it is helpful to smooth out the cash flow during the year for staffing or other reasons, extra months can be offered as an incentive for renewing or upgrading, thus moving the renewal into a different month, when the cash flow is weaker.

Dependability, Consistency, and Predictability

Membership is an implied year-round and ongoing commitment, as opposed to a single gift. Not everyone will renew, but the new member understands that the relationship can be long term if he or she finds it beneficial. If the membership program is well planned and executed, the renewal rate should be significant. This means that the income from the program is dependable, consistent, and predictable—always a positive situation in a nonprofit organization. Annual giving doesn't imply the ongoing commitment or year-round belonging that a membership program does.

Some institutions take advantage of special exhibits or controversial issues for acquisition, and they need to factor that type of acquisition into the predictability equation. There will be those who join just on the basis of that unusual event and will not be interested in a continued relationship. The issue for the organization is to make the first-year experience so good that the new members will want to continue.

Visitation

In a visitation-based institution, the membership is a keystone for attendance. Having a membership gives the organization a tar-get audience for its exhibits, programs, and events. Direct marketing to this group will bring a base of visitors to the institution. Those organizations that attract large numbers of tourists know that the tourists typically come in certain seasons. A zoo in the north will have lots of tourists in the summer, few in the winter. This may be exactly the opposite for a zoo in a southern region where northerners winter. The membership base provides a group that the organization can encourage to attend during those slow times. The membership program can expand its activities during the nontourist times to increase visitation among members and offset the lower number of tourists.

Public Issue

Public issue organizations with a membership base validate their message: "join our cause." Substantial numbers of members prove to the general public that the cause is not just that of a few, but that it enjoys widespread support. A substantial number can be 50 neighbors in an area fighting a landfill or can be hundreds of thousands—or millions—supporting either side of the gun control issue. If one side of a controversial issue has significant membership, then the opposing side will find itself trying to attract equal or greater numbers. Again, the concept of membership implies an ongoing commitment to the issue, not a one-time appeal.

MAKING THE MEMBERSHIP DECISION

To have or not to have a membership program is a question that a new organization or one that is redesigning its development program should ask. Membership is a development strategy that can be used in many organizations if there is an interest in doing so. There are differences between membership and annual giving from the perspectives of both the potential member or donor and the organization.

Membership

There are certain expectations from the potential member's perspective. The member is entering into a relationship that, by definition, lasts for a year or more. In a membership program, the member will expect benefits, regular and consistent activities and communication, and special treatment, whether it be from someone answering the telephone or when attending an exhibit. The member will expect a membership card and invitations to activities. The member will expect attention on a year-round basis. In exchange, the member will seriously consider renewing support on an annual basis. The member may become very involved in the organization, make more and generous gifts, volunteer, publicly support the cause, or do other things that reflect his or her sense of belonging.

For many members, the membership gift is the annual gift. They can be approached for a number of different types of gifts during the year, and many will give. But for most, this will be the one gift. Most interesting from the fundraising viewpoint is that long-time, value-level members will be the donors of a high proportion of planned gifts.

When an organization creates a membership program, it is making a public statement about the relationship between the members and the institution. This relationship includes providing the benefits, services, activities, communication, and recognition on a consistent basis, making the organization a worthwhile one for people to join. A good part of this value is increasing

that feeling of belonging that members expect.

An organization of any size can do this as long as there is a commitment to making it happen. The member's level and degree of expectations from a small, local organization will be far different than from one that is large and national. There would not be an expectation that a local organization's newsletter would rival the *Smithsonian Magazine*. There would be, however, an expectation for regular and consistent communication.

Acquisition and renewal of members are based on a marketing approach, emphasizing the exchange between the member and the organization. The solicitation pieces tout tangible benefits as well as the intangible ones. Once members have been members for a few years, an upgrading process can begin in those organizations with graduated dues, and in all organizations, additional gifts can be solicited during the year.

Annual Giving

From the donor's perspective, annual giving is just that, a once-a-year gift. A gift the second year is not necessarily a renewal, but rather another annual gift based on the solicitation that is made. There is not an expectation of tangible benefits, and solicitations are generally based on the intangible benefits, such as feeling good about the work that the organization is doing, giving back to the community, or personal interest. There is usually no expectation of activities or special services. Most donors do expect to hear from the organization during the year, not just at annual giving time, and that communication can be accomplished with a newsletter.

From the organization's perspective, annual giving is one of the several ways in which donors are solicited. In addition, an annual giving solicitation is not the direct marketing exchange that is used in membership. The solicitation is based on the intangible benefits that the donor receives from meeting the needs of the organization and its clients. Some annual giving programs give tangible benefits (e.g., address labels or note cards), but usually not to the extent that membership programs give them. In organizations with a long history, this means of fundraising is predictable, based on past history, just as it is with membership. The major difference for the organization is that there is no necessity for the program elements associated with membership: there is no need for a membership card, for developing significant tangible benefits, or for member service or activities. It is, however, incumbent on any strong fundraising program to develop those activities that bring donors closer to the institution.

The Decision

The essential question for an organization considering a membership program is, "why membership, as opposed to annual giving?" The critical reason why organizations have membership programs is that membership in some way supports the mission of the organization. These organizations have needs in addition to income. For some organizations, membership is what is necessary, and the need for income is minimal. As mentioned earlier, having a membership program does not preclude going back to the membership for other gifts. Membership is not an "either-or" proposition.

Tradition also plays a part. Cultural institutions almost always have a membership program in order to develop their constituency and encourage visitation, as well as create income. To those who patronize cultural institutions, a museum without a membership program would, indeed, seem unusual. And what would we think if public radio and television gave up their pledge drives for new members?

Organizations such as some museum guilds, hospital auxiliaries, and faith-based programs have traditionally used membership as a method of building their volunteer programs. Participant programs and some public issue groups need the numbers and the volunteers that a membership program brings to their activities. The raison d'être for loyalty organizations like alumni associations and fraternities and sororities isn't necessarily raising funds; it is keeping the ties that bind strong and current.

How does an organization make the decision? Those working on the project should ask themselves the following questions:

- How would a membership program support our mission?
- Why do we need and want members?
- Do we have tangible benefits that make sense and correspond to the dues we are asking?
- Are we able to distribute and provide the benefits in a timely manner?
- Are we able to solicit members during the year for other projects if income is important?
- Are we able to provide member service?
- Do we have a consistent communication program?
- Are there activities or programs that we can provide, if appropriate?
- Do we offer recognition for members including a membership card?
- Do we have the human and financial resources to keep the membership program going?

If the reason for having members is clear, and the answers to most of these questions are "yes," then implementing a membership program is the right decision. If the answers are not so clear, an annual giving program may be a better choice.

MEMBERSHIP STRATEGY

Once the membership choice is made, then the organization is able to begin planning and implementing the program. The next choice is what the membership strategy will be. The strategy can be based on growth in numbers, growth in income, or stability. Each of these strategies has numerous ways to approach it.

Growth in Membership Numbers

This strategy is based on the belief that the number of members is the most important goal. With this approach, resources are put toward acquisition and renewal, and they are aggressive, whether using direct mail, personal solicitation, or other techniques. This strategy makes sense in local areas where the program is new, or the population is growing, or where there are audiences that might be interested in the organization but haven't been approached. It also makes sense for an organization with a current, stirring issue or a museum with a new, exciting exhibit. When growth is the goal, it is also very important to make certain that the renewal process is in place and well executed. Acquiring new members is a waste of resources if they are not renewed at acceptable rates. In fact, developing a strong renewal program may be the most efficient and cost-effective way for an organization to increase its numbers.

For a beginning program, there is no doubt that the first effort is to find a critical mass. That critical mass might be 10, 100, 1,000 members, or more. It needs to be a number of members for whom, with dues, it makes sense to provide the benefits and other parts of the membership program. A book-reading group might need a critical mass of 20 to have enough people to attend regularly and join in the conversation. A new aquarium might want a beginning membership of 20,000 to make the membership program possible. Making the membership program interesting is particularly crucial for new organizations because the renewals will be critical to building the base of members.

This strategy is sensible in growing areas of the country, if the additional population is in the age range to which the organization appeals. The organization needs to find ways to reach the new people in the area and to make its presence known. For institutions that have a significant share of the people who meet their member profile, one way to increase the numbers is to find audiences that might be interested in the organization but haven't been approached. For cultural institutions, this may mean finding ways to appeal to a younger audience or to minority audiences. In either case, it will take an effort on the part of the institution to find the benefits and activities that are attractive to the group they want to reach.

Organizations with exciting issues or exhibits can often use those events as a spur to gain new members. It is very important to make the first-year membership as enticing as possible, so that renewals will be high. Some organizations find that many members who join just to see a certain exhibit or support the current cause will not stay with the organization. This is why that entire first year experience is critical. The one issue or exhibit is not enough. For some issue organizations, just having significant numbers is the key to success. AARP gains an audience for its views with more than 30 million members.

One question that always comes up is how big should, or could, a membership program be. The answer, of course, is very different for different types of programs. For loyalty programs and professional associations, the pool of prospective members can usually be counted, and the issue becomes one of marketing in ways that will appeal to the greatest numbers. For other organizations, there is no easy way to know. One way is to compare the current membership numbers with other like organizations. If the organization has a member profile, through census and other information, it is possible to find out how many people in the area fit that profile and compare. If the percentage is high, it may be time to consider appealing to different market segments.

If growth in numbers is important, and it appears that there are potential members, but the program seems to have hit a plateau, consider other approaches. Market research (see Chapter 9) can provide information about the appeal or lack of appeal of the benefits, the program, and other attendant issues. If the organization wants to appeal to new segments of the population, the research can discover what might entice them. Another consideration would be to change acquisition or renewal methods. The issue might really be a problem with renewals rather than acquisition.

There is a certain amount of energy and resources that are necessary to keep a program growing. The larger the program becomes, the more time and money it takes. Staffing becomes an issue, larger direct mail campaigns become an issue, servicing the members becomes an issue. There is a cost for growth, but for many the cost for no-growth is greater. Understand that once a membership program is up and growing, acquisition and renewals must always continue at a high level just to stay even. If the

organization is not willing to at least keep the numbers stable, the program will die from attrition.

Growth in Membership Income

For programs where membership income plays a vital role in the organization, growth in income may be more important than growth in numbers. There are several ways to increase income. Growing the number of members through acquisition and renewal is just one of them. The others include changing the dues structure, increasing the dues, changing the tangible benefits, implementing an upgrade program, and increasing efficiency.

Changing the dues structure, increasing the dues, and changing the tangible benefits will get an immediate reaction from current members. When doing any of them, inform the members that this change will happen on a certain date. Offer early renewals to keep the current rates and benefits for the next year before making the change. The organization will lose some members, depending on the size of the change. If it involves a few dollars, nothing may happen. If it involves perceived large changes, be prepared to answer questions and talk to unhappy members. The real test is what happens over the course of a year. If there is a significant loss of membership, the institution may have to reconsider the changes.

Knowing that there will be some attrition due to the changes, it is important to make the changes so that the organization will still increase income if there is a drop in membership. For example, if the dues are going to increase from A to B, and the assumption is made that there will be a 10 percent drop in membership, then income from B must be more than the current total from 90 percent of the members. Know that some members are very vocal. It is their organization. If the program has a large membership and the calls are few, do not worry. Try to calm the unhappy members as much as possible. In this day and age, people do understand that prices rise. One organization raised rates and noticed in the first two months that a large number of members downgraded to a lower level rather than increase their membership. The organization decided to offer an incentive to members who remained at their current level at the new increased dues fee. Downgrading immediately stopped, and total income increased.

It is sometimes more difficult to change benefits than to change the cost of membership. Membership has its privileges, and when privileges are removed, there can be a lot of unhappiness. If members are typically invited to an event that is very popular, and that event will no longer be held, tell them why in a small note in the newsletter. If the event is cancelled because it is not very popular, just let it fade away. If there are particular people who were very vested in the event, make certain to let them know what is happening. If there is an overall restructuring of the program—changes in the benefits and dues structures simultaneously—it may be helpful to send a letter to members explaining the changes and letting them renew with the current structure in a short time frame; then proceed with restructuring. Usually, the comments and complaints will last a year or less. No organization wants to do this type of wholesale change in benefits and dues often, but sometimes, particularly when restructuring the program, it has to be done. Small price increases every three to four years is the recommended strategy. By doing this, a major price increase won't be necessary because a program has waited too long to increase dues.

Upgrade programs for those programs with graduated dues are very effective in increasing income. This strategy for increased income does need resources put toward it. The resources may be financial, with offering an incentive to upgrade. Incentives may include anything from a product with the institution's logo to an additional two months of membership if the member upgrades. What is offered depends on the organization.

Another upgrade program that can produce increased income is a personal solicitation campaign to add members at support levels. This can be done as a fundraising campaign, with a committee and an organized way to solicit lists of potential upper-support members.

Stability

Growth in numbers or income may not be the goal for the program; the goal may be stability. The membership program is important, but in organizations where the membership program is part of the larger institution, the institution's goals are paramount. It may be that an organization's priority is a capital campaign, and that is where the resources need to be invested. In this case, the issue will be to keep the membership numbers and income at about the same level, rather than trying to increase them. Even with a strategy of stability, there is a need for acquisition and renewal. Without acquisition and renewal, the program will begin to fade. Attrition must always be countered. In the natural order of things, there will always be some attrition due to people moving, life circumstances changing, or priorities being rearranged.

It may also be that an institution does not want to add resources to the membership program, believing that it is at about the right number for the community and the organization. This is a suitable decision as long as there are enough resources to make certain that the program doesn't die from attrition. If resources are diminished, there must be an attempt to make certain that renewal and acquisition efforts are not totally reduced. In addition, an organization serving a limited geographic area will be constrained in membership size by the size of the community. If the community is not growing or declines, the membership program may reflect that reality if it already has as many members as the community will bear.

Another reason for stability may be that the organization has reached its limit of being able to service the membership. In some participant and volunteer programs, there just aren't enough projects or volunteer opportunities to take care of the number of members. When this is the case, the organization may want to limit its numbers until it has more ways to make use of the members' time. Asking people to volunteer and then having nothing for them to do is a certain way to ensure discontent.

THE MEMBERSHIP RELATIONSHIP

Even if a membership program generates only a small portion of the organization's total budget, whether 5, 10, or 15 percent, that amount may be the important difference in giving the organization some financial stability and flexibility. Remember that membership money is unrestricted money, and unrestricted funds are always the most difficult to raise. With unrestricted funds, an organization may pay the utility bills, salaries, or other unexciting (to most donors) but absolutely necessary expenses. It may also provide seed money to fund a new program or buy needed equipment. No matter how it is spent, it has significant value because the organization can make the decision to spend the money where the funds are most needed.

A well-designed membership program can be powerful in increasing the relationship with the members and turning them into donors. People who join a membership program have an interest in the organization, and they may become even greater donors over time. Strong fundraising programs are often based on a relationship being developed between the member and the organization. This relationship is based on the member's interest and involvement in the organization. Thus, the membership program should be designed and developed as the foundation of giving for the organization. The membership becomes the donor base for the institution, and it should be regarded as such.

Membership's Place in the Organization

Membership programs can be found in a variety of departments in organizations—development, marketing, volunteer—or as a stand-alone department. In order to use the membership as the foundation of an institution's fundraising program, the membership program belongs, more often than not, in the development department. If there is any question about where membership belongs, choose development.

In the Development Department

When the membership program is a part of the development office, it is, by definition, an integral part of the fundraising program of the institution or organization. With the opportunities for integration with the development program, membership fits well in this department. A single database is easily used for all projects and the driving force for all concerned is raising more funds for the organization.

In the Marketing Department

In a large organization, with separate development and marketing departments, there may a temptation to include the membership program in the marketing department. There is often the feeling that membership is more of a marketing function than a philanthropic one. Because the basic membership program begins with a marketing exchange, it would seem logical to include it with other marketing ventures. Members are profiled, surveyed, and targeted. A variety of marketing techniques are used to appeal to prospective members. Membership has all the markings of marketing. Thus the decision is made that it must be a marketing function.

Organizations that have high admission fees frequently place membership in the marketing department to try to circumvent the competition between membership and admissions that seems to occur when one person's budget is affected by the success of the other. Membership can depend heavily on the admissions staff for its on-site sales success. Thus in some organizations it may make sense to have marketing and visitor's services under one administrator.

Typically zoos and aquaria have membership programs that are placed in the marketing department. With high gate fees and the perception of a ticket package comparable to a theme park or similar venue, this placement may make sense. Also, historically, many zoos had membership programs long before they had development departments.

If this is the case, the marketing and fundraising must be carefully coordinated and work together. The membership manager must have a good working knowledge of development issues, and be certain that once a member joins, he or she receives communication that underlines how important his or her support is for the institution. The worst-case scenario is when there is competition between the marketing department and the development department or between development and a separate membership department. Competition within the institution works to the distinct disadvantage of the organization as a whole.

In the Volunteer Department

In organizations where the focus is on members becoming volunteers, the membership program can be situated in the volunteer or human resources department. If this is the case, there needs to be a link and coordination with the development office. Volunteers are often a good constituency for fundraising appeals. Some will say the volunteers already give their time and, thus, they should not be asked for money. In reality, volunteers, through their work, may well understand why the institution needs more funds. The Association of Fundraising Professionals (AFP) reports that studies show "Volunteers give more than twice the percentage of income as those who contribute, but do not volunteer" (AFP 2000, A-10). The volunteers are very close to the institution; those who are capable of making a gift may be pleased to do so.

Donated Income

With a membership program that functions as the donor base for the organization, there are numerous possibilities for increasing contributed and earned income. In some organizations, membership and development keep separate databases. This is counterproductive. If it is at all possible, the institution should have only one database.

That database should, of course, have coding to enable the selection of segments of the membership so that it can be used in a variety of ways. For most organizations, having separate databases makes it difficult, if not impossible, to use the list for multiple or cross cultivation and solicitation efforts. In an institution with a natural constituency, like a university, the alumni association would use the school's database to solicit members rather than the school using the alumni association list. This "one-way" cross cultivation is a very different situation and, as necessary, should be coordinated to suit the needs of both the development and alumni offices. In some cases, alumni may be more likely to report a change of address to the alumni association than to the school's development office. Thus, the alumni association can become an excellent source of updated contact information. With one database for both entities to share, successful, two-way cultivation would be easier.

For organizations without a natural constituency, such as a museum or civic group, offering a membership program becomes an important method for discovering who has an interest and who might become involved. The membership program is a prospecting tool, a cultivation mechanism, and the donor base from which to solicit the additional donations. There is a giving cycle for a membership program (see Figure 3–1) much as there is for any fundraising program.

Membership Giving Cycle

Benefits and Incentives

The case for a fundraising program is "the reasons why an organization both needs and merits philanthropic support" (NSFRE 1996, 28). The "case" for a membership program is first and foremost its benefits, which underscore the merit of supporting the institution. The benefits or any incentive for joining will make no difference if the potential member has no interest in the organization or its work.

Along with the package that includes the benefits and any incentive to join, a case also needs to be made for the organization itself. The potential member will be interested in the organization, but at the value levels of membership, it is the benefits and the incentive to join that are the real focus of the appeal and the major interest of most prospective members. It is that offer that is the "hook" that encourages the potential member to look further. If the offer is not one that is appealing to the prospect, then the relationship will end before it begins.

For organizations that are working to appeal to more than one market, the acquisition effort might emphasize different benefits for different groups. A school that can identify those interested in sports teams might use the benefit of access to tickets while the marketing to a group from a particular profession might emphasize certain activities like lectures and publications.

Identification and Prospecting

Organizations continually need to increase and broaden their constituency base. Some members will leave: they will find a new or different cause; they will move out of town; their personal situation will change, and they will no longer be able to contribute or participate. If new members are not found, in the long term, the program will die from attrition. Having a membership program gives a very appealing way to add to the base of support. Because the basic frame of reference for a membership program is a marketing exchange—that is, money for benefits—the appeal is broad and direct.

Finding new members to add to the base is straightforward. In fundraising, potential members are often called "suspects" and "prospects." A suspect is a potential donor whose linkage to the organization, ability to give, and interest are unknown (NSFRE 1996, 162). There are, however, demographic or psychographic characteristics that enable an organization to select a suspect pool. Places to look include magazine or catalogue lists from those publications that have a relevance to the organization's work. For example, an environmental group might consider using a mailing list from a magazine with a focus on natural areas or a catalogue mailing list from a company that sells camping or mountain climbing equipment. Those lists can be purchased on a ZIP code basis and often culled by such specifics as household make-up and income.

A prospect is identified as having "linkage, giving ability and some interest" (NSFRE 1996, 140). To reach prospects, the possibility of exchanging lists with like-minded organizations should be considered. For example, museums can exchange lists for prospecting, remove duplications (known as "deduping"), and use the cleaned list. These potential members are prospects; they have, for the most part, the interest and ability to join. Those who join one organization will often join others that are similar. With a membership program, the organization has the possibility of offering some-

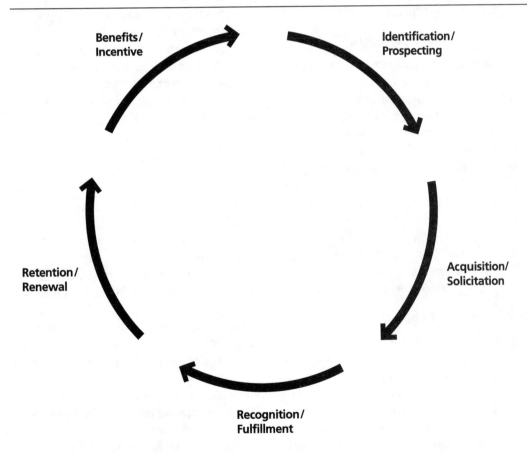

Figure 3–1 Membership Giving Cycle

thing of value to attract the member. Once a member has enrolled, the organization has the opportunity to bring that member closer to the organization, increase the linkage, and involve the member with the institution.

Acquisition and Solicitation

Acquisition is the successful act of soliciting for the membership program. When the new member returns the membership form that was included in a mailing, or purchases a membership on site, the acquisition of a new member has taken place. In membership solicitation where the program has graduated levels, the first several tiers are very straightforward. The benefits and incentive have encouraged the person to join. It is an immediate transaction.

Recognition and Fulfillment

Recognition in a membership program begins immediately with the fulfillment of the offer made in the acquisition effort. If the member does not receive, in a timely manner, a thank-you, his or her membership card, information about programs, and the incentive that was offered, the membership program will suffer in the long run. This is a part of the retention effort and, because it is the first real communication with the member as a member, it is extremely important. First impressions do count, and they are remembered. Any other recognition also needs to be timely (e.g., listing in a newsletter) and correct.

Retention and Renewal

A retention plan is the cultivation program for a membership program. It is the way that an organization "engages and maintains the interest and involvement of a donor" (NSFRE 1996, 44). A membership program is a built-in way to encourage members to become more significant donors to the institution. A strong effort will have a series of programs designed to engage and maintain the interest of the members. These programs are often marketed as some of the benefits of membership. Invitations to unusual "members-only" events (e.g., a special lecture on a topic related to the institution), individual treatment at public events (e.g., a special line to enter an exhibit), or special publications at a free or reduced cost are some of the possible opportunities.

"Special" is the operative word when describing how an organization wants its members to feel. All programs and events should be designed to encourage that feeling. If the members feel like part of the institution's "family," then the membership program and the cultivation are successful. This translates into strong support for the institution through renewed membership and increased and more frequent gifts. Feeling special also encourages the member to spread the word, advocate for the cause, and encourage others to add their support.

Pyramids of Giving

The donor pyramid of giving (see Figure 3–2) graphically represents the development process. The membership program is the pyramid's foundation for many institutions and organizations. The premise of the pyramid is that the more people become interested and involved in the organization, the more likely they are to make major and planned gifts. Some donors self-select and move from annual giving into major giving in the pyramid, while others enter at a major gift level. The challenge, however, is to involve the donors more closely in the organization. A membership program can provide the framework for that effort.

The membership pyramid of giving (see Figure 3–3) shows how the membership program in an organization with graduated dues becomes the way to develop the fundraising program.

Value Members and Support Members

An annual giving program is almost always the base for a fundraising program (refer to Figure 3–2). The hope is that once a person has made a gift to the organization, that gift will be repeated annually. Many people consider their yearly membership gift to an institution as their annual gift. And for many it is. Having an ongoing renewed membership from this group is tantamount to annual giving. The technical difference is that an annual gift is often an unrestricted donation, with the donor receiving nothing in return, while the membership gift, also usually unrestricted, is based on a marketing exchange of money for something of value (membership benefits). That something of value can be free admission, an incentive gift, or an array of other benefits with value.

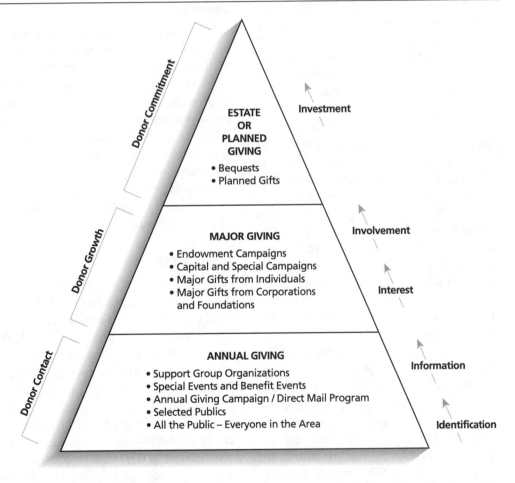

Figure 3–2 Donor Pyramid of Giving. *Source:* James M. Greenfield, *Fund-Raising,* Copyright © 1991, John Wiley & Sons, Inc. Reprinted by permission of John Wiley & Sons, Inc.

The member whose membership gift is dependent on the benefits is a value member, or one who makes the gift because it is a good value. That good value, for example, might be free admission to a museum that the member frequents—the member saves money by buying the membership rather than paying the admission price each time. Entire membership programs may be value programs. Many high-ticket-priced admission programs, such as those for aquaria, tend to be more heavily value member–based. Because the decision to join is based so strongly on the immediate benefit, gaining long-term organizational commitments and donations from this group may be difficult.

Some members at the value membership level ask not to receive the items of value and, in this case, the gift is truly an annual gift. Those who do avail themselves of the membership benefits may still equate their membership gift with annual giving. The important thing about the membership program is that, with anniversary renewal dates (yearly renewal on the anniversary date of joining), the annual giving from members becomes systematic. A member who has renewed for several years will, very often, continue this giving for many years. The predictability of this income stream underlies the importance of membership funding. The lifetime giving of a renewing member can be substantial.

Even value members can be asked for other gifts. As shown in Figure 3–3, value members are good prospects for a second annual gift, special projects, tributes, and events. Special projects can even include capital projects that can be accomplished with a small (for a capital campaign) amount, such as a brick program that asks members to buy bricks in a patio to support a building campaign.

Some members, however, become support members, moving beyond value member status to higher steps on the pyramid. Support members are those who make a membership gift at a level where benefits are no longer the only reason for giving. Where this level is for an institution depends on the benefit structure. Support members make larger gifts, make additional gifts, and, in some cases, become major donors to the institution.

Finding Support Members

Upgrades

Periodically it's important to ask members to upgrade, or to increase the amount of their annual membership. Some members will self-select and give at a higher level without asking, but asking will increase the number who do give more. Not asking is a major reason why people don't give and one of the reasons why they don't give more. The higher the gift, usually the less bearing the membership benefits have on the donor—and the gift becomes more of an outright unrestricted donation.

Donor Clubs

The higher member giving levels become donor clubs. Donor clubs usually begin at a level considered to be a major gift. In some organizations this is $100, in others $1,000, and in yet others a much higher level. Donor clubs usually have a name (e.g., The President's Club) and make special offers to the donor. These offers are often events or opportunities designed to bring such donors closer to the institution and increase their involvement and interest or provide recognition of their generosity. Opportunities might include events such as a tour with the institution's director, dinner with other club donors, a name on a plaque in the reception area of the organization's building, or a periodic "insider" newsletter.

These member/donors receive a special renewal. The renewal can be a personalized letter or a personal call or visit from a board member or the chief staff officer. These donors do receive the typical member benefits such as free admission, the publication, and discounts. Some, but not all, of these donors will opt out of taking the tangible member benefits. These donors do consider themselves members, and a number of them will have originally joined the organization at a value level of giving.

When a new donor makes a gift to the organization at a support level, it is appropriate to make that person a member at the level of his or her giving. This ensures that the donor will be on the regular mailing list and, more importantly, will be in the system to be resolicited on the anniversary date of the first gift. In addition, the new donors will be invited to events that will bring them closer to the institution and encourage them to become more involved.

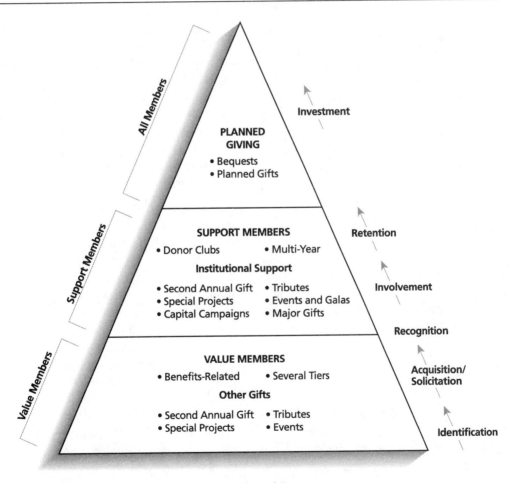

Figure 3–3 Membership Pyramid of Giving, Graduated Dues

Why People Give

Why do members make other gifts to the organization? They make these gifts for the same reasons that people make gifts to any philanthropic organization. A survey in the *Chronicle of Philanthropy* (2001, 23–24) recently reported on the reasons why people give. Of the top reasons, a number speak directly to what a membership program can provide for the organization.

Strong Feelings about the Cause/ Moral Imperative—the Right Thing To Do

When people feel strongly about a cause, they join. This can be true of almost all types of membership programs. It is particularly true for those that are issue related or faith based; there may a "moral imperative" for joining. A membership program can be an ongoing proactive way to find those who believe in what the organization does. Having membership as a constant program is a constructive way for an organization to be available to those who want to be involved. Those who feel strongly about the cause may join at a support level and also respond to additional requests for financial, and, in some cases, volunteer help. The communication part of the membership program is particularly important in bringing the messages about the important work of the organization to the members. The communication program is discussed in Chapter 4.

Personal Experience with the Organization

A well-developed program offers many ways in which a member can become personally involved in the organization. From attending events to volunteering to participating in travel programs, a membership program is a structured way to bring people into an organization. For loyalty, volunteer, and participant organizations, personal experience is required and significant. For other types of organizations, the personal experience can be increased over time. This is one of the reasons that it is essential for the membership program to have ways to involve the members.

Response to a Request

A cardinal rule of fundraising is that you must ask for a gift. Membership begins by asking people to join. Asking for other gifts is also appropriate. Those who want to contribute will, those who aren't interested won't. But those who want to contribute will not do so unless asked. Members may be asked several times during the year for different efforts. Members are the friends of the organization, and most understand the need to ask more than once for funds.

Interest in an Event Associated with a Charity

Events associated with a charity are often put on by the membership. Membership programs with a volunteer component frequently focus on fundraising. Events are one of the primary ways these groups raise funds. Whether it is a participatory event such as a walk or golf tournament, a gala dinner, or bake sale, members can create, plan, and implement events. The invitation list for the event can include the current members, lapsed members, and friends and colleagues of the members involved in the event. Events that are popular can take on a life of their own, with members volunteering in increasing numbers and attendance climbing each year.

ASKING MEMBERS

Other Requests

Other funds from members come from a variety of requests in addition to the yearly membership renewal. Members, because of their belief in the organization and their personal involvement, should always be considered as one of the groups to ask for donations for special projects. They are the ones closest to the institution and the ones with the greatest stake in it. In addition, the membership is the perfect audience for earned income opportunities.

A successful membership program provides the opportunity for successful fundraising of contributed and earned income. This successful fundraising is the foundation of support for an institution or organization. There are a number of possibilities for raising funds through other requests, as described below.

Matching Gifts

Many corporations have matching gift programs. These programs are corporation specific, with different criteria for the types of gifts that can be matched and different ratios at which they are matched. Some corporations will match gifts for membership. It is important to include asking for matching gifts on the membership enrollment form. If a matching gift is made, give the member membership at the increased level.

Second Gift

By considering the member base as the donor base, there is also the opportunity for asking members for gifts in addition to the membership. It is possible to solicit what might be called an annual gift or, in this case, a second gift. Many institutions have an annual giving fund in addition to the membership program. It needs to be very clear that this is not a membership solicitation; it is a request for another gift. This gift may be for general purposes or tied to a specific program. Often the program is one that the organization presents regularly (an education program, for example), and the organization is looking for new and additional ways to fund it.

Some members will be confused about being asked for a second gift. This confusion should not keep the institution from asking. Wording on the second gift solicitation should be clear. For example, the Missouri Botancial Garden's director writes in an annual giving letter to his members: "I realize that your membership is also due for renewal at this time, and I am truly grateful for your consideration of this special request." Or at the bottom of the response slip, print the statement, "I understand this is not a renewal of my current membership." If a member calls about this confusion and wants to make a gift but is uncertain about the difference, the member service staff should explain the differences and help the member select the option that he or she is interested in. Confusion for some members should not be used to eliminate this additional program.

Gift Memberships

There is no one better to purchase a gift membership than a current member. The gift can be for any holiday. Membership programs can promote the gift membership idea as a way to acquire new members, and this campaign is most effective with current members. Gift memberships can be publicized for the holiday season, Valentine's Day, Mother's Day, Father's Day, and so forth. The membership manager should select those commemorative days that have some connection to the institution or that can be marketed in a productive way—a Baseball Hall of Fame membership, with its Internet publications is a natural for Father's Day, as is a botanical garden membership for Mother's Day, or Smithsonian Institute membership for the holidays for someone interested in the institution and its magazine. The organization must consider the extent to which it can market the gift memberships. Even if the organization does not have the resources to publicize gift memberships, it should make them available to anyone who requests one.

Tributes

Many organizations have a tribute fund. A tribute fund allows people to make a gift in honor or memory of someone. It has become quite common for those who have a special birthday or anniversary to ask friends to make a donation to a charity of choice rather than send a gift. When people die, many families ask that donations be made rather than flowers sent. When these requests are made, and it is for a charity of the donor's choice, it is important for members to have a way to select the organization to which they want to contribute. A tribute envelope is a useful way for organizations to make certain that their members have the information and the convenience of making this type of gift.

There are at least two ways to make tribute envelopes available to members. The first is to include one with the member's information packet. This can be one of the items sent to all members. One envelope can be sent each year if the tribute program is large, or every second or third year if the program is small. Many cultural institutions and hospital groups have particularly well-developed tribute programs. The second

way to promote this program is to do a mailing once a year, at a time that is appropriate for the institution. While botanical gardens may find that the best time is in the spring, a friends' group at a social service agency might want to mail closer to the winter holiday season.

Special Projects

Seeking funding for a specific project is a great opportunity to solicit the membership. Members who have been receiving information from the organization will know about many of the programs and facilities. When there is a special project, members like to know about it, and some will be willing to support it. Over time, it will become possible to identify members who have special interests and provide them more information about their favorite areas of interest.

Capital Campaigns

Capital campaigns are also an opportunity to solicit the membership. Members who are in the support-level donor clubs will, of course, be solicited at levels appropriate for the campaign. When the campaign is in its public stage, seeking a broad range of smaller gifts, value members should be solicited for various projects. Some organizations take this opportunity to relate a special project to the membership: for example, a room may become a members' room in a new facility, or a new endowment fund for a special program might be named for members. Significant amounts of money can be raised from a large pool of value-level members.

Planned Giving

Planned giving programs are appropriate for members of long standing. This is the donor base to which planned gifts can be marketed. There are many anecdotal stories about large bequests coming from basic level members. According to Timothy Sharpe of Robert F. Sharpe & Company, the planned giving specialists, "A major misconception…is the belief that most large planned gifts are made by people of great wealth. While stories abound of six- and seven-figure bequests coming from the estates of persons who had made very modest…gifts during life, these cases are often treated as amazing exceptions. As it turns out, these gifts are more the rule than the exception."

Bequests come from members who have known the institution for a long time and believe in it. From Robert Sharpe, of Robert F. Sharpe & Company, on bequests, "There appears to be no pattern to the gifts made prior to death other than the fact that most bequests appear to come from relatively long-term donors". They have an interest, have been involved through their membership, and are ready to make an investment through their bequests or other planned gifts. Length of time of association with an organization is a significant attribute of planned givers.

Special Events

Members also provide a good pool for prospects for special events. Members are those who support your organization regularly, and when there is a fundraising event, many may want to participate. If it is an event with a modest to moderate ticket price, the entire membership may be solicited. If, however, it is a high-ticket-priced event, such as a black-tie gala, it may make sense to send invitations only to the support level members. The organization may choose to give membership at the appropriate level to those who come to such an event. Many people come to events because a friend invites them. When this is the case, the allegiance is to the friend, not to the institution.

While making the person a member guarantees that he or she will be on the mailing list and receive information and invitations, the likelihood of renewing the person is slight. This doesn't mean that sending a renewal shouldn't be done, but that the expectation of renewal should not be high. If the event is a success, some people will return to annual events but never respond to other appeals.

Special Interest Groups

For some institutions, members provide the base from which to solicit membership in special interest groups. For example, many art museums will have member groups dedicated to a certain kind of art. One group might focus on contemporary arts, another on decorative arts, and still another on classical arts. The Denver Art Museum offers seven special interest groups, ranging from the Friends of Painting and Sculpture to the Asian Art Association. Special interest groups can also be found in organizations such as environmental or hobby-related groups. For example, an environmental group might offer subgroups relating to rare plants or to endangered animals, with each providing specialized communications and events relevant to the participants' interests. Often, to belong to a specialty membership group, it is necessary to join the regular membership group first; for most programs, this should be required. There are benefits associated with these subgroups, and they are also a way to further cultivate members and increase giving levels.

Travel Programs

Membership programs may offer travel options. University and college alumni associations, museums, environmental groups, and others, from time to time, organize trips that are related to their mission. Lectures, knowledgeable guides, and special events are all a part of these tours. In addition to the cost of the trip, organizations will often include an expected donation to the organization, which is tax-deductible. This extra donation can be a noteworthy addition to an organization's budget. And, of course, many of these trips are advertised and available to members only. In addition, when a staff member accompanies the group, there is the opportunity for the members and staff to forge a relationship that carries on long after the trip is over. This relationship can be a strong motivator for further interest and involvement in the organization by the member.

Products

Logo merchandise, those caps, shirts, and mugs with the institution's logo, can be very popular. Offering these items to the membership is one way to encourage sales and to promote the use of items that bring visibility to the organization. Art museums have taken this to great levels with four-color catalogues of items based on their collections. Alumni groups make use of this with school logo merchandise; fraternities and sororities do the same.

Publications, print and electronic, insurance, and affinity credit cards are examples of other products that can also be offered to the membership.

Facility Rental

For visitation-based institutions, a member benefit can be a discount on or first priority for a facility rental. Rentals include space for meetings, conferences, weddings, and parties of all sorts. These institutions can be very desirable and in demand. If an institution is building its facility rental program, a mailing to the membership is one of the ways to make this service known.

Frequency of Requests

Overall, a member should be solicited throughout the year. How often can a member be asked for funds? There are no hard and fast rules about the number of requests that can be sent to a member. There seem to be different perceptions about the kinds of "asks" that are made. For example, a request for a matching gift, solicited on the membership enrollment form, is not really perceived as a second request. Sending tribute information can be viewed as a service because many people choose to honor or memorialize someone in this manner. Events provide ways to involve members, and different types of events appeal to different types of members. Those who want to attend will respond to those of interest. These are perceived as requests, but not in the same vein as those for contributions without participation.

Special interest groups and travel choices are both services and opportunities for members for involvement and education, should they decide to participate. These are very positive ways for the institution to interact with members, and members view them in that way. These opportunities, when done well, are popular and perceived as real benefits of being a member.

Those asks that are perceived as additional requests are the requests for a second gift, for special projects, and for capital campaigns. Again, those members who are interested will give support. For those who are not interested, the request is a form of communication, letting the members know what is happening in the organization. Planned giving information is just that—information and another way to communicate with the membership.

In Chapter 4, communication is discussed. Requests or information of any type should be considered a part of the communication package. Requests should not constitute the greatest number of pieces of mail that a member receives. A small organization might send two or three additional solicitations during the year, while a large one might send four or more, in addition to the yearly membership renewal. Additional solicitations might be for a second annual gift, the tribute fund, a special project, a special event, and one to buy gift memberships. A member might also receive an invitation to a planned giving seminar. If the organization is involved in a capital campaign, members might be telephoned for a gift in addition to the mail requests.

There are members who do not want to be solicited for anything but their membership. They will let the organization know who they are and that they do not want to be solicited for other efforts. The wishes of these members should be honored, and they should be taken off the mailing list for those fundraising campaigns. Many organizations worry about asking for a gift too often. Most organizations err on the side of not asking often enough. Always honor a person's request not to be solicited, but don't allow a few complaints to dictate the fundraising strategy.

COUNTING THE MONEY

There may be times when there is disagreement over which department gets to take credit for certain revenue; the issue should really be the overall bottom line. This is typically an issue in organizations with staff. How the money is counted can be any way the organization wants to and in accordance with generally accepted accounting procedures. But the overriding issue should be how much is raised overall. There should be cooperation among staff to provide the

best and most fundraising for the organization as a whole. No fundraising program should lead to turf wars. It is the work of the leader of the program to make certain that this doesn't happen. Everyone needs to work cooperatively toward the same end: more resources for the institution.

In an organization where membership is in the development department, the money that comes in for membership is a part of the development revenue. Some organizations recognize membership income as earned income rather than contributed income. This overcomplicates the issue, particularly since it is known that not all members use the benefits offered, and most do not use all of them (e.g., if an incentive needs to be picked up, usually one-half or fewer members actually claim them). Members believe that they have joined in order to support the organization. Count all of the funds as contributed.

In yet other organizations, there is a temptation to count lesser amounts as membership and those over a certain level as development. These organizations feel that it is important to know how much is generated by membership and how much by development. This would follow the pattern of value members being attributed to membership and support members (e.g., donor clubs) to development. This pattern, however, can set up a tension between staff members. It causes membership staff not to be interested in upgrading since they lose members. If revenues are balanced against expenses, acquisition becomes much more difficult. Is the cost prorated between the basic levels and the upper levels depending on response? Again, keep the counting simple.

Furthermore, if the membership program were not providing the donor base, then there would not be a constituency to ask for other gifts. Membership begins with many small gifts. In fundraising, it is almost always more expensive to raise small gifts than large ones. This is because direct mail, events, and the other ways that small gifts are solicited cost money. Often a volunteer with a personal solicitation and little expense will secure a major gift. These gifts, however, are typically based on a long relationship with the organization (or the solicitor) and are backed by staff efforts. The question then is, Why spend time on small gifts if they are more expensive to raise? There are several answers.

First and foremost, an organization that attracts only a small number of donors is "putting all its eggs in one basket." A strong donor base is built like the one shown in the donor pyramid of giving (refer to Figure 3–2). A large, broad donor base gives a solid foundation. With it, the loss of a major donor is difficult, but not threatening. Second, for visitation-based institutions, the organization wants a broad base to attend. Having a membership program with its events and activities is a significant way to build attendance at the institution. For other organizations, the broad base gives a core group to approach for volunteer work, educational messages, and programs. Third, if there is a planned giving program, many of these gifts will come from supporters who are not major donors.

In visitation-based organizations, it is also shortsighted for the organization as a whole to consider members attending and enjoying free admission as revenue foregone and charge the membership department for it. This view is counterproductive and provides no incentive to have a membership program, at least not one that offers any type of admission as a benefit. Revenue foregone in a visitation-based institution is a difficult concept. If a person were not a member, would he or she come as often? Anecdotal information suggests "no." The member who comes frequently may eat more often in the restaurant, may shop more frequently in the gift shop, and, as a result, provide a higher level of earned income. Those who come frequently may also tend to be those who provide other support to the institution, whether it be direct financial support, planned gifts, volunteer time, or all three.

SUMMARY

When designing the fundraising program for an organization, it is important to decide first what kind of program is required. If there are reasons in addition to or other than income involved, membership will be a good foundation for the program. In those programs where other fundraising also occurs, the membership program should be the base for much, if not all, of the activity. Membership programs can provide a solid structure for fundraising.

REFERENCES

Association of Fundraising Professionals. 2000. *AFP first course in fundraising: Building the future of philanthropy*. Alexandria, VA: Author.

National Society of Fund Raising Executives. 1996. *The NSFRE fund-raising dictionary*. New York: John Wiley & Sons.

New poll shows how wealthy view estate tax, other giving issues. 2001, January 25. *Chronicle of Philanthropy*, 23–24.

CHAPTER 4

The Membership Program

Patricia Rich and Dana Hines

Variety's the very spice of life.

—William Cowper

VARIETY IN MEMBERSHIP

THERE IS GREAT VARIETY IN MEMbership programs. It would be close to impossible to find two that are exactly alike. There are differences in structures for the programs, differences in benefits, differences in markets. This occurs because of the different types of nonprofits that develop them; nonprofits have different purposes, geography, and competition. There can also be packages within a membership program for different kinds of members. The package is the membership program that the member selects.

MEMBERSHIP PACKAGES

All membership programs have a basic membership package. For those with dues levels, such as the ones offered by most visitation-based and issue organizations, there may be several packages from which the potential member can choose.

Variety in Offerings

The Basic Package

A typical basic membership program might include admission benefits for two adults and two children under 12 years of age, a newsletter, a discount on merchandise and programs, and invitations to events. There may be different price points for this package for individuals, students, seniors, grandparents, or nannies, though the benefits would be close to the same. As the levels of membership increase, so do the benefits including more admissions tickets, tickets for special exhibits, parking, coupons for food service, invitations to more exclusive events, and so forth.

Nonresident Program

For institutions where visitation is a primary benefit, a program can be designed for those who live 100 to 200 miles or more from the institution. This works for institutions that are tourist attractions and that have special shows or exhibits that will attract visitors from a certain distance. Most often there is one level for this category, although some institutions have two—one for value members and the other for support members. The Art Institute of Chicago offers one level for those who live at least 100 miles from the museum, while the Metropolitan Museum of Art offers two levels for those who live at least 200 miles from Manhattan.

Internet Membership

With the advent of the Internet, institutions with collections online can offer an Internet membership. This program offers all information via the Internet, with little sent by postal service. The program at the Metropolitan Museum of Art provides Met Net members with benefits including screen savers, online audio features, and special members-only offers in the online Met store. There is also free admission to the museum and the incentive of a special T-shirt.

Special Interest Groups

Many museums develop special membership groups that one may join if already a member of the institution. In particular, art museums have designed these groups to take advantage of their collections and the interests of museum goers and curators. These groups offer special lectures, educational opportunities, and travel experiences. There is often a second membership fee for these groups. The Palm Springs Desert Museum offers six possible groups, all requiring museum membership, and then extra dues ranging from $15 to $400 annually.

Guilds and Auxiliaries

Guilds and auxiliaries are typically volunteer organizations that exist to provide programs and volunteers for an institution. At the Heard Museum in Phoenix, the 700 volunteers join the Guild after joining the Heard Museum. For those who want to be involved with the institution, joining a guild or auxiliary is the way to do it. Hospital auxiliaries, particularly those in rural areas, may also require membership before it is possible to volunteer.

Voting Programs

There are also membership programs with voting privileges attached. At The Art Institute in Chicago, members who are at the sustaining level of $1,500 per year for three years are granted voting membership for every year that they give at that level. These members have the privilege to vote for the trustees for the museum. At the Museum of Fine Arts, Houston, all members may vote at the annual meeting on the slate of trustees and on the budget.

Other Programs

Some visitation-based institutions have offered a junior membership program, but they appear to lack longevity. The cost of providing staffing, benefits, and other related items makes this an expensive type of program. In reality, the parents or grandparents buy the membership, so it seems to work as well to offer it to them and include benefits for children. The Saint Louis Zoo now offers a special "I'm a Zoo Friend, too!" option for children under 12 in a household that holds a membership at the family level and above.

Another effort has been teachers' membership programs. Those teachers who are very interested do join at the value level; remember that education, not income, is the best predictor for joining. Institutions that want to offer something special to get teachers involved in their education programs might consider an honorary membership for the year. The Exploratorium in San Francisco offers an educator level at the same price as the "active" or basic membership, but it also includes privileges in the Exploratorium's Learning Studio. School affiliation must be provided.

Botanical gardens often have a category for garden clubs and plant societies. This category can be tied into special privileges for their members, meeting space for the club/society, or the group's ability to stage flower shows at the garden. Yet another type of membership program relates to planned giving. Institutions with planned giving programs will often have a "Heritage Society" or "Legacy Circle" for those who have designated that a planned gift has been made. That is usually the requirement of membership, and benefits may include invitations to

special events at the institution, certificates, and other recognition efforts.

A very popular type of membership that has grown recently is the "young friends group." This membership is designed to appeal to those from 20 to 40 years of age. These groups typically plan events that attract this age range and often, but not always, are geared to singles. For visitation-based institutions, this is seen as a way to build audience in a group younger than most members. The idea of building audience is very strong and helps with fundraising and other institutional needs.

In all of these examples of special interest groups, it is important to remember that these groups exist to strengthen and promote the institution and umbrella membership group, and are not stand alone groups.

Variety in Dues

There is variety in dues as well as in programs. Construction of a graduated dues program is discussed later in this chapter and in Chapter 9. Most programs will have value levels and support levels. There are, however, other dues levels that programs sometimes offer. Make certain that dues levels are kept simple.

Annual or Multi-year

Dues are the financial part of the membership equation. If at all possible, dues should be annual. This gives the organization the opportunity to upgrade the member on a yearly basis. Some organizations offer two- and three-year memberships. The strength of this option is internal; the renewal process is eliminated for one or more years. If the institution's staff is very small, this may help. The other positive aspect of this membership option occurs in organizations that depend on blockbuster exhibits or programs that may only be scheduled every other year. For example, the two-year option, if enough people take advantage of it, might help level out the membership numbers and avoid spikes every other year. It also would keep these members on the rolls for other fundraising efforts, rather than losing them in the year when no major exhibit or program is scheduled.

The negative aspect of multi-year memberships is that there is usually a discount for the second and third years. Unfortunately, costs rise, and multi-year dues do not offer a way to take this into consideration. In the long run, the financial aspects of multi-year dues make them less attractive than annual dues. There are no known studies that test whether or not multiple year memberships increase renewal rates. For a first-time multi-year member, the entire time span should be considered as a first-year membership, until the membership has been renewed.

Flat or Graduated

For organizations where membership is not a fundraising issue—a school alumni association or a hospital auxiliary, for example—a flat structure is possible. In this case, there is one level of dues. In the school example, the school conducts the fundraising, using the alumni association to keep alumni close. For the hospital, the auxiliary is often a volunteer group that may raise funds through special events or other means; however, the main fundraising is carried out by the hospital or its foundation. Groups that have volunteers or participants as their main focus often use this method for dues because it is easy to administer, and fundraising programs may or may not be a part of the organization.

For organizations where membership is an integral part of the fundraising, a gradu-ated dues structure is essential. The dues range from basic levels to donor clubs. In a membership program, it is important to have a variety of giving opportunities for the prospective member. The basic membership level in most cases ranges from $25 to $60 annually, depending on the type of organization and the benefits offered. To increase the likelihood that people will increase their giving over time, other levels of membership should be established. These levels should be established at intervals that will facilitate a gradual upgrading of a member's giving.

For example, a dues structure of $40, $75, $150, $250, $500, and $1,000 per year paces the increases at almost double the amount of the preceding category. This allows for a stepping-stone approach based on the higher levels of membership and also makes possible the increase in a membership category if a member is employed by a matching gifts company. Such matching gifts can increase a member's membership level while also increasing their benefits.

Membership Category Options

Whether there is a flat or a graduated dues structure, there are a number of issues to decide. What kinds of membership options should be offered? Should there be individual members? Household members? Family memberships? Life members? Student members? Senior members? The list could continue. The fundamental philosophy should be to keep it simple. Simple makes it easy for everyone. The potential member (especially those who begin as value members) should not have to mathematically figure out which is the best value, should not have to send documentation of student or senior status, and should be able to make a quick decision because of convenience. On the organization side, simple makes data entry much easier. It makes reporting much easier. It makes all financial projections much easier. If the organization is a visitation-based institution, simple makes the admission staff's lives much easier. It is difficult (if not impossible) for a young, entry-level staff member to question the "family" at the turnstile. The fewer the options, the easier it is for member and organization alike. Once again, keep it simple—no "category" clutter.

Lifetime Memberships

The ultimate multi-year membership offer is a lifetime membership. Don't do it. A lifetime membership seldom makes any sense, and especially does not make economic sense unless it is very large and basically endows the membership gift for life. There are, of course, some exceptions. Lifetime membership can be used as a mark of respect or an honor. This may be appropriate for a founder, a lifetime volunteer, or a very major donor. Another possibility is to use it for major endowment gifts, which, in essence, endow the membership gift. These gifts tend to be very large and unusual, falling often into the "honor" category.

For some organizations with flat dues structures, such as alumni associations or hospital auxiliaries, the issue is to keep the person on the list, not necessarily to raise funds from him or her. If this is the case, a life membership makes sense if it will be large enough to cover mailings and other related costs for the lifetime of the member. Life members should not be an ongoing financial loss for the organization. If a large gift is made for this purpose, the prudent thing to do is to put the money into a restricted fund so that only the interest it generates is used for the membership program.

If the organization currently has lifetime members and decides not to offer this category any longer, the category can be phased out. First, remove the level from any membership literature. Second, "grandfather" all current lifetime members. Notify life members that they will always be considered a member, and list them as such on donor recognition lists. In addition, consider soliciting them for upper-level donor clubs. Many are friends of the institution and will become annual givers.

One organization decided to eliminate its life membership program because it was having a negative impact on income. It was agreed that current life members would be continued, but also solicited for the newly designed upper-level gift clubs. Life membership was no longer offered as an option. The current life members received a lengthy personal letter from the executive director explaining why they were being solicited, the need to raise more funds for important programs, and so forth. There were few complaints and most of the life members became members of the donor club.

Individual Memberships

This category offers a membership for one individual. For hobby groups, volunteer auxiliaries, and civic groups, this may be a suitable category. The organization needs to be one where the individual interest is paramount and sometimes calls for volunteer commitment. If benefits are irrevocably tied to one person, an individual membership may be appropriate. For a visitation-based institution, it should not be an option unless the demographics of the area show a preponderance of single-person households. The great majority of people visit an institution with a friend. Make it easy for the member to bring someone to enjoy the day. For membership programs that work primarily by mail, "household" will be the appropriate term since all in the household will take advantage of the communications, which will be the major benefit of the membership.

Family or Basic Memberships

"Family" has taken on new definitions during the past few decades. What is a family? There is no longer the single pattern of mom, dad, and two children. For this reason, consider other ways of describing a dual or group membership. For non–visitation-based organizations, consider naming the group "household," since many of the benefits come by way of the mailbox and e-mail, and the issue is to mail to one address, be it postal or computer. For visitation-based institutions, consider a "basic," "regular," or "household" membership that includes two adults and two children up to the age of 12, 16, or 18. Some organizations create other names such as "passport" or "active." With this basic membership, the turnstile staff need only look to see if there are two adults and two (or whatever the number of) children.

Enhanced Memberships

This level applies mainly to visitation-based institutions. If there are benefits such as IMAX® tickets or additional admissions and a need for another level, this category is a possibility. The financial impact is the consideration here. Remember that for every additional ticket included in the benefit package, there is revenue forgone on the ticket revenue side of the ledger. This is not to say that there should not be a membership program because of revenue forgone, but to say that the more tickets that are used as benefits, the more revenue that is lost. The original basic membership level needs to be sufficient to attract and keep

value members, but do not give away the store. These extra tickets and benefits will have no effect on the overall fundraising program.

Student Memberships

As the definition of family has changed, so has the definition of student. Who is a student? The organization must decide what it is trying to accomplish with this level. Is this an age issue? Or a "go to school" issue? If the real interest is in people in the 18- to 23-year-old age range or younger, then the category definition needs to reflect this. This is different than if the issue is attracting students or one of access for students.

For a non–visitation-based organization that attracts the majority of members in this age range, use a basic category at an appropriate price level, with higher-level categories available for those who can afford more. Since the organization mainly works with students, older members should tend to be support members rather than value members. For an organization that is interested in students, no matter the age, select a basic level, again, that is at an appropriate price point. In both cases, acquisition efforts would focus on those lists or sites made up of the targeted age group or student population. For example, an alumni association might have special, lower membership fee for alumni in the first few years out of college, so they become accustomed to belonging to the association.

For a visitation-based institution, this category has a direct impact on admissions revenue. Again, the decision must be made whether the issue is age or access. If the issue is age, then the student category definition must reflect this. On the whole, students are not a good source for fundraising, so the question becomes why does the organization want student members. The answer is often access. The organization may want to make certain that students have easy access to the institution. There are several ways to work on this issue. The first way is to have a low student admission price so that if a student wanted to come, he or she could come numerous times before it would make sense to become a member. If a defining characteristic is age, then that needs to be clearly spelled out in all materials. If the characteristic is being a full-time or part-time student, then student identification is needed, and this requirement needs to be clear. Admission staff need to be trained in what to ask for and how to do it in an appropriate manner. Showing a student ID is almost always a stated prerequisite for using a membership card in this category.

The second way to increase access is to identify those students for whom the institution wants access and to work on it from that perspective. For example, an art museum might want to make certain that local college and university art and art history students have access. The museum can work with the faculty and sell or donate enough admission passes to make sure that access is available. If the museum also wants students on the mailing list, the museum could ask the faculty for the students' names and addresses and add them for one year at a time. Or the museum could send the faculty enough copies of the newsletter, invitations to events, or whatever is helpful, for distribution to students.

Grandparents/Aunt-Uncle Memberships

This category is aimed at relatives other than parents or friends who bring children to the institution. Children's museums, zoos, and science centers are among the institutions that typically consider a grand-

parents category. Benefits are aimed at one or two grandparents bringing a certain number of grandchildren under a certain age. The number can range from two to unlimited; the age range goes from 12 years to 21 years of age, with most ending by 18 years of age. Benefits might also include special events. The Saint Louis Zoo offers passes to the Children's Zoo and the Zoo Railroad parking and an invitation to a special grandparent/grandchildren event, along with a shop discount, the newsletter, and a calendar. Those purchasing the membership are often asked to provide the specific names and ages of the children-involved.

Senior Memberships

Offering senior discounts has become a way of life in America. In many visitation-based organizations, seniors may make up the bulk of the membership. Senior, like the above categories, needs a definition. While always age-defined, this category can begin at 50 years old (to correspond with the AARP); however, most organizations and institutions tend to use 60, 62, or 65 years of age. This category is also based on trust; most organizations do not ask to see proof of age. The major reason for this category seems to be "everyone is doing it." The "everyone" includes movie theaters, some stores and restaurants, and a variety of other businesses.

Demographic information shows that, for the most part, this is the group that can most afford to be members. We also know that the population as a whole is aging, with the size of the senior group increasing with the aging of the baby boom population (Symens Smith et al. 2000, 4). If there is a way to avoid having this category, avoid it. Just don't offer it. If it is something that the organization must do, then make it only a little less expensive than the basic level of membership. The charge for this level should be no more than $5 less than the basic level, and at this senior rate, all costs must be covered. Some organizations offer $5 off of any level for senior members. The reason some organizations do this is that members are already locked into a senior level. Organizations feel that they cannot abandon the practice, and they want seniors who identify with a "senior" offer to know they are welcome to give at higher levels while still getting their senior discount. The other financial consideration is that the rate for this level should be the amount used when doing a cost-benefit analysis. In effect, it becomes the first level of membership.

Discount Memberships

Some organizations offer a discount on membership as an incentive to join. This is another practice that should be avoided if at all possible. By offering the membership at a discount, the offer is cheapened. It also serves value members to wait until the next discount opportunity to renew. Renewal of the regular or basic level then becomes an upgrade ask and much more difficult. If some form of incentive is desired, consider adding an extra month or two rather than lowering the price. While it may amount to the same thing, the member will be writing the check for the same amount of money when it is time to renew rather than thinking he or she is giving more.

Other Types of Memberships

There are as many categories of membership as creativity will allow. Some children's museums, such as the Minnesota Children's Museum, add the nanny to any category by adding $5 to any membership level. Some organizations have international categories for those who do not live in the United States. Others have an educator or teacher category, which is usually an individual membership with special educational benefits added.

Pricing Structure

What should be the price for each of the levels? Each organization needs to decide this for itself. Take a look at other, comparable organizations. Consider the institution's audience. Try different benefit packages and analyze their costs. In organizations for whom the membership levels move into donor clubs, it's important to know where the fundraising program places the high donor levels. As mentioned earlier, a stepping-stone approach works very well.

The same principles that apply to pricing goods and services in the open market also apply to membership dues. A part of the perception of what a product is worth is dictated by the pricing structure. If a product is bargain priced, that sometimes conjures up the notion that the product is not worth more than the price. Conversely, if a healthy price tag is attached to a product, there is a perception that it is quality and worthwhile, unless proven otherwise.

Likewise, if a membership program is found to be priced drastically under similar programs, the perception may develop that this product is inferior to the others, not that the others are all overpriced. It may also be the perception that if one institution's membership dues are above the competition in pricing, then its product is superior to the others. However, it is suggested that unless there is a dramatic difference—whether real or perceived—in an institution's quality and membership offering, its pricing structure should be in line with others offering similar products.

Dues Increases

Periodically, it is necessary to raise prices no matter what the product or service. To keep pace with inflation and other institutions, increasing dues on a three- to four-year time span is perfectly acceptable. Increasing dues more frequently may be necessary, but can present the impression that the organization is greedy. Increasing dues less frequently is literally passing up an opportunity to increase the financial support and an institution's revenues. In this case, the organization is not taking advantage of the ability and willingness of its membership to support the institution.

The mechanism and method that an institution uses to increase is dues can help soothe any ill will that is created by the dues increase. Giving ample forewarning that the increase is going to happen can appease some members. Giving members an opportunity to renew at the old dues structure rate can calm some of those irate or unhappy feelings. When carrying out a dues increase, expect that some members will write or call to complain; however, a letter or two is not an indication that the dues increase should not have taken place. A slight decline in membership renewal may be experienced during the initial year of a dues increase. These are expected responses to an increase and should not be taken as a failure or mistaken decision.

Enacting a membership dues increase can significantly increase the revenues from a membership program in one year. Increasing dues may be a way to allow a membership program to stabilize and acquire more members because of the increased revenues. If the result of a dues increase is enlarging the membership substantially through aggressive acquisition, then more power to the effort.

A new trend is appearing in membership structures at visitation-based institutions: raising the second level membership to a higher amount (e.g., from $75 to $85 or $90) and the configuration of that level into a family plus or enhanced membership level. At this new level, members are offered access to events, tickets to performances, or add guest opportunities. This level is a way to entertain extended family and friends at an institution. For example, at one museum, the IMAX® Club gives members six free tickets to all IMAX® shows. At a botanical garden, the Family and Friends Plus membership lets the member bring up to 10 guests to five increasingly popular special events. These enhanced levels of membership give members a taste of what it is like to receive a heightened level of special access, and may be the gateway to a commitment to higher levels of membership in the future.

Recordkeeping

If the organization does not have a way to keep accurate and up-to-date records, there is little reason to have a membership program. Recordkeeping is the basis for all of the work done by and for the membership. Acquisition can be expensive, with the financial rewards coming from renewals and other fundraising efforts. Thus, recording the information for a new member is essential. The questions to consider are, first, what information needs to be kept and, second, how to keep it.

The information that needs to be kept depends on the organization and the role of the membership. All organizations need to keep the basics: name, address, amount of gift, and date of gift. Related to this information may be both home and office information for address, telephone, fax, and e-mail.

If this is a dual membership, the organization may want both first names. With the proliferation of two members of a couple having different last names as well as first, it is important to keep separate names even though there is one membership. The gift level is needed to make certain that fulfillment is correct and so that, if personal renewal and/or thank-you letters are sent, the amount can be referenced. The date is essential in order to make the renewal process run smoothly. Other information to keep depends on the organization. Possibilities include names of children or grandchildren, other gifts, volunteer work, legislative district (for public issue groups), and anything else that is relevant for the institution.

How the information is kept depends on the program's size, complexity (e.g., is it part of fundraising), funding, and computer capabilities. In the past, the recommendation for a beginning program was a shoebox with 4″ × 6″ cards. This can still work for a very small program. But with the proliferation of personal computers and off-the-shelf software programs, it now makes sense for almost all organizations to keep their records on computer. Appendix E lists the questions that an organization needs to answer before buying software and includes many of the vendors who have appropriate programs. Software ranges from basic database programs like FileMaker® to sophisticated fundraising and membership programs like The Raiser's Edge® from Blackbaud.

One of the major tasks is to keep the list correct and up-to-date. This is a constant need. At least twice a year, an outgoing membership mailing should include "address correction requested," which will, for a fee, return mail with new addresses. Another option is to send the organization's list once or twice a year to a vendor who provides National Change of Address (NCOA)

service. NCOA is the process that matches the organization's mailing list to change of address information that is submitted to the post office by people who are moving. A number of vendors provide this service, and they can be found in advertising in the nonprofit publications and on the Internet at NCOA (www.nationalchangeofaddress.com).

COMPONENTS OF THE MEMBERSHIP PROGRAM

The membership program itself is made up of five components: benefits, service, activities, communication, and recognition. When developing the program, it is essential to view it from the member's perspective because it is the member who will make the decision about whether or not to join or renew. This is a marketing approach because it is concerned first with the market (the potential members) and second, with the organization. The tangible benefits are packaged for acquisition and renewal and have a substantial financial implication for the institution. The intangible benefits, the "feel good" benefits of a sense of belonging, pride, and giving back, are achieved through service, activities, communication, and recognition. These, too, have a financial implication for the institution, but the potential member doesn't necessarily see these benefits as part of the economic package when weighing whether or not to join.

Benefits

Membership at the basic levels (the first several levels of dues) most often provides benefits that make it "a good deal." Many will join at these levels because they perceive that it is good value for the money spent. Members who base their gifts on this exchange are "value members." The value member is defined as one who makes the financial calculation of benefits received versus money spent and is willing to become a member on that basis. Many members begin their relationship with the organization this way. This must be kept in mind when benefits are designed. While an organization does not want to be overgenerous in terms of benefits, the benefit package must be compelling enough to attract the prospect interested in value. If the benefits are so good that the person joins on the basis of benefits alone, it will rarely be possible to keep that member. The long-term fundraising goal is to turn value members into support members. If there are other goals for the program, such as community support, the program should reinforce those issues as well.

As discussed previously, there are many reasons why people join an organization. However, it is necessary to have the person join in the first place. It is essential to understand that, above all, those who join have some interest in the organization and the work it is doing. Member surveys cite "joining for the purpose of supporting a worthwhile organization" (Membership Consultants survey results) as the top reason why they join, followed by benefits. Even if the person is joining for the benefits—free admission to a museum, for example—the person still has to want to go to the museum for membership to be considered. The same is true for those who join organizations that have a magazine as the major benefit. The potential members have to be interested enough to want to read the magazine.

The tangible benefits are that helpful nudge to encourage people to take a look at what the organization is doing. This is the first interaction that the potential member has with the organization. The potential member must have some interest in, or at

least inclination toward, the organization for the benefits to be enticing and work in the long term.

Benefit Package

The benefit package is what the prospect exchanges for dollars. The structure of the package is very important economically and should be designed with benefits relevant to the organization. Perhaps more importantly, the structure needs to recognize basic human needs and values. People like to feel special, to have access to things and places that not everyone else can claim, to be given something that is free, to be kept informed, and to feel a sense of belonging. These are some of the issues that need to be kept in mind when constructing the membership benefits and program.

A benefit package takes on the character of the institution. Benefits are limited only by creativity and economic realities (see Exhibit 4–1). For all organizations, there is the possibility of member-related benefits: the membership card, a bumper sticker, a window decal. There can be products with the organization logo, such as a mug, a tee shirt, or a baseball cap. All of these items serve to make the person feel that they belong and can make them external advocates for the organization.

Program-related benefits can also be included in a package. These should always include a newsletter or other publication that is a regular communication vehicle between the member and the organization. Other benefits might be invitations to and/or discounts on program-related special events, lectures, classes, and tours. For example, a history interest group might invite the public to hear a famous lecturer, while members are also invited to a reception where they can meet and personally talk to the lecturer. With today's technology, it is

Exhibit 4–1 Membership Benefits

The benefits listed here are the tangible ones that programs offer to potential members. The combination for any one organization is a combination of the organization's strategy, what is appropriate for that institution, the cost of benefits relative to pricing of membership levels, and what members want from the organization. Some of these benefits are also useful as incentives, the offer that encourages the potential member to join. This list is by no means exhaustive, but it is a reference for new programs and for those that are redesigning their benefit programs.

Member-Related Benefits

- Membership card, decal, bumper sticker
- Membership directory
- Recognition on a wall, in a book, on a list
- Dinners, receptions, previews
- Logo merchandise
- Discounts in shop, catalogue, or online (10 to 20 percent or a small dollar amount)
- Gift certificates/coupons (food, merchandise, programs) to use at the institution

Program-Related Benefits

- Members-only events, free or with cost
- Lectures, gallery talks, film programs
- Tours and meetings with director, curators, staff
- Tickets to performances, films, special exhibits
- Education programs
- First opportunity—for programs, events, reservations, travel
- Special benefits for children—own membership card, birthday card, birthday parties
- Travel opportunities
- Library check-out privileges
- Legislative updates
- Members-only section on Web site
- National organization events in the member's home area
- Discount on events, programs
- Publications—books, magazines, newsletters, catalogues, videos, tapes
- Involvement in programs—volunteer for organization, be part of a testing program (e.g., plants, hunting equipment)
- Reciprocal admission to like organizations in other cities
- Resource directory
- Kit to help member become involved in issue
- Hotline for information

Visitation-Related Benefits

- Benefits can be related to admission to the institution, or to exhibits or programs within it
- No waiting; members' line to enter
- Free, discounted, or a certain number of passes
- Parking, free for a number of hours, reduced rate
- Access to early/late nonpublic hours
- Guest passes, free or discounted
- Facility rental (access to/discount)
- Restaurant or other food service discount
- Access to special dining rooms, members'/patrons' room
- Concierge service—ability to purchase house tickets to sold out performances
- Audio tours, free or discounted
- Tram/railroad or other transportation at institution

continues

Exhibit 4–1 continued

Other Benefits

- Frequent flier miles
- Discounts for:
  - Other memberships in the community
  - Relevant retailers (e.g., sporting goods store for outdoors group)
  - Community retailers, e.g., restaurants and shops
  - Real estate, home mortgage, and insurance rates
  - Business-related offers
  - Magazine subscriptions (not from the organization)
  - Hotel/motel/car rental rates

---

also possible to provide "members' only" information via the organization's Web site as well as e-mail updates on current activities or information of interest. For organizations with visitation there are the added—and usually the primary—benefits relating to visitation. These include free admission, free parking, and discounts at gift shops or for food service.

Constructing the Benefit Package

The chances are very good that the potential member also belongs to other, like organizations. Thus, in constructing a membership benefit package, one of the first tasks is to look at the types of benefits similar institutions offer to their members. Each institution is different; however, it is important to recognize that your program is competing with comparable programs. Often the comparison is geographical. For example, one museum in a city probably needs to be somewhat close in benefits and dues to another museum in the same city. Regional and national groups that attract some of the same audience need to be aware of what the others are offering.

The individual character of the institution will ultimately determine what is appropri-

ate for that institution. However, there is no sense in reinventing the wheel. Benefit programs can be modeled after one another and even a copied program will take on a character all its own. When beginning to construct the benefits package, it may seem that the organization has little or nothing to offer. Creativity then becomes the exercise, and what it stimulates can be amazing. Think from a marketing and promotional point of view. Brainstorm ideas with staff, board members, and volunteers. Hold a focus group of current or prospective members to ascertain what is important to them. And do collect membership information from other organizations to stimulate your thinking.

Value Member Analysis

The value member takes the tangible benefits package very seriously. The package needs to have a perceived value for this potential member as well as meet the economic realties of the organization. For the organization, the benefits should not cost more than about 50 percent of the entry level dues. It is incumbent on the membership manager to make sure that the benefit package is competitive without offering more than the price of membership. The perceived value is from the member's perspective and underpins the marketing of the program. The perceived value should exceed the actual dues (see Chapter 5 for a cost-benefit analysis of membership categories).

For example, the potential member for a visitation-based institution will make some assumptions. He or she will assume visiting three times a year, receiving the newsletter with information about activities, maybe attending one or two programs, and doing some shopping in the gift shop. And he or she will want the membership premium of a museum tote bag. If the potential member is a value member, he or she must feel that the organization is worth supporting and that the benefits are worth the expense.

Beyond the financial cost involved in evaluating and structuring a benefit package, there may be other concerns as well. One of the most important is deliverability. In other words, do not offer benefits that cannot be delivered easily because of the operating constraints of the organization or institution. Staffing concerns and the capacity to serve the volume of members must be considered. The benefits offered must not create any ill will. For instance, if free parking is offered as a benefit, but parking is very limited, the organization needs to make other arrangements for major events, so that members do not feel cheated. In this case, a shuttle service would be a possibility, as long as it is able to handle the demand without creating long waiting lines, an impact that would negate the positive benefit of having free parking.

The same is true for the premium that is offered. It must have intrinsic value and be easily available. On the value side, organizations need to select premiums carefully. The perceived value must be in line with what the member might picture in his or her mind. For example, a botanical garden once offered a plant as a premium. The potential members pictured the lush, large plants that the garden's gift shop sold. In reality, to keep within budget constraints, the plant premium was a very nice, but very small, houseplant. Members were disappointed. Not a good way to start a relationship.

Easily available means either by mail or at an accessible facility. One local organization without a facility made arrangements with a local department store for members to pick up premiums at the customer service counter. The organization benefited because it saved on what could have been a very high postage expense and was able to use premiums that would have been difficult to mail. The department store benefited because it increased the foot traffic from a desirable market in the store. And the members found it very convenient because the stores were located all over the region.

Support Member Analysis

Support members are those who join at higher levels, where the benefits are increasingly intangible. They are also often interested in the tangible benefits, but clearly that is not why they join. Many membership staff relate stories about support members who are interested in receiving their tote bags and other benefits. Nevertheless, all membership response slips should have a box to check for those who do not want to receive the benefits.

Service

Consumers have been trained to expect good service. Books such as *In Search of Excellence* and programs such as the Baldridge Awards have brought the concept of service to the forefront of for-profit thinking. Nordstrom has built a department store chain on this concept. Members expect no less from organizations they have chosen to join. An institution that can't provide the "service to back up the sale" will find a loss when it comes to repeat business—in this case, the renewal of the membership.

On Joining

Membership payment processing. Strong membership service is a hallmark of a strong program. The acquisition program has gone perfectly. As a result, individuals are sending checks and credit card numbers. Whether by mail, telephone, or Internet, people who want to join, flood the organization with their responses. This is when membership service begins. Now, what do you do?

Depending on the size of your staff and the number of membership responses, there are three basic ways for you to process membership payments:

1. **Internal processing.** Your organization can receive membership payments either through a post office box or directly at the office. Once received, the staff or volunteers open the envelopes, enter data into the membership computer system, and deposit or process payments. Depending on the volume of responses, internal processing may involve one volunteer with a letter opener or a team of people working in an internal lockbox environment involving sophisticated equipment for functions such as envelope opening, check extracting, check encoding, and so forth. (In the membership context, a lockbox is a service providing all handling of money, including deposits.) The principal advantage of internal processing is that it provides the membership manager with the greatest possible control over the entire membership process. The downside is that internal processing may not be timely.

2. **Bank lockbox.** If the overall annual response volume is too great for staff to handle or if the responses come at particular times of the year, it might not be beneficial to handle the membership processing internally. For example, a large spike in the number of responses at year end might overwhelm staff and yet not justify creating a year-round internal processing department. Instead, outsourcing the processing may allow for quicker deposits and fulfillment while not necessarily resulting in increased expense. Responses would go directly to the bank, where the bank's lockbox department would take care of opening responses, capturing limited data, and depositing payments. The principal advantage to a bank lockbox is that it relieves staff of a tedious function while cost-effectively ensuring that payments are processed on a timely basis. One downside of using a bank lockbox is that banks often provide data entry for limited information such as name and address, while leaving the entry of other data such as telephone number, e-mail address, etc. to the membership department. Another downside is that bank lockboxes can become very expensive as the volume of responses grows. However, when compared to staff costs and timeliness, they can be an attractive option.

3. **Independent lockbox.** A number of companies specialize in providing lockbox services, sometimes called caging or simply payment processing. Because these companies specialize in lockbox services, they will generally

offer better service and, at higher volumes, with fees far below those charged by banks. While the minimum volume handled by these companies varies, you can expect them to be a viable option once your annual volume reaches 100,000 transactions. Responses would be sent directly to the company's post office box or to the organization's post office box, where the responses will be reshipped to the processing company. The advantage of independent lockbox services is that they will process payments quickly and cost-effectively while also capturing all vital data. The data can then be downloaded electronically to the organization's database. The downside to this solution is that these companies will only service organizations with very high transaction volumes.

Stewardship. The methods of processing payments and monitoring how they are used are known as internal stewardship. The process of thanking, serving, and reporting to members is known as external stewardship.

Regardless of where membership payments get processed, good internal stewardship requires that processing be timely and accurate. Ideally, payments will be deposited within 24 to 48 hours of their receipt. To ensure that the member receives the appropriate membership benefits and recognition, the organization must also take special care to ensure that it correctly records membership information. In addition, properly capturing information will help the organization effectively evaluate the performance of its membership marketing efforts as well as the overall membership program.

Once membership payments are processed, the organization should ensure that the funds are used for the purpose outlined to the member. For example, if members are told that a portion of their membership dues will fund educational programs, then the organization should take great care in making sure that those programs indeed receive the funds indicated. Also, the organization must use the membership funds to ensure that the members receive all of the promised benefits of membership.

Soon after the organization deposits the membership payment and records it, the organization should send a thank-you letter and membership welcome package. The membership welcome package might include a membership card, guest passes, catalogue of membership services, premium, and so forth. Welcome, or fulfillment, packages can be sent directly from the organization or, if the volume is great enough, a fulfillment house can be contracted to handle this task. A fulfillment house provides the service of generating the membership packet (letter, membership card, decal or other premium) and mailing it to the member.

Thank-you. As a general rule, organizations should thank members a minimum of three times and as many as seven or more times. Members should be thanked at least when they join, as part of the conclusion to the solicitation itself, when they are sent their welcome package, and when they are solicited for renewal. In addition, organizations can thank members by publishing their names in the annual report, inviting them to special member-appreciation events, sending a thank-you letter from the chief executive officer in addition to the membership manager, or listing upper-level members on a recognition wall. You cannot thank people too much. Your only limit is your imagination.

Effective communication with members will help develop the relationship between the member and the organization. "By reporting to donors how their gifts were used, we gain their confidence. With their confidence, the opportunities for future support are greater," according to the Association of Fundraising Professionals (AFP) Survey Course (2001, E-16). The same is true for membership programs. Tell members how their funds, and even their numbers, benefit the organization. Remind them of the benefits they receive as members and encourage them to use those benefits. If members feel their membership helps support the organization in some way, and if they use the available benefits, they will be much more likely to make charitable gifts to the organization as well as renew their memberships.

Being a member means being part of something; it means belonging. The more an organization makes its members feel part of something worthwhile, the more loyal the members will be. Effective internal and external stewardship is about building relationships. Strong relationships are the building blocks of strong membership programs.

A new member should receive his or her thank-you and information within ten days to two weeks. If it takes more than two weeks to process the membership, there will be problems. There is immediacy when people join. Often someone joins because he or she wants to visit soon, is interested in the issue and wants information, or wants to become involved in the organization's activities. If the member is waiting for three weeks or a month, the initial experience is not good from the member's perspective. There may be, however, spikes in responses at certain times during the year due to campaigns and seasonality. Regardless of volume, the goal should continue to be to have responses in the mail within ten days to two weeks or sooner.

When an organization has a membership drive, it is important to be able to service the new members. It may be necessary for staff to work overtime, to hire temporary staff, or to enlist other staff to help during this busy time. When planning the calendar for the year, taking membership drives into consideration is imperative because of the time and staff involved. It is important for the new member to have a great first impression, as the renewal decision actually begins with the first impression.

Membership cards. A word about membership cards. They come in virtually any form imaginable. One vendor, Membership Cards Only, advertises that it has "more than 77 different kinds of cards" (they can be reached at 1–800–77cards, or at moreinfo@memcards.com). Membership cards can be as simple as a computer-designed and -generated card to a heavy plastic version much like a credit card. Some visitation-based institutions have begun using cards that electronically monitor tickets to activities such as movies. The tickets are subtracted from the membership card as the card is used. The electronic tickets expire with the membership.

Membership card issues include use, cost, ease of fulfillment, and potential abuse. An organization should use material that is suitable for the card's use. If the card is never really used, as might be with a fraternity, sorority, or alumni group, then a heavy stock card is appropriate. If the card is used a lot for admissions, then a plastic or laminated card might be the right kind. If the card needs to be punched for admissions, yet a different material might be used. Cost can play a major role because the more substantial the card, usually the higher the cost.

Some organizations use an inexpensive card at value levels and more substantial ones at very high support or donor club levels. Ease of fulfillment has to do with whether the card is printed or embossed, and if the card is produced in-house or by a fulfillment company. Each organization needs to make this decision based on size of membership, revenue generated, and staffing. Last but not least, membership card abuse has become a topic particularly for those institutions with high admission ticket prices. The day may come for cards with photographs, but this hasn't happened yet. However, at this time, at least a few institutions are now requiring photo identification with the member's name on it for the membership card to be used. This trend will probably grow in the next few years.

During the Year

The members view the membership department as their place to have questions answered, get information, and voice complaints. This is a major function for the organization and must be taken seriously. Whoever is in charge of answering the telephone needs to smile when picking up the receiver and be cheerful and positive. Whatever the membership department can do to answer the questions or complaints should be done.

Dealing with complaints can be difficult, but the complaints should be taken seriously. For every complaint that is voiced, there are another 10, or more, comparable complaints that aren't voiced. There are difficult members. Some will make demands that are unreasonable. Staff and volunteers need to be trained to cope with these members and situations. For these reasons, it is important to train and support the membership service workers and give them the authority to do certain things to satisfy members' demands.

At the Institution

Members expect to be treated in a special manner. While we might think that all visitors are equal, indeed, members are more equal than nonmembers. There should always be a way for members to enter without waiting. Having a list or computer access to the membership list available at the admissions desk is very helpful for those members who forget their membership card. This is not an unusual occurrence. Most members are sensitized to the fact that they need to carry their cards, but it sometimes happens that the member is without one. If having an up-to-date list is not possible, and there are no membership staff available to check, it is usually best to admit the "member." If the person is really a member, no harm done, and the person will be happy. A difficult situation can arise with a real member who is not admitted. If there is a discount in the gift shop, the membership card should be requested for purchases. If possible, the same membership list should be available in the shop. The institution should have a policy to deal with such circumstances, and staff need to be trained in how to handle these kinds of situations. Most people are honest.

For an art or other museum with a blockbuster show, it may be difficult to have easy and quick access for the thousands of members who want to see the show. Members, however, should have some way to enter that is less cumbersome and at least somewhat faster than that for the general public. In these situations, many institutions have separate lines for members, separate ticket windows, and staff in visible positions to talk with members. Members also often have access to reservations for timed tickets before the general public.

Some institutions have special members' rooms available for members. The room may be a dining room, a lounge, or a meeting room. Such a gesture is a very nice benefit for the members and can be a benefit for upper-level support members, if the numbers are such that not all members can be served.

Activities

There must be activities for all members. There are some differences, however, for first-year members and with upper-level or support members. As the program becomes more mature, other segments of the membership can also be selected for special activities. For example, there might be programs directed toward families or seniors or for those members with special interests. Activities are important. Participation equals involvement, and involvement relates to commitment, higher renewal rates, and more support for the institution.

First-Year Members

The renewal rate for first-year members is always lower than for multi-year members. Some people will "try out" the membership and decide, for whatever reason, that it is not for them. Because of the cost of acquiring new members, doing as much as possible to retain first-year members makes economic sense. Once someone is a member for three or more years, the chances are very good that the person will support the institution for many years to come. For those organizations with multi-year memberships available, the first renewal is considered the end of the first-year membership, even though the member may have belonged for two or three years. Renewal rates should be closely followed to see if there is a difference between annual and multi-year members. Additionally, there needs to be enough activity and programming so that the multi-year members will want to renew.

Developing a package of information and activities for a new member can have a significant impact on renewal rates and the level of involvement of the member. New member activities may include a phone call or e-mail from a volunteer or staff person welcoming the person to the organization, a special new-member reception to meet the director or president of the organization, or an orientation session for the new members to learn about the institution. Depending on the size of the new-member group, the activities can be held two or more times a year. Again, there is some urgency. When people first join, their interest is at a peak. If there is a new-member activity a year after someone joins, the new member no longer feels new and the reason for the activity is lost.

In an organization that wants and needs its members as volunteers and participants, involving the first-year member is crucial. The member who wants to volunteer and is not contacted to participate will go elsewhere. In any organization with a volunteer component, having a volunteer group to greet new members is very helpful. It is a great activity for the volunteers and will begin the membership program for the new member on solid footing.

Support Member Activities

Support members are treated more equally than other members. They need special activities. For a visitation-based institution, special times (without crowds) to see exhibits are a prime benefit. For all organizations, receptions, dinners, and opportunities to meet special guests of the institution are well received. As the support members become part of the institution's donor clubs, the members take ownership of the donor club activities. Coordinating these activities between membership and development is very important and is one of the reasons why it is easiest in an institution for membership to be a part of development. Remember that the support members are also invited to the general membership activities and, depending on the activity, many will attend.

General Activities

As our culture has changed, people want more and more. Movies now have to have stadium seating, special sound, and coffee bars. Theme parks have to add a new ride every year. Institutions have to keep up. Having an organization or an institution for someone to join is not enough. The membership program must provide experiences that are of interest to the members. At a visitation-based institution, just visiting is no longer enough. The blockbuster show is a good reflection of this change. Activities that members may attend are needed. As discussed in the article by Bhattacharya, Glynn, and Rao (1994, 414), members do not necessarily visit enough times for their membership to make economic sense.

Providing experiences or programs of interest is even more important for organizations without visitation. For these organizations, the experiences need to be delivered by print and electronic publications, or by events that are produced from time to time for members to attend—for example, a lecture, a discussion, a reception. This is true for both local and national organizations. An institution needs to provide activities to encourage members to attend and to demonstrate that the institution is doing a lot even if the members, personally, do not participate. A membership program without activities lacks perceived value. And, even if members do not attend, the activities have value in their eyes, they just were not able to take advantage of that valued activity.

The membership program for any kind of organization should offer some activities that are for "members only," such as a large social event, a family-oriented event, or an educational program. During the course of the year, the membership program should offer one or more of each type. The events may be free, at cost, or fundraisers. Again, there should be one or more of each. Free events might include a lecture or the after-hours, behind-the-scenes tour of the institution. An event that is at cost might be social, with a modest price associated with refreshments or entertainment. Fundraisers can be anything from a special brunch to an auction to a gala benefit. Make certain that there is a mix of activities, so that the members do not feel that the only invitations that they receive are for fundraisers.

Members should also have a special place in activities that are scheduled for the general public. As with the blockbuster events and timed tickets, it is important for members to feel that they are special; in this case, they can make their reservations before the public. For large public events with a charge, members should pay a smaller fee. In some cases, with support-level members, the fee should be waived totally. It is not so much the money involved as it is a way for the member to feel special.

Communications

A member cannot receive too many communications from the organization. The budget should be developed to include as many mailings as possible. A strong program will mail at least once a month; a large program may mail 30 to 40 times per year. For most organizations, the piece of mail in the mailbox is the major connection with the organization. Sometimes there is the thought that the member will think the organization is wasting money by sending all the mailings; this is a rare thought among members. More often the member does not renew because he or she has not heard anything from the organization since the last request for money. For the few members who request not to receive mailings, honor the request.

There should be variety in what the member receives. The effort is to create the perception and reflect the reality that the organization is doing a lot, that the work is important, and that the members are special. A communications plan should be a part of the membership planning. Often the member will receive communications from the organization that do not come from the membership department. If this is the case, the membership department should learn what is being sent in order to have a complete view of what the member is seeing.

A good exercise for the membership manager is to put his or her name on the mailing list. As each piece arrives at home, it should be dated and then put in box or bag to be reviewed later. At the six-month mark, take out all of the mail. This will give a look at what the member sees. If there is little mail, the member's perception will be that the organization is not doing much. If the mail is heavy with fundraising appeals, the member's perception will be that the organization is constantly fundraising. Conversely, if there are no fundraising appeals, it will be clear that it is time to send one. It is also helpful to have a nonmember (e.g., a friend)

take a look at the printed matter and give an honest opinion about how the organization appears.

What Should Members Receive in the Mail?

Renewal notice (one to four). Of course, a member should receive a renewal notice. The great majority of members will not renew on their own. The renewal notice should be marked on the outside of the envelope, so that it clearly notes what is inside. In the best of all worlds, there will need to be only one renewal notice. Organizations send anywhere from three to nine or more, depending on the renewal returns with each mailing; Chapter 8 details this process.

Membership cards (one or two). Once the member renews, he or she should receive a packet with new membership cards, a listing of benefits, coupons if they are a part of the membership package, and perhaps a request to volunteer or a tribute envelope to be used during the year. Each organization has its own package of information, and it should be considered a very important mailing. It is the first communication the member receives at the beginning of his or her membership year. The envelope for this mailing should also be clearly marked, so that the member knows to open it.

Invitations to events (four to fifteen). Separate invitations should be sent for the various events and activities. Invitations that appear in the newsletter may or may not be seen. Invitations that are separate are also more special. They convey to the member that sense of belonging. Invitations range from the frugal to the very extravagant. The type of invitation depends on the event and the organization. The design may range from a letter invitation for a lecture to a postcard for a members-only program to very fancy for a high-ticket-priced gala benefit. When there is little money to spend, it is best to spend available funds on design, not on fancy paper or complicated printing, and make certain that the size of invitations is a common one and uses as little postage as possible. This mailing may use bulk rate postage or first-class postage, depending on its size and on the event itself. For a very large event, bulk mail may be appropriate, but for a high-ticket-priced gala, first-class mail will be important. E-mail notices and reminders will also help increase participation; they are an even more cost effective means of communication.

Fundraising appeals (two to four or more). These are fundraising appeals in addition to the membership renewal. The most common ones are for a second annual gift, for gift membership, for fundraising events, and for special projects. Members may also be solicited from time to time for capital campaigns. If there is a planned giving program being marketed, members should receive it. The same is true of a tribute fund, if there is one. Often a special mailing once a year will encourage tribute gifts.

There will be a difference between what a value member and a support member receives. For some fundraising appeals, support members will be treated individually as major donors; for others, all members will receive the same mailings. This needs to be coordinated with the development effort. Fundraising appeals are sometimes included in newsletters. If it is not possible to send separate appeals, it can be done through the newsletter, though separate mailings can be more effective. The organization needs to test the efficacy of the two approaches. It is also important to remember that a fundrais-

ing appeal does not end until a thank-you is sent to those who respond.

Newsletter/bulletin (four to twelve). It is essential that the organization have an informational communication that is sent regularly to members. At a minimum, the newsletter should be sent four times a year. The newsletter should be published and sent as often as possible, up to once a month. A newsletter does not need to be long; it is better to send a shorter newsletter more often than to wait until a longer one can be published. The organization's newsletter is often a part of the membership/development effort. If it is not, then the membership department should have significant space allocated in the organization's newsletter for information for members. Increasingly, eNewsletters are becoming popular with Web savvy members. These condensed versions of a hard copy newsletter should not replace the traditional printed newsletter, only supplement the printed version. Such eNewsletters can provide more timely information, especially if the newsletter is on a quarterly schedule.

Other publications (one to twelve). These publications range from an annual report to a book published by the organization to a four-color magazine. For example, *Smithsonian Magazine* goes to members once a month, while the magazine, *Air & Space* from the National Air and Space Museum is published six times a year.

Miscellaneous (one to four). There are also sporadic mailings that can come from the organization. These may be planned or the result of an unexpected event. Typical might be a membership survey mailing, a special letter about something important at the institution, or legislative updates. The important thing to remember is that when something important happens, the natural audience to hear about it first is the membership.

Mailing Cost Considerations

It is apparent from the above list, which is by no means exhaustive, there is a lot that can be mailed to members. Cost is always an issue. Printed matter and postage are often among the largest budget items. They are also items that can sometimes find donors. With a plan in hand, the staff and volunteers can seek a printer who might donate some or all of the printing of a piece; a designer might be willing to design an invitation or two; or a major corporation might be willing to do a mailing. It is very important to include regular mailings, such as the newsletter, in the budget because they must be sent. For the more sporadic communications pieces, seeking funding is possible, but be aware that it may take a lot of lead time. This is one of the reasons why planning ahead is so important. All in all, because the mailbox is the major connection between the organization and the member, the rule is: the more mail the better.

Telephone

The telephone is the major way membership programs communicate electronically. This includes telemarketing for lapsed members and renewals, for thank-you phonathons, and for encouraging participation in events. Customer service is also delivered via the telephone. Membership surveys can be conducted via telephone. The telephone can provide the most personal communication that a member has with the institution. If there is an effective way to use the telephone, use it.

E-mail

As more and more of us are online, e-mail becomes a wonderful (and inexpensive) way to communicate with the membership. It is particularly useful with time-sensitive information—someone is unexpectedly coming to give a lecture, or a bill that affects an important issue for the organization is in committee, and members need to contact their legislators immediately. Some members now want to receive their newsletter online rather than through the mail. Sending event information a few days before the date may well increase attendance. To those who have e-mail, it is possible to send regular, quick updates on important projects, thereby increasing the number of communications at very little cost.

Gathering the e-mail addresses is a major project. Essentially, the organization is then keeping two mailing lists. This takes a concerted effort; keeping a list up-to-date and clean is time consuming and must be tended to regularly. The communications need to have a purpose and be of interest or they will become spam, electronic junk mail. On the membership form, the member can be asked if he or she would like to receive information by e-mail. This medium offers incredible possibilities to an organization that can take advantage of it.

It is also important to remember that e-mail is a two-way communication. When members e-mail a question, complaint, or suggestion, they need a response. E-mail is a faster medium than "snail mail." When a comment arrives, the sender expects a fairly quick response. Someone should have the responsibility for answering the mail in a timely manner. This becomes a service issue in the minds of the members. Early indications from programs that use e-mail to communicate with members are that there will be a 10 percent rate of bounce back e-mail, or e-mail that requires a response.

Web Site

The other Internet medium is the organization's Web site. It is possible for even very small organizations now to have a Web site for modest cost. It won't be fancy, but it can have the information that a member or the general public might want to have. Organizations should have a membership section on their Web site. This section should include a way to join, which is discussed in Chapter 5. Once having joined, members should be directed to the members-only section, which can be a great communications tool. A members-only section might contain a variety of information, all of which can be a member benefit. Direct access to a collection, to research papers, to the membership directory, and to information on upcoming members-only events are a few of the uses for a members-only section.

Having the membership section on the Web site is step one. Step two is to have e-commerce capability, so that prospects may join or members may donate online. Step three, and just as important, is marketing the fact that the Web site is available. The Web site needs to be advertised and touted in all of the membership communications and in or on everything that the organization produces.

Recognition

The benefits, the service, the activities, and the communications all serve to recognize members and their support of the organization. The initial recognition is the thank-you, the packet of information, the membership card, and the other items the member receives on joining. In addition, there are other things that can be done for recognition that make individual members feel particularly special.

The organization's newsletter is the most common way to recognize members. Many organizations, especially small ones, list new members. This is a nice form of recognition as well as alerting current members about who is joining the group. Some list members who upgrade. When a membership program becomes too large to do this, the organization can move to recognizing the support members rather than all members. If not using the newsletter, some groups use their annual report to do this every year. The newsletter is also the place to recognize members for volunteer work, for length of membership, and for any special activities. Often the "gossip column" about what members are currently doing is the most popular in a newsletter.

Length of membership can be recognized in other ways as well. First, those members who join "in the beginning" should be recognized as charter members, founding members, or a similar title. The Museum of Women in the Arts in Washington, D.C., has a large book with all of the names of its charter members. When members from around the country visit, they can find their names in the bound book. Some institutions use a plaque to recognize founding members. The Holocaust Museum, also in Washington, D.C., lists members in the museum's permanent "Roll of Remembrance."

If it is at all possible, it is very nice to have the membership card read "member since......" Recognizing members on special anniversary dates such as 5, 10, or 25 years of support promotes long-term relationships and shows appreciation for the value of long-time members. A reception honoring 25- or 50-year members creates nostalgia and enhances that feeling of belonging. Most importantly, it highlights the value of the members to the organization.

CORPORATE MEMBERSHIP PROGRAMS

Many organizations extend the membership concept to corporate giving. Some organizations combine all memberships together—no matter if the membership comes from an individual or a company. With this system, the person in the company who sends in the membership form becomes the member. There are no special corporate-related benefits or activities. For many organizations, this is the easiest way to manage corporate members. If the program and its staff are small or new and/or corporate benefits difficult to construct, this is the more effective way to work with companies.

For others, however, a separate set of corporate dues, benefits, and programs is desired. How an organization works on corporate membership depends on the size of the institution, the size of the dues amount, the size of the corporation, and how corporate giving is handled by the company and in the community. Just as with the membership program for individuals, a corporate program needs acquisition, renewals, and dues as well as the same basic five elements: benefits, service, activities, communication, and recognition. Although the membership manager is soliciting funds from a corporation, it is important to remember that this is still a decision made by an individual. Just as the individual program has to be viewed from the perspective of the individual member, it is crucial to view the corporate program from the corporate perspective.

There are three very important concepts to keep in mind when constructing a corporate membership program. First, do not develop benefits for the employees of a corporation that are a disincentive for individual membership. Second, the corporate program is much more like a major gifts program than a membership program and needs to be designed as such. Third, corporate members do need that personal solicitation and an individual ask. Corporate members are rarely acquired through the typical means used in programs designed for individuals.

Deciding whether or not to send additional fundraising requests to corporate members should be determined on a case-by-case basis. Most companies will consider the membership as their annual gift. Those fundraising programs that are personal in nature, such as gift memberships, planned gifts, and tributes are not appropriate for corporations. Capital campaigns, sponsorship, and special projects, however, are all possibilities for companies. Because these companies have already shown interest in the organization through the membership program, they are likely prospects for these other programs.

Acquisition, Renewals, and Dues

Acquisition is most often accomplished through personal solicitation by volunteers or staff rather than by direct mail or telemarketing. In general, the larger the company and the larger the dues amount, the more personal the appeal. A volunteer committee with members who are willing to use their contacts in the corporate world is very effective. National and major local institutions also use staff, mail, and telephone for acquisition. Renewals should be handled in much the same way.

Dues for corporate members typically start at a much higher level than those for individual members, and there tend to be fewer levels. They range from hundreds of dollars for small organizations to many thousands of dollars at large, major institutions. For some programs there is one level;

for others, up to four levels. As with the individual benefit package, it is important for the benefits to appeal to companies, be somewhat comparable to other programs (if there are comparable ones), be possible to fulfill with some ease, and bring income into the organization. Corporate programs should be designed to produce significant income.

Benefits

Corporate benefits can be linked to employees, use of a facility (for a visitation-based institution), and advertising or product promotion. Benefits linked to employees include an employee day or event at the institution, or the organization coming into the workplace to present information or entertainment for the employees. Facility use for corporate functions is sometimes limited to corporate members, sometimes free of charge and sometimes tied to a discount for their use. Advertising and/or product promotion might include the ability of the corporate member to sponsor an exhibit or program. Some of the benefits offered to individual members might also be extended to the corporation, such as a discount on purchases and products.

Service

Corporate members want the same type of service as individual members. Payments need to be processed efficiently, thank-yous sent, calls and questions answered promptly, and use of benefits (e.g., facility use) handled in a professional manner. With a corporate membership, a number of people on the corporate side may need service. The accounting department may deal with the payment, a community relations person with setting up an event, and the human re-

sources staff with membership cards for employees. For this reason, the data that are kept for a corporate membership may be much more extensive than that kept for an individual member. On the institution side, more people may also be involved—membership, facility rental, public relations, education, events. When constructing the benefits package, it is important to involve other departments that may be called upon to service the corporate membership.

Activities

The activities for corporate memberships will depend on what the corporation wants to receive and what the institution can provide. A visitation-based institution may offer an employee day for the company's staff. Depending on the size of the company and the size of the institution, this may be one day or several, or may focus on access throughout the year for the employees. In an organization that doesn't have a place to visit, the staff might design a lecture or a short course for interested employees to participate in during lunch hour or before or after work hours. For example, a service club that works with children might offer a parenting course to the employees.

Communications

Because a corporate membership is often the size of a major gift, it needs to be treated as such. It is important to communicate with all the people in the corporation who are involved with the membership. As is the case with servicing the membership, this may include the CEO's office, community relations, human relations, marketing, and others. A copy of the organization's standard newsletter should go to all the possible contacts within the company. The same may be true for invitations to certain events. Some events will include only the CEO; others may involve everyone the organization works with in the company.

In large companies, there may also be the possibility of communicating with all of the employees. If the company has a house organ (internal newsletter) or electronic messaging, these media will provide a great audience for what is happening at the institution, upcoming events, and volunteer opportunities.

Recognition

Corporate members should receive the same kind of recognition that is given to individual members. In addition, the organization might include corporate logos in print and electronic media (this may be positioned as recognition rather than an ex-plicit benefit). Corporate logos cannot be used for pieces mailed with nonprofit mail classification; check postal regulations for exact limitations. If there is an event such as an employee day at the institution, recognizing the corporation that day in every way possible should be done.

SUMMARY

Creating and implementing a strong program for members, both individual and corporate, will ensure their continued support. The membership program can be developed on any level, from very small to very large. The challenge for any membership program is to design and include the benefits, service, activities, communications, and recognition that the members want and believe are of value.

REFERENCES

Association of Fundraising Professionals. 2001. *Survey course in fundraising, faculty manual.* Alexandria, VA.

Bhattacharya, C., M. A. Glynn, and H. Rao. 1994. Membership in museums: A study of customers of cultural non-profit institutions. In *Conference Proceedings of ARNOVA* (Association for Research on Nonprofit Organizations and Voluntary Action), Session H8. Indianapolis, IN, October.

Symens Smith, A., B. Ahmed, and L. Sink. 2000. *An analysis of state and county population changes by characteristics: 1990–1999.* Washington, DC: U.S. Census Bureau, Population Division. November.

CHAPTER 5

Membership Acquisition

Patricia Rich and Dana Hines

The beginning is the most important part of the work.

—Plato

THE CRITICAL TASK

ACQUISITION IS THE BEGINNING AND the most important part of membership. Without members, there is no program. Acquiring new members is the most critical function of membership marketing. It is the membership manager's primary responsibility, a great challenge, and at times the most frustrating aspect of the position. At the same time, it is often the most costly component of the membership budget, while also being the most time-consuming and the least-predictable (and sometimes least-controllable) effort. There are a number of methods of membership acquisition, and they differ depending on the size and type of an institution, the budget, and the amount of volunteer and/or staff time available to carry out the functions described in this chapter.

Before embarking on a membership acquisition effort, it is very important to assess the organization's commitment to its membership operation. Verbalizing a commitment to membership acquisition is not enough. Sufficient funds need to be dedicated to this effort to give any statement of commitment real strength. Also, it must be understood that membership acquisition is a long-term commitment. An institution must dedicate sufficient funding for acquisition on an ongoing basis, not just for one year.

Important questions that need to be answered are: Does the leadership of the organization understand that acquisition efforts are usually a break-even proposition at best? That it may take two years to recoup the cost to acquire a member? Does the leadership understand that the benefits of membership acquisition are usually seen only in succeeding years, when membership renewal income is realized? In membership acquisition, more so than in any other area, it is critical to have realistic expectations. Expectations and projections must be attainable, or it is likely that the decision makers involved will discontinue funding membership acquisition efforts.

An on-again, off-again commitment to membership acquisition is possibly more destructive than having no commitment to acquisition at all. Without an ongoing effort to acquire new members, membership totals and revenue merely maintain an even keel or even decline over time. Spikes followed by dips occur in membership totals when funding or commitment to membership does not remain constant. If there is no commitment, money is neither spent nor generated, so garnering that initial commitment for a period of several years is a most crucial point to be made and understood.

Membership Prospects

The first major step in membership acquisition is deciding to whom your membership promotion efforts should appeal. The best way to identify prospects is by looking at people who have already been convinced to become members—current members. The easiest and most cost-effective new members to be acquired will look, act, think, and behave like current members. Trying to convince people who are very different from existing members can be quite expensive and have minimal results.

Developing an accurate member profile is achieved through a membership survey (see Chapter 9). Using a phone or mail survey, ages, incomes, and other important demographic information, such as hobbies and leisure-time activities, related to current members are pinpointed. Marketing efforts are most successful when directed at a group that very closely approximates the group of current members. A survey may also identify other, less obvious, segments of the membership.

For example, one organization had already identified the wealthier population in its community as a primary segment of its membership. After surveying its members, however, it came to realize that it had two other significant segments: retirees with significant free time to visit the institution, and families with children who belonged to the institution in order to utilize the free admission benefits for frequent family outings. This organization now had three distinct target populations to whom to target their membership promotional efforts.

To find an organization's membership prospects, it is also important to determine the best season for heaviest membership promotion. For outdoor venues in the north, that season may be spring or summer. For indoor venues, the season may be the academic year schedule—fall and winter. For alumni associations, the season may be graduation times and homecoming. Knowing when most people would naturally turn to the organization for advice, help, or the services you provide is the key.

Conditions for Becoming a Member

Before deciding whom to target as a prospective member, it is important to be aware of people's motivation for becoming a member. As discussed in Chapter 1, the need for belonging and being part of groups is one motivation. But other conditions include the prospect's interest, experience, and ability to join. These are necessary ingredients for a person to even consider the offer to become a member. The presence or absence of each of these factors should be considered when making membership acquisition targeting decisions.

Interest

Does a person have an interest in the organization that is promoting membership? Membership is unlikely if there is not some interest, on some level. People will not join a zoo if they have no interest in animals or conservation efforts, or don't care to visit and stroll the grounds. If someone has at least one of these interests, then he or she should be a likely candidate for membership.

Experience

People who have never been to a zoo are not likely to join. But once they have had this experience, they become likely candidates. On-site sales are a productive source of new members for some organizations, largely because if a person is visiting, he or she has at least one of the necessary ingredients for membership—experience.

Ability

A person must have the financial wherewithal to be a likely candidate for membership. Usually, membership does not require a major financial commitment; however, for some, a $50 donation for a membership is not possible. Therefore, it is necessary to target groups of likely members from pools of people with discretionary income.

Variety in Methods

Once groups of most-likely-to-respond prospects have been identified, the task is to decide how to reach those populations. The following is a variety of methods that are frequently used to reach various populations:

- Direct mail
- Telemarketing
- On-site sales
- Personal solicitation
- Member-get-a-member promotions
- Employee campaigns
- Brochure distribution
- Gift membership promotions
- Online membership sales
- Membership month
- Charter membership drives
- Advertising

Generally, the smaller the organization or institution, the more personalized the solicitation process can or may be, and such personalization often relies more heavily on volunteers than does a larger program with a larger budget.

Also, generally speaking, the larger an institution or organization, the larger the budget and the greater the reliance on mass campaigns (e.g., direct mail), which are costly. These large campaigns generate large numbers of members, whereas the personalized, one-on-one efforts undertaken by smaller institutions are less costly but garner fewer members. One set of circumstances is not better than the other; however, there needs to be the realization that institution size, budget, and availability and willingness of volunteers and other resources make a great difference in the program design.

Regardless of acquisition methods used or the size of the institution, diversity is the key. A membership program should not rely totally on one method of acquisition. Just as one would not commit his or her life savings to one form of investment, neither can an institution rely on a single source for new members. The more diverse the sources of acquisition, the more stability there will be in the number of new members.

As an example, one institution might employ the following methods of membership acquisition: (Each method is listed with the percentage of members attributed to that method.)

Direct mail	50 percent
On-site	25 percent
Gift memberships	15 percent
Miscellaneous	10 percent

Diversification of membership sources is important because if one method is less successful than anticipated, other methods are in place and will, ideally, make up for those that did not perform as well.

What becomes clear is the necessity to track the productivity of each membership source. In fact, in a direct mail campaign it is necessary to code responses by each list used so that the source of the new member is readily known and trackable. The same is true with the on-site methods, gift memberships, or miscellaneous methods mentioned here. If either coding or tracking is not done, it is impossible to separate successful membership promotions from unsuccessful ones. With accurate tracking of each effort, the organization is be able to evaluate the financial viability of each separate source of membership, and thus make decisions based on what is most cost effective and what is not producing at an acceptable level.

Basic Methods

Examples of how some membership acquisition efforts work or have worked at other organizations is always helpful. What is important is to realize that every organization is different, and the circumstances around an organization may be different. The membership manager may never know what will work for his or her program unless it is tested.

For large-scale acquisition efforts, there are three basic methods: direct mail, telemarketing, and on-site sales. All three can be used by any type of group, whether all volunteer or one with paid staff. Direct mail in a small organization will be personal letters from board members to prospective members; telemarketing will be a volunteer phonathon to friends and colleagues to ask them to join; and on-site sales will involve using volunteers at an event to encourage the participants to become members. At a large organization, direct mail will include many thousands of letters, telemarketing will be done by a telemarketing company, and paid professionals will staff the on-site sales effort.

Direct Mail

For most organizations, direct mail is the most popular method of membership acquisition. It is, or can be, an expensive method of acquisition, in that it requires a minimum of $5,000 to $10,000 to initiate. In some cases, a budget of $100,000 or more is needed, depending on the size, sophistication, and frequency of the mailings.

Direct mail approaches a targeted group with a specific offer and a response device that allows the prospect to act upon the request to become a member. This offer can be targeted by renting lists of people who most closely replicate the type of person the institution seeks. Cost can range from approximately \$.35 per piece (not including postage) to any amount an organization wants to spend. Typically, response rates of 0.7 to 1.0 percent are considered acceptable. Response rates greater than that are always welcome, but are not to be expected unless it is a popular institution, an organization making an appeal for the first time, or the appeal is related to a very significant event, such as a major anniversary of the organization or a blockbuster exhibition. A more complete and detailed description of direct mail acquisition is provided in Chapter 6.

Telemarketing

Telemarketing uses the telephone as another way to reach the person to be approached in a more personalized fashion. Done properly and professionally, it can be a very courteous and personable way to make contact with a prospective member. Done unprofessionally and without proper training, telemarketing can be a rude, disturbing intrusion on a person's privacy. While the cost per contact is much greater than in direct mail, the response rate and dollars generated per dollars spent can greatly exceed that generated by direct mail. Frequently, direct mail is combined with telemarketing for a two-pronged approach. When using telemarketing for acquisition purposes, only the most targeted and proven lists will be successful. In most cases, these will be in-house lists compiled by the organization or a list of lapsed members. Chapter 7 is dedicated to all facets of telemarketing.

On-Site Sales

For organizations with a place to visit, on-site membership acquisition is an opportunity to reach prospective members, with few out-of-pocket costs. There will be some cost for materials, and, if paid staff are used, there is also the cost of staff time. This form of acquisition is even less expensive if volunteers are used to staff a membership desk. This type of membership solicitation captures visitors who have already experienced some of the benefits the organization may be offering through membership. This form of membership acquisition is essential for an organization with a visiting membership. It is a form of membership solicitation that is enviable in that it is the most personal form of solicitation, and it is the least expensive.

On-site sales can be conducted in many ways, ranging from a low-cost, volunteer-run program to one implemented with a professionally staffed sales force.

Volunteer-driven programs. This type of on-site sales program is virtually 100 percent profit. It requires, however, adequate staff time to organize and manage. A core group of very dedicated volunteers is necessary on an ongoing, long-term basis. Essentially, this group of volunteers commits to selling memberships year round, at high traffic times and at events selected by membership staff. For instance, staffing will probably be required every weekend, and at other busy times when key periods during the day must be covered. The volunteers should work at a desk or in the lobby or entry area, at a position where they can influence visitors prior to their approach to the admissions desk or ticket counter. The volunteers must be well trained, personable, and willing to SELL.

The benefits of such an arrangement with a volunteer sales staff are many. First, the cost is extremely low—virtually no more than the cost of the brochures they distribute. A volunteer force is usually one of the organization's best ambassadors, or they would not be so enthusiastic about volunteering in the first place. This type of volunteer assignment is usually very rewarding—there is contact with the public, an opportunity to sell an organization that they care a lot about, and the results are quantifiable! At the end of the day, week or year, the organization will know exactly how many memberships and dollars the group generated.

The downside of a volunteer operation is that staffing may be an arduous and difficult task. This endeavor requires that volunteers give up some of the best hours in their schedules—weekends. Few people will want to dedicate a whole day to this task, so it may be necessary to fill several shifts per day. The management of a volunteer pool of the size necessary to cover all the hours needed on an annual basis may be a very significant portion of a manager's job.

The Missouri Botanical Garden in St. Louis has had the good fortune to have a very dedicated group of volunteers who have staffed and managed the Membership Services and Information Desk (MSID) for the past 15 years. The desk has about 45 volunteers and was originally a project of the Members' Board, a high-level group of selected volunteers who promote and help with membership functions, specifically this desk and events. One member of the Members' Board chairs this sales group, thereby taking some of the management responsibility for this group. The MSID volunteers sell 3,000 to 4,000 memberships a year—new and renewals. They staff the desk every weekend, year round. They also staff the desk from 10 AM until 3 PM every weekday from spring through fall. This dedicated group is a model for volunteer-run membership sales groups and can definitely quantify what their efforts mean to the Garden's membership.

Staff-driven programs. In many organizations, such a committed group of volunteers as described above is not a possibility. Therefore, it is necessary to use either existing staff or special membership sales staff to transact membership sales on-site. Paid staff that has other duties can conduct membership sales. Admission desk staff or gift shop staff may also be asked to sell memberships. These staff members are already in contact with the visiting public, so it makes sense that they may also be in a position to suggest the purchase of a membership. Just as the department store employee asks if you would like to put that purchase on your department store credit card, and is willing to open an account for you if you don't have one, so, too, should all employees of the organization mention membership to a visitor and be able to sign them up immediately. Many times, the mere suggestion of membership is all that is needed. The word "membership" should roll off the lips of any front-line person. Compare this method with that used at an upscale department store. If you are about to make a significant purchase and not using the house credit card, you will be asked if you'd like to apply for a credit card and receive 10 percent off your purchase immediately. Organizations can be just as opportunistic as department stores.

Professionally staffed programs. If neither of the above two options is a possibility, or a huge event is approaching and an organization knows it cannot handle the volume of visitors (prospective members), then professional membership on-site salespeople should be considered. These people have been professionally trained to sell memberships and are specifically trained to be knowledgeable about the institution they will be promoting. They are usually contracted to sell on behalf of the organization for a specific event (grand opening or signature event) or for an entire run of a special exhibit or expected high-traffic time period. This type of sales staff can complement an organization's volunteer, on-site sales staff and activities throughout the year.

At the Missouri Botanical Garden, even with its highly successful volunteer efforts, the membership manager knew that the organization was missing opportunities to sell memberships during some very high-traffic, signature events that are held on an annual basis. The human resources department would not permit incentive compensation, or the hiring of temporary, part-time staff. The membership department contracted with Membership Consultants to provide a team of professional membership salespeople to sell memberships at the annual Japanese Festival, which hosts 30,000 to 40,000 visitors during a three-day period. The volunteer group had sold 100 memberships during the previous Japanese Festival; the professional sales crew sold more than 900. And with succeeding years' events, they have sold as many as 1,400 memberships in those three days.

The paid sales staff and volunteers complement each other by relying on each other's strengths. Once the salesperson closes the sale, he or she escorts the person joining to the volunteer at the membership desk. The volunteer makes sure the form is filled out correctly, accepts payment, and issues the premium and free admission ticket—while the salesperson approaches more visitors. The goal of the salespeople is to talk to as many people as possible, and volunteers assist them by helping with the paperwork.

At times, with long lines of people waiting to enter the venue or to make purchases, a membership sale may not be possible. At these times, it is necessary to have a membership desk or table to which people may be referred. This desk or table needs to be staffed with people who solely sell and fulfill membership purchases. If volunteers are not available, then a paid staff person should be at this station. It may be possible to hire part-time weekend workers to fill these types of positions. The revenues generated by membership sales should more than pay for the cost to staff this position. If that is not the case, then the person may not have the sales skills necessary, or the station is being staffed at times that do not justify it based on visitorship.

Compensation may affect the productivity of the sales staff. Cash is the biggest motivator. If a sales incentive program can be put into place, such an arrangement will produce the best results. If an organization does not allow such compensation, the reason for that disallowance needs to be questioned. In some cases, publicly funded institutions do not allow for any type of incentive plan. Regardless, some form of incentive needs to be provided to drive sales. Use gift dollars in the gift shop, coupons for movies or restaurants, or pizza parties to reward the admission desk sales staff if they have a particularly productive month or weekend—whatever works.

Salespeople often rely on the knowledge the volunteers possess about the organization; thus the volunteers are an invaluable resource in the sales process.

The difference between the volunteer-run program and the professionally staffed program is the willingness of the people to sell. The volunteers sit behind a desk and wait to be approached. The professional salespeople have clipboards with applications, newsletters, and brochures in hand and approach the visitors asking them to consider joining. The pitch, highlighting all of the benefits of membership, and perhaps an incentive for joining that day, may also be more direct. The results are significant: with a volunteer, or a more passive sale, about 0.5 percent of the total visitorship will join, versus 4 to 5 percent of visitors who will join with a professionally trained staff—8 to 10 times the passive sales total.

Other considerations in on-site sales. Regardless of who is selling memberships, the tools needed for on-site sales are the same. First, there is signage. It is important for the group's sales efforts to be supported by strategically placed signage. "Join here" or "Become a member and enter free" point the visitor in the right direction and indicate what is going on that day. Signage at the admission desk might read, "Join now, save $$$ in admission." At the point of sale in a gift shop, the sign might read, "Join now. Members receive 20% discount!" Salespeople might also wear buttons or tee shirts that say, "Ask me about membership." Whatever the message, it should be one that helps make the sale by drawing attention to the possibilities of membership.

Sales tracking should include the person selling, the time period, and the day. Knowing that one salesperson has a better track record than another, or that the 10 AM to noon period is the most productive, will enhance future sales at similar events. Sales can also be tracked by new, renewal, or gift membership. On-site sales, just like direct mail, can become a science, if the proper tracking and analysis takes place. A sample on-site sales report is provided in Chapter 13 (see Table 13–17).

Other Membership Promotions

Other membership promotions such as charter memberships, member-get-a-member drives, and referrals from current members are examples of creative ways to encourage membership. Programs such as these can be designed with an organization's structure and staff capacity in mind. Creative campaigns have included rewarding the person bringing in the largest number of memberships or offering a special benefit to any person bringing in multiple memberships. These promotions can be designed cost effectively.

Personal Solicitation

Particularly in new or small organizations, personal solicitation of memberships is a way to acquire members. Some members will just ask friends and colleagues to join a group that the member believes the friend might be interested in. This may be as simple a process as a phone call or a letter. Or it may be more elaborate, with a member willing to hold an event such as a luncheon and invite potential members. The organization has the opportunity to tell its story and enroll the guests who are interested. This format can also be used at civic group meetings, where one of the group's members is willing to invite someone from the organization to speak. This type of solicitation is very much one-on-one communication.

If there is a membership manager, it is up to him or her to make certain that the solicitations are happening. Because this is a time-consuming, though inexpensive, method of acquisition, it is often used for acquiring support members rather than value members.

Member-Get-a-Member Campaign

Member-Get-a-Member campaigns have been run with varying degrees of success by many organizations. The key question is how much effort will current members extend to recruit a new member? In some cases, a member may go to great lengths to help enlist a new member (e.g., an alumnus taking a fellow alumnus friend to dinner to solicit him for membership). In other cases, a member may only be mildly committed to helping an organization expand its membership program.

One organization devised an elaborate membership sales competition with a sizable reward for the winner. The organization was known for its distinctive foreign travel programs. The incentive for the winner of the member-get-a-member campaign was a free European trip. Luckily, at least one member took this challenge very seriously and sold more than 100 memberships to win the prize. The next highest member, however, sold only five memberships. If the winner had not worked so diligently to sell memberships, this campaign would not have been a success. A second campaign based on this model would be successful only if someone were as motivated as the first member. The same person is not likely to be successful again, having already converted everyone she knew to becoming a member. Only new memberships qualified.

Another example of a member-get-a member campaign involves direct mail to existing members. A local zoo designed a campaign to reward each member who found at least one member to join. The mailing was designed around an oversized postcard with a rallying message on one side, "Your friends belong at the Zoo." The postcard had a mail panel and explanation of the offer on one side and a response mechanism on the other. Both the existing member and the new member were offered a premium if the new person joined. It was easily trackable—the existing members' name and member number were in the address section, and the new member filled out the form on the same side of the post card.

These types of campaigns usually operate on a break-even basis, which is considered a success in membership acquisition.

Yet another form of a member-get-a-member campaign was conducted for years in a southern art museum. The promotion began when the museum was in its infancy. This effort involved training volunteers in the details of membership and then motivating them to go out and sell memberships to their friends, neighbors, and business associates. Originally, the campaign was designed to sell new memberships, and it was quite successful, selling hundreds of memberships. Over time, however, with not much change in the membership of the volunteer group, it became a renewal effort, since a person's sphere of contacts does not change much from year to year.

A similar effort has been the mainstay of the membership program at the Henry Doorley Zoo in Omaha, Nebraska, for many years. The campaign presents itself similarly to campaigns initiated by the United Way. Volunteers from all major employers in the area are recruited, trained, entertained, and then turned loose to sell in their workplaces. It is a very labor-intensive effort, but it is so successful that very little direct mail is required for renewals, and none is required for acquisition. The Zoo has more than 60,000 members.

Employee Campaign

Another type of membership promotion that is similar to member-get-a-member promotions is an employee membership sales contest. It should be time limited, performed in conjunction with "Membership Month," be structured with prizes for the most sales overall by department, and be presented as a fun way for all staff to help promote the institution for which they work.

At the Saint Louis Zoo, a very successful staff membership sales incentive program was designed and implemented. Donated prizes were collected, with a television as the grand prize. Gift certificates to stores and restaurants were donated prizes. The program was designed so that everyone, including volunteers, working at the zoo could participate. One of the unexpected by-products of the program was a better understanding of the importance of the membership program by all staff.

To launch the program, the membership manager attended all department staff meetings explaining the membership program and the reason for the sales contest. As a result, staff gained a greater appreciation for the membership program and the role it plays in supporting the zoo. As the program was being launched, the primary concern was that the front-line staff would have an unfair advantage in terms of selling to the public. In the end, the person who won the contest was a person who worked in receiving in the warehouse. She asked vendors as they made deliveries to the warehouse if their companies were members. They were, after all, selling their wares to the zoo.

Brochure Distribution

Distributing membership brochures on site or via welcome wagons, point-of-purchase displays, billing statement stuffers, or enclosures in utility bills are yet other ways to spread the word about membership opportunities. They also give people a way to join a membership program by providing a piece of paper with which they can respond. The success of these programs can be measured using coded response forms to calculate the number of responses from each type of promotion. The cost of printing is often the only cost involved in these methods, since the organization is not responsible for distributing the brochures or flyers. And, an important note: brochures should not be so costly on a per-piece basis that an organization cannot afford to distribute them with abandon.

Two new aquaria that opened in the past several years grew their entire membership programs with statement stuffers. The Aquarium of the Pacific in Long Beach attracted nearly 60,000 members without ever having to incur the expense of a direct mail campaign. On several occasions, the city-owned utility company allowed the Aquarium to include a membership application in its regularly scheduled electric bill mailing to residents—and the memberships flowed in. The same phenomenon occurred at Colorado's Ocean Journey in Denver. Statement stuffers and free publicity about the Aquarium's opening on radio stations allowed the Aquarium to open with more than 40,000 members and with virtually no cash outlay to acquire those members.

Gift Memberships

Gift membership solicitation relies on a third party to purchase a membership as a gift for someone else. Membership promotions revolving around gift-giving opportunities can be designed around a variety of occasions. Appropriate times might include the winter holiday season, birthdays, Valentine's Day, Mother's Day, or Father's Day, as well as others.

Gift memberships can be promoted via direct mail to the current membership file, online as another option on the organization's Web site "join page," or by advertising in publications prior to a particular holiday or gift-giving opportunity time. These promotions are considered successful if they operate on a break-even basis when including postage, printing, artwork, and so forth. An interesting twist, especially for

Valentine's Day or Secretary's Day, is having the membership gift and the membership packet with a greeting from the gift-giver delivered to the person's office or home.

In general, the people most likely to give membership as a gift are those who have already joined the organization. They are aware of the benefits of membership and the enjoyment that results from using them. Thus, most of the promotion for gift memberships needs to be directed at this already-committed audience.

Gift memberships to cultural organizations can be promoted as a great family gift—something for everyone in the family regardless of age, size, or make-up. Memberships to a professional organization might be a nice gift from a person in a mentoring position to a professional starting out in his or her field. A gift of a membership to an alumni organization might be a great graduation gift.

It is advantageous to consider a tangible gift in addition to the membership itself, so that an actual gift that represents the membership can be physically presented to the recipient. A coffee mug, a tote bag, or something that relates to the institution or the occasion being celebrated can be used. For Father's Day, car wash coupons can accompany the gift membership. On Valentine's Day, a single red rose would be appropriately delivered with a heart shaped membership packet. For a holiday gift membership, an ornament or a packet of writing cards with a scene from the organization might be given. For Mother's day, a wind chime might be the gift.

The first and second renewal notices for membership gifts are usually sent to the gift giver. Subsequent notices are then sent to the recipients themselves. Typically, the renewal rate for gift memberships is about 50 percent.

Online Promotions

Sales of memberships online is a new phenomenon for most membership organizations, most of whom have, or are currently constructing, the means by which to offer secure transactions online. The volume of membership sales is yet to be determined for most organizations and is dependent on how computer- and Internet-savvy its target population is. The key, however, is to have a presence, have a Web site with a secure transaction page, and then promote the idea of joining or renewing online in all printed material the organization distributes.

The number and percentage of members joining online is a moving target for most organizations. Until the site and the act of joining online are promoted, the number of people who join online will be low. But once the promotion begins, the numbers should increase. The Woodland Park Zoo in Seattle reported that its sale of online memberships took a sudden leap in October 1999 to about 100 per month, perhaps because of the first-ever heavy promotion of buying online that seemed to permeate the airwaves on television commercials around the holidays. The National Baseball Hall of Fame and Museum acquires about 20 percent of its new members online. For others, the percentages are infinitesimal, yet growing exponentially every month or year.

The Metropolitan Museum of Art has one of the leading membership sites among cultural organizations. Not only can a member join or renew online, there is a special Net Met membership where benefits are delivered online—online newsletter, a screen saver membership premium, a Net Met–only membership, online virtual tour of the collection, and special access to member-only areas of the Web site.

The membership potential of the Internet is that it exposes an organization to the entire universe. An organization that does not have the budget to become national or international can attract members worldwide if it can offer something of value to its members online. An organization might offer special access to information, an "Ask the Expert" feature to current members online, discounted shopping from its online store, or up-to-the-minute news flashes delivered by e-mail on whatever the most recent discovery, acquisition, or breakthrough research information might be. Members can also be cultivated and communicated with by participating in forums and surveys—all online. This medium may also make traditional institutions be perceived in a totally new light to a younger, more connected population than these organizations have appealed to in the past.

Membership Month

Membership never seems to get the attention it deserves—internally or externally. One way to change that situation, at least for one month out of the year, is by hosting a membership month. Pick a high-traffic time during the year and designate it "Membership Month!" To add hoopla to the month, schedule special entertainment on weekends, create big "Membership Month" banners, invite radio stations to do live remote broadcasts with on-air contests and free memberships as prizes, and invite people to come to your venue to become a member. Other events such as a membership appreciation night can be moved to this month.

Perhaps an already scheduled direct mail campaign can be moved to this month. An employee sales incentive contest can take place during Membership Month. Suddenly you have an event for which you can get free media coverage. Also, you might even get the local newspaper's business section to do an article on the business of membership organizations in your area—with your program as the lead, or course.

Charter Membership Opportunities

For new organizations, or organizations with new beginnings, a charter membership program may be in order. A charter membership program is one in which the original group of members will receive special designation and forever be remembered as the founding mothers and fathers of an organization. The key is to impress upon people that to remain a charter member, they must keep their membership intact year after year, without lapse. Charter members may sign on at an increased monetary level, should get memorabilia that connotes their status, and should be reminded of their status at all future fundraising times. This group has the potential of being a loyal group of supporters for many years to come if properly treated.

Advertising

Generally, it is not recommended to use stand-alone advertising to promote membership. There are two reasons: first, advertising is very expensive, and second, it is not targeted enough. If the marketing department has a budget for advertising for the purposes of driving attendance, it is recommended that they collaborate on a theme and have the advertising support the direct mail acquisition campaigns. This is usually done quite well when museums are sponsoring a major exhibition, and the entire organization works together to plan the opening, including media buys, free publicity, and membership direct mail. Also, many zoos coordinate their spring attendance push and memberships drives with each form of media—direct mail and print ads—supporting one another.

What usually does not work is advertising for membership alone. It is not targeted, nor is the impact measurable. For most organizations, the exception to this rule would be advertising specific gift memberships in targeted publications. This would include ads in a business journal around the holidays, when businesses are gift buying for clients or employees, or in an alternative newspaper for a Valentine's Day gift membership promotion. Another possibility might be to advertise through a service such as Welcome Wagon or other group that welcomes new residents in town.

The other exception to the "no advertising" rule is very large organizations, such as the AARP and the World Wildlife Fund, that have large enough budgets for advertising. For large, national and international organizations such as these, advertising is also a way to reach many more people than by any other means. Advertising needs to be well done and to be well placed. It needs to be in print and electronic media where potential members may see or hear it. Market research is the primary way to discover what current members read and the other media they experience. Advertising placed without the research beforehand puts significant funds at risk.

MEASURING ACQUISITION SUCCESS

The success and productivity of each method of membership acquisition can be measured in both immediate and long-range terms. As mentioned earlier, membership acquisition on a break-even basis the first year is very successful. In his book *Fund-Raising,* James Greenfield (1991, 67) notes that when acquiring new members or donors, it may be necessary to spend $1.25 to $1.50 for every dollar raised. The profitability in membership acquisition comes in succeeding years, when membership renewal monies begin to flow. In calculating succeeding year income, memberships from any acquisition source should be income producers by the second or third renewal year and should produce a surplus in revenues, over the cost of acquisition, when considered over a five-year basis. To conduct this kind of multi-year revenue evaluation, it is necessary to determine renewal rates by source and by year. Careful coding and attention to detail is a necessity, and it is important to know how each source produces over time to evaluate fully its success or failure as an acquisition method.

To calculate membership income over time, follow the mathematical process shown in Exhibit 5–1.

This equation can be extended as many years into the future as necessary. Also, if only the overall renewal rate is known, that rate can be used. In the example illustrated in Exhibit 5–1, a per-membership acquisition cost of $75 could be justified, but an acquisition cost of $100 or more would be poor economics, since it would take three years to recoup the cost to acquire the member. In general, the cost to acquire a member should be recouped by year two.

Membership acquisition will probably be the largest single line item in a membership budget. It will most likely outpace the salary line item. And the membership manager's job may be in jeopardy if the acquisition line item doesn't produce expected results. That is why understanding the true cost of acquisition is so important, as is realizing that it will most likely cost more to acquire a member than that member produces in the first year. And it is the mem-

Exhibit 5–1 Five-Year Income from a Member

Membership dues rate year one	$50
+ (Dues × 1st year renewal rate—60% in this case)	+ ($50 × .6)
+ (Dues × 1st year renewal rate × 2nd year renewal rate)	+ ($50 × .6 × .75)
+ (Dues × 1st year renewal rate × 2nd year renewal rate × 3rd year renewal rate)	+ ($50 × .6 × .75 × .85)
+ (Dues × 1st year renewal rate × 2nd year renewal rate × 3rd year renewal rate × 4th year renewal rate)	+ ($50 × .6 × .75 × .85 × .95)
= Five-year income	**= $139.80**

Exhibit 5–2 Membership Acquisition Math

Response Rate	Number of responses divided by the number mailed Example: Received 50 divided by 5,000 mailed = 1.0% response rate
Average Gift	The average of all gifts received. Example: $5,000 in donations divided by a total of 50 gifts = $100 average gift
Cost per Dollar Raised	The cost to raise $1 in donations. Divide the total cost of the campaign by the total amount raised. Example: Cost of $4,000 divided by $5,000 = $.80 cost per dollar raised
Cost per Response	The cost of generating each response. Divide the cost of the campaign by the number of responses. Example: $4,000 cost of campaign divided by 50 responses = $80 cost per response
Return on Investment (ROI)	The return on the money invested in a campaign or the amount that will be returned to the organization for every dollar spent. Divide the total amount raised by the total amount spent. Example: Divide the $5,000 raised by the $4,000 spent = $1.25 ROI
Five-Year Income	What a campaign produces financially if the five-year life of a donor or member is taken into consideration. First, second, third, and fourth year renewal rates must be known and taken into consideration. For an example, see Exhibit 5–1 Five-Year Income from a Member.

bership manager's job to educate everyone else in the organization about this concept. Overall membership will decline if too few new members are attracted on an annual basis. Therefore, as mentioned previously, the acquisition of new members is perhaps the most important function of a membership manager.

The keys to acquisition are to be creative, cost effective, and yet confident enough so that membership growth can occur. Exhibit 5–2 is an example of membership acquisition math that might be useful when planning membership drives and new member acquisition.

Which of these is most important? This depends on the organization and its strategy. If the organization is small and beginning a membership program, the most important issue is to develop a critical mass of members. For this group, the response rate will be most important because gaining members is the strategy. If the institution has a long history and many members, the five-year income projections may be most important. If the organization has mainly corporate board members who work with return on investment on a daily basis, this may be the most important number because it helps the board members understand the program. When budget is an issue, average gift becomes important and the basis for knowing whether or not an upgrade program is working or not.

Because of the many ways that the numbers can be figured and counted, it is important to decide ahead of time what is significant for the organization. That is the only way that an honest evaluation can be made about any acquisition or membership program. Once that decision is made, the organization may proceed to determine the strategy, implement it, and measure the results accordingly.

REFERENCE

Greenfield, J. 1991. *Fund-raising: Evaluating and managing the fund development process.* New York: John Wiley & Sons, Inc.

CHAPTER 6

Direct Mail

Patricia Rich and Dana Hines

Letters, we get letters, we get stacks and stacks of letters...
—The Perry Como Show

PROACTIVE ACQUISITION

DIRECT MAIL IS THE MOST PRO-active, controllable source of new memberships that an organization can have. It is proactive because it initiates the action with the prospect. It is controllable because the timing and the number of new members generated is determined and controlled by the manager. If 1,000 new members are needed during the month of March, the manager plans a campaign of 100,000 to 120,000 in February. Other acquisition methods may be dependent on factors out of the membership manager's control, such as weather, attendance, or the independent decision of a person to join on his or her own without invitation or suggestion.

Direct mail is a form of direct marketing that is just that—direct. It's a direct ask to join. Direct marketing attempts to create behavior in the present. Its goal is to persuade the prospect to overcome inertia, to encourage him or her to indicate, "I'm interested." This call to action means that direct marketing messages tend to be highly conversa-

111

tional and explicit because direct marketers must supply ample justification for the prospect to take immediate action.

It also means that direct marketing involves database work. Because responding involves returning a response card, joining online, or using a toll-free telephone number, human behavior can be tracked, recorded, and analyzed. Program results are objective. Direct marketing analysis determines which lists, packages, ads, or premiums work and which do not. A larger test of the programs that prove to be successful can be accomplished with confidence while eliminating the unsuccessful ones. It is the combination of these elements of testing, trackability, and measurability that is the great appeal of direct mail.

DIRECT MAIL COMPONENTS

There are three basic components in any direct marketing program:

1. The list
2. The offer
3. The creative execution

Experts argue continually over which of the three is the most important element. There are certain truths, however. The list is important because without it, there would be no one to mail to. The offer is important because it triggers a response. The creative execution, or form the offer takes, can help or hinder the physical involvement of the customer or prospect.

Direct mail experts attach 60 percent of the success or failure of a campaign to the lists, and 30 percent to the offer. That leaves 10 percent of a campaign's success dependent on the creative execution. Ironically, most managers spend the bulk of their time laboring over the creative part of the campaign—the design and copy.

The List

Most people are on hundreds of lists, including compiled business and professional lists, magazine subscription lists, hobby or club lists, enthusiasts lists, financial lists, credit approval lists, catalogue lists, and resident lists. The challenge in selecting a mailing list for a particular group or organization is to develop first an accurate profile of the current member, donor, or customer and then proceed to target future mailings to prospect lists with like profiles. This is the concept of marketing to strength rather than spending time and money trying to convert the unconvertible.

One good way to create a profile is to survey current members. Ask them who they are, what their interests are, what publications they subscribe to, and what organizations they belong to. It will be surprising to find the number of people who will complete the survey and provide vital information. When surveying a loyal membership base by mail, it is possible to obtain a 33 to 50 percent response rate (see Chapter 9). This is a phenomenal response. Market researchers in the for-profit world are usually very pleased with a 10 percent rate of response. The information gleaned from a survey is especially important in our fast-paced world, where lifestyles change rapidly and where last year's target market is this year's marginal market.

Another way to profile members is to have the current membership list demographically or psychographically enhanced. A list can be broken down by numerous characteristics, such as median income, home ownership, education level, retail spending index, number of family members, age, and number or types of automobiles. This demographic profiling (usually done for large lists) will identify the most prevalent subgroups within a larger database, and describe the target audience using descriptions, such as "shotguns and pick-ups" or "blue-blood estates."*

To acquire lists for mailing, the first step is to look at establishing reciprocal list trades with similar institutions or organizations. Surveying the organization's members, asking them which other organizations they support, identifies the similar institutions. The more frequent responses will be the organizations to use. Frequently, list exchanges can be made on a name-per-name basis at no cost to either institution, thereby circumventing expensive list rental costs, which sometimes exceed $100 per thousand names rented.

By exchanging lists, the appeal reaches people who are already predisposed to belonging or donating to similar organizations. As mentioned, list trading can cost very little and requires only the spirit of cooperation when it comes to timing of mail drops among the participating institutions. One caution, however, when trading: a name duplication factor of as much as 50 percent is possible since the lists being collected are like-minded in nature. Thus, the lists must go through a deduping process, which means merging lists to eliminate this duplication. It should be noted that the higher the duplication rate, the more certain it is that a good list has been identified, since that list has almost the same profile and many of the same people.

Some organizations have a policy against list trades. This type of policy is a major impediment to a direct mail program. Traded lists from like-minded organizations will perform at twice the response rate or more, than any other lists that are rented. So, right away, without cooperative list trades, the response rate has just fallen by half, without even having been mailed.

*Example of PRISM cluster, Claritas, Inc.

To circumvent such a policy and to make all involved more comfortable with the concept of list trades, a mailing list exchange letter of agreement (see Exhibit 6–1) should be used. Such an agreement specifies the number of times the list can be mailed (usually once), that the list is for mailing purposes only (not telephoning), that it may not be reserved or incorporated into the user's database, that no coding be used that identifies the source of the mailing. A review of the mailing package may also be required.

It should also be noted that when an organization agrees to be involved in list trading, it still reserves the right to trade with whomever it chooses, such as not trading with commercial entities. It may trade with some organizations and deny others. Non-profit organizations should not exchange lists with political organizations lest they risk the loss of their tax-exempt status.

In renting lists, demographic information is accessible on all lists available for rental, and it is necessary to match those lists as closely as possible to the current membership list. The profile of the rental list is provided on a data card. This card lists the percentage of male and female respondents, the income or educational level, and perhaps most importantly, names of other organizations who have rented the file. One can determine by viewing the list of other users whether or not these may be like-minded organizations and whether the list is desirable or not. In some cases, the list manager may even have data on how the list performed for some organizations that used the list previously.

Another type of list that is readily available is the compiled list. Compiled lists are lists of people who have probably filled out information from a warranty card and listed their demographic information as well as interests, hobbies, and likely future pur-

Exhibit 6–1 Mailing List Exchange Letter of Agreement

{NAME OF LENDING ORGANIZATION}
Mailing List Exchange Letter of Agreement

Organizations or companies interested in exchanging mailing lists with the {Name of Lending Organization} agree to adhere to the following policy:

Confidentiality. Organizations or companies participating in the list exchange agree to ensure confidentiality of the list. Membership databases will be sent directly to the mail house of the mailer's choice. Information will not be entered into the database of the borrowing organization, company, or their representatives. The {Name of Lending Organization} mailing list will remain the property of the {Name of Lending Organization}. Prospects responding directly to the mailer may be entered into the mailer's permanent database. Mailer agrees not to distribute, provide, or sell the list to any individual or corporation.

Reciprocity. Mailing lists will be shared only when there is mutual interest in exchanging lists. Names and addresses will be exchanged on a name-for-name basis. The mailer agrees to limit the usage of {Name of Lending Organization}'s list to a one-time mailing solely and exclusively for the agreed specific offer as described in the sample mailing piece.

Common Bond. Mailing lists will be exchanged only when it is presumed that the {Name of Lending Organization}'s members share a common bond with the organization or company using its mailing list.

Content Approval. {Name of Lending Organization} has the right to approve the concept and content of mailings by the organization or company borrowing the {Initials of Lending Organization} membership mailing list.

Telephone Numbers. The {Name of Lending Organization} will only provide names and addresses of members in its database. Telephone numbers, fax numbers, e-mail addresses, and other confidential information will not be shared.

Purging of Duplicates. The mail house authorized by {Name of Lending Organization} will merge all lists prior to mailing, and duplicates will be purged.

Source. The source of the list must not be divulged. If addresses are coded in the mailing, the code cannot reveal its source, including abbreviations or initials of the organization.

Mail Date. The date of the mailing is: _____.

My signature below indicates that I have read the above list-exchange guidelines and agree to abide by them in every way.

Signature: _____

Name: _____

Title: _____ Company: _____

Address: _____

Telephone Number: _____ Date: _____

---

chases. Many compiled lists are just that, compiled from some source, but not necessarily from a source of purchasers such as subscribers or catalogue buyers. Usually compiled lists are not advisable to use unless all other list options have been exhausted. The reason for this is that in direct mail, the important factor is that a person is direct mail responsive, meaning he or she has taken action by mail to purchase something. That is the action that needs to be repeated. With a compiled list, that past action is not guaranteed. A marketer, however, may recommend a compiled list to a membership manager because it is the easiest list to acquire, and the marketer makes a commission on the list rental. In reality, however, a list trade may work much better, but it is more labor intensive to acquire and provides no revenue for the marketer.

One of the best lists an organization can use is a list that the organization itself has compiled. If the organization hosts events, names should be collected and added to a database for future use. Each such event or group of names should be coded, so the list can be tested for productivity in the next membership acquisition mailing. In-house lists of class registrants, shop purchases, or even names from a free membership drawing should be collected, entered, and tested as a mailing list.

To summarize, the type of lists, in order of productivity, that an organization should use when prospecting for new members, is shown below, along with their projected average response rates:

1. Lapsed member file: 2 to 3 percent response
2. Trade lists from like-minded organizations: 1 to 1.5 percent
3. In-house compiled lists: 0.75 to 1.25 percent
4. Consumer rental lists: 0.5 to 1 percent
5. Compiled lists: 0.1 to 0.5 percent

Merge/Purge Processes

Duplication of names is an issue when more than one mailing list is used in a prospect mailing. It is a waste of money for the organization and an annoyance for the recipient, if he or she receives more than one piece of mail from a single mailing. It is even worse if a current member in good standing receives an invitation to join the organization. Merge/purge processing removes duplicates between and within lists. List deduplication is very sophisticated now; however, there will always be some duplicates that slip through. These are usually people who are on every conceivable list, spouses with different last names, or people who are on one list at home and another list at the office. Names with appendages such as Jr., Sr., or Dr., or addresses containing different spellings, such as Ave. or Avenue, should not be reasons for duplicates.

One very important list that should be compiled by every organization using direct mail for new members prospecting is a "do not solicit" list. In every direct mail campaign that is conducted, the organization will receive "hate mail," mail from people who make it known that they do not want to receive any future solicitations from the organization. This is typical. To save money and future annoyances, it is best to list all of these people in a "do not mail" file that will be used as a "kill" file in the deduplication process. This means that any name on this file will be automatically removed ("killed") from all lists being used.

Compiling your own "do not mail" file is just the first step in complying with the "Privacy Promise" sponsored by the Direct Marketing Association (DMA). (see www. the-dma.org/consumers/privacy.html for greater detail.) This program is a nationwide effort to remove from mailing lists people who really do not want to receive solicitations by mail. It is also an act of self-policing by conscientious direct marketers. The components of the program are these:

- A person who does not wish to receive mail notifies the Direct Marketing Association (DMA) in New York. The name is added to a national "do not mail" list.
- Responsible marketers have free access to this national "do not mail" list, and use the national list as a kill file with every prospect mailing.
- Organizations compile their own "do not mail" file and also remove those people from any mailing the organization sends.
- Organizations that trade or sell names make people on their own database aware of this fact, giving them a chance to write, call, e-mail, or fax the organization to place themselves on a "do not mail" list.

This type of self-policing is good for everyone: for the people who do not want to receive mail, for the organization that will not waste money on mailing to nonresponsive households, and for the industry as a whole. Organizations should ask their marketing firms and mail houses if they adhere to the Privacy Promise.

Mail Quantities

Determining the appropriate number of pieces to mail is sometimes a difficult task. Every organization probably has a range of mail quantities within which it will be most successful. Sometimes this range is arrived at by trial and error, sometimes, by using the expertise of a direct mail professional. It is best to start small. The larger a campaign, the lower the response rate may be. The larger the mailing, the further from the target audience many of the prospects may be, thereby decreasing the response rate. Thus, it is best to start small and increase the quantity from one campaign to the next until the optimum mail quantity is found.

Different situations may call for different mail quantities. What is happening in an organization—whether it is a major event, activity, or anniversary, or nothing in particular—will dictate campaign size. For instance, an art museum may have a major exhibition on the horizon and be very justified in doubling its usual mail quantities. In an organization's slow season, however, a decision may be made to mail a smaller quantity. With every organization, there is a target audience that is within its service area. Finding that audience, and then mailing to those prospects time after time with new offers and new information is what is recommended to find the optimal size of a mailing in a targeted geographic area. The Missouri Botanical Garden in St. Louis found that one mailing of 240,000 pieces at one time in the St. Louis region (population 2.5 million) was too large. But a mailing of 140,000 was optimal, and mailing 240,000 pieces over three campaigns every spring worked very well (January mailing of 60,000, March mailing of 140,000, and May mailing of 40,000 equals 240,000 pieces over three mailings). This strategy entailed mailing to some of the same lists all three times.

Sometimes it is difficult to find sufficient numbers of names to mail to in rollout (the larger mailing implemented after testing smaller quantities) quantities. List brokers often require purchasing a minimum number of names, usually 5,000. What may seem like a perfect list may not have 5,000 mailable names in the target area. Sometimes the minimum name requirement can be made flexible by working with the right list broker. If a list performs well, it should be used time after time. This is in keeping with the direct marketing principle that states: You can mail the exact same package to the same list three to five times without the risk of lessening the effectiveness of the offer or creative execution.

Where some organizations fall short, literally, is in gauging the number of mailable names available after the merge/purge process. In planning a campaign, an estimated mail quantity is established at the beginning of the effort. When mailing lists and mail quantities are amassed in preparation for the campaign, the total number of mailable names collected must exceed the intended mail quantity. Because some prospects will appear on multiple lists, excess names must be included in the merge/purge process to allow for the duplication. In other words, it may be necessary to collect 70,000 names to reach a target mail quantity of 50,000 names.

The duplication rate may not be known in advance when an organization is planning its first-ever direct mail campaign. In this case, an educated guess or the experience of a seasoned direct mail consultant may be necessary. The duplication rate will vary by the size of the mailing and the size of the target area. For organizations that serve a limited geographic area and are aggressive in their direct mail strategies, a duplication rate of 50 percent may not be uncommon. For an organization mailing nationally, however, the duplication rate may be minimal, closer to 5 percent. Knowing this number is critical. In some campaign scheduling, the printing and the list deduplication may occur at the same time. An undesirable outcome would be to print 50,000 mail pieces and have only 30,000 names to which to mail. Hence, planning and knowledge of the mailing universe is critical.

Some large national mailers, who mail solicitations by the hundreds of thousands or even millions, do not perform a merge/purge on, or "dedupe," lists. The thinking may be that the chance for duplication is minimal and that when prospecting for value level members, they will take the risk of alienating people who receive multiple pieces rather than go to the expense or the time delay of merge/purge processing. This practice is not recommended. Alienation of potential members is one consideration, as is alienation of some trade list sources. In fact, the best prospects may be on many like-minded lists if they are very committed to a particular cause. For instance, a single prospect may contribute to the World Wildlife Fund, the National Wildlife Federation, and the African Wildlife Federation. If a like-minded organization used these three files in its prospect mailing and mailed three pieces to this generous prospect, it may well alienate the prospect and lose the donation.

List Hints

Some important points to remember when implementing a direct mail campaign are as follows:

Duplication. Anticipated duplication means, of course, that there must be an overage in purchase of names in order to have enough names to meet the projected mailing quantity. It also means that particular attention must be paid to computer work so that as many duplicates as possible are removed from the mailing. The current membership file is used as the primary source file, against which all lists are run. There may also be a special file of people who do not want to receive mailings. This becomes your purge file. A good merge/purge program should not only be run between the lists, but also *within* the lists, removing intrafile duplicates

A multi-hit list matrix shows the duplicate names appearing on each list. It can be a valuable way of judging the quality of the lists. If there is a lot of duplication between the lists, it demonstrates that the selected lists are similar, thereby ensuring success. If few duplicates are found, it is an indication that either the list is not a good one to use because it does not mirror the type of prospect being sought, or it is an indication that the merge/purge process is faulty.

Coding. Ensure that all lists are coded so that response rates by list can be tracked. This will determine which lists should be used again.

Variety. In a test mailing, use the minimum of 5,000 names from a variety of lists. Depending on each list's success, use larger quantities in a rollout. Using all the available names on a large list without some idea of how that list is going to perform is a gamble. NEVER pin the hopes of a campaign on just one list. Spread the risk around; use five lists of 5,000 names each rather than one list with 25,000 names. This is like investing in the stock market: If one list does not perform, you hope the others will do well enough to make the mailing a success.

Repetition. Continue using the most successful and productive lists. It takes many mailings to "wear out" a list, if in fact that happens at all. Some organizations have used some of the same prospect files for 15 to 20 years and will continue to use them as long as those lists keep producing good response rates.

Multi-hits. "Multis" are the names of people that show up on several lists. They receive only one mailing, but the names have come from several organizations. This group may be the most productive since they were on several lists. Thus, this group can be mailed to again as a follow-up to the first campaign, since permission to send mail to that person was given by each organization that person's name appeared on.

The Offer

The offer is the "deal" that is presented to an individual in the direct mail package. Examples are:

- "Join now and receive a free tote bag!"
- "If you're not satisfied, you'll get all your money back—guaranteed!"
- "Respond now and get 2 months free!"

The offer is the "hook" that, ideally, entices the prospect to respond. There are numerous offers that can be made to enhance a program and overcome human inertia. There are examples of various types of offers available in magazines, on the Web, and on television. Free trials, free samples, free gifts, sweepstakes, money-back guarantees, easy terms, yes-no involvement devices (affix a stamp indicating "yes" or "no" to indicate acceptance of the offer), expiration dates, two-for-one offers, discounts, charter memberships, and exclusive terms—these are but a few of the many offers encountered any day in today's world.

One way of determining the more productive of two offers is to test them by mailing simultaneously to the same list and changing only one item in the package: the offer. Results can be compared and the winner determined by response rate and dollars generated.

Premium items (also known as incentives) are a great way to enhance membership offers. Tangible premiums provide a great way for a person to show his or her affiliation with an organization, to say, "I belong." These premiums are also a good way for the organization to obtain a bit of free publicity while also offering something of value that is appealing to the prospective member.

Here are a few examples of premiums that have proven successful for many membership organizations:

- Tote bags
- Umbrellas
- Mugs
- CDs, tapes, videos
- Note cards
- Posters
- Bookmarks
- Books
- Backpacks
- T-shirts
- Baseball caps embroidered with a logo

The key is to find a premium that is related to the type of organization. A history museum might give books on historical topics; a botanical garden might give seeds, gardening tools, or an umbrella. It is also important to find premiums that are attractive to the widest possible audience, young and old, male and female.

Premiums do work. No matter what people may say, when a package without a premium is tested against a package that offers a premium, the package with the premium will most often win. Premiums can also be used to boost average gift sizes by offering them for upgrades or for joining at a certain level. For example, a premium can be offered to anyone who agrees to move to a higher level of membership; the premium will produce better results than a package that asks without the premium.

The Creative Execution

The third component of the direct mail campaign is the creative execution. Once the list decisions and the offer have been determined, it is time to package them all in the physical form that actually carries the offer to the intended parties. But before the creation of the graphics and copy for a direct mail campaign can begin, some fundamental decisions with respect to the number and size of pieces to be included in the package must be made.

Format of the Package

It is important to understand some direct mail formats and remember that there are some environmental differences between direct mail and other media. People read the newspaper, watch television, surf the Web, or listen to the radio while sitting down. Be it good or bad, most people tend to sort through direct mail before they even open it—while standing in the kitchen near a wastebasket. The first order of business, then, for a successful direct mail piece is to sustain enough interest to be included in the pile to be opened.

Unlike other media, direct mail is not restricted to time or space. Large or small formats can be used for brochures with multiple folds and numerous inserts. The only limitation is budget and maintaining a look that is in keeping with an organization's image. Many other media, like billboards or commercials, make an impression and build an image, but are not good for eliciting a decision.

The classic direct mail format is a letter package. It may simply consist of a single-page letter, a response form, and the reply envelope or it may be a multiple-page letter with a brochure response form, a lift letter (an extra note included in the mailing), and other inserts. These types of formats have evolved through numerous tests over the course of many years.

Themes and Copy

Every direct mail campaign needs an overriding theme. A consistent message that relates to the theme helps readers comprehend what is being proposed and how and why they might want to participate in the cause. Arriving at or creating a theme is one of the fun and challenging parts of formulating a campaign. The theme is what the copy is wrapped around; it is the glue that holds the copy, the offer, and the message together. Examples of complete creative packages are seen in Figures 6–1 and 6–3. Figure 6–2 is an example of an envelope that worked well in a direct mail campaign.

The potential member's most frequently asked question is: "What's in it for me?" Membership prospecting copy should highlight membership benefits first and foremost over the "good" the prospective member will be doing by supporting the organization. Focusing on "What's in it for the individual?" is more important in the acquisition campaign, when the prospect is being engaged for the first time.

Copy is very important in direct mail prospecting for membership. Within the copy of the letter, for example, it is important to appeal to a number of basic human desires, such as to be smart, have pleasure, take advantage of special opportunities, save money, save time, or be part of a selected group. All of this can be achieved with well-written copy. It is also important to realize that such things as underlining, highlighting, and indenting can draw a reader's eye to important statements.

Other components of the package that make it easy and desirable to respond should also be considered. Perforate pieces that need

Theme: "Open Your Eyes to a Desert Surprise." "Open Your Eyes to a Desert Surprise" produced a response rate of .87% and an average gift of $40.93. This piece highlighted the seasonality and surprises that await visitors and members at the Desert Botanical Garden when the cactus blooms are at their peak. It also mentions the year round opportunities at the garden.

Figure 6–1 Desert Botanical Garden Package. Courtesy of Desert Botanical Garden, Phoenix, AZ.

The desert flower motif encouraged potential members to open it. "Open Your Eyes to a Desert Surprise" produced a response rate of .87% and an average gift of $40.93.

Figure 6–2 Desert Botanical Garden Envelope: "Open Your Eyes to a Desert Surprise." Courtesy of Desert Botanical Garden, Phoenix, AZ.

to be torn out, encourage telephoning in a membership using a credit card, date the offer to create a sense of urgency, use a postscript (P.S.) in the letter to highlight an important note, use real-life testimonials from people who are recognizable in your area or region.

Outer Envelope

The purpose of the outer envelope is two-fold: to prepare the prospect for what is inside and to generate enough interest for the prospect to open the envelope. In direct mail, a highly illustrated envelope tied to an offer inside or a plain white envelope (with nothing on it but the name, address, and a stamp) will most likely ensure that the package is opened and, thus, increase the number of responses. The aim is to involve the recipient in the process of exploring a direct mail piece.

There is a variety of sizes and types of envelopes, both standard and custom. There are no hard facts about which size to use. What must be considered are the overall objective, the look of the mailing package, where it will be opened (home or business), and the competitive environment. This last point deserves elaboration. In many cases, an organization is in competition with others. Colorful graphics, catchy teaser copy, a plain white envelope, or an interesting return address might catch a person's attention and increase the likelihood of one piece being opened before, or instead of, another one.

Four-color graphic envelope versus plain white envelope package: that is the question. The answer is in the testing. What works for one organization may not work for another, but this is a hotly debated issue in the membership acquisition world. A consensus may be reached by going to one extreme or the other to have the package opened. A plain white envelope is used to raise the level of curiosity: "Who is writing to me and why?" is a question the reader may ask when looking at a package that appears to be personalized or does not give the reader a hint of who/why/what on the outer envelope. On the other hand, a very bright, lively, and visually appealing package may jump out at a reader and scream, "Open me first!"

Membership Consultants tested the plain versus four-color envelope for three of its clients. The results are shown in Table 6–1. In this test, for these organizations, a plain envelope brought a greater response. This is not always the case, which is why it is so important for each organization to test. Envelopes that have worked well are shown in Figure 6–2, Figure 6–4, Figure 6–5, and Figure 6–6. It should be noted, however, that after the anthrax scare in 2001, plain white envelope packages were abandoned for "safer," more illustrative mail packages that did not scare the recipient.

The Letter

The letter is the personal appeal to the prospect. In keeping with what has been proven to work in direct mail, always include a letter, even if that letter is not personalized. Personalization includes addressing the letter to a specific person. In direct mail membership acquisition, personalization is not necessary. What is necessary is to keep the costs as low as possible, and personalization costs money. Begin to use personalization after someone has been acquired as a member, and the solicitation is for another gift from the member. At the prospecting stage, after all, there are no relationships with the prospects; prospects are anonymous, and a "Dear Friend" salutation is appropriate.

An age-old debate in direct mail circles is "What should the length of a letter be?" The answer to that question may be answered by considering what type of organization this letter represents, and how familiar people are with the organization. For some organizations, a one-page, graphically enhanced letter might be sufficient. For very small organizations that are using personal solicitation from a known friend, one page with the friend's signature and a personal note should work well. For organizations that already have a connection to their prospects, such as alumni associations, a two-page letter may be appropriate. The alumni are already familiar with the alumni association and the concept of the organization. For an organization that has a physical presence in a geographic area and a fair amount of awareness surrounding that organization, such as a well-known museum, again, a two-page letter is sufficient. Organizations that are national, do not have a physical presence, or are cause related, usually require a four-page letter. Organizations such as the Nature Conservancy or the World Wildlife Fund usually require a four-page letter, or longer, to explain all that they are doing to conserve green spaces or endangered species.

The issue for the organization is to test different letters to see which one works the best for that particular organization.

It should be noted that direct mail copy is very different from the verbiage used in

Table 6–1 Direct Mail Package Tests: Four-Color vs. Plain Envelopes

Client	4-Color Envelope		Plain Envelope	
	Response Rate	Average Gift	Response Rate	Average Gift
Client 1	0.59%	$54.94	0.69%	$56.23
Client 2	0.85%	$65.96	0.93%	$67.34
Client 3	0.47%	$49.25	0.70%	$65.71

Theme: "Join the Bloomin' Garden!" This members appeal, with an attractive umbrella offer as the premium, produced a .85% response and an average gift of $56.11.

Figure 6–3 Missouri Botanical Garden Package. Courtesy of Missouri Botanical Garden, St. Louis, MO.

brochures, proposals, or everyday business communication. Direct mail copy breaks all the rules. There may be incomplete sentences, slang, and "fluffy" copy. To be certain, copy for direct mail letters is not usually part of the communications repertoire of the President, Executive Director, or whoever the letter's signer may be. Thus, there is often reluctance on the part of the signer the first time he or she is asked to sign a well-written direct mail letter. In fact, the sign of a great direct mail letter designed for membership acquisition purposes is that someone will complain, "It does not sound like a letter from the President!"

The Reply Envelope

Including a reply envelope will *always* increase the response rate. In fact, no package should ever be mailed without a return envelope. Without a return envelope, the prospect has to do too much in order to join. The business reply envelope is not fancy because its graphics are regulated by the post office. The post office should be consulted about the appropriate barcodes for the organization's particular mailing address. These are the vertical lines that are printed on business reply envelopes. Always have the envelope approved by the post office prior to printing to avoid having problems crop up after printing has already been completed. Although not required to do so, it is advisable to print these envelopes in black. Some colors are made up of other colors, and certain reds in inks can cause problems with the post office's readers. So do not get fancy here; just print in black.

If possible, use a postage-paid envelope to preclude the barrier of the prospect not

This envelope emphasized the premium of the Garden umbrella. This had good "open me" appeal, as this offer produced a .85% response and an average gift of $56.11.

Figure 6–4 Missouri Botanical Garden Envelope: "Join the Bloomin' Garden!" Courtesy of Missouri Botanical Garden, St. Louis, MO.

having a stamp. There is debate about providing the postage for the reply. Unless there is money in the budget to test this, it is recommended that the postage-paid business reply envelope (BRE) be supplied, avoiding the possibility that the prospect, while paying bills and making donations, has one too few stamps and omits the organization.

Membership Consultants tested a BRE versus a non-BRE in a direct mail renewal program for one of its clients, Missouri Historical Society. The findings were more related to the timing of the responses than to the difference in response rates: money and memberships arrived more quickly in the BRE group than in the non–postage-paid group. This factor alone saves money for an organization because of the smaller mail quantity that is required for subsequent renewal mailings.

Another option is to use a BRE, but print a message on the envelope such as, "Your stamp here will save the organization money."

Then, when members use a stamp, the organization can save those stamped envelopes, return them to the post office, and receive a refund. A common misunderstanding is that this refund happens automatically, but it doesn't. The envelopes must be returned to the post office for the refund.

The Response Device

Include all information on the response device that will make processing and servicing a member as simple as possible. When possible, the label or name and address should be printed on the response device so that processing personnel do not have to read handwriting or printing. The list code should be on the response device for easy tracking. Ask the prospective member to include information such as telephone number, e-mail address, children's ages, matching gift employers, and any other information important for future direct mail efforts to the member.

This envelope did double duty—the same design was used for a membership acquisition piece and for the museum's annual fund appeal. The copy and the appeal were different, but the result for both were good, with the annual appeal being the best ever for the museum. The membership acquisition package produced a response rate of .72%, with an average gift of $45.24. The annual appeal had a 4.24% response, raised $35,319, with an average gift of $88.74.

Figure 6–5 Missouri Historical Society Envelope: "Meet me at the Fair!" Courtesy of Missouri Historical Society, St. Louis, MO.

This compelling appeal to members for a second gift had a strong endangered species theme. The design "had legs," in that the design was used for several years, with only the face of the animal changing from year to year. So the design became synonymous with the zoo's annual appeal campaign. This produced the best-ever results, with a 3.22% response, $58,738 raised, and an average gift of $84.64.

Figure 6–6 Saint Louis Zoo Envelope: "Kingdoms lost are gone forever." Courtesy of Saint Louis Zoo, St. Louis, MO.

If there is room on the response device, repeat the offer, picture the premium, and list the benefits and categories (use the reverse side if necessary). Consider presenting the categories of membership by listing first the most popular category or the category you want people to join. Highlight the category that is a level up from the entry-level category, and note that this is the "Best Value!"

IMPORTANT CONSIDERATIONS IN THE DIRECT MAIL PROGRAM

Seasonality

Each organization needs to establish its own seasonality in mailing. A museum may find that the back-to-school mood in the fall is a prime time of the year, thereby making a direct mail rollout at that time most successful. This would leave the spring or winter for test mailings. On the other hand, a zoo or botanical garden may feel that spring is the best time for a large direct mail campaign, leaving fall for the test time. Each institution is different, and testing should be done to determine the most effective mailing time for your organization.

To take full advantage of an organization's seasonality, testing should be performed in the off season so that winning packages and offers can be rolled out, or mailed in larger quantities, during that organization's best-performing season. Direct mail results for a particular organization may be from 10 to 50 percent higher in the best time of the year. However, other key times in an organization's lifespan can be the exception to the rule of seasonality. For instance, if an organization is celebrating a major anniversary or is opening a new facility in a season that is not considered its

peak season, that event and the heightened attention and publicity can overcome or surpass its typical seasonal response.

Testing

Testing results in the learning that makes or breaks an organization's direct mail productivity. Testing is the scientific component of direct mail that needs to be conducted to demonstrate what really works and what doesn't. The true enemy of a direct mail program is the "gut feeling" that people sometimes impose on a campaign. Sometimes managers of campaigns or committees will impose what they like or dislike about direct mail on a campaign. To be successful, direct mail campaigns cannot be run on gut feelings or personal whims, but must be based on industry standards and test results.

Testing is the scientific presentation of two or more opposing elements of a direct mail package to target audiences under controlled conditions, to determine which element of the package will produce the better results. For instance, in an offer test of a free tote bag versus a free umbrella, the only variation in copy is the description of the item being offered. The remainder of the package must be identical, with the same graphics, the same copy, the same number of inserts mailed to the same lists that are randomly divided into two equal groups. The tote bag offer is mailed to one of the randomly selected groups; the umbrella offer is mailed to the remaining group. The results will speak for themselves: whichever group produces the most responses, the highest average gift, and, in the end, the lowest cost per dollar raised and greatest return on investment (ROI) will be the winner. This information can then be applied to the next mailing in the annual cycle of campaigns using the winning element and testing another one.

This description may be an oversimplification of the testing process, but in general, that is how testing works. Test cells (a cell is a test group) need to be at least 5,000 pieces in size for a reliable test. That means that for testing an umbrella against a tote bag, at least 5,000 of each offer would need to be mailed. In some cases, one of the test cells may produce a higher response rate and the other may produce a higher average gift. The umbrella may cost twice as much as the tote bag. In these cases, all costs of the package and the cost of the premium need to be taken into consideration. When this is done, it will usually be possible to determine a winner. If the results are inconclusive, repeating the test may be necessary. Verifying the results with a subsequent test is usually advisable.

Other elements that can be tested and examples include:

- Messages or themes: a philanthropic message versus a benefits message
- Package size: a 6″ × 9″ package versus a #10 (business size) envelope package
- Offer: a discount offer versus a premium offer
- Outer envelope: a plain envelope versus a four-color graphic envelope
- Appeal: a two-color package versus a four-color package
- Letter: a two-page letter versus a four-page letter

In almost every case, it is recommended that an organization conduct its own testing. What has been tested and proven to work for one organization may not be the case for another organization. What has been proven to work for one group at a given point in time may need to be retested several years later as the direct mail community changes and other trends may apply.

Tracking

You have mailed the piece; now it is time to track results. Tracking the results allows for future decisions that are based on concrete and objective information. Tracking the responses by the day and by the week helps the organization predict future campaign results. For instance, sometimes the number of responses received within the first 10 days after the mailing (starting with the first *heavy* response day) multiplied by 2 is an indicator of the total number of responses once the campaign is complete. It is important to determine response rate, cost per response, and cost per piece. Then compare the cost per package to the income over the life of the member. Looking at all of these factors helps determine what was successful in a campaign and what changes should be made in upcoming campaigns.

Analysis

Perhaps the most important part of any campaign is not how much money is collected, but what is learned in the process. The analysis of a campaign is critical, and yet it is the part that is most frequently overlooked. The purpose of every campaign must be to learn as much as possible, so the organization can mail smarter the next time around. If a comprehensive analysis is not performed after every campaign, then what was learned or overlooked might be repeated or deleted in the next campaign. For instance, if a list performed poorly with respect to response rate, but had a high average gift in one campaign, that list might be deleted from the next campaign if the lists are judged only on response rate. Some organizations might be married to a particular offer, even though a less expensive offer proves to work just as well in a test of the two offers. The lesson is: don't test what you don't want to change. An organization that delights in its fabulous design that so beautifully depicts what the organization stands for may be reluctant to give up those graphics when a plain, white envelope is proven to "pull" better (produce better results) than those gorgeous, four-color envelopes. Hence, use what is learned to build a foundation for the next campaign. This type of ongoing testing, analysis, and learning is what makes great direct mailers and separates the professionals from the amateurs.

A complete direct mail report (Table 6–2) usually occurs about 60 to 90 days after a campaign has "dropped" (mailed). This time allows for the full measure of a campaign's response to be received, processed, and tabulated.

The data needed to perform a spreadsheet analysis include:

- Number of pieces mailed: in total and by list segment
- Number of responses: in total and by list segment
- Amount contributed: in total and by list
- Costs: of creative, printing, processing, mailing, lists, premiums

With these numbers, a response analysis spreadsheet can be developed. No analysis is complete, however, without a narrative to accompany the spreadsheet. Such a narrative is needed to point out the subtle nuances that may be missed by those people who are not well versed in the minutiae of direct mail, especially direct mail used for membership acquisition purposes. Often, budget decisions are made by individuals who do not have a good working knowledge of direct mail, so the role of the analysis becomes the justification for some rather large expenditures. In fact, direct mail campaign budgets usually rival staff costs as the largest items in the membership department's budget.

Campaign Size

The size of a direct mail acquisition campaign has significant impact on the results: generally, the smaller the campaign the higher the response rate. This is due to the fact that smaller mailings tend to be more targeted and the prospects are usually comparable to current members. The larger the mailing, the farther from the target the prospects will be, hence responding at a lower rate.

Some organizations have thought that if they want 2,000 new members, and if a 1 percent response is what should be expected, then all they have to do is mail 200,000 pieces. It is not that simple. The organization may be able to get a 1 percent response if the campaign is 50,000 or 100,000 pieces, but if there is one mailing of 200,000 prospects, the additional quantity may not be—and won't be—as targeted as the prospects in the first 50,000 pieces, and the response rate will be lower.

In St. Louis, with a population of 2.5 million, one membership group mailed 200,000 pieces and found that the response rate fell off precipitously from the campaigns it had been doing at the 150,000 piece level. However, the organization was able to achieve its desired results by mailing two campaigns that added up to the 200,000 quantity.

Winning Campaigns

The definition for a "winning" campaign will vary from organization to organization, depending on the response rate, the average gift, or the total number of new members or new donors that a campaign

Table 6–2 Direct Mail Campaign Report: Spring 2000 Membership Acquisition Results, Drop 1—March 30, 2000

Code	List	Number Mailed	Number of Responses	Response Rate	Revenue	Average Gift	5-Year Income	Cost per Response	Cost per $ Raised	Return on Investment
FOML	Lapsed	386	10	2.59%	$505.00	$50.50	$1,411.92	$19.38	$0.38	$2.61
FOMP	Prospects	4,164	53	1.27%	$3,680.00	$69.43	$10,288.82	$39.44	$0.57	$1.76
MG1	Natural History	2,939	26	0.88%	$1,540.00	$59.23	$4,305.65	$69.97	$1.18	$0.85
MG2	Smithsonian	3,886	21	0.54%	$1,060.00	$50.48	$2,963.63	$114.54	$2.27	$0.44
MG3	Parents Magazine	5,044	26	0.52%	$1,430.00	$55.00	$3,998.10	$120.09	$2.18	$0.46
MG4	Ranger Rick	4,510	27	0.60%	$1,205.00	$44.63	$3,369.03	$103.40	$2.32	$0.43
MG5	Parenting	3,825	12	0.31%	$640.00	$53.33	$1,789.36	$197.31	$3.70	$0.27
OM1	Exploration	778	26	3.34%	$2,535.00	$97.50	$7,087.54	$15.02	$0.15	$6.49
OM2	Museum of the Region	489	1	0.20%	$100.00	$100.00	$279.59	$245.48	$2.45	$0.41
OM3	Museum of Art	2,434	53	2.18%	$2,285.00	$43.11	$6,388.57	$23.05	$0.53	$1.87
OM4	Symphony	1,609	37	2.30%	$2,480.00	$67.03	$6,933.77	$21.83	$0.33	$3.07
OM5	City Museum	255	6	2.35%	$295.00	$49.17	$824.78	$21.34	$0.43	$2.30
OM6	World Wildlife Fund	4,148	48	1.16%	$2,640.00	$55.00	$7,381.11	$53.49	$0.97	$1.03
OM7	Planetarium	533	11	2.06%	$585.00	$53.18	$1,635.59	$24.32	$0.46	$2.19
	Total	**35,000**	**357**	**1.02%**	**$20,980.00**	**$58.77**	**$58,657.46**	**$57.55**	**$0.98**	**$1.02**

generated. Sometimes success is declared when a new package beats the control package that may have been a perennial winner in the past. It is also important to view the results in context to what is a success for that particular organization. One organization might be disappointed with a response rate of 0.75 percent while another organization would be very pleased with that response. For a full analysis of what is deemed a success and how to measure success, refer to Chapter 13.

"Winning campaigns" may also refer to the fact that the packages where actually "Award winning!" A successful campaign and package can be submitted to local Direct Marketing Association or other professional marketing or fundraising groups for annual award programs. Some of the direct mail samples included in this chapter were indeed "Award winning" as determined by the St. Louis Chapter of the Direct Marketing Association's annual Arrow Awards. In fact, the Missouri Historical Society envelope "Meet Me at the Fair" (see Figure 6–5) won the "Best of Show" award, beating out its better funded, for-profit challengers!

DIRECT MAIL USES

There are a variety of uses of direct mail in the membership and development areas of an organization. For the most part, the advice given here has been for direct mail acquisition of new members. Mail is also used for renewals and other gifts to an organization. Included here are some rules of thumb for other uses of direct mail in nonprofit membership organizations.

Renewals

Many of the same rules apply to renewal mailings as those recommended for acquisition. There are, however, a few differences relating to renewals. First, the letter for renewals can be shorter. For the most part, because a person has had an experience with the organization, there is less convincing to do; hence a shorter letter. A letter is advised because it does not presume the renewal decision, but kindly asks the current member to consider it. A renewal letter allows for another thank-you for past support, something that is always important. A renewal letter

---

Exhibit 6–2 Acceptable Ranges of Response Rates by Type of Campaign

Acquisition, first time members:	0.6% to 1.2%
Membership renewal:	10% to 50% per renewal mailing; usually at least 3 renewal mailings are performed for a renewal rate totaling 70% to 80%.
Annual or special appeal:	5% to 15% of the membership solicited, less if to nonaffiliated groups (then it becomes an acquisition campaign). May be as high as 50% to 80% if segmented and prior donors are solicited.
Lapsed member mailings:	1.5% to 8%, depending on the aggressiveness of pursuing lapsed members; the more aggressive, the lower the response rate.

also allows an organization to talk about upcoming events and the reasons for renewing the relationship. Some organizations use an invoice format, without a letter, in an attempt that presumes the member will renew and just pay the "bill." If there is a question about a campaign like this, it should be tested, just as an acquisition package would be tested.

Another element of renewals that can be tested is personalization versus nonpersonalization. Some organizations with very high renewal rates do not use a personalized renewal package. Timing of the renewal mailing should also be tested.

Annual or Special Appeals

Direct mail can also be used to ask for other gifts to the institution. In fact, direct mail is probably the preferred way to determine whether a member has the interest and capability to make commitments to an organization beyond the membership commitment. Direct mail is an important technique for the development program, with the membership program providing the pool of prospects to solicit.

Anticipated Responses

The response rates vary depending on the type of campaign, the history and aggressiveness of a mailer, and the expertise of the staff or consultant performing the direct mail campaign. Exhibit 6–2 provides examples of acceptable ranges of response rates per specific type of campaign.

Chapter 7

Telemarketing

Michael J. Rosen

That's an amazing invention, but who would ever want to use one of them?
—Rutherford B. Hayes, 19th U.S. president, after participating
in a trial telephone conversation, 1876

ADVANCEMENT THROUGH PERSONAL COMMUNICATION

ALMOST IMMEDIATELY FOLLOWING its invention, the telephone became a uniquely personal communications medium. It remains so today. People share gossip, learn of the death of loved ones, receive news of births, arrange vacations, schedule appointments with doctors, purchase entertainment tickets—all through the telephone. In short, people use the telephone to receive and convey personal information on a regular basis. Marketers recognize this fact. They also know that the more personal the communication, the more positive the outcome.

While face-to-face communication is usually the most effective way to market because it is the most personal, it is often not the most practical or cost-efficient. That leaves the telephone as the next-most-personal method for communicating to carefully targeted populations. For this reason, savvy organizations use the telephone as an important part of their marketing mixes. These organizations use less personal means to reach broader audiences.

Negativity Toward Telemarketing

When the subject of "telemarketing" comes up, most development and membership personnel, not to mention boards of directors, give it a less-than-enthusiastic response. Despite the benefits of communicating personally with target audiences, savvy organizations carefully weigh the benefits and potential downsides of implementing telemarketing campaigns. Often, organizations will implement such campaigns while still harboring some reservations about the general appropriateness of telemarketing, in part because it is such a personal medium. While known by a number of other names, we will use the broad term "telemarketing" to describe the organized use of the telephone medium for the purpose of contacting individuals to solicit donations or sell memberships.

To understand why organizations are cautious about implementing telemarketing campaigns, consider the following:

1. Most people do not like the general practice of telemarketing, as it is used by both the nonprofit and for-profit sectors. At the close of 1999, Yankelovich Partners (1999) released the findings of a survey on "Life in the Year 2010." When asked, 73 percent of those surveyed stated they would like to leave telemarketing behind as the world prepared to advance into a new century.

2. The U.S. Federal Trade Commission (FTC 1996) adopted strict regulations for telemarketing (Telemarketing Sales Rule) following negative press for the industry and increased public pressure. In 2001, following the September 11 terrorist attacks in the United States, Congress instructed the FTC to promulgate new regulations to govern telemarketing for nonprofit organizations. According to the FTC's 1996 article "Straight Talk about Telemarketing," telemarketing fraud costs the public over $40 billion a year (U.S. Federal Trade Commission 1996).

3. Responding to complaints from citizens who receive unsolicited telemarketing calls, several state governments have adopted laws and regulations creating state-based "do not call" lists. Such lists allow members of the public to register their desire not to receive telemarketing calls. These states then require companies that use telemarketing to purge these names from their telemarketing prospect lists.

4. The continued growth of the use of call screening devices indicates the public's displeasure with unsolicited telephone calls. Today, answering machines, caller ID devices, and electronic telephone watchdogs all permit consumers to effectively screen their calls. As a result, many telemarketing agencies report a decline in the number of contacts they can make as a percentage of the number of call attempts.

5. The Center on Philanthropy at Indiana University's *Report on the December 2001 Philanthropic Giving Index* revealed the decline in perceived effectiveness of the telephone as a medium for fundraising. Between the December 1998 and December 2001 survey summaries, there has been a 10 percent decline in the reported effectiveness of the telephone for fundraising, not including membership programs. During this same period, direct mail saw an 11 percent decline. The Report reveals the perceptions of development professionals (The Center on Philanthropy at Indiana University 2001).

Telemarketing Works

The five items listed above reveal a less than positive perception of telemarketing on the part of the general public and some segments of the nonprofit community. In light of this, why does any nonprofit organization choose to implement telemarketing campaigns? The answer: Telemarketing can work most effectively from both the economic and public relations perspectives when properly implemented. Telemarketing remains a powerful marketing tool.

One can think of telemarketing as the flip side of the direct response coin, with direct mail on the other side. Telemarketing has many similarities to direct mail, including the attitudes surrounding it, particularly during the early days of its use. Many organizations have received complaints about "junk mail." Despite, or perhaps because of, these complaints, organizations began designing tasteful and targeted direct mail appeals that achieved fundraising and membership goals. Just as the nonprofit sector looked past personal biases to let results justify the use of direct mail, today's membership professionals are doing the same where telemarketing is concerned; otherwise, they risk losing ground to the more nimble competition.

Most fundamentally, the telephone remains an effective medium as evidenced by the fact that organizations continue to use it. According to *Giving and Volunteering in the United States: Findings from a National Survey,* 1999 Edition, (Independent Sector, Kirsch et al. 2001), nearly half of those surveyed reported that they have seen an increase over the past year in the number of telephone solicitations they receive. If telemarketing were ineffective, its use would certainly be discontinued. This is not to say that telemarketing is an appropriate technique for all organizations or all populations. Telemarketing is a technique that can work but only when carefully implemented for an appropriate audience with a compelling message, just as with direct mail.

Independent Sector also reported that 73.1 percent of survey respondents who gave money indicated that receiving a telephone call was important or very important to their decision to support a particular nonprofit organization (Kirsch et al. 2001). While the survey primarily addresses fundraising rather than membership initiatives, these remain related endeavors. Because donors remain responsive to telephone calls, nonprofit professionals believe that the telephone will continue to be about as effective a fundraising tool in the near future as it was at the close of 2001, according to a survey of development professionals reported in the Philanthropic Giving Index (The Center on Philanthropy at Indiana University 2001).

While telemarketing remains a vital communications tool, the government will continue to enact new consumer protection laws and regulations related to the practice. An outright ban is unlikely, however, for several reasons. Nearly six million people were employed in telephone marketing positions in 2000, according to the Direct Marketing Association (2000). The annual job growth rate for the telemarketing industry is projected to be nearly 4 percent per year through 2005. This means that the telemarketing industry impacts the livelihood of a tremendous number of voters. Politicians are not likely to put so many voters out of work. Politicians are also not likely to ban a fundraising medium upon which they themselves rely. Furthermore, a series of U.S. Supreme Court decisions in the late 1980s found that nonprofit organizations are entitled to greater first amendment protection than purely commercial telemarketing endeavors.

Many organizations continue to find telemarketing campaigns just as effective for membership programs as for fundraising. Organizations use telemarketing effectively to reclaim previously and recently lapsed members, acquire new members, solicit members for contributions, and survey members.

Because it works, telemarketing will remain a vital communications tool for reaching large numbers of people in a personal way.

Neutralize Pitfalls to Ensure Success

While many complaints of telemarketing are valid, there are techniques that can be used to neutralize problems before they arise. As with any marketing technique, poorly executed telemarketing will produce poor results. By contrast, well-executed campaigns will produce excellent results. The following list presents five common complaints that people voice about telemarketing and ways to neutralize the potential for negativity:

1. Calls Are Poorly Timed

Perhaps the most common complaint about telemarketing is that the calls always seem to come when the recipient sits down to dinner. Unfortunately, callers cannot know whether they are about to intrude on someone's dinner, favorite television program, or quiet time after the children are tucked into bed. People simply do not keep the same schedules, so interruptions are inevitable. To neutralize the potential for negative impact when calling someone, the caller simply needs to ask permission to speak immediately after introducing himself or herself. By asking the prospect for their permission to proceed, the caller has

empowered the recipient of the call. By granting permission to proceed, the call recipient invites the caller into the home rather than having the caller simply barge into the living room. If the call recipient cannot deal with the call or simply chooses not to, the caller can schedule a specific appointment to call back at a mutually agreeable time. By giving the call recipient a degree of control early in the conversation, the caller is much more likely to maintain control of the outcome.

2. Calls Are Uninvited

Many people simply do not like telemarketing calls in general and have taken action to virtually eliminate such calls from their lives. Answering machines, caller ID devices, and electronic telephone watchdogs allow people to screen their calls. However, most screeners do not screen their calls all the time, seven days a week. By changing the time of day and day of week that call attempts are made, the caller will eventually be able to reach many so-called screeners.

At the point of contact, then, the call recipient will likely be very defensive given their general stance against telemarketing. The caller will have just 10 to 15 seconds to sound different from every other telemarketing call, so as to engage the other party. To accomplish this, the caller must be calling for an organization that will interest the recipient, must sound natural rather than canned and, as mentioned above, must ask permission to speak. By sounding different and by calling on behalf of an organization the recipient cares about, the caller will neutralize the potential negativity that could result from making an uninvited call. Uninvited need not be equated with unwelcome.

Make certain, however, to check state and federal laws and be certain to comply with all regulations, including any "no call" rules.

3. Callers Are Pushy

The public frequently complains that callers are pushy and do not listen. While many telemarketing calls fit this description, the most effective calls do not. By asking call recipients open- and closed-ended questions, by listening to them, by speaking to their interests and concerns, and by engaging them in a true dialogue, the caller will achieve the strongest possible results, and the call recipient will actually appreciate the contact.

4. Offers Are Inappropriate

The public also complains about receiving calls from organizations that do not interest them. Consider the couple with no young children at home who receives a call to join a children's museum. Of course they would not appreciate the call unless they want to visit the museum with their grandchildren. As with direct mail, organizations will find that one key to telemarketing success is carefully selecting the target population. By making certain that the call will be of interest to the recipient, the organization will neutralize the potential for negativity.

5. Calls Are Impersonal

Ironically, many people complain that telemarketing calls are impersonal despite the uniquely personal nature of the medium. There is a difference between personalization and personal. Organizations that simply personalize each call by using the recipient's name do not use the telephone to full advantage. Since the call is person-to-person, the caller can and should tailor the call to each prospect. For example, a science museum might ask a call recipient if he/she has young children. If the recipient does

have children, the caller can discuss the membership benefits that appeal to families such as free admission. If the recipient has grown children, the caller can discuss the membership benefits that appeal to adults such as travel opportunities and educational programs. By using different responses within calling scripts, depending on the prospect's reaction (see Figure 7–1), and by using available data to customize the call (database marketing), organizations can make each call personal and effective.

By being sensitive to those on the receiving end of the call, by designing the calls to ensure that each is as personal as practical, by working to ensure that each call is placed to someone with a reasonable expectation of interest, the organization implementing a telemarketing campaign will achieve some level of success.

THE OTHER DIRECT RESPONSE APPROACH: TELEMARKETING

As with direct mail, there are three basic components to any telemarketing program:

1. The list
2. The offer
3. The creative execution

Rather than restating information on these three subjects, already covered in other chapters, this section will focus on these areas as they relate specifically to telemarketing.

The List

The lists used in telemarketing efforts are critically important to the outcome of such efforts. Telemarketing can overcome many difficulties that direct mail cannot. For example, a caller can customize the message to each recipient in real time, which is some-

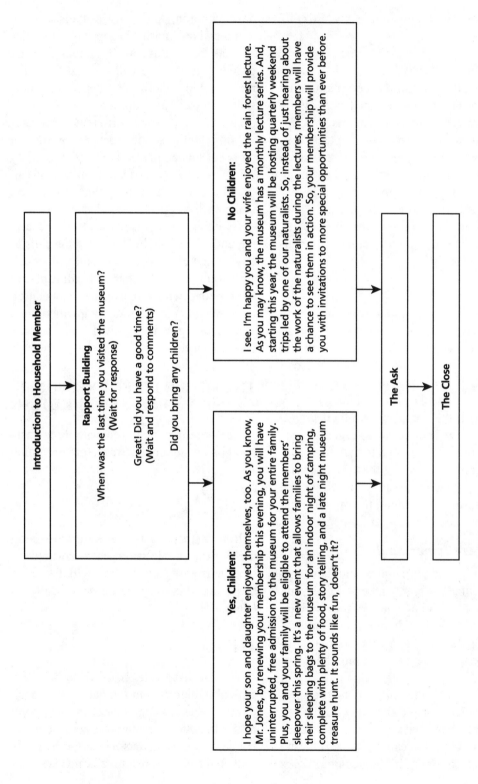

Introduction to Household Member

Rapport Building

When was the last time you visited the museum?
(Wait for response)

Great! Did you have a good time?
(Wait and respond to comments)

Did you bring any children?

Yes, Children:

I hope your son and daughter enjoyed themselves, too. As you know, Mr. Jones, by renewing your membership this evening, you will have uninterrupted, free admission to the museum for your entire family. Plus, you and your family will be eligible to attend the members' sleepover this spring. It's a new event that allows families to bring their sleeping bags to the museum for an indoor night of camping, complete with plenty of food, story telling, and a late night museum treasure hunt. It sounds like fun, doesn't it?

No Children:

I see. I'm happy you and your wife enjoyed the rain forest lecture. As you may know, the museum has a monthly lecture series. And, starting this year, the museum will be hosting quarterly weekend trips led by one of our naturalists. So, instead of just hearing about the work of the naturalists during the lectures, members will have a chance to see them in action. So, your membership will provide you with invitations to more special opportunities than ever before.

The Ask

The Close

Figure 7–1 Dynamic Telemarketing Script Branching.

thing direct mail cannot do. Even with all its power and flexibility, however, the telephone as an outreach tool cannot compensate for the use of an appropriate list. Just as mailing to the wrong list will produce poor results, so too will calling the wrong list.

There are several telemarketing applications related to membership (Exhibit 7–1) for which the quality of the list is extremely important:

- Membership renewal: This includes calls to members whose memberships are about to expire as well as calls to members who have lapsed. Lapsed members can typically be called cost-effectively for two to three years after their date of membership expiration. And, if they decline by telephone, they can be called again one year later. After that, it is generally best not to call again.
- Affiliated acquisition: This involves calls to individuals who have had some point of contact with the organization. For example, the individual might have visited a museum without joining. Or, the individual might have requested information. In any case, the individual is familiar with the organization and may have even received service.
- Unaffiliated acquisition: This is by far the most challenging type of campaign because it involves calls to individuals who are not known to have had prior contact with the organization. These individuals may belong to similar organizations or have a similar demographic and/or psychographic profile to the organization's existing membership base.

For membership renewal efforts, the house list should be used. Renewing members should be called as part of the normal

Exhibit 7–1 Telemarketing Applications Related to Membership

- Renewals
- Acquisition
  - Affiliated
  - Unaffiliated
- Annual fund
- Lapsed member campaigns
- Capital campaigns
- Customer service call
- Boost participation

direct mail renewal cycle, either as the final renewal notice or the second-to-last notice. Lapsed members can be called up to 2–3 years from the membership expiration date, and called cost-effectively for up to two consecutive years.

If current telephone numbers are not available for the house list, there are various telephone number research firms that can find them. Computerized research is less costly but also less accurate. While computerized research is good for a first pass through the list, a manual research firm should be used to acquire numbers for as many others as possible. Some research companies offer both manual and computerized searches. Whether or not an institution has plans for telemarketing efforts, telephone numbers should be collected at any opportunity. For example, day and evening telephone numbers can be collected on new member enrollment and member renewal forms. These will be helpful if the organization wishes to use telemarketing in the future.

For an acquisition campaign, organizations should acquire lists the same way they do for direct mail campaigns. List trading and list rental are two effective ways to build a telemarketing prospect list. Unfortunately, organizations may find it difficult to identify a list trading partner or list rental source because of concerns about having those lists used in a telemarketing campaign. However, analyses by many nonprofit organizations prove that a properly conducted telemarketing effort will not erode support for the list-lending institution anymore than a direct mail campaign would. The individuals on a given list will generally maintain their primary loyalty to the original source organization.

Generally, if a list performs well with direct mail, it will perform well with telemarketing. Because of this fact, a successful direct mail program is a prerequisite for a telemarketing effort. Direct mail is the list prospecting process that identifies the best lists to use in a telemarketing program while ensuring massive outreach and generating important results itself. Identifying the productivity of a list is less expensive in the direct mail process than through telemarketing. Once an organization identifies the prime performing list segments, it can then use telemarketing to increase market penetration. For example, instead of being content with a 1 percent response rate through a direct mail acquisition effort, an organization can realize an additional 10 percent response by following the direct mail effort with calls.

Various Uses for Various Lists

Organizations can also use telemarketing for fundraising efforts such as annual fund or capital campaign appeals. Telemarketing can also be used for nonfundraising calls to provide member service (a thank-you call or information on legislation of interest, for example) or to boost participation in an upcoming activity. For such campaigns, the organization can very cost-effectively call current members. Depending on the organization and the nature of the appeal, other segments from the house list can also be used. A house list might consist of lapsed members, individuals who have received service but are not members, individuals who have requested information, and so forth.

Deduplication

While not deduplicating ("deduping") a list may at times be an acceptable shortcut for direct mail efforts, deduping is an essential component of all telemarketing efforts. Various computer houses are available to perform this service. Deduping can also be done in-house without a great deal of difficulty. Always dedupe the list to ensure that individuals do not receive multiple calls. Duplicate calls will do more than almost anything else to ensure ill will during the campaign. Deduping, while seemingly expensive, actually saves money by eliminating unnecessary, expensive multiple calls to the same individual or household.

The Offer

In a membership campaign, the offer might involve different levels of membership, multi-year membership discounts, highlights of current special exhibitions or events, trips, giveaways, or premiums. Like direct mail, telemarketing campaigns can be used to test different offers. The advantage of testing through telemarketing rather than direct mail is that the population of each test cell can be much smaller. And, once the organization identifies the most effective offer, it can immediately begin promoting that offer during the remaining campaign rather than waiting for the next effort. Telemarketing has another advantage over direct mail: The caller can make more than one offer during a single telephone conversation by being responsive to the call recipient.

For example, if a museum sends a direct mail membership solicitation highlighting family membership and the museum's new dinosaur exhibition, it might not have any impact on a single man who is not particularly interested in dinosaurs. A telemarketing call, however, might start with a similar offer but could easily shift the offer to meet the needs of the individual. The single man, for example, might be delighted to learn that the museum sponsors many field trips including bird watching. He might be interested in meeting other single adults with similar interests. Now, telemarketing has done something that direct mail cannot do well: dynamically match the needs or desires of the prospective member with the specific benefits that will be of interest.

Another example is a voluntary professional association that offers a wide array of benefits. A telephone call can draw the call recipient's attention to the key membership benefits that will be of greatest value to him or her, as determined by a mini-survey at the beginning of the call. In this way, the prospective member need not be overwhelmed by the array of benefits. This technique eliminates the risk that the prospective member will overlook those benefits that are of greatest personal value.

When preparing the offer for telemarketing, be flexible. By its dynamic nature, the telephone call becomes more than a solicitation or sales call; it becomes a service call. When calling for membership renewal, less time will be needed to explain the mission of the organization. After all, the call is to someone who at one time, perhaps recently, was committed to the organization. In this situation, the offer should highlight some of the new benefits of membership, new things happening at the institution, or upcoming news. In many cases, the call will be the gentle, extra nudge needed to encourage someone to rejoin. In other cases, objections will be raised. By honestly and knowledgeably responding to questions and objections, the caller will once again be able to do something that direct mail cannot: match specific needs with specific benefits.

For membership acquisition efforts, the call will need to be more detailed than would be required for membership renewal. Also, the call will likely need to involve more probing, so the caller can better match the benefits of membership to the call recipient's desires, concerns, and aspirations. For an unaffiliated acquisition effort, the increased level of detail may even have to include a description of what the organization is or does. Fundraising calls will also be somewhat longer because, while they will be made to those who are affiliated with the organization, the caller will need to establish the case for support.

A well-designed call will also result in the collection of valuable market research data that can be used to improve retention rates in the future, even if the call recipient does not renew or contribute. For example, the caller can learn why the individual is not renewing. Or, if the call recipient does renew, the caller can learn which membership benefits are most valuable. In any case, the call will also help promote the organization and its activities. For these as well as general public relations reasons, it is essential that every call be handled with utmost care.

In addition to the direct quantitative results, a well-conducted telemarketing campaign will have a valuable qualitative, and even indirect, impact. For example, a professional association might promote its upcoming conference during the membership marketing call. Even if the prospective members choose not to join, the organization will still want them to attend the conference and, perhaps, later they will become members. A city zoo found that a number of those who refused to join as members during a telephone solicitation, visited the zoo shortly thereafter and joined at the gate.

The key to success is to meet the needs of the individual contacted. The telephone is a personal medium; this quality is its primary benefit as a marketing tool, and it should be used to its fullest.

The Creative Execution

The telephone can be used to generate donations, acquire new members, renew the memberships of those about to lapse or whose memberships have already lapsed, and survey attitudes of existing or lapsed members.

Pre-call Letters

Before the call requesting the donation, members should first receive a letter outlining the case for support. Depending on the nature of the appeal, a capsule case statement brochure can also be included. Ideally, the letter will be personalized and sent in a closed-face envelope. The letter will inform the member about the campaign and tell the member that he or she will be receiving a telephone call. In some cases, calling without a pre-call letter may work as well or better. Each organization will need to test the two approaches to determine which will work best. In addition, certain types of campaigns, such as emergency appeals, must happen with immediacy and, therefore, do not lend themselves to the pre-call letter approach.

When the telephone call is made, a pledge of support will be negotiated. Following the successful call, a personalized pledge confirmation letter should be sent with a pledge card and business reply envelope to those who have not committed with their credit card. Testing will determine whether personalization of the letter is essential or whether a business reply envelope is necessary as opposed to a courtesy reply envelope. However, as a base-line rule, a personalized letter works best because it is in keeping with the personal nature of the call. Another general rule is to make responding as easy as possible for people; a business reply envelope saves people the time of finding and affixing a postage stamp.

In one pre-call letter test, Membership Consultants divided a file that was being called to solicit donations from the membership for an annual appeal campaign. One half of the recipients received a pre-call letter that mentioned that they would be receiving a telephone call. The other half received the pre-call letter, too, but the coming telephone call was not mentioned. The letter that mentioned the call pulled a greater response, and subsequently, so did the telephoning to that half of the list.

Pre-call letters should always be sent first-class to ensure timely delivery and proper timing with the telephone call. The letters should be sent 7 to 10 days prior to the call. Generally, the letter will be informational and will not contain a response device. Confirmation letters should also be sent first-class to ensure timely delivery since any delay could significantly impact negatively on the fulfillment rate. To help ensure strong pledge fulfillment, confirmation letters should be mailed within 24 hours of the pledge commitment. Reminder letters, sent to those who do not respond to the confirmation letters, should be sent first-class at 21-day intervals to those whose pledge payments are past due. It is worthwhile to send three reminder letters in addition to the pledge confirmation letter. Generally, sending fewer reminders will leave money on the table, while sending more reminders will alienate people. Confirmation and reminder letters can be sent in window envelopes. However, they should be letters and not billing statements alone. Each letter will, once again, make the case for support, thereby reinforcing the campaign message.

When using the telephone to renew or acquire members, no specific pre-call letter should be sent; however, renewal calls can, and should, follow the standard direct mail renewal notice process. Acquisition calls can be made any time after one month following an acquisition mail drop. Membership purchases tend to be impulsive decisions based on emotion. The mailing of a pre-call letter over-intellectualizes the process and detracts from the telephone call. Membership renewal or acquisition calls should present an offer, promote key benefits, and negotiate the level of commitment. The follow-up mail process should be the same as for fundraising calls. However, a great effort should be made to secure payment by credit card to maximize fulfillment. Even though there is a fee for the credit card transaction, it secures the gift immediately and eliminates any second thoughts or the costs of continued mailing to fulfill the pledge. To those who do not wish to engage in a credit card transaction, sending letters along with the membership billing statements will remind members of key benefits or other important elements of the offer in a way that preserves the personal touch established by the telephone call.

When using the telephone for survey work, no letters need to be sent. However, as a courtesy to participants, this might be a nice touch. A letter could be sent to alert them to the upcoming call, for example. At the very least, thank you letters to participants are a good idea. The telephone polls should be brief and designed with great care. The way a question is phrased or even positioned in the context of the broader survey can impact the results.

The following story illustrates the importance of surveying with caution: A new aquarium asked its first-time members if they planned on renewing their memberships. Two-thirds of those surveyed responded that they would renew. However, when renewal time came, only one-third in fact renewed. To discover the reason for this discrepancy, the aquarium re-surveyed first-time members. Once again, the aquarium found that two-thirds said they would renew. But, then they asked, "When will you renew?" They found that only one-third of the overall respondents planned to renew by the expiration date, as actual result trends indicated. The balance said they would renew at some point in the future, 12 to 24 months. People will only answer the questions asked. Asking the right questions in the right way is critical.

Whatever type of telemarketing effort an organization implements, staff will need to establish systems to respond to the feedback provided by those contacted. For example, a university athletic club member may not know where to park when attending a university basketball game. In response, both the member and the athletic office would be well served by sending the member a map illustrating the location of area parking lots. The telephone is a two-way communications tool. If used effectively, it will present organizations with further opportunities to meet the needs of members.

Callers

Regardless of the nature of the telemarketing program, the organization will need to determine who is best suited to make the calls. Some organizations have effectively employed volunteer telephone callers. Because all calls must first involve building rapport with the call recipient, volunteer callers can be an excellent choice. However, because volunteers are seldom well trained or experienced, they often have difficulty effectively asking for commitments. In addition, a ballet company found that paid callers can produce more than twice the net income of volunteer callers. Therefore, organizations must be aware that while volunteers may be able to build rapport and, by definition, are free labor, they can be very expensive in terms of foregone income. Also, few organizations can recruit a volunteer calling corps large enough to meet the demand. Few volunteers will commit to successive nights of calling, thus making it necessary to train a new group every night. This is time consuming and can have an impact on the efficiency and efficacy of the calling program.

An alternative to volunteer callers is paid callers. There are two types of paid callers: those hired and trained by an institution's staff, and those whom an outside agency hires, trains, and manages. In either case, it is important to employ only callers who can identify with the organization and who are committed to respecting those they will call.

Whether an organization implements a telemarketing program in-house, off-site, or on an outsource basis, calls should be generated from a room set up for telemarketing. The telephone room should have ample workspace for callers and ensure a compromise between caller privacy and a communal atmosphere. Monitoring equipment is essential for training and for maintaining quality in the well-run telephone room. Monitoring equipment allows a manager to hear both sides of a conversation, and helps the manager fine tune calling scripts after hearing how they are received in a live environment.

Scripts

Calling scripts are essential to telemarketing campaigns. They help callers make the appeal and respond to questions or objections. However, the script should not be read verbatim. Instead, the script should be put into the words of the caller. While following the general guidelines, the caller should converse with the prospect rather than read to the prospect aiming for a natural-sounding conversation. This will produce a greater number of favorable responses while engendering goodwill. By using dynamic branching within calling scripts as discussed earlier in the chapter (refer to Figure 7–1), and by employing database marketing, organizations can make each call very personal and very effective. Exhibit 7–2 gives a good overview of guidelines for a script. See Figure 7–1 and earlier text, above, for more description of these techniques.

RESULTS

The points reviewed in this section represent general guidelines. Actual results will vary, depending on the type of organization, the external environment, whether the telemarketing campaign is conducted with volunteers or professionals, and other factors. Graphic presentations of the level of difficulty and the financial viability of telemarketing campaigns are shown in Figures 7–2 and 7–3.

Exhibit 7–2 Telemarketing Script Checklist

The following is a guideline for developing a script for a telemarketing call:

INTRODUCTION

_____ Identify caller.
_____ Identify organization.
_____ Request to speak with the designated prospect.
_____ Ask permission to speak.
_____ Adhere to any state legal disclosure requirements.

The introduction to the call involves exactly what you would expect. The caller should introduce him- or herself, mention the name of the organization, and ask to speak with the designated prospect. Once the designated prospect is on the line, the introduction should be repeated and any legally mandated disclosure language should be used. Then the caller should ask permission to continue.

In order to be effective, the introduction must capture the attention of the prospect and put the prospect at ease, all within the first 15 to 30 seconds of the call. By asking permission to proceed with the conversation, the caller puts the prospect in the position of inviting the caller into his or her home instead of putting the caller in the position of barging into the prospect's living room. The very act of asking permission to speak will make the call sound different from most other telemarketing calls, will make the prospect feel more comfortable, and will get the call started on a friendly footing. Almost no one will refuse the caller's request without good reason. If the prospect truly cannot speak at the time of the call, the caller can schedule an appointment to call back at a time convenient to the prospect, thereby building goodwill, which will help lead to a positive outcome during the subsequent call.

RAPPORT

_____ Thank the member for his or her past membership.
_____ Engage the prospect in a dialogue.
_____ Promote the organization.

While the caller does not have to be best friends with the prospect to gain his or her commitment over the telephone, the caller does need to establish a basic level of rapport. To build rapport, thank the member for his or her past membership. Also, ask open- and closed-ended questions that are designed to elicit positive answers and/or reactions. By engaging the prospect in a dialogue, he or she will be much more willing to stay on the line and actively listen. If presented with a monologue, most people will either hang up the telephone or mentally tune out. The script might ask the prospect "throw-away" questions such as "When was the last time you visited the museum? Did you enjoy your visit?" Or, the script might ask "mini-survey" questions for which you may capture and analyze the responses. An example of a mini-survey question is "What is your favorite membership benefit?" You can also design questions around the promotion of your organization. For example, you might ask the following series of questions: "Did you see the news story about the new cheetah cubs? They're really cute, aren't

continues

Exhibit 7–2 continued

they? Well, make sure you visit the zoo to see the cubs before they get much bigger; after all, they're growing fast!" This is the section where the passion of the caller must shine. The prospect's interest in the rest of the call will largely be determined by both the message and the delivery. If the caller is disinterested, the prospect will be, too.

REASON FOR CALL

_____ Make the case for membership by focusing on benefits and/or a problem that can be solved through membership.

This is where the caller will state the reason for the call and set the stage for the "ask." If the benefits of membership are the driving force motivating individuals to become members, then the purpose should provide people the opportunity to acquire those benefits that you believe will be of greatest value. Do not list all the benefits; list only the key benefits. If the membership motivation is more philanthropic or advocacy oriented, focus on what the problem is and how an enhanced membership base will address the problem. For example, an advocacy group might talk about its lobbying efforts in Congress. The caller could highlight a key piece of legislation and discuss how an increased membership base gives the organization greater clout when dealing with lawmakers. The key is to show prospects how a membership will be of either tangible or intangible value to them.

ASKS

_____ Develop a three-tier ask ladder.
_____ Develop transitions between asks that continue to build the case.
_____ Identify and script responses to anticipated common objections or questions.

People are most likely to join or give when asked two or three times. By asking first for a $150 President's Circle membership, then a $75 Sustaining membership, and then a $45 Household membership, you will receive far more Household memberships than if you simply asked just for the Household membership in the first place. In addition, you will be surprised at how many upper-level memberships you close as well.

The first ask should be two levels above the prospect's last membership level or, in the case of acquisition, two levels above the most popular membership level. Of course, if your organization does not have tiered membership levels, then go with what you have; however, you can still put multiple asks on the table by offering, for example, payment terms. A successful ask will invite the prospect to join. Once the caller mentions the dollar amount, the prospect will stop listening. Therefore, the last word in the ask should be the dollar amount. Then, the caller must remain silent to give the prospect a chance to think. Put the word "PAUSE" or "SILENCE" into the script so that the caller is reminded to wait. If the caller speaks first, the caller will not close. If the first ask is rejected, the caller should transition to the second ask. The transition text will continue to make the case for membership. Failure to include a transition could result in a call that sounds more like a membership auction rather than a conversation. Also, make sure to prepare callers to respond to common questions and objections. Once the caller

continues

Exhibit 7–2 continued

responds to a question or objection, it is imperative that they immediately move back to an ask or otherwise risk losing control of the call.

CONFIRMATION

_____ Confirm the membership level at least once.
_____ Confirm the membership dollar amount at least two times.
_____ Confirm the address of the prospect.
_____ Gather any relevant information (e.g., size of household).
_____ Confirm twice the credit card number, expiration date, and name as it appears on the card.
_____ Confirm a payment due date for non–credit card users.
_____ Thank the member profusely.

If the caller has done everything well, and if your list was properly selected, the prospect will perceive the conversation as a service call. As a result, many will commit. However, the caller's job is far from finished. The membership commitment must be fully confirmed to make sure that there is no misunderstanding and to ensure collectability of the payment. Finally, the call should end with a hearty word of thanks to the member. The duration of the call will depend on a number of factors, including the complexity of the offer, the relationship with the prospect, the interest of the prospect, and the demographics of the prospect pool. As a general rule, calls will last 3 to 10 minutes.

Annual Giving and Capital Campaigns

Telemarketing campaigns have achieved pledge rates of 25 to 40 percent for annual giving and capital campaigns when non-donor members have been contacted. The rates can be 60 to 100 percent when contacting donor members. The average gifts are usually a match of the membership level to a gift 30 percent higher than the membership amount. For example, if someone is a member at the $50 level, that individual's donation will likely be between $50 and $65. Among donors, the new gift will be, on average, the same as the last gift up to 20 percent greater. Fulfillment rates on pledges can surpass 80 percent. Annual fund telemarketing efforts usually cost $0.20 to $0.60 per dollar generated. The cost per dollar generated will depend, in large part, on the average membership value because this value correlates with the average contribution amount. Thus, the higher the average membership value, the lower the cost per dollar raised and the greater the net income.

Membership Acquisition

For membership acquisition, pledge rates range from 15 to 30 percent. The average membership dollar value is usually just above the most popular membership category in the overall membership program. The fulfillment rate will range from 40 to 80 percent. The actual response rate can be 10 times the direct mail response rate to the same list. So, if a list achieves a direct mail response rate of 1.2 percent, the telephone response rate could be 12 percent after the

Figure 7–2 Telemarketing Level of Difficulty.

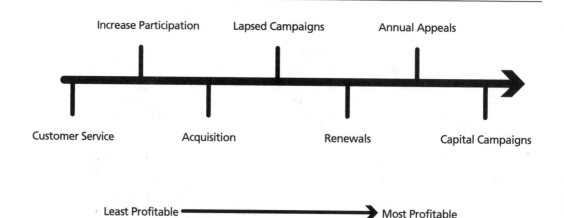

Figure 7–3 Telemarketing Financial Viability.

fulfillment process concludes. Acquisition telemarketing efforts usually cost $0.70 to $1.20 or more per dollar generated. The cost per dollar generated will depend, in large part, on the average membership value. This cost is less than the accepted direct mail guidelines, which recognize that it can cost up to $1.25 or even sometimes $1.50 to raise a new dollar. The payback to the organization comes with renewals and the lifetime giving of the member for membership and other activities. Direct mail is used more frequently than telemarketing because of the availability of address lists versus telephone number lists and the difficulty of telephoning thousands of prospects. Acquisition calls are by far the most difficult and the riskiest of telephone fundraising options.

Renewals and Lapses

Telemarketing is particularly useful for renewals and lapsed-member campaigns. For membership renewal, the pledge rates range from 20 to 50 percent, depending on how long the membership has been lapsed and on how many years the individual had maintained a membership before allowing it to expire. The average membership dollar value is usually just above the most popular membership category in the overall membership program. The fulfillment rate typically ranges from 50 to 90 percent. Lapsed member renewal telemarketing efforts can cost $0.30 to $0.70 per dollar generated, but it is not uncommon for them to approach the break-even point. The cost per dollar generated will depend in large part on the average membership value. Table 7–1 illustrates projections for a sample lapsed-member campaign.

Other Considerations

If pledge or fulfillment rates are very low or the per–dollar-raised costs very high, it may be time for trouble-shooting. For example, a low pledge rate may indicate a prospect file that is too old, callers who need further training, an offer that is not

Table 7–1 Telemarketing Projections: Sample Lapsed Member Campaign

Item	Projection
Number in pool	1,000
Percent with telephone numbers	80%
Number to be called	800
Percent reached	80%
Number reached	640
Pledge	25%
Number pledged	160
Average pledged	$65
Total pledged	$10,400
Percent fulfilled	70%
Total received	$7,280

compelling, timing that is inappropriate for events in the community, or other reasons. If costs seem to be running too high, the full range of options needs to be explored to achieve the right balance between cost and revenue.

Securing commitments on credit card will enhance the fulfillment rates for development and membership telemarketing programs alike. Use of credit cards can vary widely, ranging from 12 percent to as much as 75 percent. This depends a great deal on the demographics of the membership. If implemented properly, telemarketing efforts will always produce more net income, or a smaller loss, than a direct mail effort targeted at the same lists.

The acceptable cost per dollar raised for a telemarketing campaign should be the same as the ratio considered acceptable for a comparable direct mail effort. Again, telemarketing and direct mail are just two different sides of the direct response coin. Take for example, an acquisition effort: if it breaks even in the first year, the organization is making progress because memberships can be renewed and, as this happens, the membership base will continue to grow cost-effectively. Many organizations observe that members acquired or renewed through telemarketing can be renewed at roughly the same rate as members acquired or renewed through direct mail when direct mail and telemarketing contacts were made.

Tracking Costs

When evaluating telemarketing performance, tracking costs is essential to containing them, thereby helping to ensure the cost-effectiveness of the effort. An effective way to track costs is to develop a telemarketing program budget (see Table 7–2) and then monitor costs as they compare to the budget on an ongoing basis. In addition, when looking at results, a wide variety of statistics should be reviewed. While some tracking statistics will vary from organization to organization, most nonprofit institutions should consider the following basic statistics:

- Total number of calling hours
- Cost per hour
- Cost per contact
- Total number of contacts (pledges; those considering; refusals)
- Total number of credit card commitments
- Total number of billed pledges
- Total number of commitments (credit card plus pledges)
- Total dollars committed (with breakouts by credit cards and pledges)
- Average pledge value (total dollars divided by total commitments)
- Average dollar per hour (total dollars divided by total calling hours)
- Average dollar per contact (total dollars divided by total contacts)
- Fulfillment rate (paid pledges plus credit card dollars, divided by the total dollars committed)
- Pledge rate (number of paid pledges plus credit card commitments, divided by total contacts)

SUMMARY

As with any direct response medium, there are pros and cons to implementing a telemarketing campaign. With careful planning, tight management, and appropriate design, telemarketing programs can produce more money, greater numbers of members and donors, and much goodwill for organizations of every description.

Table 7–2 Sample Telemarketing Budget Worksheet

Budget Item	Dollar Amount
Personnel Costs	
Caller recruitment	_____
Caller training hours	_____
Caller wages	_____
Caller incentives	_____
Clerical wages	_____
Word processor compensation	_____
Data processor compensation	_____
Management compensation and benefits	_____
Telephone Costs	
Local charges	_____
Long-distance charges	_____
Mailings	
Stationery	_____
Word processing	_____
Postage	_____
Data Processing	
Data conversion	_____
List rental	_____
Prospect cards	_____
Telephone number research	_____
Deduplicating	_____
Report generation	_____
Capital Expenses	
Telemarketing room set-up: includes equipment, furniture, office space, etc.	_____
Grand Total	_____

REFERENCES

Direct Marketing Association. The WEFA Group. *Direct marketing total employment by medium and market. Direct Marketing Association.* New York, 2000.

Kirsch A.D., S. Saxon Harrold, M.S. Weitzman, E.A. Crutchfield, and A.J. Heffron. 2001. *Giving and volunteering in the United States: Findings from a national survey,* 1999 Edition. In press. Independent Sector,

The Center on Philanthropy at Indiana University. December 2001. *Report on the December 2001 Philanthropic giving index,* Indianapolis, IN: Indiana University.

U.S. Federal Trade Commission. 1996. "Straight Talk about Telemarketing." www.ftc.gov/bcp/conline/pubs/tmarkg/straight.htm

Yankelovich Partners Inc. *Life in the Year 2010.* December 1999.

CHAPTER 8

Membership Retention and Renewals

Patricia Rich and Dana Hines

It's like déjà vu all over again.

—Yogi Berra

THE IMPORTANCE OF RENEWALS

MEMBERSHIP RENEWALS ARE VERY much like "déjà vu all over again." Once the organization has found the right renewal combination, the renewal process is repeated over and over and over again. The key is finding what works best for the members, the organization, and the staff structure.

Renewals are the backbone of the membership program. It is much less costly to retain a member than to acquire a new member. It costs pennies on the dollar to renew a member, but it may cost the entire amount of the membership dues, or more, to acquire a new member. According to customer satisfaction researchers, it will cost 5 to 15 times more to acquire a new member than to keep a current one (Farber Sirkin and McDermott 1995, 7). If membership growth is a priority, then membership renewals at a fairly high and consistent rate are essential. For every member who does not renew, a new member must be acquired to replace him or her, just to stay even, and two members have to be acquired to grow.

The successful membership renewal process is a combination of motivation and mechanics, motivating people to renew their memberships and employing the mechanics needed for the motivated members to actually renew their membership.

RETENTION

The ability to retain the greatest number of members is the key to growth in membership. The process of retention is one that is ongoing, inherent in the management of the membership program, and is a direct result of the philosophy of the organization. Retention is the process of keeping members engaged, involved, and in a positive mindset with respect to the organization or the cause that they support. Such engagement is a result of the organization's treatment of the member, or the organization's ability to successfully deliver benefits and services at a level acceptable to the member. Retention is also dependent on a member's judgment that an institution is remaining true to the mission to which the organization and the individual are committed.

The act of retaining members is a matter of keeping members satisfied, content, and pleased with their membership experience in a way that motivates the member to continue the membership relationship. Membership retention results when the cultivation of existing members has been a success. The ingredients of membership retention include quality customer service, successful stewardship, and a "member first" orientation on the part of membership staff. Membership retention is a yearlong process. It is the day-by-day process of responding to members' needs, anticipating those needs, dealing with members in a

friendly, professional manner, and delivering a quality product that will translate into membership retention.

Benefits and Value

The member's decision to renew or not to renew is dependent on myriad factors. A member consciously or subconsciously asks, "What was my membership experience like? Did I use my membership? Was I happy with my membership experience?" The issues of benefits, value, use and involvement, communication, and membership service provide answers to those questions that the members are asking themselves when deciding whether or not to renew.

Efforts to renew a member begin the moment a person joins. Every experience that a member has during the membership year will help determine that member's likelihood of renewing his or her membership. The factors that influence a person's decision to renew include the benefits they have been offered, their frequency of use, the number of visits to the institution, the treatment received during the membership year, and the quality and frequency of communications received during the membership year.

Use and Involvement

The quality of the membership experience can be affected by the benefits offered. For acquisition, it is important to create an appealing benefits package; however, it is as important to plan as many benefits as possible that encourage member involvement during the year. Events and activities such as lectures, educational opportunities, and, most importantly, those occasions that truly entertain the member, can also affect membership renewal. In recent years, museum professionals and membership personnel have begun to realize that it is permissible and necessary for museum programming to be "fun."

The success of many alumni organizations located far from their alma mater is involvement of alumni in activities in their current city of residence. This allows involvement with other alumni who have a commonality, their college or university. Scheduling and planning programming that is entertaining, while sometimes also educational involve both visitors and members in a way that provides memorable and satisfying experiences that will draw those people back to the institution again and again.

Even though few members will take advantage of every activity or benefit, the mere offering of such opportunities can affect membership renewal. For instance, if an institution has a wide range of activities and publicizes those happenings with frequent announcements and invitations, members may feel the programming is there for them to take advantage of if they so chose. It is the perception of activities, especially among members, that is important.

Communicating with Members

The frequency with which an organization communicates with its members greatly affects the decision to renew or not to renew a membership. Frequent communication in a variety of forms brings an institution close to its members. Frequent communication, just as in friendship, is a way to keep a relationship strong. These communications should be timely and attractive, but need not be expensive. Communications can take the form of newsletters, postcard reminders of events, and course brochures, as well as other fundraising communications relating to annual

funds, tribute gifts, or special projects (see Chapter 4).

A recommendation for the frequency of mailings ranges from one to three mailings per month. As long as there is a reason to mail, there is not a reason to be concerned about too many mailings. It only solidifies the relationship. It is almost impossible to mail too often. Most organizations err on the side of not communicating often enough.

E-mail communications are a recent addition to the communication mix. As long as the member has given permission for this kind of communication, and the frequency and content are at an acceptable level, then this is an easy and cost-effective way to stay connected to members.

Membership Service

Another key factor in a member's decision to renew is the quality of service received during the membership year. Whether or not membership materials were received on a timely basis, whether or not phone calls or letters were answered promptly, and whether or not the response they received when calling or visiting the institution was courteous—all of these aspects affect the membership experience and the decision to renew or not to renew. Service in membership, as in any other consumer experience, has a negative or positive effect on a person's decision to continue doing business with the organization.

There are also conditions that cannot be controlled that affect a person's willingness to renew. These include personal financial state, health, and change of residence. To achieve the greatest success in membership retention, the organization should focus on those factors that can be controlled.

RENEWALS

Anniversary Membership or Calendar-Year Membership

Memberships are best managed when they are based on an anniversary-year membership rather than a calendar-year basis. In other words, a person should receive 12 months of membership in exchange for his or her donation, not a prorated portion of a calendar-year membership. Spreading the memberships and thus the renewal dates throughout the year evens the workload for membership processing staff. There is seasonality to memberships. Some members will tend to join and renew their memberships at certain times of the year. Members should not have to make decisions at a specific time of the year for the organization's convenience. In a large organization, if all members were due to renew at the same time of the year, the workload would be unbearable and impossible. The exceptions to the anniversary dues rule are very small organizations with little change in membership. For example, in a group of 50, it will be much less work to ask the members for their dues at the same time.

Renewal Rates

No matter what the membership effort is, there will be 10 to 25 percent of members who will not renew. This portion of the membership is lost due to moving, death, or some other personal situation that prohibits them from continuing as members. These are the conditions that are beyond the control of the membership program and are a fact of the human condition.

Depending on the type of organization, it is possible to renew 60 to 80 percent of current members. This is obviously a wide range to be considered acceptable. However,

a great deal depends on the type of organization. In a non–visitation-based organization, it can be more difficult to renew members because the entire relationship revolves around exchange of information by mail. This lack of personal contact or experience at a physical place may significantly affect the renewal behavior. National or professional organizations can make membership a prerequisite for attendance at conferences or for professional certification. This requirement can be strong "encouragement" for renewing and is effective as long as the certification, conference, or meeting is a sought-after product.

Non–visitation-based organizations need to communicate in stronger, more consistent ways. It may be incumbent upon these organizations to occasionally communicate by phone, not only for fundraising purposes, but also for membership service and market research purposes. Some national organizations host annual conferences or local or regional events. Alumni organizations invite members to come to homecoming events and join local booster clubs that encourage lifelong affinity. A major national conservation organization connects with its midlevel members by hosting receptions at various sites across the country, which are held at the homes of donors or at local zoos that share the mission of preserving endangered species.

Even in organizations with a site and a visiting membership, the renewal rates can vary greatly. If an institution depends heavily on major exhibitions to recruit or retain its members, renewal rates can be closer to the 60 percent range. The same is true of an institution that has exhibitions or offerings that are generally static in nature, such as an aquarium. Organizations that appeal to young children such as youth museums and science centers face a special challenge:

when the children are too old for what the institution has to offer, it is difficult to keep the family engaged in membership.

Institutions that are constantly changing and offering new opportunities and exhibitions are blessed with the ability to attract their members to the institution again and again during any given year. These institutions are able to achieve renewal rates in the 75 to 80 percent range.

It is also important to note that the length of membership and the level of membership also affect the likelihood of renewal. A member who is new to the institution is less likely to renew than someone who has been a member for a period of several years. A member who has committed to a higher membership category is also more invested and therefore more likely to renew than someone in a lower membership category. Both length of time and amount of financial commitment correlate to the member's overall commitment to the institution. The more commitment expressed, the greater the likelihood that the member will continue to support the institution through its membership program. For first-year members, a renewal rate of 45 to 50 percent is common. Renewal rates can exceed the 90 percent mark among members who have surpassed the 3- or 4-year mark as members. A renewal rate that is 85 percent or above can be a warning sign that an organization may not be doing enough to attract new members. This is because new members renew at lower rates, decreasing the overall membership renewal rate. In the absence of a significant number of new members, renewal rates can be very high.

Another issue that must taken seriously is the consistency of the renewal effort. One midwestern zoo had a renewal rate of about 68 percent compared to other venues in the same market with mid-70 percent renewal rates. The zoo had 15,000 members, but only one staff member to send and process all the memberships. Thus, the person was overburdened and always behind. The staff person would send renewal notices whenever the pile of data entry became manageable. Thus, June 1 renewals were being sent in July or August rather than in May. An additional staff member was added, along with some more efficient procedures, and renewals were put on a very specific and rigid schedule. The renewal rate improved by 6 percentage points.

Special Situations

First-Year Membership

First-year members are special, and they need special treatment. First-year renewal rates are always less than multi-year renewal rates. The long-time member knows the organization and has made a commitment through time and money. The first-year member may be "trying out" the organization to determine if it is a group he or she wants to be associated with for years to come. The organization wants to be careful not to "overpromise" in its membership acquisition program, a cardinal sin of marketing. If the acquisition program promises the new member all kinds of programs, events, and volunteer opportunities and then is not able to fulfill the expectations, the member will certainly not renew. For organizations with multi-year memberships, a first-year member is really any member who has never renewed. This means that the first-year programming needs to continue until at least one renewal cycle has passed.

For first-year members, special events and activities, communications, service, and recognition are helpful in bringing the new member closer to the institution and increasing the chances of the member's becoming involved. While a strong membership program is essential for keeping all members, if the organization can do even more for the first-year members, their retention rate will be higher than expected. These special activities can be as modest as a telephone call thanking the member for joining or calling midway through the year to find out if the member has been attending events or enjoying the publications. More elaborate activities might include a new-member behind-the-scenes tour for a visitation-based facility or a reception to meet the director.

If an institution finds that the first-year renewal rate is 40 percent or less, something needs to be done. The membership manager should consider a survey of those who did not renew to discover what the issues are. The benefit package should be reviewed to make certain that it is not overpromising. The premiums should be examined to ensure that receiving a tangible gift is not the only reason that people joined. It may be necessary to sweeten the renewal offer for first-year members, to increase the renewal rate.

Lapsed Members

While not as high as renewal rates for active members, the rate for renewing lapsed members can be significantly higher than acquisition rates. An organization needs to determine whom it considers to be a lapsed member. One definition is that lapsed members are those who joined and then did not renew within six months of the membership expiration date. Some organizations consider any member who did not renew during the renewal cycle lapsed. Lapsed members should always be included in all new member acquisition mailings.

When trying to renew lapsed members, send renewals that recognize their past relationship with the organization. Every organization should do at least one lapsed-member mailing per year. The mailing should be personalized and directed at lapsed members. This is in addition to including the lapsed members in the new member acquisition campaign.

Do not overlook these past members. Consider a lapsed-member mailing or telephone campaign every six months to recontact those who have not renewed. If using telemarketing, calling once a year for two years can be successful (see Chapter 7).

Upgrades/Downgrades

Renewal time is the time to suggest upgrades in those organizations with graduated dues levels. If renewals can be personalized, suggest an upgrade to a member who has been a member for two or, preferably, three years. Once someone has been a member for three years, they have made a commitment. First-year members should not be asked to upgrade; the issue with first-year members is to encourage them to renew.

If upgrading within the value levels (those most dependent on benefits), discuss the additional benefits that an upgraded level will bring. Because this level becomes more of a charitable gift, also talk about the important work of the organization. Other ways to promote the upgrade include mentioning it in the postscript (P.S.) of the letter and offering a premium to upgrade. If it is not possible to personalize renewal requests, and all members receive the same request, a premium will be very helpful in encouraging upgrades.

Downgrades will also occur. Downgrades happen most frequently when the membership rates increase, especially if they increase by a large amount. This will be an issue with value members more than with support members. If this is the case, it is important to do something quickly. Consider using a premium for members who remain at the same level during the year of the increase. For example, if a member is a "regular" member at $50, and the regular level is increasing to $60, offer the premium to those who remain regular members at the new rate.

As with renewals in general, it is very important to track upgrades and, of course, downgrades. By tracking, the membership manager can see, on a month-to-month basis, whether an offer is working or not. If the upgrade effort is working, keep it going. If not, make changes to see if a different effort will work. If downgrades become too prevalent (there will always be some), it is time to make a change to stop the trend.

Renewal Efforts

Just as in membership acquisition, there are several avenues available for renewing the existing member. As in acquisition, the primary method of renewal is by mail. In addition, there are the possibilities of a member renewing through telemarketing or in person at a visitation-based institution. Although the use of the Internet for renewals

is still in its infancy, increasingly, online renewal opportunities are becoming a renewal tool as well. The methods suggested here can be used in any size organization.

Direct Mail

The greatest effort to renew a member should be directed to mailing notices to members. Figure 8–1 shows a typical renewal schedule. The content and timing of the mailings are the most crucial factors in this effort. There should be a minimum of three renewal mailings, with four to five renewal efforts being the norm. The timing of the mailings should be tested and customized to the particular audience that an institution serves. For instance, an institution that serves an older population may find it advantageous to mail its first renewal notice several months in advance of the expiration date. In general, older people may be more likely to renew ahead of time so that their membership does not lapse because of delayed renewals. Younger people may be more spur-of-the-moment and delay payments until the last possible moment. Therefore, it is necessary for each institution

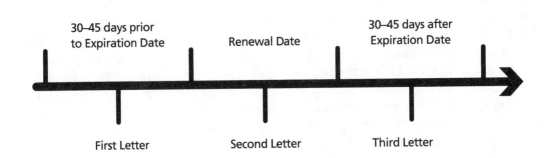

- Test schedules.
- Find a renewal schedule that works for you.
- Stick to the schedule, don't alter it for any reason.
- Using first class or bulk rate postage can affect your schedule.
- Your speed of processing can affect your schedule.

Figure 8–1 Renewal Schedule

to decide what timing of mailings will work best for that institution. Regardless of the time frame, it is necessary to allow enough time to lapse between mailings, so that the member has a chance to

- receive the mail
- respond
- have the renewal processed before a second renewal notice is sent

If a membership office can provide quick turnaround in processing memberships, it is possible to mail renewal notices within six weeks of one another. This timing will also depend on whether first class or third class mail is used and the workload of the data processing personnel. One word of caution: members who renew early should have the same renewal date as the year before. For example, if a June renewal sends in the renewal in May, that member's renewal date should remain the end of June. If the renewal comes in July, the new renewal date should be the end of July.

In general, the membership renewal package should include a renewal letter signed by the director of the institution or by the leader of the membership or friends group, a renewal application, and a return envelope. The letter personalizes the renewal effort, and the response form and envelope make it as easy as possible for the member to respond. Other materials can be included in this mailing, including notices of upcoming events that will entice the members into renewing so that they may attend. A window sticker or other small, inexpensive premium item that will encourage them to reenlist as a member or other reminders regarding premiums for renewing or for upgrading memberships are always beneficial.

Just as in the acquisition mailing, the copy is promotional in nature. It should be upbeat, and the benefits of membership should be highlighted. Special pleas can be successful, especially if the member was a charter member, a long-term member, or if a special institution anniversary is coming up. The letter should contain several suggestions that the member renew, along with a suggestion that the member do so immediately by charging their membership via the telephone or online. A "P.S." is needed to highlight a very special or crucial message. The renewal form, if possible, should include the current level of membership, the length of time he or she has been a member, and an encouragement to upgrade the membership level in exchange for increased membership benefits. The member's name, address, and ID number should be preprinted on the reply device.

The reply envelope should be a postage-paid, business reply envelope (BRE) whenever possible. This will only enhance the member's likelihood of renewing the membership, by overcoming the need for a postage stamp. If a person is one stamp short when paying bills with a deadline, and "nonessential" items such as the membership notice are in the stack, the membership renewal will not be mailed if a choice needs to be made. Providing a postage-paid envelope removes that obstacle. Providing a BRE also quickens the response time of members.

The second, third, and subsequent renewal letters should be increasingly more urgent than the first, highlighting even more of what the member will miss if the membership is not renewed. You may also request a note to let you know why he or she is deciding not to renew, if, in fact, that is the case.

It is possible to continue subsequent renewal mailings as long as the dollars generated from a particular mailing exceed the cost of actually doing the mailing. Some institutions employ three, four, five, six, or more membership notices, depending on the profitability of such efforts.

Telemarketing

Telemarketing is another means for renewing members. This more personalized contact with members is sometimes more successful than mail. In some cases, a telephone call merely serves as a reminder that will trigger the member into making a personal commitment to renew the membership. In other cases, for a member who has decided against renewing, it is a way to gauge any dissatisfaction with the membership program or other reasons for not renewing. Frequently volunteers or staff with training, a script, and proper supervision can conduct a renewal telemarketing effort. However, the best results are seen when a professional telemarketing firm is hired to reach the lapsed members. Substantial volume is one reason to use a professional firm rather than volunteers. The quality of the call and the ability to make the sales ask are other issues to consider. Many volunteers feel uncomfortable making a financial ask.

Unlike other forms of telemarketing, renewal telemarketing is not a cold call. There is past experience between the member and the institution. This relationship provides more positive results than if there had been no relationship at all. Again, the profitability of using telemarketing is determined by comparing the dollars raised to the cost if professional telemarketers are employed.

On-site

On-site renewals are also possible with a visitor-supported institution. Again, the one-to-one personal experience of asking a member to renew can be advantageous. Such an experience is especially successful when someone with an expired membership visits the institution and is denied free admission unless the membership is renewed. This is an excellent time to "catch" that member and gain another year's support.

Online

Online renewals are a new addition to the renewal mix. Online renewals can be proactive, sending a renewal request via e-mail prior to the mailing of the first renewal notice. The member can be encouraged to "renew now, save time, and eliminate the need for future mailings." The ability to renew online can also be promoted in renewal letters: "Save the cost of postage, renew online, get immediate confirmation, and visit tomorrow, hassle-free!"

Renewal Fulfillment

The end of the renewal process, but the beginning of the next cycle for retention is the renewal fulfillment. Just as a new member receives a packet of information, so should a renewing member. The packet should include a thank-you, acknowledging the member's continued support and, if possible, referencing the length of the membership. The membership card should also have this reference, if it can be done. This is one of the reasons why it is very important to keep records, especially in a beginning membership program. In the packet include information about the membership benefits, upcoming events, and anything else that might be of interest to the member. If there are special interest groups within the organization, offer membership in them in the fulfillment packet. This is also a good opportunity to send the member a tribute envelope for future gifts, if the organization has this type of fundraising program. Last, but not least, it is also a great time to solicit volunteer help, detailing the volunteer opportunities that are available at the institution.

The fulfillment packet should be looked at as the first step in the continuing retention of the member. The packet should make a good impression, reinforcing the members' feeling that they have made a wise choice in renewing and in supporting the organization.

Tips to Try

- Do all that you can do (see Exhibit 8–1)!
- Always have a P.S. on the letter, and use it to promote the idea of upgrading.
- Offer an upgrade incentive. It will double the number of members who upgrade.
- Offer a renewal premium. It will boost renewal rates. If you send coupons so members have to pick up the premium, a coupon redemption rate of 30 to 50 percent is typical. Premiums can be purchased according to redemption. Calculate the cost of the premium versus the percentage increase that the offer of a premium will generate. It may only be necessary to increase the renewal rate by 1 percent to cover the cost of the premium, and yet a premium may raise renewal rates several percentage points.

Exhibit 8–1 Renewals: Do All That You Can Do!

- Renewal mailings: 3 or 4
- Telephone: in place of third or fourth mailing
- Lapsed member telephone campaigns: to all lapsed members every 6 to 12 months
- Lapsed member mailings: 2 times a year
- Include in all direct mail campaigns
- On-site renewals when visiting

- Print only the member's current membership level and above as options on the renewal form to encourage upgrading and discourage downgrades.
- Track your mailings. Tracking renewal mailings is a must. A form like the one shown in Table 8–1 is helpful to track mailings. This form and a monthly query of number of members with renewal dates of past months will determine renewal rates month by month.

Table 8–1 Monthly Renewal Tracking Report: Renewals Sent as of May 31, 2000

Month	First Renewals Sent	Second Renewals Sent	Third Renewals Sent	Fourth Renewals Sent	Still Not Renewed
January	1,215	801	550	402	335
February	897	705	556	367	267
March	567	399	285	142	112
April	413	345	234	196	154
May	998	768	564	342	228
June	1,254	865	456		
July	986	654			
August	439				
September					
October					
November					
December					
Total	**6,769**	**4,537**	**2,645**	**1,449**	**1,096**

REFERENCE

Farber Sirkin, A. and M. P. McDermott. 1995. *Keeping members*. Washington, DC: Foundation of the American Society of Association Executives.

CHAPTER 9

Marketing the Membership Program

Patricia Rich and Dana Hines

Virtue has its own reward, but has no sale at the box office.

—Mae West

A MEMBERSHIP PROGRAM, AT ITS basic level, is a direct exchange with the member—benefits for the membership dues. The key concept is exchange. The marketing exchange refers to the method by which "the organization can offer something of value to resource owners in exchange for the needed resources. As long as an organization continues to produce value in the minds of resource owners, it is likely to attract the needed resources and survive," says Philip Kotler in *Marketing for Nonprofit Organizations* (Kotler 1982, 37).

In order for the membership program to market itself successfully, it needs to have a marketing orientation. Kotler defines a marketing orientation as determining "the needs and wants of target markets and [satisfying] them through the design, communication, pricing, and delivery of appropriate and competitively viable products and services" (Kotler 1982, 23). For a membership program to be successful, it needs to have this marketing orientation.

Who are the target markets and what do they want? How can the organization find

163

out? It can be difficult for membership staff (whether paid or volunteer) to determine what a prospective member wants. The membership manager has preconceived notions based on institutional history, what the institution can afford in terms of time and funding, and his or her own interests. And all members are not the same. We all want something different from the box office.

TARGET MARKETS

Every organization has one or more target markets for its programs and activities. One or more of these markets may be appropriate for the membership program, but probably not all of them. For example, a health-related organization may want to introduce its programs to elementary school children—clearly the right market for the programs, but obviously not for the membership program.

It is essential to understand who the target market is before marketing the membership program. If there is a membership program in place, the primary target market includes those people who are most like the current members. To know what the current members are "like," ascertain membership characteristics from data collected in a market research project (discussed below), and compile it into a member profile. The mix of promotional activities should always be designed to include this target market for membership.

If the program has been in existence for some time and it is time to add a new market, it is helpful to gain as much information about that market as possible before designing marketing materials. For example, a museum might decide that it would like to attract members who are younger than the typical member. In order to do this, the membership manager will first need to determine what appeals to this group. He or she can ask people, read publications such as *American Demographics*, and do research in a library and on the Web. The membership program then has to reflect and incorporate the kinds of benefits, services, and events that are of interest to this group. Marketing to a group that is different from those the organization already appeals to takes more than just mailing to a new list. In fact, that kind of mailing rarely works.

If the program is new, gather as much information as possible from like organizations to determine the characteristics of those most likely to join. If direct mail acquisition is possible, talk with list brokers about the possible lists to use. If the group is starting small, ask friends, relatives, and colleagues who might be interested. Have board members submit lists of potential members.

MARKET RESEARCH: FINDING NEEDS AND WANTS

Determining the target market's needs and wants is done through research. Market research is the method by which an organization can determine current and former members' needs and wants—along with a host of other information. Kotler defines it as "the systematic design, collection, analysis, and reporting of data and findings relevant to a specific marketing situation or problem facing an organization" (Kotler 1982, 156). According to David Lipke (March 2001, s4) in *American Demographics*, "the ability to make better decisions is the point of all research." Market research is important to a membership program so that informed decisions can be made about how the limited resources of time, money, and energy can be expended most effectively.

It is essential that the organization determine the answers to a number of questions before beginning a market research project: What information is needed? Who should be surveyed? What method should be used? Who will do the research work? What funding is available?

What information is needed? This question is the most important. Defining the issues to be researched is the first step. We are a nation of curious people. Magazines like *People* and newspapers like the *National Enquirer* have enormous audiences based on this curiosity. Above all, there needs to be a reason to ask questions and take the time of those who are willing to participate. Because of limited time and dollars, the information needs must be determined and prioritized.

Market research gives two kinds of information: quantitative and qualitative. Quantitative information can be measured and includes the demographic information. Qualitative information uses questions like "How do you feel about...?" or "Why did you visit...?" This information reveals the members' perceptions about why they are members, former members, or visitors. This information can be generalized to a total population, but not with the statistical accuracy of quantitative information.

You can ask about virtually anything. Information can be gathered on benefits, events, the newsletter or other communications tools, member services, exhibits, programs, and volunteer opportunities. Ask questions only about those areas and issues that can be changed. Ask about the newsletter if redesigning it is a possibility; if redesign won't happen in the near future, don't ask until redesign is a possibility. The same is true of events, educational offerings, and other programs.

Demographic information should always be collected in order to develop the member profile. Include questions about gender, age, education level, income level, and ZIP code. Age and income are usually asked in terms of ranges. Not everyone will answer, but enough people will, to give a fair picture of those answering the questions. Because an organization is interested in acquisition, public relations, and marketing, information about which radio and television stations are listened to and watched, what newspapers read, magazines subscribed to, and popular catalogs used is very helpful. This information can be used in planning acquisition programs, buying or exchanging lists, and determining where and how to advertise, and where to direct public relations.

Who should be surveyed? Current members and former members will give the most direct information relating to the membership program. For a visitation-based institution, visitors can be surveyed. If they are members, they can be asked member-related questions. If they are not members, they can be asked "why not." They can also be asked to which other organizations they belong. This information can be used to determine if there is an opportunity to increase the membership program. If a significant number of visitors are members of comparable organizations, but not the one they are visiting, there is room for growth.

Research Methods

There are a number of ways to obtain the research information. Mail surveys and focus groups are the two methods that are most often used in membership programs. Other ways of obtaining information can also be helpful in certain situations. Exhibit 9–1 asks the kinds of questions that a survey should ask, no matter the method used.

Exhibit 9–1 Sample Member Survey

Missouri Historical Society
Member Survey, March 2001

1. HOW LONG HAVE YOU BEEN A MEMBER? (Check one)
    ___ (1) Less than 1 year   ___ (3) 3–5 years   ___ (5) 11–20 years
    ___ (2) 1–2 years   ___ (4) 6–10 years   ___ (6) More than 20 years

2. WHAT IS YOUR CURRENT MEMBERSHIP LEVEL? (Check one)
    ___ (1) $45 Senior Member   Platinum:
    ___ (2) $50 Regular Member   ___ (6) $500 Sponsoring Member
    Patron:
    ___ (3) $75 Family Plus Member   ___ (7) $1,000 Thomas Jefferson Society
    Silver:
    ___ (4) $125 Contributing Member ___ (8) $2,500 Thomas Jefferson Society
    Gold: ___ (9) $5,000 Thomas Jefferson Society
    ___ (5) $250 Sustaining Member   ___ (10) $10,000 Thomas Jefferson Society

3. HOW DID YOU FIRST BECOME A MEMBER? (Check one)
    ___ (1) Received a membership offer in the mail.
    ___ (2) Joined while visiting the Museum/Library.
    ___ (3) Joined at the recommendation of a friend or member.
    ___ (4) Received membership as a gift.
    ___ (5) Joined online.
    ___ (6) Other (please specify) _____

4. I JOINED THE HISTORICAL SOCIETY BECAUSE: (Check up to three)
    ___ (1) Interest in history   ___ (6) Value of membership benefits
    ___ (2) Interest in political/social issues   ___ (7) Enjoy programs
    ___ (3) Visit Museum/Library frequently   ___ (8) Other (Please specify)
    ___ (4) Major exhibition(s)
    ___ (5) To meet others who share my interests   _____

5. THE MOST IMPORTANT BENEFITS OF MEMBERSHIP ARE: (Check two)
    ___ (1) Free or reduced admission to special exhibitions for adults
    ___ (2) Free or reduced admission to special exhibitions for children under 18
    ___ (3) Exhibition previews
    ___ (4) *Meriwether's* restaurant discount
    ___ (5) *Louisiana Purchase Shop* discount/gift certificate
    ___ (6) Subscription to MHS Members' Magazine
    ___ (7) Subscription to *Gateway Heritage*
    ___ (8) *"Time Travelers"* reciprocal benefits at other historical societies
    ___ (9) Membership gift item
    ___ (10) *Pastimes* and other lectures and events
    ___ (11) Discounts on education programs and classes
    ___ (12) Children's and family programs
    ___ (13) Other (Please specify)_____

continues

Exhibit 9–1 continued

6. PLEASE RATE YOUR EXPERIENCE WITH THE FOLLOWING:

	Excellent	Good	Adequate	Poor	Don't Know
Exhibitions	___	___	___	___	___
Meriwether's restaurant	___	___	___	___	___
Louisiana Purchase Shop	___	___	___	___	___
Visitor Services desk	___	___	___	___	___
Overall museum experience	___	___	___	___	___
Membership benefits	___	___	___	___	___

7. HOW LIKELY WOULD YOU BE TO:

	Very Likely	Somewhat Likely	Not Likely
Recommend MHS Membership to a friend	___	___	___
Give a gift membership	___	___	___

8. HOW OFTEN DID YOU VISIT THE MUSEUM IN THE PAST 12 MONTHS? (Check one)

___ (1) More than 20 times   ___ (4) 3 to 5 times
___ (2) 10 to 20 times   ___ (5) 1 or 2 times
___ (3) 6 to 9 times   ___ (6) Did not visit

9. IN WHICH OF THE FOLLOWING HAVE YOU PARTICIPATED IN THE PAST 12 MONTHS? (Check all that apply)

___ (1) Opening of the new museum building
___ (2) Special exhibitions (*Unseen Treasures/Nazi Olympics/1904 World's Fair*)
___ (3) Permanent exhibitions (*Seeking St. Louis*)
___ (4) Members' exhibition previews
___ (5) Festivals and celebrations
___ (6) African American history events
___ (7) St. Louis Rams Super Bowl trophy exhibition
___ (8) Twilight Tuesdays
___ (9) *Pastimes*, monthly members' programs
___ (10) Hands-on workshops, lectures, or educational programs for adults or children
___ (11) Bus tours to historic sites and communities
___ (12) Urban Forum
___ (13) Holiday Fair
___ (14) General visit to museum
___ (15) Other (Please specify)_____

10. WHEN ARE YOU MOST LIKELY TO ATTEND MHS EVENTS? (Check all that apply)

___ (1) Weekdays   ___ (3) Saturdays
___ (2) Weeknights   ___ (4) Sundays

11. HOW DO YOU LEARN ABOUT MHS EVENTS? (Check up to three)

___ (1) MHS Magazine   ___ (6) Radio
___ (2) Members' invitations/postcards   ___ (7) Newspaper
___ (3) From visiting the Museum   ___ (8) MHS Web site at **www.mohistory.org**
___ (4) From other members and friends   ___ (9) Other (Please specify)
___ (5) Pastimes mailings   _____

continues

Exhibit 9–1 continued

12. WHAT IS THE LIKELIHOOD THAT YOU WILL ATTEND THE FOLLOWING UP-
    COMING EXHIBITIONS?

	Very Likely	Somewhat Likely	Not Likely
Many Voices: Reflecting on American Indian Objects (opens March 2001)	___	___	___
Miles: A Miles Davis Retrospective (opens May 2001)	___	___	___
Can You Tell Me How To Get to Sesame Street? (opens December 2001)	___	___	___
Charles Lindbergh: The World's Passion for One Man (opens May 2002)	___	___	___
Through the Eyes of a Child: African Americans in St. Louis (opens Fall 2002)	___	___	___
Lewis and Clark: The Bicentennial Exhibition (opens January 2004)	___	___	___
World's Fair Centennial (opens April 2004)	___	___	___

13. WHAT KINDS OF NEW PROGRAMS WOULD BE OF INTEREST TO YOU? (Check
    up to three)
    ___ (1) Film series and classic movies
    ___ (2) Informal coffee/tea discussions with curators
    ___ (3) Theme dinners
    ___ (4) Orientation tours of Library and Collections Center
    ___ (5) Travel programs
    ___ (6) Discounts on Historyonics season ticket subscription
    ___ (7) Other (Please specify)_____

14. WHAT ARE YOUR FAVORITE TOPICS OF HISTORICAL AND CIVIC INTEREST?
    (Check up to three)
    ___ (1)   The Civil War
    ___ (2)   Genealogy
    ___ (3)   History of St. Louis
    ___ (4)   River lore/steamboats
    ___ (5)   Native American culture
    ___ (6)   1904 World's Fair
    ___ (7)   African American culture
    ___ (8)   Lindbergh and aviation history
    ___ (9)   Lewis and Clark
    ___ (10) Historic Architecture & Communities
    ___ (11) Issues affecting the St. Louis region today (transportation, land use, education, etc.)
    ___ (12) Other (Please specify)
    _____

15. ARE YOU A MEMBER OF ANY OF THE FOLLOWING ST. LOUIS CULTURAL
    INSTITUTIONS? (Check all that apply)
    ___ (1)   Saint Louis Art Museum
    ___ (2)   Saint Louis Zoo
    ___ (3)   Missouri Botanical Garden
    ___ (4)   St. Louis Symphony
    ___ (5)   Channel 9
    ___ (6)   St. Louis Science Center
    ___ (7)   Forest Park Forever
    ___ (8)   City Museum
    ___ (9)   Laumeier Sculpture Park
    ___ (10) Butterfly House
    ___ (11) Magic House
    ___ (12) Other (Please specify)
    _____

continues

Exhibit 9–1 continued

16. TO WHICH RADIO STATIONS DO YOU LISTEN MOST OFTEN? (Check up to three)
    ___ (1) KMOX AM 1120   ___ (10) KLOU FM 103
    ___ (2) KMJM FM 108   ___ (11) WSIE FM 88.7
    ___ (3) KFUO FM 99.1   ___ (12) WALC FM 104.1
    ___ (4) KWMU FM 90.7   ___ (13) KSHE FM 94.7
    ___ (5) KTRS AM 550   ___ (14) KEXZK FM 102.5
    ___ (6) WEW AM 770   ___ (15) WSSM FM 106.5
    ___ (7) KATZ FM 100.3   ___ (16) WGNU AM 920
    ___ (8) WIL FM 92.3   ___ (17) Other (Please specify)
    ___ (9) KYKY FM 98   _____

17. TO WHICH MAGAZINES/NATIONAL PUBLICATIONS DO YOU SUBSCRIBE?
    ___ (1) *New Yorker/Atlantic Monthly*   ___ (8) *Vanity Fair/Cosmopolitan*
    ___ (2) *Time/Newsweek/U.S. News*   ___ (9) *Smithsonian*
             and World Report   ___ (10) *New York Times*
    ___ (3) *Better Homes and Gardens*   ___ (11) *Wall Street Journal*
    ___ (4) *National Geographic*   ___ (12) *American Heritage*
    ___ (5) *Fortune/Money*   ___ (13) Other (Please specify)
    ___ (6) *Gourmet/Bon Appetit*   _____
    ___ (7) *Business Week*

18. DO YOU HAVE ACCESS TO THE INTERNET AT WORK? AT HOME?
    At work: ___ (1) Yes   ___ (2) No
    At home: ___ (3) Yes   ___ (4) No

19. HAVE YOU EVER VISITED THE MHS WEB SITE AT **www.mohistory.org**?
    ___ (1) Yes   ___ (2) No   ___ (3) Don't know

20. IN THE FUTURE, IF SERVICES ARE AVAILABLE, WOULD YOU LIKE TO RECEIVE
    ANY OF THE FOLLOWING BY E-MAIL? (Check all that apply)
    ___ (1) Event notices/confirmation
    ___ (2) Other MHS news   E-mail address (optional)_____
    ___ (3) Membership renewal notice   Name (optional)_____

21. IF THE FOLLOWING BECOME AVAILABLE IN THE FUTURE, WOULD YOU USE
    THESE ONLINE SERVICES? (Check all that apply)
    ___ (1) Online museum shop   ___ (3) Event registration
    ___ (2) Events calendar   ___ (4) Other (Please specify)_____

22. WHAT IS YOUR ZIP CODE?_____

23. WHAT IS YOUR AGE?
    ___ (1) 29 or younger   ___ (3) 46–65
    ___ (2) 30–45   ___ (4) Over 65

24. WHAT IS YOUR MARITAL STATUS?
    ___ (1) Married   ___ (4) Divorced
    ___ (2) Single   ___ (5) Separated
    ___ (3) Widowed   ___ (6) Other (Please specify)_____

continues

Exhibit 9–1 continued

25. NUMBER OF CHILDREN UNDER AGE 18 LIVING AT HOME:
    ___ (0) None   ___ (3) 3
    ___ (1) 1   ___ (4) 4 or more
    ___ (2) 2
    Please specify ages of children under age 18 living at home_____

26. WHAT IS YOUR GENDER?
    ___ (1) Male   ___ (2) Female

27. WHAT IS YOUR HIGHEST LEVEL OF EDUCATION?
    ___ (1) High school graduate or less   ___ (3) College graduate
    ___ (2) Some college   ___ (4) Postgraduate

28. WHAT IS YOUR ETHNIC BACKGROUND?
    ___ (1) White, non-Hispanic   ___ (4) Hispanic American
    ___ (2) African American   ___ (5) Native American
    ___ (3) Asian American   ___ (6) Other (Please specify) _____

29. WHAT IS YOUR TOTAL ANNUAL HOUSEHOLD INCOME?
    ___ (1) Under $40,000
    ___ (2) $40,000–$49,999
    ___ (3) $50,000–$74,999
    ___ (4) $75,000–$99,999
    ___ (5) $100,000 and over

30. WE WOULD APPRECIATE ANY ADDITIONAL COMMENTS OR SUGGESTIONS
    THAT YOU MAY HAVE.
    _____
    _____
    _____
    _____

THANK YOU FOR TAKING THE TIME TO SHARE YOUR OPINIONS WITH US!

Courtesy of Missouri Historical Society, St. Louis, MO.

Mail Survey

Purpose: To gather a large amount of data. The data can be both quantitative and qualitative. With a mail-in survey, an open-ended section can be included for "other comments." In a membership program, this is the most efficient and can be the least costly of the research methods. Members often take a proprietary interest in their organizations, and everyone loves to be asked for advice.

Technique: A survey is sent to a sample of the membership. It is also helpful to include a cover letter (see Exhibit 9–2) and thank-you gift (e.g., a coupon for organization merchandise, a free ticket for an event) to increase the rate of return. A reminder postcard can be sent to those who received the survey if the rate of return needs to be increased. Most membership groups can expect a return rate of 30 to 50 percent, far greater than the rate for a for-profit business. The information is then collated and analyzed.

Cost: Expense is related to the number of surveys printed and mailed, the tabulation, and the design and the analysis of the data.

Time needed: Mail surveys can be accomplished quickly with a deadline for return. The project will take 3 to 4 months to complete.

Focus Groups

Purpose: A focus group is conducted to generate or to test ideas. It is called a focus group because the facilitator focuses the dis-cussion. For membership programs, focus groups are a very good way to test ideas about events, programs, exhibits, or membership benefits. They are also valuable in brainstorming for new ideas about these subjects. For a new program, holding several focus groups to discover what members of similar organizations like about their membership experience would be a productive way to determine what should be included.

Technique: A randomly selected group of eight to twelve people is brought together for approximately two hours. A script is developed to elicit the information wanted

---

Exhibit 9–2 Sample Membership Survey Cover Letter

March 2001

Dear MHS Member,

As we look back on the opening of the expanded Missouri History Museum and make plans for the exciting future that lies ahead, your opinions are very important to us.

Your participation in the enclosed Members' Survey will help us learn more about how you perceive MHS and your experience as a member. This information will guide us in developing new features and programs for our members and the public. We would be grateful if you would please take a few minutes to complete the survey and return it in the enclosed envelope by April 30.

As a token of our appreciation, enclosed please find two complimentary beverage coupons for Meriwether's restaurant at the Museum. We hope you will visit the Museum again soon.

Thank you for your support as a Member and for taking the time to share your thoughts with us.

Sincerely,

Robert R. Archibald
President

   Courtesy of Missouri Historical Society, St. Louis, MO.

during the session. Using a professional meeting facilitator ensures objectivity and coverage of the material. Often more than one group is convened to make certain that the information is corroborated. It is also possible to convene groups with different characteristics. For example, one group might be longtime members and another, first-year members.

Cost: The cost ranges from very little to very expensive, depending on how much professional help is used. The information is more reliable if professionals conduct the sessions. An organization can also use a professional focus group facility that has a special room with one-way glass, so that the organization's representatives can watch the group's reactions. If necessary, the sessions can also be videotaped. Very often the participants are given a financial incentive to participate.

Time needed: Focus groups can take weeks or months in order to confirm the attendance of a random sample, develop the script, and analyze the results.

Exit Surveys

Purpose: To gather information from visitors to an institution. This type of survey is particularly useful for information about the visitor's experience. If a visitation-based institution is planning exit surveys, the membership program should be represented by several questions and have input into the demographic information being collected. Because this is typically an all-institution survey, membership needs to select a few very important questions to ask. Remember that a visitor survey is not a membership survey. It is possible, however, to extract member information if enough of the visitors who fill out the survey are members.

Technique: A survey form is distributed to visitors as they leave the institution. It can be completed on location (in which case it needs to be short) or it can be completed at home and returned by mail. Filling out the survey on site guarantees a completed survey, but many people are not willing to extend their stay, especially if visiting with others and especially if visiting with children. A mail-back survey is far preferable. It allows for more random distribution because even those people in a hurry to leave can participate. If distributed effectively, the return is good. Last but not least, it eliminates any bias that might occur with a live survey-taker. A live survey-taker needs to be trained to remain neutral, not express any feelings about the institution and not to engage in conversation with the interviewee. Any comments or expressions could bias the survey.

Cost: The cost depends on staffing the distribution, printing, mailing, and analysis of the surveys. Exit surveys conducted with paid interviewers greatly increases the costs.

Time needed: Several weeks or months depending on survey design, the number of surveys, distribution schedule, and analysis.

In-depth Interviews

Purpose: This format is used to obtain in-depth, qualitative information about the interviewee's perceptions of the membership program. A membership program might use this format if there were major issues that needed to be resolved. For example, a professional might be hired to do a study of why a program was not growing when similar programs were steadily increasing. The professional might interview members of other, similar organizations to determine what needed to be done to spur growth.

Technique: One-on-one interviews with a selected group, usually conducted by a professional. It takes the time of the professional and the interviewee. Interviews last from 20 minutes to an hour or more.

Cost: Dependent on professional costs. It is less expensive and tempting to use an organization's volunteers or staff, but the objectivity and candid answers that the organization wants from the interviewee would be lost.

Time needed: It can take several weeks to gather the information and write the report, depending on number of interviews and availability of interviewees.

Telephone Surveys

Purpose: To talk to a random sample of members about the membership program. The information is both qualitative and quantitative, though there is not time for many in-depth comments. This method is becoming somewhat more difficult because of the use of answering machines and people's reluctance to spend time on the telephone. Fortunately, happy members are often very willing to talk about their experience and answer questions. This method can be inexpensive if there is a volunteer corps that can be trained and is willing to do the work. Whether or not the callers are paid or volunteer, tight supervision is necessary, so that the questions are not asked in a way that promotes a bias in the answers.

Technique: A survey form is used over the telephone. It needs to be fairly short. The callers can be professional or volunteer, and they must be trained to ask the questions in the correct manner. The survey will give more quantitative than qualitative information because of the time involved. For example, a person will usually be asked to rate something on a scale of 1 to 7, rather than answer open-ended questions. The downside is that there may not be enough time to ask as many questions as might be included on a written survey.

Cost: Cost includes the expense for the callers, designing the survey, and analyzing the survey.

Time needed: This method can gather a great deal of information quickly. Time needed depends on number of members contacted as well as the time to design and analyze the survey. Survey results may be available in a short a time span as two weeks.

Mail-Back Surveys Included in a Newsletter or Other Publication

Purpose: To gather information by using an existing communication vehicle. Membership programs want to use this method because it is less expensive than sending a separate survey. This research effort, however, is not very reliable because participants are not randomly selected. It is also difficult to ensure a significant return or to meet deadlines because many members do not read the newsletter immediately, and some, not at all. This type of survey is survey of the people who read the newsletter, and hence not representative of the entire membership.

Technique: A mail-back survey is published in the organization's newsletter. Members are asked to fill it out and return it by a deadline.

Cost: The cost includes the design, printing, and analysis of the survey. It becomes an internal accounting matter if a portion of the mailing cost of the newsletter or publication that contains the survey is attributed to the membership department.

Time needed: Timing depends on the newsletter mailing. There is often a six- to eight-week lead time for publishing the newsletter. If this is the case, the survey must be ready, then be inserted and mailed, and responses received. The deadline on the survey should be at least six weeks after the newsletter's mail date. With sometimes unforeseen delays with the newsletter, the survey deadline should allow enough time to make certain that it can be returned within the appropriate time frame. It will take four to six weeks after the newsletter is mailed to determine if enough surveys have been returned for analysis.

Web Surveys

Purpose: To gather information from those who are Web members. For those organizations with Web memberships, using e-mail for a survey would be appropriate since this is the main route of communication. An organization might also use a Web survey to determine if there were an interest in a Web membership program. The rate of return is dependent on the use of the Web site. An organization would have to try this to see if enough of a return were generated to give any statistically valid information. Remember, just as with the newsletter survey, this will be a survey of those people using the Internet; a total of 35 to 50 percent of the membership will not be included.

Technique: The survey is posted on the Web site, either in a section open to anyone who is on the site or in a members-only section if it is to be a membership-only survey. Design the survey so that it can be e-mailed back to the organization.

Cost: This is a very inexpensive way to survey a portion of the membership because the distribution is virtually free. Costs will center on design and analysis and on any technical issues that arise with the use of the Web site.

Time needed: The Web is an instantaneous medium. Once the survey is on-line, those who visit the Web site will see it. Responses from those who fill it out are received immediately. This type of survey could be ongoing, with no deadline: the organization could just receive information as it arrives. Or there could be a deadline, so that at some point an analysis can be done.

Use of Professionals

For any of the methods discussed above, it is important to talk to a market research professional, to make certain that the method has validity for the information that is desired. Professionals are particularly helpful in selecting the sample, designing the survey, and collating and analyzing the results.

The sample needs to be large enough to be statistically valid. The researcher can determine the number of surveys that need to be mailed to generate the appropriate sample size. The sample also needs to be selected in a way that makes sense for the information and for the organization.

To encourage people to complete or mail back a survey, an incentive may be used. A small incentive included in a mailing can help generate a significant return. Incentives used in mail surveys may be items such as a coupon for purchasing something from the organization (food, publications, and so forth) or a small item such as a bookmark, or anything that can be mailed easily. This incentive is really a thank-you gift and should be front-end, or included in the mailing with the survey, so that surveys can be returned anonymously. Incentives used to ensure focus group attendance are usually money and/or food. Incentives are usually not used for telephone, mail-back, or one-on-one surveys. If an incentive is used with a Web survey, it needs to be something that can be redeemed on the Web, such as a discount coupon (in reality a coupon number that is e-mailed back to the responder) that can be used for logo merchandise or publications. If a visitation-based institution uses the Web, a coupon that can be printed and used on-site for a discount would be an appropriate front-end incentive.

The design of the survey will be the key to whether the data are useful or not. It is very difficult to write good, clear questions that elicit the information desired. If staff or volunteers do the survey design, it is worthwhile to have a market research professional review and edit the questions. The questions should also be tested on a few staff and volunteers to make certain that they draw out the appropriate kinds of answers. The physical design also needs to be considered, so that the data entry is easy to accomplish. No matter who writes the survey, it should look professional, as it is reflective of the organization conducting it.

Collating and analyzing the data are projects that should be given to a professional. Between the number of questions and the number of respondents, the data to be entered can be overwhelming. It is also necessary to code open-ended questions so they can be analyzed. It is a time-consuming task. Special software programs are often used to analyze the data, and a professional research organization will have such software. With professional tabulation, it is possible to analyze the data in many more dimensions. For example, many professionals use tab and banner analyses, which allow various questions and answers to be analyzed by, and in comparison with, a variety of segments. Someone familiar with statistical methods is best qualified to do the analysis.

Issues of Cost

Research can be very expensive. Estimated costs for most member/lapsed-member surveys are in the range of $10,000 to $25,000. There are ways for a membership program to reduce or eliminate the cost. Is there a board member or a member who is a professional market researcher and is willing to donate the services pro bono? Is there a board member or member whose company uses a lot of market research and the company he or she uses is willing to do some pro bono work? Is there a local research firm that is willing to do the work pro bono? Is there a local college or university with a business curriculum that would take this on as a class project? Or last, but not least, try negotiating with a professional market research company. Remember that staff or volunteers can always do some of the work, and professionals may be used for those essential tasks that make the research valid.

If it is appropriate, include an article in the organization's newsletter or another communication vehicle, so that those who have sent in responses or received the questionnaire will know what has happened with the information. This is also the opportunity to thank them for replying.

Using the Information

As mentioned earlier, the point of all research is to make better decisions. The information needs to be used when making decisions about the membership program. The member profile developed from the demographic information becomes an important base for marketing and other institutional programs. If this is the first membership survey (or the first in a very long time), consider a survey two years in a row to establish a baseline of information; then repeat and update the survey approximately every three years.

It is important to use the results as soon as possible to inform decisions that are relevant to the information gathered. For example, if a desire for more benefits was expressed in the survey, restructure that part of the program. If certain kinds of events bring positive responses, try more of them.

Use the demographics to determine where to find potential members. Use the radio, television, and magazine information to place stories and advertise.

Information about members can also be used in the development of the fundraising program. For example, if the average age of the membership is found to be more than 50, a planned giving program would be appropriate. The demographics can also be used in securing corporate sponsorships if the member profile is one that the corporation wants to reach. If it is clear that a significant portion of the membership watches or listens to a certain station, it is possible to approach that station for in-kind media exposure.

DESIGNING PRODUCTS AND SERVICES

In membership, the product is what is presented to the potential member. It includes the benefits, both tangible and intangible. In marketing, there is much written about selecting the right message. The message is how the product is presented to the prospect. If the message is not clear, consumers will not buy—and marketing is, first and foremost, about buying. Or in the case of nonprofits, when it comes to membership, marketing is about joining. There are also messages that create an image of the organization, and these are very helpful in persuading potential members that the organization is worthwhile and one that should be supported.

The primary marketing message for membership programs is about the exchange of membership dues for benefits. The first benefits that are expected and weighed in the mind of a potential member are the tangible ones, and those should be first in any message for an institution with tangible benefits. Whether it is admission, a

publication, or a discount, the easiest and clearest message for a potential member to hear and understand is about tangible benefits. Messages about the intangibles can be woven throughout those about the tangible ones ("See the award-winning exhibit about Picasso for FREE and learn how he influenced other artists!") Or they can be stated separately in another part of the direct mail, public service announcement (PSA), or brochure ("Your membership helps support our educational programs for the schools").

Market research gives a basis for what new benefits should be developed or how the current ones should be changed. For example, when the Arts & Education Council in St. Louis decided it was time to take a look at benefits, it held a focus group that discussed this issue, among others. The facilitator had the group discuss the current practice of sending a ticket strip to members, which included tickets to a variety of arts events in the community. Without exception, the two focus groups dismissed the ticket strip as too cumbersome, easy to lose in a drawer and, basically, never used. When shown a potential membership card to replace the strips, the response was unanimously favorable—the Council changed the benefit.

COMMUNICATIONS

Communications are what most people think of when marketing is mentioned. However, communications represents the advertising, the public relations, events, and all of the other ways that an organization offers and promotes its membership program.

When most organizations think about membership, they think about how it will be promoted. The promotion is actually how the program will be "sold." Promotion activities are the tools used to enlist members, retain members, and pique the interest of nonmembers. There are as many promotional opportunities as there are creative thoughts. What works for one institution may not work for another. Deciding which activities to pursue, which are worth the time and money, takes planning and knowing whom the organization wants to reach.

Rules

In order to select the promotional vehicles that make sense, it is important to follow a few rules. In *Marketing Workbook for Nonprofit Organizations,* Gary Stern (1992, 77–78) talks about principles to help choose an effective combination of techniques. Several are particularly useful for membership programs and are discussed below in the next three paragraphs.

"Gear tools to the audience." Make certain that techniques you choose will reach potential members. If the effort is to attract a particular group—for example, a younger audience—then any advertising needs to be on radio stations that have an audience in the appropriate age range, and speaking appearances should be sought at meetings of this age group.

"Pick the right mix of techniques—within your budget." The operative words here are mix and budget. Mix is important because not everyone sees, listens, or reacts to the same media. Budget is a concern because every membership program has one. For mix, it is key to decide which of several efforts will be best to use for reaching members or potential members at an affordable price. A small, inexpensive brochure may be the basis of the marketing plan. It can be used in numerous places. Added to this might be proactively seeking speaking engagements with groups of potential members. A third effort might be one-to-one sales efforts carried out by board members and

volunteers. All of these efforts can be carried out with time rather than a lot of money. In an organization with a large budget, the brochure might be a four-color, direct mail piece sent to thousands of households; advertising might be used; and PSAs might be developed for radio and television.

"If it worked, do it again." This rule is true for everything that a membership program does. If direct mail is working, keep doing it. Do not change it because you are bored with it. If you want to try something new, test the new direct mail using the current package as a control. If a special event is successful, keep doing it until the response to it seems to be falling. (Many special events have a life cycle.) Marketing of the program must be evaluated on an objective basis (e.g., number of responses), not on someone's whim. Marketing tends to be one area where everyone thinks that they are the experts. Know what you are doing, why, and stick to it. Persistence is fundamental.

By the same token, if something does not work, do not do it again hoping that it will work. With activities like direct mail, telemarketing, and on-site sales, it is very easy to tell what is working. With those like advertising, PSAs, and speaking, it is not often quite so clear. Before doing these activities, decide how you will measure success.

Promotional Activities

The promotions fall into two main categories, direct and indirect marketing activities. The categories are not mutually exclusive. The direct activities are those that actually "sell" the membership and are used for acquisition or renewal. The indirect activities are those that raise the profile of the membership program, so that when potential members are approached, they will join. For those who are already members, this is an affirmation that they belong to a great organization.

The emphasis for the activities, whether direct or indirect, will depend on the type of organization and on the geographic boundaries. An international organization will spend more time and effort on direct mail, for example, while a local visitation-based institution may emphasize on-site membership sales. Exhibits 9–3 and 9–4 display the major direct and indirect activities that visitation-based and non–visitation-based organizations may use for membership. The activities discussed below are not a complete list, but rather those that are used most frequently by membership programs. There are also other ideas discussed in the chapter on acquisitions (see Chapter 5).

Direct Promotional Activities

Direct promotional activities are those that include a call to action. They provide the means for a potential member to join. The means may include an enrollment form, a telephone number, an address, or an online Web site membership page. These activities are meant to generate membership, and their effectiveness is measured by how well they do that.

Direct mail. Direct mail is used for acquiring new members and for renewing and upgrading current members. The direct mail pieces need to have a marketing orientation, so that the potential and current members will immediately understand the value of their membership. The exchange needs to be explicit. Direct mail can also be used to increase members' involvement in the organization by encouraging attendance at programs and events. It is also a good vehicle for educational and policy-related information. Mail is still the most effective way to reach members on an individual basis. (For more information, see Chapter 6.)

Telemarketing. While many people do not like to be called, and answering ma-

---

Exhibit 9–3 Direct Promotional Activities

Direct promotional activities are those that include a call to action. They provide the means for a potential member to join. The means may include an enrollment form, a telephone number, an address, or an online Web site membership page. The following activities are meant to generate membership, and their effectiveness is measured by how well they do that:

- Direct mail
- Telemarketing
- On-site sales
- One-on-one sales
- Advertising
  - Print
  - Paid television
  - Paid radio
- Billboards
- Brochures
- Business cards

- Public service announcements
  - Television PSAs
  - Radio PSAs
- Employee house organs
- Newsletters
- Point-of-purchase displays
- Public speaking engagements
- E-mail
- Web site
- Special events

chines are ubiquitous, calling still works. The telephone is the next best thing to being there in person. It is particularly good for renewals and for non–fundraising calls that market the membership program. Calling to tell about upcoming events, to thank the member for his or her membership, or to give information about an issue are all ways to communicate about the program. (For more information, see Chapter 7.)

On-site sales. This acquisition method has become increasingly popular for visitation-based institutions and for those organizations that hold large events. The cost per dollar raised can be significantly lower than direct mail. Well-trained sales people become a marketing force themselves. There is nothing better than one person selling to another person. Benefits can be explained, objections overcome, and an emotional appeal made. This can be very effective at those times when there are enough potential members to make promotion financially viable.

One-on-one sales. Much like on-site sales, this means of marketing the program is inexpensive and personal, and can be very effective. Because it is one-on-one, it does not generate large numbers of members, but those who do join have had a solid introduction to the program.

Advertising. Advertising occurs in a variety of media—print, radio, and television among them. A number of national organizations use print advertising to help with their membership programs. They tend to be large organizations that can afford to place advertising in national publications. The advertising may have a coupon to send in, may have a telephone number, may give the Web site address or, most likely, will do all three. Sometimes local publications will make space available to a local institution either

for free or at a reduced price. Local membership programs rarely have the resources for print advertising. If the local institution is advertising for other reasons, such as to increase attendance, then, if appropriate, the membership program can piggyback on the advertising and use it as reinforcement for direct mail or telemarketing.

Paid television advertising is too expensive except for the largest of organizations. Paid radio advertising tends to be less expensive than television because the audience is smaller. If an organization has done market research and knows the stations that potential members may be listening to, radio is a possibility. An offer needs to be included in the advertising spot, so that the potential member is driven to action ("two free months if you call within the next hour"). More likely, especially for visitation-based institutions, is that an exhibit will be advertised with membership mentioned—"Join today and receive free tickets"—or there will be on-site sales. No matter the medium used, the ads must be frequent. Advertising is not a one-time effort. Stern discusses the advertising formula that says "Frequency Over Time = Reach" (Stern 1992, 78).

Public service announcements (PSAs). While paid advertising on radio and television is usually too expensive, PSAs are advertisements that are run free of charge on television or radio. They can be effective because they have the potential to reach a large audience. There are some caveats. It can be expensive to produce well-done PSAs that will move someone to action. Because the action needs to be fulfilled immediately, the organization must be able to react when the viewer or listener calls—which can be at any time, day or night. Often the free time that is donated is not during business hours. PSAs are also good for image building. And remember the frequency over time = reach equation mentioned in the above section on advertising.

Billboards. For large organizations such as the YMCA or Boy Scouts of America, billboards encouraging people to join can be helpful. Billboard companies will sometimes donate space, though it may be space available rather than space in desired locations. The organization then pays for the actual billboard. Because it is difficult to call someone to action while he or she is driving on the highway (though with cell phones, this is changing), billboards are used more for image building than for actual sales. Visitation-based institutions will usually use billboards to drive attendance and then have on-site sales for membership.

Brochures. It is hard to find a nonprofit that does not have a brochure. For membership programs there are two issues: first, there should be a membership brochure; second, membership should be mentioned in the organization's general brochure. The membership brochure is a very important marketing tool. It can be used in all of the membership sales efforts. It is essential to design the membership brochure to be affordable enough to print and distribute in great quantities.

Business cards. Zoo Atlanta prints a mini-membership form on the back of its business cards, including membership phone number and address to which the filled-out card may be returned. Every card handed out becomes an ad for membership as well as an enrollment form.

Employee house organs. If the organization has a good relationship with any corporations, those companies may be willing to advertise the organization and/or its membership program in the company's house organ. If the organization's mission is related to the corporation's work or its consumer market base, it may be possible to work out membership arrangements for employees. A company may be willing to pay a portion of the membership fee if it feels that it is important to offer this as a benefit to employees who are interested. This is similar to matching gift programs, some of which will match membership monies.

Newsletters. The organization newsletter should always tout the membership program. People who are not members will see the newsletter. Those who are interested should be encouraged enough by the newsletter to find out how to join. Some newsletters make space for a membership application, especially if the newsletter goes to a large number of nonmembers. Having an application in the newsletter is particularly helpful if the organization is going to have a "membership month." This allows members to cut out the application and pass it along to a friend.

Point-of-purchase displays. Signage positioned at strategic points at which a professional purchaser might notice are called point-of-purchase displays. At a visitation-based institution, point-of-purchase displays for membership should be at the ticket booth, in the gift shop, in the restaurant, and anywhere else that is appropriate. Marketing the program where the benefits are immediate, such as at the ticket booth and the gift shop, is very effective.

Public speaking. Any time anyone speaks on behalf of the organization, a "pitch" should be made for membership and brochures given to the attendees, if possible. An enthusiastic speaker who can talk about the benefits and the organization makes membership exciting. This is an effective way to encourage membership. If an incentive is used ("Join today and get two free months"), and the audience is large enough, this can be a very cost effective way to increase membership.

E-mail. If the organization has a way to collect e-mail addresses from potential members (for visitation-based organizations or for organizations with events, this could be through an on-site raffle), this is a very direct and inexpensive way to solicit membership. E-mail is perceived as more personal than direct mail and could be effective. If the membership brochure is on-line, it can be included in or attached to the e-mail. Again, an easy-to-fulfill incentive can be a great encouragement.

Web site. Every organization's Web site should have a page on which to join. If having a secure page is too expensive, there are services that will supply the secure page for a fee. If this is still too expensive, have a membership page that can be printed and then mailed or faxed. The membership page should include the brochure or a description of the membership benefits and the institution. This is a very economical marketing tool.

Special events. At all of the organization's events, there should be on-site sales with volunteers or staff. If that is not possible, everyone should be offered a membership brochure to take home. An organization might have a members' event in which members are encouraged to bring potential members, and membership is one of the topics of the event program.

Indirect Promotional Activities

These are the activities that put forth the image of the membership program. There is no direct call for action, but there is the intent of making the membership program desirable. When the membership program is a part of a larger institution, many of these activities are done in conjunction with the

---

Exhibit 9–4 Indirect Promotional Activities

Indirect promotional activities are the activities that put forth the image of the membership program. There is no direct call to action, but there is the intent of making the membership program desirable. Many of these activities are done in conjunction with the total institution when the membership program is a part of a larger institution. For those membership programs that are the organization, these activities are a very important part of the organization's image in its community. Indirect promotional activities include:

- Annual report
- Editorials
- Feature stories
- Letters to the editor/op-ed pieces
- Merchandising of public relations
- News releases
- Posters/Flyers

- Specialty advertising
- Talk shows
  - Radio
  - Television
  - Cable
- Word-of-mouth advertising
- Public displays/Events

total institution. For those membership programs that are the organization, these activities are a very important part of the organization's image in its community.

Annual report. The annual report can be used to tout the successes of the membership program. Those programs that are a part of a larger organization should ask for space for the membership program in the annual report. Numbers, if good and impressive, can be used, as well as comments about member programs, activities, and services. In organizations with small membership programs, this may be the place to provide recognition by listing members, new members, or those who have upgraded to donor clubs.

Editorials. For organizations with a message that concerns a public issue that is current, meeting with a newspaper's editorial board to encourage a favorable editorial for the organization is a very good way to bring the issue—and the organization—to the attention of the public.

Feature stories. These stories can be about the organization, about the membership program, or any combination. A group of local institutions might convince a reporter to write an article on the importance of membership to the organizations or on the "business" of membership.

Letters to the editor/op-ed pieces. If there is an editorial that has relevance to an organization or a membership program, take the opportunity to respond to it. Try to include a reference to the membership program.

Merchandising public relations. No matter how many people read an editorial, a feature story, or an op/ed piece, the piece can be used in a number of ways. Referred to as "merchandising public relations," this technique involves giving the piece more lives. Copy the article and send it to the membership, so that they know it has been printed. A particularly relevant piece may be included as part of the acquisition and renewal campaigns. Use it when trying to gain a spot on a talk show. When it is necessary, make certain to obtain permission to reprint the article. Contact the publisher if it is not clear whether or not permission is needed.

News releases. These are the basis for almost all public relations efforts appearing in the print and electronic media. As possible and appropriate, include an invitation to join in releases. This can be done in the body of the release, depending on the subject matter, or it can be a "footer" on all releases. The footer would be printed at the end of each release stating, "Be a part of our effort. Join today. Call …."

Posters/flyers. Posters and flyers are great, if there is a distribution system in place. Designing and printing them is fairly easy, and cost can range from inexpensive or very expensive depending on the design, color, and quantity. The issue with posters and flyers is delivering them to sites that will take them and making certain that they are, indeed, posted. They are particularly useful to bring people to an event, meeting, or other gathering. Membership then becomes an on-site solicitation.

Specialty advertising. This type of advertising is fun. Specialty advertising is the pen, the cap, the tote bag, the mug, and so forth—all with the organization's logo and name. Often used as premiums, incentives, and thank-you gifts for membership programs, specialty advertising items are intrinsically a marketing and promotional tool. When people see the item, they are reminded of the wonderful work of the organization. On a per-view cost, they are relatively inexpensive. Cost decreases as quantities increase. For this reason, buying many of an item is preferred. Many organizations produce logo merchandise for sale to members and/or the public, and the marketing value of this endeavor should not be overlooked. For member gifts, the items should be for members only. Do not sell the specialty items for members to the public; this would take away its exclusive appeal.

Talk shows (radio, television, cable). For membership, target those talk shows that reach the potential membership audience. If the organization has a spokesperson on a show, make certain to remind him or her to mention the membership program, benefits, and how to join. In most instances, talking about membership will be a part of a larger message that the institution wants to impart to an audience. If there are particular talk shows that reach the potential member audience, be proactive in trying to place a spokesperson on those shows.

Word-of-mouth. This is always the best promotional technique. At visitation-based institutions, visitors most often cite "family and friends" as the way they heard about the institution. Word-of-mouth communication becomes the one-on-one marketing that is so effective. This is why it is so important for members to have a positive feeling about the organization. A member who is negative, for whatever reason, will find ways to tell others about it. As we all know, if we have a bad experience, we tell many more people than we would if we have a positive one. Create positive member experience, service, and benefits, and word-of-mouth advertising will work as a strong marketing technique.

Public displays/events. Sometimes an organization is offered the opportunity to place a display or have a table at an event. There may be many reasons to do this. If membership is the major reason to do it, make certain that the event draws the correct profile for potential members. Have a point-of-purchase display with the brochure. Consider having a raffle for a free membership to gain names of potential members. If the event does not permit sales or people, but is, rather, a display of photos or other objects from the organization, do try to have at least a point-of-purchase display so that attendees can take the brochure.

EFFECTIVE PRICING

Pricing the membership program is a part of the marketing. Membership, at its basic level, is a direct exchange with the member—benefits for the membership dues. For a value member, this is the marketing equation. Designing the benefit package is a combination of what the institution is able to offer and what the potential member wants.

The major issue for the institution is making certain that the benefits (tangible and intangible) are commensurate with the price charged. The organization needs to decide what position it wants to take on the dues structure. An organization can decide that it wants to offer an expensive program and charge a higher fee than others; or it can position itself within the generally accepted range of other like organizations; or it can decide that it wants large numbers at a low price. There are examples in all categories.

If the price is low, not much can be offered unless the numbers are enormous. AARP, with $10 annual, dues can offer a lot with more than 30 million members. There are not many organizations that can offer as much. Most visitation-based organizations price their membership in line with other like, local organizations, unless they are offering something for which they can charge a high price to nonmembers, such as a high admission fee. In this case, the organization can charge more for membership than other organizations in the same area. This is particularly true for institutions that attract a large tourist base.

One word of warning: do not ask about the price of membership when conducting a survey. Information about pricing is rarely accurate. If moviegoers are asked about the price of popcorn at the movies, it is always too expensive—but many people buy it. What people want to pay and what they will pay are two different things. Everyone would like to pay less for whatever it is they want to buy; however, if really interested, people will pay the price. The best way to determine price is to look at competing programs, at the cost of providing benefits, and decide where the organization wants to position itself. If the cost seems to be decreasing the total numbers or total revenue, whichever is more important, then the price can be adjusted to a lower level. As with any part of the program, price can be tested. Test two different pricing structures, determine which works best, and use that pricing structure.

DELIVERY

Delivery, with regard to the membership program, has to do with the ability to bring the membership program to the members. For national organizations, this means trying to find ways to bring the membership program to the local level where members live. Many national groups have meetings and events in different cities in order to keep in contact with their members. AARP has now set up offices in all 50 states, all the better to serve and reach members across the country. Mothers Against Drunk

Driving (MADD) has more than 600 chapters nationwide.

Local membership organizations have done this as well. In large cities, the League of Women Voters, a national organization, holds monthly meetings in many and diverse locations designated by local Leagues. Museums now consider having satellite locations not only to serve more of the public, but also to encourage membership for those who do not live near the main location. Technology has offered the ultimate in distribution. Becoming a Web member at the Metropolitan Museum of Art allows the Web member to browse the collections from anywhere in the cyberspace world. This is also a new membership opportunity.

SUMMARY

For the marketing and the membership program to work effectively and serve the institution or organization, it is necessary to have viable products and services that meet the needs and wants of potential members. Market research is conducted to develop a member profile, help select the target markets, and discover their needs and desires. With this information, the membership program can design the offer, price it appropriately, use effective promotional techniques, and provide services that the members want and in the areas they want them. When all of this is done well, the markets will respond in kind by joining, renewing, and becoming ever more involved. Having a marketing orientation in the membership program, which means taking into account all of these efforts, will result in a program that does meet the needs of the market and motivates people to join. If the membership program is run with marketing in mind, it will have a lot of sales at the box office.

REFERENCES

Kotler, P. 1982. *Marketing for nonprofit organizations.* Englewood Cliffs, NJ: Prentice-Hall.

Lipke, D. J. March 2001. Ready for a close up: Market research moves into the spotlight. *American Demographics 23*, No. 3.

Stern, G. 1992. *Marketing workbook for nonprofit organizations.* St. Paul, MN: Amherst H. Wilder Foundation.

CHAPTER 10

Volunteers

Patricia Rich and Dana Hines

*Volunteers are not paid—not because they are worthless,
but because they are priceless.*

—Unknown

MEMBERSHIP AND VOLUNTEERS

VOLUNTEERS IN AN ORGANIZATION may or may not be a part of the membership program. Many institutions have developed volunteer programs and opportunities that are not connected to membership. However, in others, volunteers are an integral part of the membership program. Their role in membership ranges from being the fundamental core of the program to operating a program to being a group that enhances the fulfillment of the organization's mission. The difference in roles depends on the type and size of membership program and on how the organization views volunteers. The volunteer component can be a valuable and essential part of a successful program. This chapter first discusses the independent volunteer membership organization often, and here, called a Friends Group. Then the discussion considers the many sides of the member-volunteer equation in different types of programs: the membership program that offers volunteer opportunities for members; the membership program in which volunteering is a requirement for membership; and the membership program run by volunteers in an all-volunteer organization.

INSTITUTIONS AND INDEPENDENT FRIENDS GROUPS

The most important concept about volunteer member groups for institutions is that they need to be a part of and owned by the institution. Some volunteer member programs, often called Friends Groups, have been started as an adjunct to an institution. A museum, for example, might have a Friends Group that is basically volunteer run and that contributes its income to the institution it is serving. In this case, the Friends Group has its own 501(c)(3) status rather than being a part of the museum itself. In the best of all worlds, this arrangement would work very well.

The intent of this effort is clearly to help the institution; however, this configuration provides many avenues for conflict. The conflicts arise over use of name, expenses, use of funds raised, use of lists, and relationship with the fundraising efforts of the institution, and relationships with the members of the Friends Group. All of these issues, of course, have to do with control and responsibility. As one might say, this arrangement is "fraught with peril," and is one to be avoided. The issues that make this arrangement difficult are considerable.

Government-owned institutions often have a Friends Group in which the membership is separately governed and provides financial, volunteer, and other support to the publicly owned facility. Many zoos, for example, are owned by their municipality and,

thus, have independent Friends Groups. This is also true with the newly developing alumni associations for public schools.

Use of Name

The moment a Friends Group uses the name of the institution, it becomes synonymous with the institution. Members of the Friends Group believe that their money is going directly to the institution. Vendors and others believe that they are signing contracts and making commitments with the institution. When everything goes smoothly, this is not a problem. But the minute there is difficulty, the institution will be seen as the cause of the concern. When the membership cards arrive late, when the bills are not paid on time, when the customer service is below par, it reflects on the institution. Even when the circumstances are explained, there will still be a perception that the institution is to blame.

Expenses

Having a separate organization can engender extra expenses. For example, if the friends' program has its own administrative structure, reporting structure, and general overhead, the fundraising will not be as cost effective as it would be if the work were done under the auspices of the institution. The institution may also be expected to pay the bills and provide the upfront money for events and programs, but has no control over how the money is spent. This can lead to a rocky relationship.

Use of Funds

One of the positive aspects of an institutional membership program is that they raise unrestricted money: the institution can use the funds for the needs that are the most pressing. Funds raised through separate membership programs, however, are almost always restricted to something that the membership group wants to do. If there is a very close relationship between the institution and the Friends Group, these conflicts may be avoided. In most cases, the Friends Group knows that it has raised the money (it has) and, thus, it should be able to say what the money is used for.

Use of Lists

The membership program should be the basis of the fundraising program for an institution. The membership list becomes the donor base for the organization. When another organization—for example, the adjunct Friends Group—holds the list, using it becomes more difficult. Difficulties can involve the format for the recordkeeping, what information is kept, how up-to-date the list is, and how available it is. Although the Friends Group is separate, the two organizations need to be using the same recordkeeping or database system, so that the list is easily transferable for mailings and other fundraising efforts. If this is not the case, for whatever reasons, one of the most important purposes for having the Friends Group is lost.

Relationship with the Fundraising Effort

As stated above, there needs to be smooth flow of lists and other information between the two organizations. If there is any issue with "turf," this exchange becomes difficult, if not impossible. The best situation is that the Friends Group works within guidelines set by the institution itself.

Relationship with Members

The perception among members is that they are members of the institution itself. This means that the work of the Friends Group needs to be seamless with that of the institution. If the Friends Group wants to offer new benefits, they need to be coordinated with the institution. Communication between the two organizations needs to be constant and strong. A change in one organization needs to be known in the other. It is even better if the two consult with each other before making any changes that would have any impact on members.

Considering all of the pitfalls of a separate Friends Group, it is recommended that, if at all possible, the Friends Group be a part of the institution itself, however sometimes this is just not a possibility. Where a separate organization is necessary, with everyone working very hard to cooperate and coordinate, the Friends Group can prosper.

VOLUNTEERING IN MEMBERSHIP PROGRAMS

Opportunities Within the Membership Program

The structure of the volunteer part of the member program differs by organization. A common structure includes a board called "the Friends' Council," the "Members' Board," the "Auxiliary," or another, comparable name. The board will have bylaws (see Exhibit 10–1) and operating policies (see Exhibit 10–2). Some organizations also have a code of ethics (see Exhibit 10–3), which is recommended here and in Chapter 14. The board is made up of members who volunteer to work for the membership program and the institution. The board members volunteer on this members' board and

Exhibit 10–1 Sample of Bylaws

BYLAWS OF THE HEARD MUSEUM GUILD
(AMENDED 4/2001)

ARTICLE I: NAME

The name of this organization shall be THE HEARD MUSEUM GUILD.

ARTICLE II: OBJECT

The object of this organization shall be to further public interest in The Heard Museum, and to support and aid the work of the Board of Trustees and the Staff of the Museum.

ARTICLE III: MEMBERSHIP

SECTION 1: Membership in The Heard Museum shall be a prerequisite to membership in the Heard Museum Guild.

SECTION 2: There shall be five classes of membership: (A) Active, (B) Associate, (C) Honorary, (D) Complimentary, (E) Life. Active members shall be those who dues are current and who participate in the activities of the Guild. Associate members shall be those whose dues are current and who may participate but are not obligated to do so. Honorary membership may be conferred for life by the Board of Directors in recognition of distinguished service in the Guild. Complimentary membership may be conferred by the Board of Directors for one year. Life members shall be those who have paid the amount designated and who may participate in all activities of the Guild, but are not obligated to do so. Heard Museum Staff members may not become members of the Guild, but may volunteer for special events.

ARTICLE IV: DUES

SECTION 1: Dues for active membership shall be $18.00 per year. Dues for associate members shall be $25.00 per year. Life members shall pay the amount of $250.00 and shall be exempt from annual dues. If a life member's Heard Museum dues should lapse for more than one year, the life membership fee shall be considered a donation to the Guild.

SECTION 2: The fiscal year shall be July 1 to June 30 each year, and dues shall be due June 1 and delinquent July 1.

SECTION 3: Membership dues received after March 1 shall be considered as dues paid for the ensuing year.

SECTION 4: Honorary members shall not pay dues but shall have a vote and may hold office.

SECTION 5: Complimentary members shall not pay dues and shall not have a vote or hold office.

ARTICLE V: OFFICERS AND DUTIES

SECTION 1: Officers of The Heard Museum Guild shall be: President, President-Elect, Secretary, Treasurer and Assistant Treasurer.

SECTION 2: The officers shall be elected at the April meeting to serve for one year or until their successors are installed. Their term of office shall begin when they are installed at the annual meeting in May, except the Treasurer and Assistant Treasurer, whose terms begin on July 1.

SECTION 3: The President shall preside at all meetings of the Guild, its Board of Directors and its Executive Committee; shall represent the Guild on the Board of Trustees of the Museum; shall be an ex-officio member of all committees except the Nominating Committee; shall appoint six Coordinators and with their assistance appoint chairmen of standing and special committees; shall appoint the Parliamentarian; and shall perform such duties as may be assigned by the Board

continues

Exhibit 10–1 continued

or prescribed elsewhere in the Bylaws. The President may sign checks, drafts and contracts.

SECTION 4: The President-Elect shall assist the President and fulfill such duties as may be assigned by the President or the Board of Directors. The President-Elect shall preside in the absence of the President. The President-Elect may sign contracts.

SECTION 5: The Secretary shall keep the minutes of all meetings of the Guild, the Board of Directors, and the Executive Committee and shall submit to the Guild members the minutes of the Guild business meetings; shall notify the Board of Directors of their meetings and shall keep a roll of the attendance; shall conduct the official correspondence of the Guild; and shall be the custodian of the permanent records of the Guild.

SECTION 6: The Treasurer, who will be aided by an Assistant Treasurer, shall receive all funds of the Guild and deposit them in a bank or banks designated by the Museum Controller and shall disburse payments in accordance with the budget. The Treasurer shall make a report to the Board of Directors and to the Guild at each monthly meeting; the report shall be filed and retained for future reference. The Treasurer shall be chairman of the Finance Committee and shall submit the proposed budget prepared by the Finance Committee to the Board of Directors at its September meeting, and shall present the final budget to the Guild for ratification at its September meeting. The Treasurer shall have records available for the Museum audit. The Treasurer may sign checks, drafts and contracts.

SECTION 7: The Assistant Treasurer shall assist the Treasurer and shall manage the financial transactions for specific Guild projects as assigned by the Treasurer.

ARTICLE VI: MEETINGS

SECTION 1: Regular meetings of the Guild shall be held on the third Wednesday of each month, September through May, unless otherwise requested by the Board of Directors.

SECTION 2: A majority of the members present and voting, whose current dues have been paid, shall constitute a quorum at any meeting of the Guild.

SECTION 3: The annual meeting shall be held in May for the purpose of installing newly elected officers and for any other business to be transacted.

ARTICLE VII: BOARD OF DIRECTORS

SECTION 1: The Board of Directors shall be composed of the President, President-Elect, Secretary, Treasurer, Assistant Treasurer, Nominating Committee Chairman, Long Range Planning Chairman, Parliamentarian, Heard North Liaison, Guild Communication Coordinator, Museum Service Coordinator, Museum Education Coordinator, Community Programs Coordinator, Guild Programs Coordinator, and Membership Service Coordinator.

SECTION 2: The Board of Directors shall be responsible for the property and business of the Guild. It shall notify the Guild membership of the report of the Nominating Committee at least ten (10) days prior to the April meeting.

SECTION 3: The Board of Directors shall meet at the call of the President or any two Board members.

SECTION 4: A majority of voting Board members shall constitute a quorum.

SECTION 5: The Board of Directors shall fill any vacancy in the elective offices or in the Nominating Committee from a single slate submitted by the Nominating Committee.

ARTICLE VIII: EXECUTIVE COMMITTEE

SECTION 1: The Executive Committee shall consist of the President, President-Elect, Secretary, Treasurer and Assistant Treasurer.

continues

Exhibit 10–1 continued

SECTION 2: The Executive Committee shall conduct business when the Board of Directors cannot be convened.

SECTION 3: The Executive Committee shall meet at the call of the President or any two members of the Executive Committee.

ARTICLE IX: MEMBERS AT LARGE

SECTION 1: The Coordinators shall be the liaison between the Board of Directors and the committee chairmen under their respective jurisdictions; shall be voting members of the Board of Directors; and shall fulfill such duties as may be assigned by the President or Board of Directors.

SECTION 2: A Coordinator also may serve as the chairman of a committee in the same jurisdiction.

SECTION 3: The Parliamentarian shall be an ex-officio member of the Executive Committee and shall serve on the Board of Directors in an advisory, non-voting capacity.

ARTICLE X: STANDING AND SPECIAL COMMITTEES

SECTION 1: Standing Committees shall function as outlined in the job descriptions.

SECTION 2: A single slate shall be presented by the Nominating Committee for the following offices: President, President-Elect, Secretary, Treasurer, Assistant Treasurer, and Nominating Committee. Nominations may be made from the floor provided consent of the nominee has been obtained.

SECTION 3: If there is more than one nominee for an office, election shall be by secret ballot and a majority vote shall elect.

ARTICLE XI: NOMINATIONS AND ELECTIONS

SECTION 1: The Nominating Committee shall consist of five members of the Guild elected at the April meeting. Only the Chair shall have served on the Nominating Committee the previous year, the other members coming from a wide range of Guild activities. The outgoing President and the President-Elect shall not serve as members of the committee (Article V, Section 3) but shall be invited to attend the first meeting to offer non-binding suggestions and ideas.

SECTION 2: A single slate shall be presented by the Nominating Committee for the following Offices: President, President-Elect, Secretary, Treasurer, Assistant Treasurer, and Nominating Committee. Nominations may be made from the floor provided consent of the nominee has been obtained.

SECTION 3: If there is more than one nominee for an office, election shall be by secret ballot and a majority vote shall elect.

ARTICLE XII: PARLIAMENTARY AUTHORITY

The rules contained in Robert's Rules of Order Newly Revised shall govern this organization in all cases to which they are applicable and consistent with these Bylaws.

ARTICLE XIII: AMENDMENTS

These Bylaws may be amended at any regular meeting of The Heard Museum Guild by a two-thirds vote of those present, provided that at least thirty (30) days prior to the vote each proposed amendment has been submitted in writing, first to the Board of Directors and then to the Guild membership.

Courtesy of Heard Museum Guild, Phoenix, AZ.

Exhibit 10–2 Sample of Operating Policies

THE HEARD MUSEUM GUILD POLICY STATEMENT

ADMINISTRATION

1. Any change in policy must be approved by the Guild Board of Directors. Any action requiring a change in policy must be approved by the Board of Directors prior to the action being taken.

2. All Board meetings are open to the general membership of the Guild.

3. Any Guild member wishing to speak before the Board for the purpose of introducing ideas, raising questions or presenting proposals, should notify the Guild President and request inclusion in the agenda for the intended meeting.

4. The May Annual Meeting minutes may be read and approved at the next Executive Committee or Board of Directors Meeting, whichever comes first.

5. Elected Officers: **a.** The President shall have served a minimum of two years on the Board of Directors, one of these years as a member of the Executive Committee. **b.** The President-Elect shall have served in a voting capacity on the Board of Directors for a minimum of one year. **c.** The Nominating Committee Chairman shall have served on the Nominating Committee the previous year.

6. The Nominating Committee Chairman shall present the slate of candidates to the Board of Directors at the February meeting, publish the slate in the March Newsletter and announce the slate at the March Guild meeting.

7. The term of office for all members of the Membership Committee shall begin on July 1 to coincide with the Heard Museum's fiscal year and with the Guild Treasurer's term of office.

8. All committee members must be officially registered Guild members. Under certain circumstances, the President or Board can modify this policy.

9. Field trips shall be confined to the continental United States. Trips will be limited to Museum members only, Guild members being given first choice.

10. The Code of Ethics of the Heard Museum Guild is used as the guide for all volunteer activity undertaken by the Guild.

11. A volunteer whose responsibilities require his/her presence at an event, with the exception of the Indian Fair and Market, shall pay for admittance to that event. Other exceptions may be made at the discretion of the Guild administration.

12. An artist, when paid as a guest speaker at a Guild meeting, may not bring art wares to sell at the presentation.

FINANCE

1. No charge shall be made to any organization requesting a speaker through the Speakers' Bureau. Donations will be accepted.

2. The spouse of the Heard Museum Director shall be a complimentary member of the Guild.

3. The Heard Museum Guild Endowment Fund is available to honor family and friends or to commemorate events.

4. Non-budgeted expenditures in excess of $50 shall be incurred and paid only upon approval of the Board of Directors.

5. Guild accounts shall not change financial institutions without due cause. Any branch of the depository may be used for the convenience of successive Treasurers.

continues

Exhibit 10–2 continued

6. All fundraising activities should be developed in consultation with the Museum Director and staff.

7. The Guild may make a discretionary contribution to the Museum each May at the Guild Annual Meeting and Luncheon and at any other time that the Executive Committee decides that there are sufficient funds to support an item to be contributed or an amount of money to be contributed. Any contribution at a time other than the Annual Meeting and Luncheon should take into account the amount of an already projected contribution. The amount of all contributions shall be decided by at least the Executive Committee after review of all financial accounts, less the Student Art, Note Cards, and the Book Sale accounts. Each year in August/September the Guild President gives the Museum Board of Trustees a projected amount of our contribution for that year.

8. The proceeds of the Book Sale shall be used to support the activities of the Heard Museum Library within the guidelines set down by the Guild Board of Directors and reported to the Guild Board of Directors.

9. The proceeds of Student Art and Note Card sales shall be disbursed by the Student Art Committee within the guidelines set down by the Guild Board of Directors and reported to the Guild Board of Directors.

10. The Guild Treasurer will maintain a Special Events Account of not less than $10,000 and not more than $12,000 to be used as start up money for any event the Guild Board of Directors wishes to start.

AWARDS

1. The Heard Museum's Board of Trustees recognizes the value of service and quality of work of Guild volunteers by awarding Ketohs* in Service, Education and Special Achievements. All volunteer service hours should be carefully recorded and filed with the Guild Administration as a means of aiding the Museum in preparation of grant and sponsorship proposals. It is the goal of the Museum and Guild that awards be granted on a fair and equitable basis.

    I. The **SERVICE KETOH** shall be awarded to any Guild member who has given 500 hours of service to the Museum and/or Guild.

        A. All types of service to the Museum or the Guild, whether performed at the Museum or away from the Museum, shall be included in the volunteer's time record. These services include Museum Shop service, Guide service, Speakers' Bureau assignments, COMPAS assignments, Information Desk service, service as aide to the Museum staff in the Curatorial Department, Library and Administrative Offices, as well as work on specific Museum or Guild projects.

        B. Volunteer time shall be recorded on the prescribed Volunteer Time Record form kept in the volunteer's possession and may be mailed or given to the Service Awards Committee Chairman at any time during the year, but all hours received after April 1 will be totaled for the following year. Two Volunteer Record forms will be included in the Guild Directory each year. Additional forms may be obtained from the Service Awards Chairman or in the Guild Room.

        C. It shall be the duty of the Service Awards Committee to total all Volunteer Time Records and record the cumulative total on the Guild computer. Completed records shall be kept on file in the Guild Room.

continues

Exhibit 10–2 continued

    D. There shall be no time limit for earning an award. Volunteer Time records will be kept as long as the volunteer maintains continuous membership in the Guild.

    E. The following guidelines are presented to clarify the definition of "SERVICE" to the Museum or Guild:

        1. Service time to the Museum of Guild begins at the time of arrival at the place of assignment and ends at the finish of that work session and includes round trip travel time from the volunteer's home.

        2. Actual time spent at Board meetings, committee meetings, work sessions, etc., relating to Museum or Guild projects shall be considered service time.

        3. On-the-job training in the Museum Shop, Library, Curatorial Department and at the Information Desk is considered service time.

        4. Training time required for maintaining or improving proficiency in any service area may be included as service time; workshops are included.

        5. The Las Guias Training Course must be completed prior to guiding and pursuing an Education Ketoh. It is, therefore, not considered hours toward a service award.

        6. Staffers and committee chairmen are expected to enter estimated telephone time on a weekly basis on the time records.

        7. Attendance at Guild meetings, lectures, gallery openings, etc., is not considered service to the Museum or Guild.

II. The **EDUCATION KETOH** shall be awarded in accordance with the requirements included in the Las Guias Handbook.

III. Candidates for **SPECIAL ACHIEVEMENT AWARD KETOHS** shall be recommended to the Museum's Board of Trustees by the Service Awards Committee.

IV. The name of any Guild volunteer who has given 2,500 hours of service shall be inscribed on the **SERVICE AWARDS PLAQUE** in the Sandra Day O'Connor Gallery.

V. Any Guild volunteer who has given 5,000 hours shall be granted the status of **HONORARY MEMBERSHIP** for life. The Board of Directors may grant the status of **HONORARY MEMBERSHIP** to any Guild member for exceptional service.

The Heard Museum Guild Policy Statement shall be reviewed by the Bylaw Review Committee. Changes shall be recommended to the Board of Directors for approval.

*Ketoh is a Native American item used to protect skin when hunting with bow and arrow. It is used by the Guild as its logo and for awards.

Courtesy of Heard Museum Guild, Phoenix, AZ.

also work with the organization in a variety of other volunteer capacities. For a national organization, there may be chapters or groups that volunteer for the organization on a local or regional basis. This is true of university alumni groups, sororities and fraternities, many national issue based groups, and many interest groups.

This board is often self-perpetuating, with suggestions of new board members coming from current members and from staff. Diversity in this group is important because many of its activities require outreach into many parts of the community. Members who are interested in being on this board volunteer to be on committees

Exhibit 10–3 Sample Code of Ethics

THE HEARD MUSEUM GUILD CODE OF ETHICS

The Heard Museum Guild makes an essential contribution to fulfilling the mission of the Museum. Volunteers share with staff and members of the Board of Trustees a responsibility to support a code of ethical behavior consistent with the public trust accorded the Museum. Guild members should accept responsibility for understanding the policies and programs adopted by the Museum Trustees and support the achievement of these policies and programs. Volunteers should abide by relevant portions of the ethics statement as it is contained in THE COLLECTION AND COLLECTION MANAGEMENT POLICY of the Heard Museum.

Access to the Museum's inner activities is a privilege, and the lack of material compensation for effort expended in behalf of the Museum in no way frees the volunteer from adherence to the standards that apply to paid staff. Conflicts of interest restrictions placed upon the staff must be explained to volunteers and, where relevant, observed by them. The volunteer must work toward the betterment of the institution and not for personal gain other than the natural satisfaction and enrichment of participating in the Museum.

While the Museum may accord certain special privileges to volunteers, they should not accept gifts, favors, loans or things of value from other parties in connection with carrying out duties for the institution.

Volunteers who deal with the Museum's collections and interpretive programs work in areas that are especially sensitive. In particular, volunteers may find that they have access to confidential information and should respect that confidentiality as part of the vital support they render to the Museum.

Museum volunteers should consider themselves obligated to fulfill their responsibilities in the same spirit as though they were a part of the paid staff.

Courtesy of Heard Museum Guild, Phoenix, AZ.

---

and become involved in the activities of the group. The membership or development department often staffs the board. In some organizations the staffing is provided by public relations, the marketing department, or the director's office. The relationship between this board and the board of the institution should be close. One model that works well is for the chair of the members' group to sit on the institution's board, ex officio, reporting to the board on the group's activities. This relationship gives status to the members' group and signifies its importance for the institution.

The board's raison d'être is to assume responsibility for projects and tasks, all in support of the membership program and the organization. The responsibility often includes increasing membership and fundraising for the institution. In fulfilling these responsibilities, there are many volunteer opportunities. These opportunities are both within the membership program itself and within the larger institution. The Heard Museum Guild is a well-developed member organization for the very respected Phoenix museum that showcases the heritage and living cultures and arts of native peoples, with an emphasis on the Southwest. Exhibit 10–4 shows the Guild's organization chart and all of the functions it provides for the institution. These services range from docents programs (e.g., Las Guias) to an enormous Indian Fair each spring to helping in the library. In a beginning program, a few of these types of activities would be tackled, with others added over a span of years.

Opportunities Within the Membership Program

No matter what the size of the membership program is, members can be very helpful as volunteers. Remember that the same thing is true of large membership programs as well as small ones—involvement is positive for the institution. The discussion below presents some of the possible volunteer activities within a membership program.

Acquisition

Members who are willing to recruit new members are invaluable. This can be done in a number of ways.

House parties. A member may be willing to hold a meeting in his or her home for the purpose of informing others about the organization and encouraging membership. Many issue-related organizations have started in this way. For an organization that wants to promote growth in a certain geographic area where membership is low, this may be an effective way to do it.

On-site sales. Every visitation-based organization should have a way to promote membership on site. This may mean a desk at the front gate, a table at an event, or a cart at the turnstiles. Whatever the location, there needs to be a person to take the new membership forms. Even if a staff person

needs to be in charge of the financial aspects of the transaction, a well-versed membership volunteer can persuade those entering that a membership is worthwhile.

"Every member get a member" campaign. Design an acquisition campaign using a volunteer corps. Have a contest challenging current members to ask their friends and colleagues to join. Those who recruit the most new members can be eligible for prizes. With a great volunteer group, this is very cost effective and can be fun for the volunteers. This can also be particularly effective at upper levels of membership, for which the volunteers may be willing to make personal calls to solicit members.

Calling New Members

Calling new members a few months after they have joined can be an especially helpful part of the retention effort for first-year members. The experienced member can answer questions, point out events and programs of interest, and, in general, make certain that the new member is aware of all of the benefits of membership as well as the important work that the organization is doing.

Renewals

Every program must renew its members to continue. If mail is used to renew members, there is often the possibility of following up with a telephone call. A member telephone bank set up to make those calls can be very effective. If members cannot be in one place, those who are willing to may make calls from home. Having an enthusiastic member-volunteer offers an opportunity to make contact with members and to bring them up to date on the wonderful accomplishments of the institution.

Exhibit 10–4 Heard Museum Guild Organization Chart

EXECUTIVE COMMITTEE*				
President	President Elect	Secretary	Treasurer	Assistant Treasurer

Curatorial Aides Library Committee Library Archives Library Slide Library NAARC Library Oral History Library Book Sale & Library Friends Museum Shop Information Desk	Museum Services Coordinator	Museum Education Coordinator	Las Guias Training Las Guias Continuing Education New Exhibit Training Las Guias Touring Touring at Heard North Performance Review School Liaison Speakers' Bureau Short Course
Indian Fair Lecture Series Special Events Student Art Note Cards Cookbook COMPAS	Community Programs Coordinator	Guild Programs Coordinator	Field Trips Holiday Luncheon Hospitality Guild Programs Spring Luncheon
Guild Room Guild Technology Historian Newsletter Marketing	Guild Communications Coordinator	Membership Services Coordinator	Data Processing Directory Membership Service Awards
Nominating Chair*	Long Range Plans Chair	Heard North Liaison	Parliamentarian

*Executive Committee Officers and Chair of the Nominating committee are elected, the rest are appointed.

Courtesy of Heard Museum Guild, Phoenix, AZ.

Thank-You Telephone Calling

Another use of telephone calling is to thank members for renewing or for being a member for a certain length of time. Many volunteers like to make these calls because they are friendly, there is not a solicitation involved, and it gives them a chance to wax eloquent about the exciting things that are going on at the organization. For those members who have been members for five, ten, twenty years, or more, having someone call to acknowledge their membership is a reminder that the organization knows who they are and cares about their involvement.

Development of Materials

There may be very talented people among the membership who would be willing to help in developing materials for the organization. Volunteers can be involved in writing, design, or graphics. There may also be a printer who would be willing to help with this part of the project. Be careful with this arrangement, however. Projects with a deadline such as direct mail that must be mailed by a certain date, need to be assigned to volunteers who can meet the deadline and not want to write copy or design by committee.

Helping with Surveys

If it is time to do a member survey, there may be a market research professional within the membership who would be willing to help with concept, questions, collating the data, or analysis. If the surveying is conducted with telephone or exit interviews, volunteers can be trained to administer the surveys. If there is an exit survey to be distributed, volunteers can also be trained to help with this important step in the process.

Recordkeeping

Recordkeeping is an essential component of any membership program. Volunteers willing to work on the database and other tasks associated with the recordkeeping are enormously valuable. These volunteers are serving in a role that otherwise would have to be filled by a staff person. It is imperative that the volunteers receive appropriate training and supervision, as the database becomes the foundation for future fundraising in the institution. Sometimes an organization is tempted to have a volunteer do the recordkeeping at home. This should be avoided at all costs. Records should be kept in one location only, usually the office. Anything to do with the financial aspects of the organization, including all records, needs to be stored in a safe place.

Member Events

Member events present a prime opportunity for volunteer involvement. A substantive membership program will offer a variety of events and programs for members. Many volunteers enjoy the challenge and creativity involved in designing, developing, and implementing events. These events may be free to members, may have a charge so that the event is breaks even, or may raise funds. Those that are typically members only are the ones that are free or break even in their fee. Fundraising events are more often open to a large audience in the community, not necessarily just members.

Member events are usually associated with the organization. They may be lectures or demonstrations in the institution's area of interest. They may feature the opening of an exhibit at a museum or the construction of a new area at a school or hospital. National organizations might have local groups bring in noted speakers on the subject of interest.

First-year members might be invited to a behind-the-scenes tour of the institution or lunch with the director. Any or all of these kinds of events can be in the purview of the volunteer corps.

Volunteers as Assets

The possible ways to use volunteers in the membership program are limited only by imagination and creativity. Membership programs grow by viewing volunteers as an asset to the program. They take advantage of the enormous opportunity to support the mission and broaden the volunteers' involvement in the institution. With limited resources, using volunteers is a major way in which the membership program can increase its reach and offerings.

Opportunities Within the Organization

There are a number of activities within an institution that can be accomplished by the membership program. The membership provides a ready base of interested people who may be willing to help in a number of ways.

Information Desk

Visitation-based institutions and visitor-friendly organizations with a facility often have an information desk located where visitors enter. Staffing this desk is a function that can be handled by the members' program. Volunteers from the membership have an interest in the organization and can easily be updated on current activities. The bonus for this arrangement is the ability to sell memberships at this desk and to use it for members who want to pick up their premiums.

Public Relations

Media relations. Because membership groups frequently develop events for the or-

ganization, having members who are willing to be public relations ambassadors is a real advantage. When an event needs publicity, the members who are involved are great representatives for the institution. The media often like to talk to and feature the volunteers who are intimately involved in the event and the organization.

Speakers' bureau. Another membership program project is a speakers' bureau for the institution. The members speak for the institution at civic groups, luncheon meetings, and other functions where a speaker is needed. This is an opportunity to tell the story of the organization as well as to solicit memberships, if the group is appropriate. A slide show, video, Powerpoint™ presentation, or flip charts can be used to picture the work being done by the institution and to make it very easy for the member to feel comfortable making the appearance.

Public events. Members may want to plan and implement events and programs to which the public is invited, in addition to those for members only. This provides important visibility for the organization in the community. At a visitation-based institution, the events are usually planned to bring people on site. For organizations with a facility, events may take place at the facility or at other locations. As organizations grow, the number of events and programs escalates. With the larger number of activities, the membership group can provide significant help in this arena.

Advocacy

For an issue-based organization, or one that finds itself in the middle of an issue, the membership is an effective voice for the cause. Given the availability of e-mail and other high-speed communication opportunities, voices can be heard quickly and counted effectively. Not only can the membership work on behalf of the institution, but also the fact that there is a significant membership proves to the community involved that many people care. The complexity for the institution is in the organization and management of this effort. It does take time and energy, but when the stakes are high, the member response can be impressive and successful.

Grassroots work. For some issues, the most effective thing to do is mobilize neighborhoods or groups of people. With many members interested in the issue, the connections can be extensive. The mobilization may be to get people to a city hall meeting, to a rally, to a legislative day, or to a related event. Having this network can be invaluable to the organization.

Letter writing. A frequent advocacy project for members is to encourage them to write to their legislators, the newspapers, and anyone else relevant to the issue at hand. Much of this is really an educational effort so that those contacted and the public at large understands the basis of the issues and what is involved. Volunteers doing this work can be much more effective than paid staff.

With the advent of e-mail and faxes, members can be mobilized in a very short time. There is the ability not only to encourage members to write, but also to include a significant amount of information for them, particularly through the organization's Web site, so that they feel comfortable in this activity. This is one of the reasons for gathering additional addresses and numbers. Not only can the members be energized, but also their communication with the appropriate officials can now be sent and received in record time, or in virtually no time at all, and at little or no cost.

Speaking. The same is true of speaking to relevant groups such as the legislature, the city council members, or the editorial board of the newspaper. The members can be passionate about what they are saying with no real self-interest—a very powerful message.

Fundraising

Members make a major contribution to the organization by working on fundraising. The roles for members include working on fundraising events, personal solicitation, and participating in other fundraising efforts.

Fundraising events. Members are often in the forefront of fundraising events. A wide distribution of members, each of whom has a network in the community, is the key to success. This ensures a large volunteer committee to work on the event as well as people who will support and attend the event. Fundraising events range from bake sales to black tie galas to everything and anything in between. The type of fundraising event depends on the organization, its mix of fundraising events, its resources, the interest and willingness of members to work on a project, and the community. The volunteer component may include creating, designing, and implementing the event as well as selling tickets and tables and finding the underwriting. These events bring funds to the organization and visibility in the community.

Personal solicitation. Upper-level members are ideal to help with the responsibility of soliciting others to join at these levels of support. The most effective solicitation takes place in person. Staff provides materials and names of potential members, and the member makes the appointment and visits the prospect. Telephone or letter may also be used, though neither is quite as effective as the personal visit. In whatever way members are willing to increase the upper-level membership, this volunteer activity is a benefit to the entire institution.

Having members partner with staff to make the solicitation call can be very successful. At times, the volunteer is very happy to make the contact and the appointment, but is not comfortable in the "asking" role. When this is the case, a staff member can be the solicitor, while the volunteer is the entrée to the potential upper-level member. This team approach affords the opportunity for the volunteer to provide the social context for the setting, while the staff person provides the answers to any detailed questions they may ask. Because these calls are time consuming for both the volunteer and the staff, in most institutions they are best used when working with potential upper-level members rather than those who might join at the basic level.

Other fundraising efforts. The members' group may initiate or respond to requests for other fundraising projects. The opening party for a new store, a benefit performance at a theater, or selling a product are examples of fundraising possibilities that the members may be willing to undertake for an organization. Many of these kinds of projects are not possible without a volunteer group willing to help implement the event, sell the tickets and, in general, provide the support that events like this need to be successful.

Recruiting Membership Volunteers

In order to fill volunteer opportunities, there must be efforts to recruit members as volunteers. Recruitment is a primary responsibility of the members' group, but should also be augmented by staff and the institution.

Person-to-person

The participants in the members' group will know many people throughout the community. The extended networks of this group are a good starting point for recruiting others to work on the volunteer projects. The participants can ask those they know to help with specific projects. This is also a good way to work with volunteers who have the potential to be asked to become board members. Every happy volunteer is a potential recruiter for another volunteer.

Newsletter

The newsletter or other communication pieces that are sent to members should have an ad for volunteer opportunities. One project might be featured, or a satisfied volunteer highlighted. Emphasize the positive aspects of the volunteer positions.

Brochure

If there is a great need for volunteers, design a brochure that describes the opportunities in an appealing way and includes an application section that can be returned. The brochure can be used with mailings, distributed through the information desk, or sent to those who call or otherwise express an interest.

Renewal Mailings

Incorporate information on the volunteer possibilities in the renewal mailings. Include a return slip that the member can fill out and send back with his or her renewal. Follow up on any returns as quickly as possible, so that the member can be included in a current project.

Signage

If the organization has a facility, display signage that advertises the volunteer opportunities. Design the signage to make it appealing and inviting. If possible, include a brochure or return application on the signage.

Speaking Engagements

If the members' group has a speakers' bureau to provide visibility for the institution, include the volunteer options as part of the presentation. When a member is very excited about what he or she is doing for the organization, that enthusiasm is contagious and results in membership and volunteers.

VOLUNTEERING AS A CONDITION OF MEMBERSHIP

There are two types of membership programs in which volunteering is the reason to belong. The difference between them is that, in one case, the program is a part of an institution that defines services that are provided by the volunteers, while in the other, the membership organization itself determines how and where the volunteers will spend their time. (See Table 1–1 in Chapter 1 for further insight into volunteer and participant programs.)

In the first type, the membership program has the mission of providing the volunteers for the institution of which it is a part. This type of membership program exists for this reason. There may be a small membership fee, usually a flat fee. The program can be associated with any nonprofit, including hospitals, arts organizations, or other groups that need volunteers in order to provide its services. The institution is the focal point for the work and provides staffing for the group, and there is a very close working relationship between the two entities. The Heard Museum Guild (Phoenix) is a 700-member volunteer group that works in almost every facet of the museum. (The guild originally started the museum.) To be a guild member, membership

in the museum is required first, then membership in the guild. There is a dues charge for each. For this popular museum and guild, belonging to both organizations does not pose a problem.

In this type of membership program, however, there is sometimes the issue of someone who wants to volunteer for the organization but may not want to be a member of the group—for whatever reason. The group and institution need to have a way to work with these nonmember-volunteers. Possible solutions include encouraging the person to become a member, giving the person an honorary membership after a certain number of hours of volunteering, or just not worrying about it.

The issue looms large if a great number of volunteers do not want to belong, and the institution has to have yet another way to work with volunteers outside of the member-volunteer structure. Good volunteers are too valuable to let slip away because of a turf problem and institutional infighting. This situation needs to be worked out between the institution and the membership group. If it cannot be worked out to everyone's satisfaction, then the institution needs to decide how it will proceed in the future. There are times when the institution must say that its interests are such that the entire volunteer program will be redesigned. In this case, the program will then become a volunteer program integrated into the institution rather than run as a membership program.

In the second type of volunteer organization, the participant membership program, the reason to belong is to volunteer for the volunteer organization. In these organizations, volunteering is a requirement and a condition of membership, not an option. If the member does not want to volunteer, then this is not the group for him or her. This happens in organizations such as service leagues, Junior Leagues, some civic groups, and some sororities. Some groups may have an ongoing program staffed with volunteers (although there may be paid staff to help with administrative issues) who might work in a gift shop or thrift shop or hold a holiday bazaar. Others may hold a variety of events during the year, often for fundraising. In order to be a member in good standing, the member volunteers a certain number of hours or gives time in other comparable ways. The funds raised may go to the organization itself to disburse to charitable endeavors and to pay expenses; or the funds may be raised for a selected nonprofit, sometimes the same one, sometimes different ones.

Finding Volunteers

The issue for both of these types of groups is to be able to find people who want to volunteer. Times have changed. The organizations that have met the challenges of the changing volunteer world have prospered; those that have not are becoming smaller, merging with others or, in some cases, disappearing. In the past, many of these groups relied on the homemaker who was interested in volunteering. This cadre of volunteers had time, was often well educated, and virtually always female.

First and foremost, the issue is to determine the profile of the volunteer. What kinds of people does the organization want to attract as volunteers? And do the current members know where to find them? It may be that the organization has to change its definition of who can be a volunteer. All-women's groups need to decide if they want to attract men, and vice versa. An organization of older members will need to decide if it wants younger ones. The group must also decide what it is willing to do and how

much change is possible and acceptable. This discussion needs to take place during the planning phase of developing volunteer acquisition programs.

There are trends in the environment that give some answers to how to find volunteers. One answer is the retiree. Both men and women are retiring at younger ages, and looking for something meaningful to do (Putnam 2000, 131). All studies point to the fact that Americans (as well as others in the developed world) are living longer (Putnam 2000, 131). In addition, this segment of the population has "above-average wealth and relatively few demands on their time…"(Cetron and Davies 2001, 33). While this group spends time on travel and other leisure activities, there is time available for volunteer activities if they are appealing and speak to the individual's needs.

Another answer is the restructuring of the volunteer commitment. If the target group for membership is those who work, activities may have to be held at night; if the target is a parent with small children, daytime activities with day care may be the answer. If the organization wants both groups, it may have to hold activities at both times. With many retirees having second homes, being "snowbirds" by going south in the winter, or just having a lengthy stay in a second location, it is incumbent on the volunteer organizations to structure the volunteer activities to take this into consideration. Organizations in the south may find new groups of three-month volunteers; organizations in the north may have to limit their projects in the winter.

MEMBERSHIP PROGRAMS IN ALL-VOLUNTEER ORGANIZATIONS

Many small nonprofits are completely volunteer organizations. Volunteers make up the entire organization and are in charge of all programs. Can there be a membership program in an all-volunteer organization? Absolutely. In these organizations, the membership program should function exactly like one that is run by staff. Members do not necessarily know if staff or volunteers manage the program; but they know whether or not it is well run.

Guidelines for Volunteer-Run Membership Programs

Policies and Systems

It is very important to develop policies and systems for every part of the program. A written handbook should be created with all of the policies and systems in it. When one volunteer gives the responsibility of the program to another, the transition should be seamless for the members. Written guidelines go a long way to making this happen. The policies and systems include how membership funds are used, use of the membership list, directions for recordkeeping, the methods used (and their success) for acquisition, how renewals are handled, and any other information that is relevant to keeping the program running smoothly.

Keep It Simple

Time is limited in all organizations; it is especially limited in an all-volunteer organization. All parts of the program should be kept simple. New member acquisition can begin at a board or committee meeting when participants bring their address books to help put together the acquisition list. Mail renewals can be folded and stuffed at a monthly committee meeting. Phone call follow-ups can be done from the volunteers' homes on a timely basis. Recordkeeping should be limited to very basic information including name, address, telephone and fax numbers, e-mail (if the organization has this capability), amount and date of membership gift, and when the renewal effort should begin. Membership events can be created by the membership committee or by another committee within the organization.

Operating the Program

In these types of organizations, volunteers have three basic models for how to operate the program. The three are

1. Volunteer Membership Chair
2. Division of Responsibilities
3. Membership Committee

Volunteer Membership Chair. In this configuration, one volunteer commits to doing all of the work involved. The volunteer designs an acquisition program, develops materials, creates a system for recordkeeping, and sets up the renewal process. This can be a very efficient and effective method for staffing the program when the volunteer is willing to make an ongoing commitment to the work.

The acquisition program in this situation is often based on an every-member-get-a-member campaign or on a letter writing/telephone calling effort. Current members ask their friends and acquaintances to join in supporting their work. Materials may be fairly simple, giving basic information about the organization, the membership program, and how to make the donation, along with a return envelope. A recordkeeping system may begin with $4'' \times 6''$ cards in a box or with a user-friendly database system. In either case, only a minimal amount of information about members needs to be kept. Renewals should be as simple as acquisition, and much of it done with personal letters and phone calls. In a small organization, this system can work very well with that all-important personal touch.

Division of Responsibilities. If there is not one volunteer who is able to commit to the work of the membership program, the work may be divided among volunteers. One volunteer might be responsible for acquisition, another for developing the materials, another for the recordkeeping, and yet another for renewals. This can also work well as long as the group doing the work communicates frequently and the systems that are in place (e.g., how to do the recordkeeping or when renewals go out) are followed. Someone in the group or in the organization's leadership will need to make certain that the process is running smoothly.

The Friends of the Kirkwood Library (a suburb of St. Louis) is a small all volunteer group that has developed comprehensive job descriptions for roles. See Exhibit 10–5 and Exhibit 10–6 for how this organization divided the responsibilities.

Membership Committee. In many organizations, this is the preferred method. The work can be divided among a number of volunteers, the group can work together to plan the program, and brainstorming can generate new ideas for the program. The chair of the committee is responsible for leading and managing the effort, dividing the work, and making certain that it is performed in a timely manner. Having committees is a tried and true method for volunteer organizations

Exhibit 10–5 Job Description: Volunteer Membership Chair

Friends of the Kirkwood Public Library
Volunteer Membership Chair
Job Description

Duties are:

1. To create, write, and mail membership renewal letters.
2. To create, write, and mail renewal thank-you letters.
3. To create, write, and mail late follow-up letters.
4. To create, write, and mail new member welcome letters.
5. To maintain membership files.
6. To maintain membership list and provide updated lists for Greentree Books volunteer handbook, board members, FKL liaison, and files.
7. To provide names of volunteers to appropriate chairpersons.
8. To provide names of new members to Newsletter Editor for each issue.
9. To maintain membership labels.
10. To create, write, and mail contributor letters and thank-you letters including matching gift correspondence.
11. To purchase postage and supplies and arrange for copying as needed.
12. To develop and provide membership analysis twice a year to FKL Board.
13. To track membership expenses and provide cost projections to Budget Committee.
14. To lead and implement long-range membership development effort.
15. To serve as chair of the Membership Committee.

Courtesy of Friends of the Kirkwood Public Library, Kirkwood, Missouri.

to involve their members. While the meetings take time and add a level of input into the program, they also provide a way for members to feel a part of the organization and to become closer to it. This involvement is crucial to the long-term building of the organization and its donor base.

The committee structure should include a chair (or co-chairs, if one volunteer does not want to do this alone) and three to six committee members. If there are not many who are able to participate, three plus the chair will give some diversity of views and help with the work. Six committee members, along with the chair(s), provide enough people to do the work and have good discussions, and not so many that it becomes unwieldy for the chair(s) to communicate and effectively use everyone's time.

Having a membership committee also creates a larger group with a commitment to the program. A strong committee will have more community connections for acquisition, more time to make the personal calls for renewals, and more of a sense of camaraderie that will help move the program forward.

For organizations that remain small (a local hobby group, for example), the program may always be a volunteer effort. For a growing program, however, at some point the workload requires too large a time commitment for the volunteer corps. This becomes the occasion to hire paid

---

Exhibit 10–6 Job Description: Volunteer Database Manager

Friends of the Kirkwood Public Library
Database Manager
Job Description

Duties are:
1. Maintain membership and Book Fair databases, which are both on Microsoft Access.
2. Receive updates from membership chairperson (approximately monthly) and update membership database accordingly.
3. Receive updates from Book Fair Chairperson (approximately biannually) and update Book Fair database accordingly.
4. Provide newsletter editor with listings of new members for publication in newsletter.
5. Generate reports:
    A. Monthly report to membership chairperson for monthly membership renewal letters.
    B. Full membership report to membership chairperson as requested (approximately several times a year).
    C. Board members' reports printed and distributed at February meeting and August meeting.
    D. Generate other reports on an ad hoc basis as requested by officers and board members.
6. Generate mailing labels:
    A. Four times a year for newsletter mailings.
    B. Once or twice a year for Book Fair.
    C. As requested for other mailings (membership drives, etc.).

Courtesy of Friends of the Kirkwood Public Library, Kirkwood, Missouri.

staff to provide the day-to-day operation of the membership program. Often the first hire is someone who can take on the tasks of recordkeeping, maintaining the list (database), and working on the renewal program. The volunteers may keep the task of acquisition, with staff helping to send mailings, print materials, and work on all the other pieces that go into the basic program. Events and other member-related programs remain as tasks for the volunteers. The volunteers will also continue to determine the direction for the program, develop policies, supervise systems changes, and, in general, keep an eye on the program.

How Organizations Have Adapted

Organizations have adapted in a variety of ways. Those that have changed have responded by enlisting members from a broader range of ages, including recruiting retirees. They have moved from being totally or predominately female to signing up both men and women. They have looked at hiring staff for those tasks that volunteers are no longer interested in and those for which volunteers cannot make the full-time commitment to accomplish. They have looked at how they do business, adding or moving meetings to evenings rather than daytime, and thus, not automatically eliminating most of those who work. They have divided tasks so that someone in the workforce would have time to do them and contribute to the organization. They have added or enhanced programs so that they appeal to a larger group of potential member-volunteers. The successful membership organizations in this category have learned and acted on the premise that to add and keep members, change must occur.

VOLUNTEERS WHO ARE NOT MEMBERS

Many organizations have volunteers who are not members. The organization might be a museum or a hospital with a very large volunteer program. The volunteer might be someone who wants to work for the organization, but for whatever reason has no interest in joining the membership program. Because volunteers throughout the institution might or might not be members, the membership program should solicit the volunteer corps first for memberships. Who better to want to support the institution than those who know it well? The volunteer corps should be considered a pool of prospective members. The membership program is a good way to bring the volunteers into the donor base of the organization. While some say that this is an imposition, that the volunteers are already giving their time, the reality is that most will understand that the institution also needs money in order to operate. This is not meant to be a pressured approach, but rather giving the volunteers an opportunity to help support the work that they know so well.

Another way to attract more volunteer-members is to give volunteers who donate a certain amount of time a membership in recognition of their hard work. For example, the volunteer program might use a basic level membership as a gift for those who give at least 100 hours a year, with higher-level memberships for those who give even more time. Those who are given a membership might still be solicited for a second annual gift. The Association of Fundraising Professionals (AFP) states, "volunteers give more than twice the percentage of income as those who contribute, but do not volunteer" (AFP 2000, A-10).

The two concerns that are addressed by these approaches are including the volunteers in the donor base and making certain that they are on the mailing list for information about the organization. As fund-raising theory maintains, involvement leads to greater and greater support of an organization. In addition, keeping volunteers well-informed increases their knowledge about the organization and their ability to serve.

THE VOLUNTEER DEPARTMENT

The institution's volunteer program may be located in any of a number of organizational departments: sometimes it resides in the membership program, sometimes in human resources, sometimes as a stand-alone department, or sometimes in another configuration. The membership department is not the best choice for the volunteer program. While some members will be volunteers and some volunteers will be members, the two groups have different goals, particularly in those institutions where membership serves as the basis for the fundraising program. The two areas should communicate and work cooperatively, but maintaining a vibrant volunteer program for an institution is very different than maintaining the membership program.

REFERENCES

Association of Fundraising Professionals. 2000. *AFP first course in fundraising: Building the future of philanthropy.* Alexandria, VA.

Cetron, M. J., and O. Davies. 2001. Trends now changing the world: Economics and society, values and concerns, energy and environment. *The Futurist,* January–February, 30–43.

Putnam, R.D. 2000. *Bowling alone: The collapse and revival of American community.* New York: Simon & Schuster.

CHAPTER 11

Leadership, Management, and Staff

Patricia Rich and Dana Hines

There are three kinds of people: those who make things happen, those who watch what happened, and those who wonder what happened.

—Unknown

LEADERSHIP AND MANAGEMENT

MEMBERSHIP PROGRAMS WITH STRONG leadership and management make things happen. They are proactive rather than reactive; they try new and different activities while keeping the successful ones fresh. Effective leadership and management are the hallmarks of successful membership programs. Who provides that leadership and management in a membership program? As with almost everything involved in a membership program, there are a variety of answers. The answers are interwoven with the type of membership program, the founders, the strength of volunteer involvement, the quality of staff, and the role the membership and membership program play within the total organization.

In a large institution with a strong membership program, leadership may come from the members' board and management from staff. In a large, staff-driven organization, staff may provide both. In a small, participatory or volunteer organization, leadership and management will both come from the members.

Leadership shows itself during the planning process for the membership program, where those who have a vision for the organization make it known. It shows itself in the willingness of staff or volunteers to take on projects, persuade others to participate, and implement them successfully. Effective management makes certain that goals are set and met, that day-to-day operations of the program run smoothly, and that the members are well served.

STAGES IN THE GROWTH OF MEMBERSHIP PROGRAMS

Typically, a membership program will start small, and many will stay small. The support group for a library in a small town will never be very large. On the other hand, Mothers Against Drunk Driving (MADD) is a good example of a small group that grew very large. Started by several women in California when they were angered about a drunk driver who had killed a child, it has now grown to many thousands of members and 600 chapters across the country.

There are four stages that a growing program will go through, although a program might always remain at any one stage, or, if there are problems, return to a prior stage. We are calling the stages initiation, growth, expansion, and comprehensive. The descriptions below are meant as a general guide describing what happens in programs. Most organizations will reflect parts of more than one stage. Every organization will evolve differently and at its own speed. The only constant is that all programs will change over time.

Stage 1: Initiation

Someone has to initiate the program. That person is the founder, and most often a volunteer. Sometimes there is a group of founders, the founding members, though usually only one or a few consider themselves the founders. Founders have a special pride in what they have accomplished, as they should. They had the vision to begin the program, implement its first activities, and watch it begin to prosper. Many founders work tirelessly, giving of themselves with time as well as finances. They bring together their friends, family, and colleagues to support the cause. For some, it is their life's work.

The initiation stage revolves around the founders. These are the people who are leading the group. One is the president of the group. The founders will continue to help in leadership roles, sometimes in a leadership position, sometimes behind the scenes; they are the ones who provide the glue that keeps the group together. At some point, this structure isn't enough. Typically, the program will begin to grow. Membership acquisition increases slowly but surely. Programs are developed for the members. There is a newsletter. The group is now up and running and there is an active, vital program.

Difficulties begin when there is more work than the group can manage on its own. This is often linked to growth in numbers and the ability to process the membership applications and serve the members in a timely and efficient way. It may also be related to the ability to have a presence and to be able to answer members' inquiries by phone, fax, or e-mail. This time comes when the organization has between 500 and 1,000 members. By the 1,000-member level, some staff becomes essential unless there is the luxury of consistent, ongoing volunteer staffing. The tasks that need to be done must be done in a timely manner to keep the program running smoothly and keep members satisfied with the level of service they are receiving.

Stage 2: Growth

This is a major step in the membership program's evolution. The program has begun to be institutionalized, and the active members share the work and power. This is point at which the founders know that they can't do it all by themselves, and there is considerable delegation of tasks.

The greatest rite of passage is that the organization has to hire paid staff. The management of the membership program has become too large a task for volunteers. The institution has made the commitment to the program and is willing to fund it. As the numbers increase, the processing becomes more and more burdensome. It is important to keep donor records, do the financial bookkeeping, issue membership cards, issue tax-related information if necessary, send out renewals on a timely basis, conduct acquisition programs, produce events, and more.

Hiring staff is a large commitment, both of time and money. Time is necessary to train the person, making sure that he or she understands the program and what needs to be done. While a new membership manager will be learning and able to help from the day of hire, it will take a full calendar year for him or her to be conversant with all of the operations of the membership program. This position, sometimes titled the membership coordinator or membership assistant, is a jack-of-all-trades with the staff, doing data processing as well as working on events. If part of an institution, the mem-

bership program becomes more integrated into the institution when the staff arrives since there is someone available at all times.

At this point in the evolution, it is important for the volunteers to stay involved at a very high level. Hiring one person will not take the place of myriad volunteers who believe in and are passionate about the program. With staff, however, the program can be more persistent with acquisition and renewals, and provide better customer service to the membership. Many of the tasks of the membership program can be delegated to the staff member.

Stage 3: Expansion

With everything running smoothly, the volunteers and staff may decide that it is time to drive growth more, add more programs and, in general, expand what the program offers. It may take more paid staff to implement the activities. An assistant for the membership manager may be the next person hired in order to help with inquiries, some processing duties, and other tasks. With membership growth, by the time the numbers reach 4,000, it is time to add a full-time data processing staff member. This will free the membership coordinator's or assistant's time from the processing tasks to concentrate on other projects. The membership coordinator or assistant may be elevated to manager status. That person has now become the full-time manager of the program and may also be providing some of the leadership.

At this stage, acquisition and renewal efforts become very aggressive and may increase with a phonathon and on-site sales. The membership software may become more sophisticated, with the ability to track all acquisition and renewal efforts. A membership survey may be instituted. A Web site might be started or a membership page added to the institution's Web site. A small fundraiser may be held. New people are included in leadership positions. In all, the program is becoming institutionalized, with systems in place, and day-to-day operations moving at a healthy pace.

Stage 4: Comprehensive

This is a fully mature program, staffed with a number of paid people, all dedicated to serving the membership and its volunteer activities. With growth, one data processing person is needed for approximately every 7,500 members. By the time the total reaches 15,000, there will probably also be a need for part- or full-time supervision of the computer operation, including reporting and supervising the data entry personnel. The membership manager manages and works in partnership with the volunteers to provide leadership for the membership program. More staff may be added to handle additional projects, including a large fundraiser, a membership month of activities, or a membership desk in a visitation-based institution.

Other membership programs may be added, such as Internet memberships or special interest groups. More complicated benefits may be negotiated, such as travel, insurance, or concierge service. The Web site is enlarged and upgraded. An upper-level membership solicitation program is added. The volunteers have become an integral part of the institution, and their contributions of time, energy and money are greatly appreciated. The program is fully institutionalized, not dependent on any one person or group, and there is a guarantee that it will continue into the future.

As the program matures during this comprehensive stage, the membership manager

position is again upgraded to membership director.

RELATIONSHIP BETWEEN STAFF AND VOLUNTEERS

There may be tension between paid staff and volunteers in any organization. In the membership program, where often the volunteers have created the program and there is a sense that it is "their program," this feeling may be very strong. The vast majority of membership programs are either volunteer-run or have a volunteer component, and many have, or will have, paid staff if growth occurs. The issue is the volunteer time available. By the time a group reaches a critical mass of 1,000 or more members, staff becomes essential. The relationship between staff and volunteers is one that must be managed carefully and carried out thoughtfully by both the staff member and volunteers.

At some point—and this is the point at which issues arise—the program becomes managed much more by staff than by volunteers. In addition, activities that may be valued by volunteers can no longer be handled in the same way because of the size of the program. For example, the personal touch of hand addressing invitations to a members-only event or providing homemade refreshments may no longer be possible with thousands of invitations to send and hundreds of people to feed. There is a loss. The loss is that of the personal touch and of the feeling among the volunteers that their work is valued. Many will also feel that they have lost control of a program that they may have created. This feeling of loss needs to be overcome with a bright vision for the future, interesting volunteer activities that work to increase the personal touch (for example, having greeters and hosts at events, calling new members), and a staff that meshes well with the volunteer workers.

If this is an institution deciding to add staff to the program, and there was a founder involved who is still present, it is important to enlist his or her help and understanding. There are times when the strength of the founder is such that the program belongs to him or her; he or she wants to manage it with help from friends, and staff is not welcome. It is important for the founder to understand that the management of the program needs to grow with the program. When programming develops and the management side does not, there can be problems of service for the members and difficulty in keeping the processing running smoothly, and the volunteers can become overwhelmed. When this occurs, the program is suffering from what has been called "founder flounder." Much as a business entrepreneur provides the vision and the passion to begin a company and then needs managers to take it to the next level, the developing membership program has the same growing pains.

When staff is added, there are several possible outcomes. No matter how well the situation is handled by the staff, there may well be some volunteers who feel that they are no longer needed and will decide to volunteer elsewhere. While this isn't what an organization wants, the priority becomes managing the program well, and that will include a staff component. If not handled well, the program may lose all of its volunteers, which is not a desirable outcome. It is vital for the leadership of the organization to work with the volunteers to make certain that there is a smooth transition. It is also essential that the staff are people who have excellent interpersonal skills. The mandate for the staff is to involve and include the volunteers as much as possible and in as many activities as possible.

From the staff viewpoint, involving volunteers increases the amount of time that an activity takes. For example, it may well take the membership manager longer to coordinate a volunteer group to hand address invitations than to print and affix computer labels; however, there will be instances when working with the volunteers on this project is time well spent. The volunteers who are involved in the hand addressing will make certain to ask their friends and colleagues to attend the event. They now have a stake in it. The same is true with organizing events. The membership manager can organize an event fairly quickly; however, volunteer involvement is often essential in order to guarantee an audience. It is necessary for the membership manager to make certain that volunteers are involved in an appropriate way wherever possible.

On the volunteer side, those volunteers who are not happy about the addition of staff have two choices: they may find a different organization with which to work, or they may partner with the membership manager and work together. The point is that the volunteer must make the decision; it is not helpful to anyone to have an irritated volunteer involved who participates by grumbling. When this happens, the volunteer leadership needs to speak with the unhappy volunteer and resolve the situation in as pleasant a way as possible.

For staff and volunteers to work together in harmony takes work on both sides. There needs to be mutual respect, a delineation of roles, and the commitment of all to work for the organization together. When this partnership works well, the membership program and the organization will flourish. If it is not working well, the staff and volunteer leadership need to sit down and talk through the situation to resolve it. The challenge is for staff and volunteers to become a team to carry out the work of the membership program.

STAFFING THE MEMBERSHIP PROGRAM

Tasks

There are numerous tasks in the membership program that need attention. It is irrelevant whether the membership manager or the volunteers accomplish the tasks; they just need to be accomplished. The tasks run the gamut from keeping records to developing and implementing events to developing the long-range plans for the membership program. Each of these tasks can be done at a minimal, basic level or at a very high, sophisticated level. All of them should be done at the basic level to keep the program running smoothly and effectively. As the program progresses through its stages of evolution, more of the tasks will be done in a sophisticated and comprehensive manner. Below is a recommendation for the amount of time to be spent on each of the major tasks.

Time and Effort

The time suggested is a percentage of the effort spent on the program by the membership manager, assuming the entire program takes 100 percent. It is not necessarily related to the importance of the task, because some tasks just take longer than others, even though they might be less important. For example, acquisition is the most important task for any program because bringing in new members is imperative; however, a program may well spend more time on events because they are extremely time consuming, and the acquisition is contracted out to a direct mail professional. Furthermore, the time spent will vary depending on the day, week, or month. Juggling and setting priorities become important skills. And, of course, there is overlap between the activities. For example, an event might be planned for acquisition, or volunteer coordination may be needed for planning. Look at the time suggested with these caveats. The times suggested are guidelines based on experience.

1. Acquisition: Regardless of the type of acquisition program, it must be planned and implemented. This task also includes planning the benefits for the program. *Time: 15 percent*
2. Renewals: There must be a schedule for renewals. They must be sent in a timely manner with as much follow-up (letter and telephone) as possible. *Time: 10 percent*
3. Processing and recordkeeping: Someone must process the membership applications and keep the records of who joined when, membership level, and information such as addresses and telephone numbers. Processing may include sending a welcome letter, a membership card, and a list of benefits. The recordkeeping may be a 4″ × 6″ card file or on a computer with sophisticated software; how it is done depends on the organization and the size of the membership. If memberships cannot be processed in a timely manner and the records kept with accuracy, there is a real question about whether or not there should be a program. This task also includes providing monthly reports on new members, renewals, and upgrades. *Time: 10 percent*
4. Member services: Members need someone to call. If a membership card is lost, information wanted about an event, or an RSVP required, there needs to be someone who can answer the questions and provide the information and service. *Time: 10 percent*

5. Communications: Where the membership program is a part of the larger organization, another department may handle this. In this case, the membership program needs to coordinate with the other department so that the appropriate communications vehicles have membership information. When the membership program is the organization, one of the largest tasks is handling the communications with the membership. *Time: 15 percent*

6. Activities and programs: At a minimum, there should be three to four events and/or programs a year planned for members only. They can be as easy as a lecture or as complicated as a major fair. There may also be events that the volunteers want to plan for the public. Additionally, there may be interest in having the membership volunteer's work on fundraisers for the organization. *Time: 20 percent*

7. Coordinating volunteer activities: For a program with an active volunteer component, the membership manager is often called on to coordinate the volunteer work. This can be very time consuming, but it is very important to have the volunteer corps involved; they give enormous amounts of time and energy. *Time: 15 percent*

8. Planning: Every year an operational plan based on the program's strategic plan must be developed. This includes planning all of the work for the year, the budget, and the calendar. At least every three years, the organization should take a look at the program to determine if any strategic changes are necessary. With a plan, small changes can be made at any time. Strategic changes are major changes, such as beginning direct mail acquisition when there has been none, increasing the number and type of communications, or deciding to appeal to a new market segment with a new acquisition program, events and services. *Time: 5 percent*

9. Other: There are myriad other tasks that can be a part of the program. These include tasks such as market research, travel programs, interest groups, or Internet programs. Time: *whatever is left*

Possible Staff Configurations

Programs that add staff usually do it slowly but surely. The following configurations will give some idea of what can be accomplished by adding staff. Size of the membership and the amount of volunteer help available are the two variables that make the greatest difference in what can be accomplished by staffing. The configurations are meant as a guideline; each program needs to decide for itself how to succeed at the work at hand. A general but loose rule of thumb for staffing is one staff member for every 5000 members and one full-time data entry person for every 7500 members. This "rule of thumb" will vary depending on the use of volunteers, staff assignments and responsibilities, and size of the parent organization.

1. A very part-time staff person: When a small program reaches the point that it needs help with recordkeeping, renewals, and mailings, a very part-time staff person can be a great help. With this type of staffing, the volunteer responsible for membership would have the tasks planned so that the staff person could accomplish them in the limited time available.

2. One half-time staff: This might be some of the time of the development director or the public relations staff person, or it might be a half-time membership manager. Volunteer coordination, recordkeeping, part of the acquisition and renewal work, and some member service would be the first tasks for a new staff person.

3. One full-time equivalent: All of the tasks could be tackled at the levels suggested above. Exhibit 11–1 outlines the job duties.

4. Two full-time staff: One staff person would be assigned the acquisition, renewal, recordkeeping, and member service tasks. The other would be responsible for the communications, volunteer coordination, events, and planning tasks.

5. Three full-time staff: By this time, the program would be large and require a full-time person working on recordkeeping, renewals, and member services. The other duties would be divided between the other two staff. The director of membership would have supervisory responsibilities by this time. Exhibit 11–2 lists the various responsibilities of the director of membership, large program.

6. Four full-time staff: At this stage, one staff person might be totally committed to working with the volunteers and events. Two might be assigned to the recordkeeping, renewals, and services. One of the recordkeeping staff (by now data processing) would be the supervisor of this area.

7. More staff: As time goes by and the program becomes larger, more time must be spent on data processing, reports, and analysis. More members require more events and communica-

tions to reach the different segments of the membership. Additional programs, such as interest groups, can be added. The sky's the limit. Two sample organizational charts involving membership are shown in Figure 11–1 and Figure 11–2.

In both of these charts, the membership department is a part of the development effort. The major difference is who is in charge of information services, which is the information technology (IT) staff. In Figure 11–1, membership staffing chart #1, the manager of development information services department is listed and is responsible for carrying out recordkeeping, including the data processing and reports for membership and development. In Figure 11–2, membership staffing chart #2, this person is at a higher level, meaning they play a larger role in developing reports and research methods for membership, development, the capital campaign, and other development and visitor services needs. On both charts, no matter their position on the chart, the events coordinator is responsible for member and donor events and the membership service staff person is responsible for phone calls and dealing with member issues. The on-site sales assistant may be full-time or part-time. There are, of course, many ways to design the organizational chart for membership.

Hiring Staff

The first effort in hiring staff is to develop a position description that outlines the responsibilities of the staff person (Exhibit 11–1 and Exhibit 11–2). The volunteer group can do this in conjunction with the current staff person responsible. If this is the time when the volunteer-founded membership program is first hir-

Exhibit 11–1 Membership Manager Job Description, Small Program

Job title:	Membership Manager
Reports to:	Executive Director
Results Expected:	That the ABC Center's membership program grows to support the Center's work and mission.
Job Duties:	1. Develop plans to increase the membership.
	2. Create and implement acquisition, renewal, and upgrade programs.
	3. Develop at least three activities for the membership during the year.
	4. Write a membership article for each newsletter.
	5. Keep the membership database up-to-date.
	6. Generate labels for mailings as requested.
	7. Coordinate membership bulk mailings as necessary.
	8. Prepare monthly reports for board meetings.
	9. Staff the volunteer membership committee.
	10. Provide services needed by members.
	11. Develop the membership budget.
Qualifications:	1. College degree or equivalent experience.
	2. Ability to work with diverse groups of people.
	3. Ability to develop and analyze membership numbers and reports.
	4. Ability to budget.
	5. Organizational skills.

Exhibit 11–2 Director of Membership Job Description, Large Program

Job title:	Director of Membership
Reports to:	Development Director
Results Expected:	That the XYZ Museum's membership program builds a constituency for the Museum's mission and increases income for the Museum's work.
Supervisory Responsibility:	This position supervises two data entry personnel and one assistant, and works cooperatively with other development staff.
Responsibilities:	1. Membership Strategy
	a. Work with development director and volunteers to determine strategies for program.
	b. Design and implement acquisition efforts including direct mail, on-site sales, and membership desk.
	c. Design and implement renewal upgrade efforts including direct mail and telemarketing.
	d. Develop and implement a support level membership campaign.
	e. Design any needed membership materials.

continues

Exhibit 11–2 continued

     f. Staff the volunteer membership committee and organization.

     g. Create and implement membership activities with the membership organization.

     h. Work with the newsletter editor to include membership information in each issue.

     i. Represent membership within the institution.

     j. Make certain that the membership office provides needed services to members.

2. Database Work

     a. Supervise data entry staff.

     b. Stay up-to-date on the processing software.

     c. Develop reports for membership organization and board on a monthly basis.

     d. Analyze reports and relate them to the annual plan.

     e. Train data entry staff on membership service.

3. Development

     a. Work with development director to find sponsorships for membership activities and needs.

     b. Write grants as necessary for the membership program.

     c. Coordinate fundraising efforts to membership with development director.

     d. Produce membership portion of the budget for development.

Qualifications:

1. College degree or equivalent experience.
2. Five years of membership or related experience.
3. Supervisory experience.
4. Experience working with vendors of services such as direct mail.
5. Ability to work closely with volunteers.
6. Ability to develop and analyze membership numbers and reports.
7. Ability to budget.
8. Organizational skills.

ing staff, the volunteers should be directly involved. Since it is some of their work that will go to the staff person, they should determine which tasks to move to staff. The position description should include specific tasks for which the new person will be responsible, to whom he or she reports, and any results that are expected. If the membership program has a plan, the goals and objectives in the plan should be discussed with the potential new staff person so that he or she has an idea of what is expected.

Those involved in the hiring need to determine the skills needed. The position description will make clear the required skills. If work on a computer is necessary, then computer skills are essential. Computer skills can include word processing, database management, and spreadsheet work for reports. Determine which skills are necessities and which can be learned. Some-

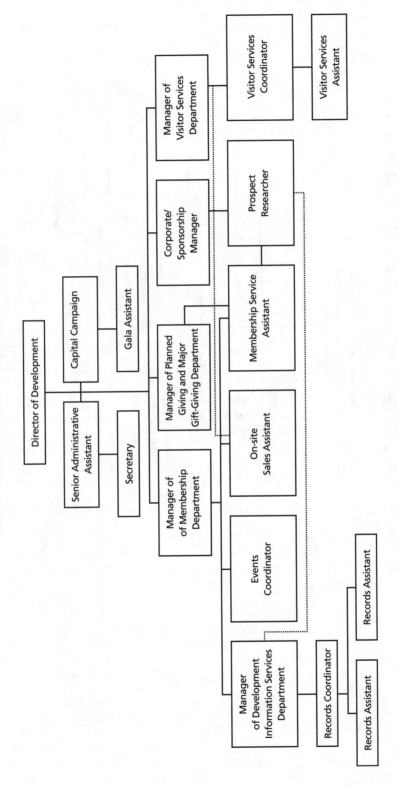

SCENARIO #1 – DEVELOPMENT GROUP

Figure 11–1 Membership Staffing Chart #1: Development Group

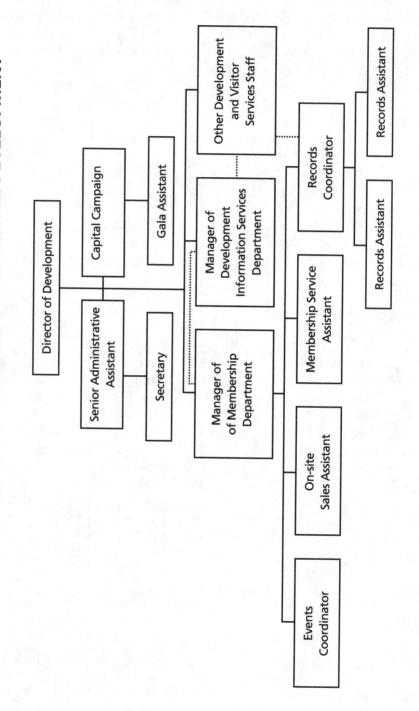

SCENARIO #2 – MEMBERS GROUP WITHIN DEVELOPMENT

Figure 11–2 Membership Staffing Chart #2: Membership Group within Development

one who is conversant with computers can be sent to training on membership software. Other skills and abilities will include being able to juggle a number of tasks at the same time, enough math to be able to develop and read reports, and writing skills for letters and reports.

As important as skills are the personality traits of the person to be hired. He or she must have excellent interpersonal abilities. These are the traits that enable a person to work well with others. Membership is about working with other staff, volunteers, and the members. The appropriate person will enjoy working with people and know how to do it skillfully. It's also always good to have someone who is cheerful and enthusiastic about the organization and its mission.

Finding the person who is the right fit for the organization can take some time. Look in all the usual places, including the volunteer and member ranks of the organization. Someone who is already a volunteer or member knows about the organization and has already made a voluntary commitment to it. It is sometimes difficult to make the transition from volunteer to staff, but it is often done very successfully. If the person is the right fit, consider it. Other usual places include advertising in the newspaper, placing the position opening in the appropriate place on the institution's Web site, and networking with groups in the community to find out who might be available. It often can take up to three months or more from beginning the search to having someone in place.

Staff Orientation

Once the person is in place, it will take time to train him or her. If it is necessary to train the person on the database, take the time and money to do it; it will pay rewards in the future. If the person has never worked in membership before, consider sending him or her to a seminar on membership programs; two days at a seminar will shorten the learning curve considerably. It takes one calendar year for anyone to be completely familiar with a job. This is because so many activities are calendar dependent. It is necessary for the person to experience the ebb and flow of membership over the course of a year in order to understand the position.

Staff Evaluation

The new staff person should be evaluated at the end of a probationary period, often three months. This is the time at which the person can be terminated if it is determined that he or she is not the right fit for the organization. Assuming that all is well, the next evaluation will be at the end of the first year. Every organization should have some form of performance appraisal to evaluate the employee.

Once the membership manager has become a part of the membership team, it is important for him or her to establish personal objectives based on the membership plan. The membership manager and his or her supervisor should agree on what the membership manager needs to accomplish. This process becomes an ongoing activity.

When to Increase Staff

As the program grows in numbers and activities, the time comes to add more staff. In the data processing area, a new staff person is needed with each addition of 7,500 members. In activities, it will depend on the amount of volunteer help and extent of the programs. Large public events and fundraisers may signal the need for additional help.

The need for more staff is often a signal that it is time to review the plan for the membership program. The plan will detail the work for the year and allows the current staff and volunteers to decide what is needed. This is very much an individual situation, with each organization needing to find its own level of staffing for what it wants to accomplish, as shown in the membership plan.

CHAPTER 12

Membership and the Internet

Patricia Rich and Dana Hines

Any sufficiently advanced technology is indistinguishable from magic.
—Arthur C. Clarke

THE INTERNET IS REVOLUTIONIZING the world. It is making instant access, instant information, and instant decisions possible for all who use it. It is like magic. *Membership programs have the potential of being revolutionized by the Internet as well.*

The backbone of a membership program is its activities directed at servicing and retaining its members. The Internet provides a whole host of means by which an organization may add a new layer of service for its members. The Internet also provides a way to enlist new members and donors and a source for prospects. Many organizations are concerned with the aging of their donor base, and the Internet is capable of supplying new audiences that are younger and not necessarily tied into older, traditional ways of engaging audiences. Thus, the Internet just may provide a new means for gaining new audiences in a way not previously possible.

This Chapter will address the current state of membership's use of the Internet and the possible uses by a membership office, and present some case studies of how some membership organizations are using the Internet to attract, service, and communicate with their members.

AN ADDITION, NOT A SUBSTITUTION

The Internet and the services and features that it provides should be an addition to current ways of delivering services and of attracting members, not a substitution. The Internet should complement existing face-to-face, telephone, and mail activities.

In terms of providing services and information to existing members, the membership manager needs to continue to manage programs with mailed newsletters and invitations, but there are additional services that can be provided online to supplement printed and mailed communications. While many members will still want personalized service from organizations, whether face-to-face or via the telephone, the Internet may be one way of answering questions that others will prefer to use. The same is true of acquiring new members. There are people who have suggested that the Internet would be the end of direct mail for membership acquisition; however, this is not likely to be the case any time in the foreseeable future. Prospective members will still require that the idea of membership be suggested to them, usually by an invitation, either in person or via direct mail. To date, direct e-mail to audiences without some prior connection to the organization has not been successful.

WHAT IS POSSIBLE?

The possibilities may be endless for e-commerce, but here are the features that membership managers should strongly consider for online capability:

- To acquire and renew members—via a secure transaction page
- To communicate with members—via online newsletters and group e-mails to members
- To increase participation—using e-mails and online invitations
- To service members—using members-only access pages

EARLY IMPACT OF THE WEB ON FUNDRAISING

It is important to understand the current situation with regard to the Web. Although the Web has monopolized attention recently, the economic impact is really quite small: $1 of every $100 raised is being raised over the Internet (Rick Christ, www.rickchrist.com).

That said, there is a lot of money being donated via the Web: 3.5 million donors gave $192 million to nonprofits (DMA Nonprofit Council Annual Conference, 2001) in 1999, with an average gift of $55 (just the right amount for a membership program). In the for-profit world, there were $5 billion in sales in the fourth quarter of 1999, and yet this was only 0.6 percent of all retail sales (Rick Christ, www.rickchrist.com).

There are already some strong online giving records for nonprofits. Listed below are the amounts raised online by some of the largest and most far-reaching of the nonprofits. Note that the amounts shown are donations, not necessarily memberships (except the amount shown for WAMU, which represents all memberships). Clearly, these are organizations with large budgets and the capacity for developing online giving capabilities (Rick Christ, www.rickchrist.com):

- The American Red Cross: raised $1.2 million in the first six months of 1999 for the Kosovo crisis.

- The Heifer Project: raised $1 million dollars in 1999—a sixfold increase from 1998.
- WAMU (public radio in Washington, DC): raised $227,000 in one day of its online/on-air campaign and suspended its on-air campaign for a day.
- Woodland Park Zoo (Seattle): has sold about 100 memberships online per month since October 1999.

Of course since September 11, 2001, online giving has skyrocketed to phenomenol levels—at least to relief agencies serving the families of victims and rescue workers.

STATE OF THE MEMBERSHIP

The holiday season in 1999 was the first time that a Web address and shopping online was promoted in practically every television ad. Larger membership organizations, such as alumni groups and one of the leaders in the museum world, the Metropolitan Museum of Art, had e-commerce capabilities at that time. But most membership programs have been developing online capabilities at a slower pace, with many still in the process of finding ways of making the Internet work for them.

Surveys conducted by Membership Consultants, Inc., one each in 2000 and 2001, illustrate the rate at which two segments of the membership arena are embracing e-commerce capabilities.

In the fall of 2000, 36 zoo and aquaria Web sites were surveyed for their ability to allow prospective or current members to join online with a secure Web transaction page. The results were that 8 of 36 sites allowed for a secure transaction to take place. The remainder required downloading a form to mail or fax, or simply asked the prospect to call the membership office during office hours to join or renew—definitely not new ways of doing business. Of those zoos and aquaria surveyed, the size of the institution and the budget had no bearing on whether it had secure online capabilities. Larger organizations were surprisingly lacking in the online capabilities, and some very small zoos had surprisingly sophisticated capabilities.

In March 2001, Membership Consultants conducted a survey of art museums. In this case, size and budget did matter, as well as position and order of listing on Web engine searches. Larger organizations were more likely to have secure online e-commerce capabilities. In this survey, 12 of 30 sites surveyed had online giving or joining capabilities. This 40 percent rate was higher than the zoo percentage six months prior, but clearly, the majority of small to midsized membership organizations are still working on their online capabilities.

Larger membership organizations have an advantage. In some cases, with memberships in the 100,000-member range or larger, portal services are available and designed to look like the organization has developed a full range of online membership capabilities just for its members. The best example is alumni organizations. With large memberships and an even greater pool of very targeted prospects, alumni associations have the advantage of being able to attract some Internet portal service providers who will design and service their sites for free, just for access to this very large, highly educated, and presumably high-income audience for advertising purposes. Hence, alumni associations have the ability to sign with a service provider and have a site immediately available to their members, and all they have to provide is content for the site that relates to their program. The size of membership organization required is approximately 100,000 members. Others can buy into these services, but at a very high price.

SECURE TRANSACTION PAGES

The ability to provide a secure transaction page is the first priority for an organization that wants to be able to transact membership purchases online. The "s" in the "https" at the top of a Web address indicates that the membership transaction form is on a secure site designed for e-commerce. With such a secure page, prospective members can transmit their membership applications and credit card numbers with relative comfort, knowing that the site is protected. Such sites are protected by firewalls that are designed to make the information contained therein secure via encryption. It provides an accepted level of security for online transactions that exceeds the level of security of general Web sites.

People who are accustomed to transacting business online—buying stocks, making online store purchases, or performing banking transactions—expect this level of security. It is a level of security that membership organizations must provide if they want to be part of the e-commerce community and that members using e-commerce capabilities expect from their membership organizations. Membership programs that want to be a part of this new world of the Internet must, at a minimum, make secure transactions possible for new and renewing members.

These secure transactions pages may be provided in a variety of ways. Table 12–1 graphically represents the four choices:

1. in-house construction
2. outsourced construction and off-site hosting
3. e-charity portals
4. Net Solutions® via Blackbaud's Raiser's Edge database software

In-house Construction and Maintenance

As with many operations in membership, there is often the philosophy or need to do membership work in-house. As programs grow, organizations often realize that it is not always cost effective to do everything in-house. Doing projects using in-house staff, which was once presumed to be less costly than outsourcing, may no longer be economically feasible—nor time efficient either. This

Table 12–1 The Pros and Cons of E-Commerce Solutions for Membership

Item to Consider	Choice of Solution			
	In-house	Outsourced	Portals	Net Solutions
Hardware	−	+	+	−
Software	−	+	+	−
In-house Expertise	−	+	+	+
Cost	+	−	−	−
Flexibility	+	+	−	−/+
Development Time	−	+	+	+
Interconnectivity	+	+	−	+

can be true for direct mail campaigns for acquisition, graphics production, telemarketing, and now e-commerce capabilities. Each organization must weigh time, money, and staff capabilities to determine what is possible.

An organization may elect to construct its own Web site to ensure that design standards are consistent or content is current. The same rules may not apply to e-commerce capabilities. To construct an e-commerce site or page requires the purchase of additional servers and software, and the organization must possess the expertise necessary to build firewalls to protect the sensitive information being transmitted. Also, the time required for an information technology (IT) professional, who may be responsible for an institution's entire technology needs, to learn and construct an e-commerce site, may be less than an optimal use of resources. However, if this route is chosen, the organization will have the utmost in control of its site and its capabilities.

Outsourced Construction and Off-Site Hosting

Outsourcing the construction and hosting of an e-commerce site may make the most sense for many small to medium-sized organizations with limited, or nonexistent, IT staff in-house. An e-commerce site can take as little as two weeks to construct, and much of the time used is dependent on content and approvals from the membership manager and organization. If in-house resources cannot produce a site that is up and running in a timely manner, then the site should be outsourced. The best scenario is to have the site constructed and hosted by a vendor, with the in-house staff trained to make minor changes to the site as needed. A membership transaction page can be designed fairly reasonably and hosted for an affordable monthly fee, de-

pending on volume. Also, other e-commerce pages can be constructed at little additional cost. For instance, an annual fund page can be developed, or pages for other special fundraising campaigns added. The mechanism for accepting donations remains the same, no matter how many donations are placed in a shopping cart.

Membership or donation transactions are transmitted to the organization via e-mail or fax, at timed intervals determined by the host site. Donations can be electronically transferred to the organization's bank account, or the organization can transact its own credit card transactions. The "forms" are then processed by the same means as mailed forms and are added to the organization's database, or the transaction can be set up to automatically update on the organization's database.

One experience demonstrates what can easily happen in an organization. The membership department presented its needs to its two-person IT team. Other departments presented their e-commerce needs at the same time. The requests included membership and donor transaction pages, an online store, class registrations, and a members-only access page that would allow members to ask curators questions. An outsourced proposal was compared to that of the in-house IT team. The in-house team stated that it could do all of the requested services at no cost, though taking far more time than an outside firm (18 months versus 6 weeks). The organization decided to do the work in-house. Twelve months later, the in-house staff had all left the organization for other positions without completing the wish list. This scenario, in hindsight, could have been prevented if the organization had been more realistic. While outsourcing costs more in the short run, it can save time and provide long-term benefits.

e-Charity Portals

This option is changing rapidly. Initially, e-charity sites, or portals, have been touted as allowing charities and membership nonprofits to collect online donations without having any internal e-commerce capabilities. The cost is generally 8 percent of all transactions or donations, plus setup or construction fees. While that may seem like a reasonable amount, if credit card charges that may be 3 percent are considered along with 8 percent of all donations, forever, this may turn out to be significant in terms of dollars, if online donations are expected to increase. Hence, the e-charity solution may be a temporary one until an organization can develop its own capabilities, whether in-house or outsourced. Transactions from members are faxed or e-mailed to an organization's membership processor on an hourly, or daily, basis for processing by standard means. Funds are deposited electronically from the host to the organization's designated bank account.

Another issue is the temporary nature of some of these resources, with some of these service providers having already gone out of business. If an organization is depending solely on one independent solution, it may learn one morning that the organization no longer has e-commerce capabilities. Organizations might consider taking advantage of as many donation portals as possible, so that many potential members can find the organization on the Web; relying solely on a single portal can be risky.

NetSolutions® via Blackbaud's Raiser's Edge Database Software

The fourth option allows for total integration of the donation process. Users of Blackbaud's Raiser's Edge software have the option of utilizing a service that is offered as an add-on to their database capabilities. Called NetSolutions,® this service allows for a membership transaction page to be hosted by Blackbaud for a monthly fee. Just as described above in the discussion of outsourced hosting, when a member is surfing the organization's Web site and clicks on "join here," the member is taken to what appears to be the organization's transaction page, but is, in fact, an off-site–hosted secure transaction page, or e-commerce site. The members complete the transaction, click submit, and the transaction is automatically and seamlessly updated on the organization's database, with no hand processing necessary on the part of the membership organization. The other costs associated with this capability, in addition to the cost of being a Raiser's Edge user, include the purchase of the NetSolutions® module, a one-time setup fee, and a monthly hosting fee. Other database vendors may offer comparable services.

E-MAIL COMMUNICATIONS WITH MEMBERS

Communicating with members is a must and a key to keeping members a part of the membership family for many years. E-mail communications are one way to make that connection. The issues are the quality and timing of those communications. First and foremost, this must be an "opt-in" situation. In fact, the organization would not have their members' e-mail addresses if they did not willingly provide them. But some members may do so without knowing what the organization's intentions are, so care should be taken to honor all requests to opt out once the e-mail program is in place. Also, the development and adherence to a privacy policy with respect to e-mail address usage is vital. E-mail programs, like secure transaction pages, can be developed in-house, be off-the-shelf programs, or be part of an integrated software package. The time, expertise, and cost can also vary greatly.

E-mail communications are an excellent way to send timely or last-minute information to members. E-mails can serve as a means of boosting attendance at events, serving as reminders about class registrations, or highlighting institutional information to members before that information appears in the traditional press. Members especially appreciate receiving tips on visiting during major events or other high-traffic times, or on the best way to get tickets to popular events. E-mail is particularly useful for public issue organizations that need members to write or telephone legislators on any particular issue in a very timely manner.

Organizations that have begun to use e-mail as a means of communicating with their members usually take a year to collect e-mail addresses. The effort should begin in earnest with adding a line for e-mail addresses on acquisition and renewal forms. Every effort should also be made to collect addresses when talking with members on the telephone or in person. Organizations who report using these methods state that they may have started their campaign with only 10 percent of their members' e-mail addresses and in a year's time increased that penetration to 60 to 80 percent. There will always be members who do not have access to the Internet or who do not want to receive communications in that fashion.

Online Newsletter

A more formalized way of communicating information to members online is via an online newsletter. This requires the collection of e-mail addresses. Online newsletters may take the form of a text format or a more graphically pleasing format. Generally, it is not a good idea to send a newsletter in *pdf.* format, since that may require more download time. Some organizations e-mail a note to members with a hotlink to a newsletter Web page that is a condensed version of the organization's newsletter.

A case study of the development and growth of an online newsletter is the Detroit Zoological Society (DZS). The Zoological Society is the organization that supports the Detroit Zoo through its membership and fundraising. DZS wanted a more timely way to communicate with its members than was available through its traditional quarterly publication. The membership department decided to attempt an online newsletter. This undertaking was performed in-house with nontechnical membership employees.

Step one was condensing the more salient points of the newsletter into a one-page document. This took three to four hours after the regular newsletter copy was approved. The next steps involved preparing the e-mail file and sending the text version newsletter. It should be noted that the nontechnical membership staff used a relatively inexpensive off-the-shelf e-mail program. It should also be noted also that e-mail addresses, because of constraints of the membership database, were stored in a separate database.

The day after the newsletter was sent, the morning was spent answering e-mails from recipients of the e-mailed newsletters. The newsletter increased the level of e-mail communication between members and the membership office. There was much more one-to-one communication with members who were on the e-mail mailing list. This is both a positive and a negative. There was more communication with members (good), but it took considerable staff time to respond (bad—or at least unplanned).

After the first few issues, it was apparent that the membership staff had a successful venture. Members loved it. Some said they didn't want to receive information any other way. Others stated that they felt their connection to the Zoo was stronger than ever because of this new way of keeping up with what was going on at the Zoo.

At the outset, the Society had about 2,500 e-mail addresses from its 40,000 members, or about 6 percent. After one year, the number increased to 60 percent, or 25,000 addresses. The quality of the newsletter improved as well. Rather than the original text version, the society now produces a four-color, one-page newsletter complete with photos. It is still produced in-house by membership staff, with a digital camera and a few hours of training by the Zoo's IT staff. And it is still managed with the inexpensive e-mail software package.

The e-mail addresses were collected everywhere—on site, on the telephone, via the mailed response forms. The staff know that not all recipients are members because it is still not linked to the membership database; however, the feeling is that those non-members who receive the online newsletter (available via that hotlink in a text message) are in a position to be solicited for membership by the closer connection developed by this new form of communication.

MEMBERS-ONLY WEB ACCESS PAGES

Perhaps one of the best ways to engage members who may not be able to physically visit an organization is via members-only Web access pages. These pages can be part of the organization's Web site, but accessible only with a member access code and member password. This type of page also gives non–visitation-based membership organizations a way to have their members "visit." Members want to have special access and privileges not available to the public. These pages fulfill that desire for exclusivity.

Private access areas provide a variety of "members-only" information and services. They are designed specifically for each organization. Features might include:

- a question-and-answer page for member chats
- an "ask the experts" page
- a calendar of events open to members only
- an online newsletter for members
- a plant/object/work of art of the day/week/month or any other feature that members would value

A model for this type of service is the Internet membership at the Metropolitan Museum of Art, which was one of the first museums to go online with many membership opportunities. Not only do prospective members join online, but they also receive membership benefits online. The Met created an online membership category: Net Met.

These members receive an instant membership benefit: the opportunity to download a Metropolitan Museum of Art screen saver. The Net Met members have a separate dues structure and their own set of benefits. Other benefits include members-only access to a virtual tour of the museum. Such access to areas not available to the general Internet surfing public provides the kind of exclusivity that many joiners relish. After joining online, a Net Met member can customize the types of online information he or she wishes to receive from the Met by signing the member guestbook. A Net Met member can get information from the museum's Web site on selected areas from the museum's art collection, or information on events or acquisitions.

INTEGRATION OF OLD WORLD AND NEW WORLD

Membership and Internet professionals are just seeing the beginnings of what is possible in combining the needs of members with what the Internet can provide and how the two worlds will interact. What is known is that current methods of acquiring, renewing, and servicing members will not be abandoned, just supplemented by the capabilities of the Internet.

A few facts are now known, and there has been some experience and testing in this area. It is currently known that if Web addresses are included in direct mail, and joining online is suggested as an option, then direct mail response rates will be depressed. Some experience is now showing that response to direct mail pieces without an online suggestion is greater than response via the mail or by the Internet with pieces that suggest joining online. Evidently the online suggestion encourages some people to put the direct mail piece aside, perhaps with the intention of joining online at a later date, but then apparently never doing it. Thus, integrating online suggestions with acquisition and renewal efforts should be done carefully and with some testing. Some organizations are just beginning to use e-mail reminders for membership renewals. Data are not yet available on the productivity of e-mail renewal reminders.

The world of Internet giving, including managing and serving members online is

just beginning. Taking advantage of every opportunity to attend conferences and workshops on this topic is recommended. According to Rick Christ (www.rickchrist. com), who follows these trends, "All information at this point is anecdotal."

To keep pace with the technological world around us, membership programs must address the demands of our existing audiences as well as appeal to totally new audiences who respond and relate to the electronic way of life.

Here are some other options for servicing our members' needs online:

- Event reservations and ticket sales: Special events are often major projects for nonprofits and reservations and ticket sales can be difficult and stressful. An online ticket sales and reservations Web sales page can minimize the difficulties. Transactions occur online without taking staff time and acknowledgments are automatic.
- Member chats: Make the possibility of chats among members possible online. If an organization is comprised of like-minded individuals with common interests, it may make sense to offer this service.
- Calendars: It is possible to post all relevant organizational activities on a calendar, including members-only events posted in the members-only section. Events can be listed on the calendar or the dates can be clicked for information of events happening on any given date.
- Online store: Sell the organization's merchandise online. An organization can expand its gift shop or bookstore without construction or new employees. By outsourcing this to a vendor, a store can be developed very quickly and relatively inexpensively. As traffic

to the Web site expands, so will online sales of merchandise.

- "Ask the Expert": This is a nice feature to make available to members only, especially if the organization's strong point is that it has experts in a particular field, whether they are staff or other members. Members can post questions and have them answered online.

- Member surveys: Conducting a member survey online can be a resource for marketing staff and gives members a chance to make their opinions known. Online surveys return instant information. Remember, however, that the information provided is a survey of online members; members who are not connected may feel totally differently about a topic.

- Virtual tours: Virtual tours provide interactivity with the site. This feature allows the organization to serve populations who may live far away from the organization's main site or office. This has the potential to drastically increase the time spent on a site.

The more features on a site, the greater the likelihood that members will return to the organization's site again and again, making it a benefit of membership in its own right.

REFERENCE

Christ, Rick. 2001. Direct Marketing Association, Nonprofit Council Annual Meeting, January.

CHAPTER 13

The Math of Membership

Patricia Rich and Dana Hines

A million here and a million there, and pretty soon you're talking real money.

—Senator Everett M. Dirksen

UNDERSTANDING THE MATHEMATICS of membership is one of the most important pieces of managing a membership program, and yet, it often a misunderstood or overlooked part of the program. Everyone in the organization who is involved with the membership program should have an orientation to understanding the membership numbers. Whether the program is very small, very large, or somewhere in between, the numbers are important. This chapter will solve the mystery of the math of membership.

THE DEMANDS ON MEMBERSHIP

The organization's strategy is often "more members" or "more money." Understanding what it takes to make "more" happen involves a discerning look at all of the relevant numbers. A lack of this understanding can make life difficult for membership managers in their attempt to make "more" happen. In the best situations, as described in Chapter 2 on Planning, there will be both institutional and departmental planning, and staff and volunteers will work together to arrive at reasonable goals for the program and understand what has to be done to make it happen.

However, in larger organizations, it does happen that membership goals are handed down from above. The board and management will sometimes pluck a number out of the clear blue sky: "Let's get to 20,000 members by our 50th anniversary in two years" is a familiar refrain. These goals might be realistic, but achieving them requires money, effort, a plan, often a consultant, possibly outsourcing direct mail services, and usually additional staff to service the growing numbers of members. Substantial growth just cannot be achieved without an investment of these resources.

THE FINANCIAL SIDE OF MEMBERSHIP

Membership managers and their supervisors are always looking for benchmarks by which to compare their program to those in similar organizations. A benchmark in servicing a healthy membership program—one beyond the start-up phase and yet one that is not so huge that great economies of scale are in operation—is that it takes one dollar for every two dollars a membership program generates to adequately serve current members and to do enough marketing to replace nonrenewing members, attract others, and continue growing.

The ratio of one dollar of expense for two dollars of income holds for organizations that range from about 3,000 members to about 50,000 members. Smaller programs produce a much higher ratio, mainly because, typically, volunteers manage them and much solicitation is handled on a person-to-person basis. Costs become greater

as staff and direct mail are added to the program. Recordkeeping (e.g., data entry) also becomes more of an expense because of the need for more sophisticated computer software to keep track of the gifts and staff to enter the data. As programs reach the 50,000 mark, there are greater economies of scale. Fixed costs (e.g., some salaries, computers) are amortized over many more members, ordering in large quantities lowers the cost per member of many items such as the newsletter and other printed matter, and virtually all mailings can be done as bulk mail.

For example, a membership program with 20,000 members and revenues of $1,000,000 a year would need a budget of about $500,000. If a program is spending less than this 50 percent ratio of budget to revenues and has a program that is operating well and still growing, then a closer examination may be necessary to make sure that there aren't issues that need to be addressed for this phenomenal success to continue.

When more revenue is being produced with fewer dollars, it's important to ask a number of questions to make certain that this kind of economic viability can be sustained.

1. **Staffing: Is the program adequately staffed?** With current technology, it takes approximately one data entry person to manage every 7,500 records. The program mentioned in the example above should have three data entry people plus a manager of the database, plus the membership manager. A program with too few staff may alienate members in high volume times, when membership cards or correspondence are too long in coming. Overworked staff can cause low morale and hence grumpy customer service—not a good thing.

2. **Salaries: Are staff members adequately compensated?** Often not. Membership positions are frequently entry level and attract young staff that have little experience. Good membership managers are hard to find, so keeping them should be key to a successful program. (See eMemberships.net, a Web site for a salary survey, job postings, and search service for membership managers.) Nothing holds a membership program back more than losing its manager, letting a program remain static while a search ensues, and then allowing it to potentially stagnate while a new person goes through what is usually a one-year learning curve.

3. **Benefits: Are the member benefits enough to keep them engaged? To acquire them?** The membership benefits are important, especially in the early years. Carry out the cost-benefit analysis detailed later in this chapter (see section entitled "Cost-Benefit Analysis Methods") to see if the program offerings are appropriate. A high retention rate is also a good measure for determining that the service and benefits are at an acceptable level, at least for current members.

4. **Marketing budget: Next to staff, this may be the largest budget item, but is it enough?** If the program is to grow, there must be enough money to make it happen. It may be necessary to spend 25 to 50 percent of the budget on the marketing aspects of membership, such as direct mail, on-site sales, telemarketing, special promotions, and the like.

Sometimes organizations spend more than 50 percent of the revenues generated on servicing the membership program. There may be a variety of reasons for that as well.

1. **Size or tenure: Is the program small or in a start-up phase?** If the answer is yes, then that may explain the high level of expenditures. A start-up program may take several years to break even, possibly three years. No matter how many members an organization has, it needs a database, someone to run the program, the necessary printed materials, and a marketing budget. However, with fewer members and revenues to bear the expense, the financial viability of a membership program may not be evident in the short term. The institution should be ever mindful, though, that a loyal membership base is usually what supports programs, annual giving, capital giving, and planned gifts.

2. **Unusually high expenses: Is there an unusual benefit or burden on the program?** Some organizations deliver a highly expensive, signature publication that can weight the membership revenue scales. Examples include historical societies whose mission is to publish and distribute historical writings; the *Smithsonian Magazine* is another example. Yet another is a museum that publishes a definitive collection of booklets on its collection and the care of the collection, which members receive quarterly. These examples represent complicated situations: yes, the publications are benefits of membership, yet they also fulfill the organizations' missions. Should the costs be allocated to membership and thus tip the scales of the percentage of revenues spent on membership, or should they be part of an

institutional program budget, and thereby return the membership to its 2:1 ratio of revenues to budget expenditures? These are decisions that the organization must make.

Spend Money to Make Money

If membership is charged to grow, then it needs money to help it grow. If a program is challenged to bring in 1,000 more members, the membership manager must determine where those members will come from. If all possible channels for acquiring members are being pursued, then a new source of members must be developed, or an existing source must be supplemented. A 100,000-piece direct mail campaign may be a possible way to acquire those 1,000 new members. The cost for such a campaign might well be $50,000. Or if on-site membership sales are not being fully implemented, a new staff person to concentrate on such sales may be necessary to do this. Or if on-site sales are fully maximized, then creating a new weekend event may be necessary to attract enough visitors who can then be transformed into members, and that can be costly.

Whatever the goal for membership, it is not enough to announce the goal; it is necessary to find the ways to make that goal a reality.

The Budget Numbers

Staffing and marketing are the two largest expenses in a membership budget. In both cases, these line items must increase as the size of a membership program increases. Sufficient numbers of excellent staff who are paid appropriately (or volunteers who are shown appreciation) is the way to ensure good member service, low turnover, and a program that meets the needs of the members. The marketing budget must be adequate to attract enough new members to sustain growth in membership or to remain stable from year to year. Depending on the program, staffing and marketing can absorb 50 to 75 percent of the membership budget.

Counting Members

Counting members sounds easy, but it isn't. It can mystify many a membership manager and board member alike. First, members should be counted at the end of a month in order to count consistently, which is the key. Second, 14 months of members should be included in the totals. The reason for this rule of thumb is that it takes several months for the renewals due in any given month to come in (after the three notice or more renewal cycle has run its course). Hence, since renewals for the most recent two months are still arriving and in batches waiting to be processed, it is advisable to count these members as current for a 60-day grace period. This practice is an industry standard and is usually built into the logic of the most prevalent membership database's queries and reports. If an organization were to count only 12 months, then the result would be that many more people would be deleted, only to be reentered in the next two months.

Another reason for counting 14 months and keeping these members in a semicurrent state is for continuity purposes, especially for mailings being sent to current members. For instance, if the current date is March 5, and the membership expired on February 28, chances are, the membership renewal is "in the mail." If a mail file is being prepared on March 5, it would be advisable to include the January and February members in the file, so they don't miss upcoming events or miss important institutional information; the assumption is that those members are going to renew, and they shouldn't have a lapse in the flow of information. For visitation-based institutions, however, there is a major exception: there is no grace period for entry after the actual expiration date. If a member attempts to enter after the expiration date, he or she should be asked to renew at that time or forego the free admission.

A third point to remember about counting is that members should be counted as households, not as individuals. A few organizations have attempted to swell their membership numbers by counting actual people that the membership represents. In other words, they count one family membership as two to four people, and then multiply the number of households by two to four. This is not typically how memberships are counted and will only confuse the process when trying to link a dollar amount to the number of members, which is how most membership projections are produced.

Another misunderstanding when it comes to counting members is the fact that membership totals will go up and down from month to month throughout the year. With seasonality and major marketing efforts during different months or seasons, it is natural that the number will fluctuate if membership totals are compared at the end of each month. Thus, the important—and fair—comparison is from year to year at each month's end. For example, compare this May's numbers with last May's numbers, not May with April or June. The numbers for this year should always outweigh the numbers for last year in same-month comparisons, if growth is the objective.

Once an organization has developed good monthly reporting and has done this for some time, it will be able to identify annual patterns of membership increases and decreases (this is known as seasonality). For instance, one botanical garden, with a relatively set pattern of acquisition efforts in the spring and fall, sees the total build through spring, to peak by the end of May each year. The totals then decline through the summer (when there are no special promotions), rise again in the fall as new members are added with special events and lapsed members are recaptured with seasonal efforts, and reach another peak by year end. After tracing the numbers for several years, this pattern became evident. Patterns, individual to the organization, will be seen in those organizations that have consistent, aggressive marketing and management of their membership programs.

It is important for staff and board members to understand these "counting phenomena," so that they have realistic expectations and can make decisions accordingly.

Growth

Growth is one strategy that a membership program can follow. Growth of a membership program is dependent on two factors: renewal rates and the acquisition numbers for new members. Knowing those two numbers makes it possible to predict the future. In general, it is safe to assume that if there is a certain level of renewals or new members in one year, then it is possible to achieve that same level the next year, barring unusual circumstances. If an organization was able to renew 75 percent of the members and attract 3,000 new members in one year, it should be safe to assume the same is possible next year. Using these numbers, Table 13–1 shows the calculations for growth over time for a membership beginning with 10,000 members.

Table 13–1 shows that even with great consistency, something significant must be added to marketing efforts to increase membership totals more than a few percentage points from year to year. Of course there is nothing wrong with slow, steady growth. However, the larger a program grows, the more difficult growth becomes, and the more it may cost to acquire more members. This, of course, depends on the organization, the size of the metropolitan area for local groups, and the amount of funding the organization wants to spend on acquisition and renewal efforts. The reality of diminishing returns may apply, and it may be time to change the membership strategy from growth to stability, and to upgrade current members so that revenue will grow even with a stable number of members.

Projections

Constructing membership totals and revenue projections also needs a realistic approach. Often an institution's planning for membership starts with: "We increased membership by 5 percent last year, let's do the same this year!" Or, "We need more revenue because of decreasing attendance figures, so let's increase the membership revenue expectations to compensate!" This is not the way to plan (see Chapter 2).

To manage the numbers, it is important to evaluate each source of new members for the previous year. If all is the same—the economy, the number of pieces of direct mail, another blockbuster exhibit, the same media attention for the organization—then it is safe to say that the same numbers can be achieved again. Not more, the same. If the organization is committed to growing the membership, then more resources must be added for new or increased acquisition methods or stronger renewal efforts.

To produce accurate revenue projections, start with certain number and percentage calculations as follows:

- the number of new members acquired last year, by source and by month
- the number of new members the program expects to attract next year, by source and by month
- the number of members due to renew for the coming year, by month
- the percentage distribution of members by category
- the dollar value of each membership category
- the renewal rate
- the "flow" of renewals response by mailing; for example, 40 percent of renewals come in on the first mailing, 20 percent come in on the second mailing, and so forth

With these numbers, it is possible to calculate a fairly accurate set of projections, assuming:

Table 13–1 Six-Year Growth

Item	Year 1	Year 2	Year 3	Year 4	Year 5	Year 6
Total members as of January 1	10,000	10,500	10,875	11,158	11,367	11,527
Renewal rate	75%	75%	75%	75%	75%	75%
Renewed members	7,500	7,875	8,158	8,367	8,527	8,642
New members	3,000	3,000	3,000	3,000	3,000	3,000
Members as of December 31	10,500	10,875	11,158	11,367	11,527	11,642
Percent growth	5%	3.5%	2.6%	1.8%	1.5%	1%

- The number of members acquired is in keeping with what was projected, and all acquisition efforts planned are actually executed.
- The projected renewal rate is accurate.
- The flow of renewals is accurate.
- Renewals are sent out on time every month.

The sample projections in Tables 13–2, 13–3, and 13–4 illustrate a typical projection spreadsheet.

Note that the exercise begins with new members. Use the history of the program as a guide for what may be possible in the future. If there were 432 memberships via a gift membership program last year, then it is assumed that, with a repeat effort, the same result can be expected. However, if a new dimension is added to the repeat effort, then increase the numbers in the gift membership line in proportion to the offer. Never assume that there will be an automatic 5 or 10 percent increase from year to year unless there is a new initiative or an addition to current efforts.

By tracking projections by source and by month, a month-to-month actual analysis is possible. If one source is not performing as well as expected, then, ideally, another source will be doing better than expected. It is very important to be honest and realistic when constructing projections. Numbers that are overinflated by a heavy dose of optimism or wishful thinking will cause only disappointment a year from now.

Calculating Renewals

When calculating renewals, it is important to look one year ahead. How many people are due to renew in each of the upcoming months for the next year? Start with these monthly numbers. Then review the last year's flow of renewals. For instance, if there

are 1,000 members due to renew in March, the first renewal notices were probably sent out in early February. Determine the overall response by renewal mailing by keeping track of the number of pieces mailed. If that group of March renewals required a second mailing of 600 pieces in March, then the first mailing had a 40 percent response. Likewise, if a third renewal notice quantity of 400 were mailed, then it is evident that another 20 percent of the original group responded to the second mailing. Finally, it is also important to look back occasionally to find out how many members, by month, still have not renewed. For example, examining the sample month of March several months later shows that there are still 300 who did not renew. With this finding, it is apparent that the renewal rate for the month of March is now 70 percent.

Renewal Math and Cash Flow

To calculate accurately the cash flow from renewals, it is necessary to pay attention to the flow of members plus their level of membership as shown in Tables 13–5 and 13–6. With flow, there will be a loyal group of members who renew their memberships the first time they are asked. They respond to the first suggestion of renewing: they renew on the first renewal notice. There are other, well-intentioned members who need a little nudge to renew and/or who have a bill-paying schedule that is out of sync with the renewal mailing schedule. These members respond to the second renewal letter. Then there are the procrastinators. They will eventually renew, but with a lot of reminders, encouragement, and pursuit. These members will renew when they are ready. It is the job of the membership manager to predict when people will renew. While this sounds difficult, it is fairly easy.

Table 13–2 Museum of Art New Membership Projections—2002

	Oct	Nov	Dec	Jan	Feb	Mar	Apr	May	Jun	Jul	Aug	Sep	TOTALS
Projections–New													
Events		30			25			100					155
Personal Solicitation													
Board		15				15			15				45
Docents	5	5	5									5	20
Member get a Member							40	40					80
Direct Mail	200	300		200	200		100	200					1,200
On Site													
Professional	100					100						100	300
Staff and Volunteers	10	10	10	10	10	10	10	10	10	10	10	10	120
Store	10	10	10	10	10	10	10	10	10	10	10	10	120
Brochures	5	5	5	5	5	5	5	5	5	5	5	5	60
Online Memberships	5	5	5	5	5	5	5	5	5	5	5	5	60
Total New	335	380	35	230	255	145	170	370	45	30	30	135	2,160

Courtesy of Membership Consultants, St. Louis, MO.

Table 13-3 FY2002 Projected Membership Renewals by Month*

	Oct	Nov	Dec	Jan	Feb	Mar	Apr	May	Jun	Jul	Aug	Sep	TOTALS
Memberships by Month													
Due to Renew	224	189	204	159	145	190	210	162	134	159	225	425	2,425
1st Notice—32% (1 month prior)	60	65	51	46	61	67	52	43	51	72	136	276	981
2nd Notice—25% (month of)	56	47	51	40	36	48	53	40	33	40	56	106	606
3rd Notice—13% (month after)	55	29	25	27	21	19	25	27	21	17	21	29	315
Total Renewing	172	142	126	113	118	134	129	111	105	129	213	412	1,902

Table 13-4 FY2002 Projected Revenues Total Members*

	%		Oct	Nov	Dec	Jan	Feb	Mar	Apr	May	Jun	Jul	Aug	Sep	TOTALS
Total Members			507	522	161	343	373	279	299	481	150	159	243	1,047	4,562
Individual/senior	30.0%	$ 40	$ 6,081	$ 6,260	$ 1,937	$ 4,112	$ 4,473	$ 3,343	$ 3,587	$ 5,767	$ 1,804	$ 1,910	$ 2,915	$ 12,560	$ 54,748
Family Dual	54.0%	$ 60	$16,418	$ 16,901	$ 5,231	$ 11,103	$12,076	$ 9,025	$ 9,684	$ 15,570	$ 4,872	$ 5,157	$ 7,871	$ 33,912	$147,819
Contributing	9.0%	$ 125	$ 5,701	$ 5,869	$ 1,816	$ 3,855	$ 4,193	$ 3,134	$ 3,363	$ 5,406	$ 1,692	$ 1,791	$ 2,733	$ 11,775	$ 51,326
Sustaining	5.0%	$ 250	$ 6,334	$ 6,521	$ 2,018	$ 4,283	$ 4,659	$ 3,482	$ 3,736	$ 6,007	$ 1,880	$ 1,990	$ 3,037	$ 13,083	$ 57,029
Fellow	1.0%	$ 500	$ 2,534	$ 2,608	$ 807	$ 1,713	$ 1,864	$ 1,393	$ 1,494	$ 2,403	$ 752	$ 796	$ 1,215	$ 5,233	$ 22,812
Associate	1.0%	$ 1,000	$ 5,067	$ 5,217	$ 1,615	$ 3,427	$ 3,727	$ 2,786	$ 2,989	$ 4,805	$ 1	$ 1,592	$ 2,429	$ 10,467	$ 44,121
Total Revenue			$42,135	$ 43,375	$13,425	$28,493	$30,992	$23,161	$24,853	$39,958	$11,000	$13,234	$20,199	$87,030	$377,854

*Total revenue for each month was rounded to the nearest tenth.

Courtesy of Membership Consultants, St. Louis, MO.

Track the percent response received from each renewal mailing sent. To do this, simply track the number of renewal notices sent every month, the first renewal reminders, the second renewal letters, and so on. Armed with these numbers, it is possible to find the average rate of response to each letter throughout the year. And it is important to take an average of the year, since, during an organization's high season, renewals may come in more rapidly than during the off season.

If the first renewal notice is sent two months prior to the expiration month, and elicits a 30 percent response, then plot 30 percent of March's members to arrive in January. Likewise, if the second notice is sent the month before the expiration date, and that reminder draws a 20 percent response of the number originally due to renew, then plot 200 of March's 1,000 renewing members to arrive and be processed in February. To follow this example to its completion, understand that 15 percent of the members will respond in the month that they are actually due to renew, 10 percent the month after, and another 3 percent even

later. Thus, March's members may actually be spread over the preceding and succeeding months, as shown in Table 13–5.

March has a renewal rate of 78 percent. However, it is important to understand that 78 percent of March's members do not all renew in March. Hence, March's revenue is a total of new members, plus the renewals that were due from months before and after March.

Calculating Revenues

Once the flow of renewals is determined, and those members renewing during any given month are added to the number of members predicted to join during that same month, it is then time to calculate revenues. Membership programs with graduated dues have a variety of membership levels. It is important to know the percentage of members at each dollar level, and apply those numbers to the total numbers of members processed that month. In this example, if there were 1,000 members projected to be processed during this month, the revenues would be anticipated as shown in Table 13–6.

Table 13–5 Monthly Renewal Flow, March Members

Renewal Status	January	February	March	April	May
Due to renew			1,000		
Actually renewed	300	200	150	100	30

Table 13–6 Monthly Financial Projections by Membership Level

Membership Level	Percentage Distribution of 1,000 Members	Calculation of Revenues	Revenues
Regular Member	60%	600 members @ $50	$30,000
Sustaining Member	20%	200 members @ $100	$20,000
Patron Member	10%	100 members @ $250	$25,000
Supporting Member	5%	50 members @ $500	$25,000
Director's Circle	5%	50 members @ $1000	$50,000
Total Monthly Revenues			**$150,000**

The Pitfalls of Projections

No matter how diligent and clever the membership manager is with membership projections, from time to time there may be an inconsistency that forces a review of the membership numbers and the revenues.

One organization offered "one month free" as an incentive to encourage members to renew on the first renewal notice. It was a fine idea and it seemed to be working. The percentage of members renewing on the first letter increased. In fact, the overall renewal rate increased. But the year-end ramifications of the successful offer were discovered when the revenue projections were not met. After making the offer and giving that free month of membership, the projections did not take into account that a month's worth of revenue had been shifted into the next year.

It is not possible to anticipate everything that might happen in the coming year, but there definitely are occurrences that can affect renewals or people's willingness to join an organization at certain times. One organization found itself in a public relations uproar over the construction of a parking lot (pictured as a "tear down the trees to put up a parking lot" situation) and found members writing angry letters and voicing their opinions by not renewing their memberships. Another organization found itself in the midst of a natural disaster, massive flooding in the community, which caused a two-month change in its renewal rates; apparently everyone was writing checks to the disaster relief rather than the organization. Yet another organization had problems when a major employer announced it was moving out of the area. The employer was also a matching gifts company, so the organization had a loss of members who were employed with the company, plus the loss of the matched gift.

These examples illustrate show the unknown can challenge the best, most accurately determined, set of projections.

MEMBERSHIP REPORTS AND BENCHMARKS

Reports are essential for tracking results and evaluating the objectives in the membership plan. But reports are self-evaluation, and therefore everyone is also looking for benchmarks from others to which to compare his or her organization. Every organization is different and will have its own patterns; however, there are some general numbers to measure performance. Each organization should consider its special circumstances when reviewing the reports and benchmarks discussed below.

Reports

Membership management and reports go hand in hand. For anyone responsible for managing a membership program, a significant portion of time must be spent reviewing and interpreting reports. The reason that some people find membership to be such a rewarding endeavor is that it is measurable. The membership manager can see the fruits of his or her labor. It is possible to see how a program measures up—or doesn't.

Reporting is how all of this is done. Reviewing reports on a monthly basis is a must. If it is not done on a regular basis, then the manager is not managing the program. Reports should be run at month's end, or when the last of the month's donations and membership gifts have been entered. Month end is an important time because it is a snapshot in time when numbers can be compared accurately. Running reports in midmonth gives an inaccurate view of the status of the program. For instance, if a report is run on membership totals, it must be done at month's end. That is the time when a previous month, usually the month two months prior to the month being closed out, is dropped, and the totals will be accurate. If reports are run midmonth, before the prior month has been dropped, the report will generate a number that is higher than reality. There is no other time than at month's end to capture an accurate count of what the membership totals are.

As an example, assume that it is the end of June. At this time, members should be counted with a formula in the computer query that asks for all members with a renewal date of greater than April 30. In this query, members who have yet to renew, but may be in process of renewing during the months of May and June, are still counted. For a true picture of the number of members at that point in time, reports must be run after all of June has been processed and before July begins to be processed. If the report is run on July 15, before the month of May is dropped, then the report will show higher numbers than if run at month's end on July 31, when May is dropped.

Reports are run for two reasons: to effectively manage the program and for the history of the program. If a direct mail campaign has not performed well, reports will illustrate that. Running the campaign reports regularly will signal problems in time for the manager to find another source of new members before the fiscal year ends, and it is too late to reach the goal. If reports are run just once a year, at year end, a program manager has waited until it is too late to effect change in the program and to correct the situation. With monthly reporting, a manager knows the victories and defeats as soon as possible and can alter the membership action plan promptly, as needed.

Here are samples of reports that membership managers should be reviewing on a monthly and campaign basis:

- Monthly basis:
  - Monthly new member report by level with revenue (see Table 13–7)
  - Monthly new member report by source with revenue (See Table 13–8)
  - Monthly membership totals by level, versus last year (see Table 13–9)
  - Monthly renewals, with revenue (see Table 13–10)
  - Membership upgrades by month (see Table 13–11)
  - Membership downgrades by month (see Table 13–12)
  - Renewal rates by month (number mailed on first renewals minus the number still due to renew by month, divided by number mailed in first mailing). This report should be done monthly for the current fiscal year and the previous full fiscal year (see Table 13–13).
- Campaign reports:
  - Direct mail campaign report (see Table 13–14)
  - Telemarketing campaign report (see Table 13–15)
  - Lapsed-member mailing report (see Table 13–16)
  - On-site sales report for recent events (include attendance figures) (see Table 13–17)

Benchmarks

Renewal Rates

Renewal rates should be between 60 and 85 percent, with a 70 to 80 percent renewal rate considered good. A lower rate of 50 percent may be seen for first-year members. If the organization serves a population that

Table 13–7 Monthly New Members by Level

Membership Level	Number	Revenue	Percent of Total
Senior	154	$6,930	37.84%
Regular	208	$10,100	51.11%
Enhanced	31	$2,160	7.62%
Contributing	11	$1,400	2.70%
Sustaining	2	$555	0.49%
Sponsoring	1	$250	0.25%
Director's Society	0	$0	0.00%
Total	**407**	**$21,395**	

Table 13–8 Monthly New Member Report by Source

Source	Memberships	Revenue	Average Gift
Direct mail	254	$13,240	$52.13
On-site sales	142	$7,600	$53.52
Gift memberships	5	$250	$50.00
Web site	6	$300	$50.00
Totals	**407**	**$21,390**	**$52.56**

Table 13–9 Monthly Membership Totals by Level Versus Last Year

Membership Level	Last Year	This Year	Variance	Percentage Change	Percentage of Total Membership
Senior	2,215	2,822	607	27.40%	39.32%
Regular	2,522	3,154	632	40.88%	43.94%
Regular Plus	0	399	399		5.56%
Contributing	413	434	21	5.08%	6.05%
Sustaining	116	124	8	6.90%	1.73%
Sponsoring	28	26	−2	−7.14%	0.36%
Director's Society	204	218	14	6.86%	3.03%
Total	**5,498**	**7,177**	**1,679**	**30.54%**	**100.00%**

Table 13–10 Monthly Renewals, With Revenue

Membership Level	Number	Percent of Total	Revenue
Renewed at same level	357	81.32%	$28,030
Number of upgrades	49	11.16%	$4,745
Number of downgrades	33	7.52%	$7,665
Total	**439**		**$40,440**

people outgrow (e.g., children's museums), then the renewal rate may be lower. The same will be true of public issue organizations when the issue no longer provokes an intense response. Renewal rates higher than 80 percent may be seen for professional associations, where a member's accreditation or livelihood depends on belonging, and the

Table 13–11 Membership Upgrades by Month

Membership Level	Number	Percent of Total	Revenue
Regular	20	40.82%	$1,000
Enhanced	20	40.82%	$1,400
Contributing	5	10.20%	$520
Sustaining	2	4.08%	$325
Sponsoring	1	2.04%	$500
ABC Society	1	2.04%	$1,000
Total	**49**		**$4,745**

Table 13–12 Membership Downgrades by Month

Membership Level	Number	Percent of Total	Revenue
Senior	21	63.64%	$945
Regular	5	15.15%	$250
Enhanced	2	6.06%	$95
Contributing	3	9.09%	$375
Sustaining	0	0.00%	$0
Sponsoring	0	0.00%	$0
ABC Society	2	6.06%	$6,000
Total	**33**		**$7,665**

only way people would not renew is if they die or retire. Loyalty organizations may also see very high renewal rates because the members want to continue to belong.

If renewal rates exceed 85 percent, then an organization must ask itself if it is doing enough to attract new members. A healthy program that is adding new members at significant rates will find that new members' first-year renewal rates will decrease the overall renewal rate.

Distribution of Membership Categories

In organizations with graduated dues, typically, the lowest level of membership, the beginning value level, will contain 80 to 85 percent of the total membership. The next category will probably be 10 to 12 percent of the total number of members. The support categories, in the $250 to $500 range, will occupy 2 to 5 percent of the total. The highest levels will have a few tenths of a percentage point of the total.

Membership Upgrades and Downgrades

If nothing is done to encourage upgrades, then upgrades and downgrades usually cancel each other out. If upgrades are encouraged, then upgrades should outpace downgrades by 2 to 1. An aggressive upgrade program can actually serve to decrease downgrades. It may be possible, with the right offer, to upgrade 6 to 12 percent of the renewing members. It is also typical that 3 to 6 percent of those renewing will downgrade their membership levels.

Membership Acquisition

Direct mail. Response rates will range from 0.6 to 1.5 percent. Response rates of less than that suggest problems with the offer,

Table 13–13 Renewal Rates by Month, 1999 and 2000

1999

Month	Number Due to Renew	First Renewal Rate	Number of Second Renewals	Second Renewal Rate	Number of Third Renewals	Third Renewal Rate	Number of Fourth Renewals	Current Number of Nonrenewals	Current Renewal Rate
January	307	58.31%	128	64.17%	110	73.94%	80	35	88.60%
February	515	46.21%	277	57.09%	221	62.52%	193	141	72.62%
March	479	54.70%	217	63.05%	177	70.15%	143	90	81.21%
April	246	52.85%	116	64.23%	88	70.73%	72	43	82.52%
May	451	54.32%	206	61.42%	174	68.96%	140	96	78.71%
June	356	62.08%	135	70.79%	104	76.69%	83	59	83.43%
July	117	41.03%	69	58.12%	49	64.96%	41	31	73.50%
August	515	64.08%	185	70.49%	152	75.15%	128	76	85.24%
September	362	67.13%	119	70.99%	105	76.24%	86	44	87.85%
October	445	69.21%	137	78.43%	96	84.72%	68	57	87.19%
November	372	69.09%	115	77.15%	85	81.99%	67	48	87.10%
December	645	64.96%	226	72.40%	178	79.53%	132	98	84.81%
Total for 1999	**4,810**	**59.88%**	**1,930**	**68.00%**	**1,539**	**74.37%**	**1,233**	**818**	**82.99%**

2000

Month	Number Due to Renew	First Renewal Rate	Number of Second Renewals	Second Renewal Rate	Number of Third Renewals	Third Renewal Rate	Number of Fourth Renewals	Current Number of Nonrenewals	Current Renewal Rate
January	217	61.75%	83	78.80%	46	81.57%	40	38	82.49%
February	754	50.00%	377	53.71%	349	63.79%	273		
March	446	61.21%	173	73.77%	117	79.82%	90		
April	315	45.08%	173	63.81%	114	68.57%	99		
May	337	63.20%	124	68.25%	107				
June	413	58.60%	171						
July	189								
August	417								
September									
October									
November									
December									
Total for 2000	**3,088**								

Table 13–14 Direct Mail Campaign Report: Spring 2000 Membership Acquisition Results, Drop 1, March 30, 2000

Code	List	Number Mailed	Number of Responses	Response Rate	Revenue	Average Gift	5-Year Income	Cost per Response	Cost per $ Raised	Return on Investment
FOML	Lapsed	386	10	02.59%	$505	$50.50	$1,411.92	$ 19.38	$0.38	$2.61
FOMP	Prospects	4,164	53	01.27%	$3,680	$69.43	$10,288.82	$ 39.44	$0.57	$1.76
MG1	Natural History	2,939	26	00.88%	$1,540	$59.23	$4,305.65	$ 69.97	$1.18	$0.85
MG2	Smithsonian	3,886	21	00.54%	$1,060	$50.48	$2,963.63	$114.54	$2.27	$0.44
MG3	Parents Magazine	5,044	26	00.52%	$1,430	$55.00	$3,998.10	$120.09	$2.18	$0.46
MG4	Ranger Rick	4,510	27	00.60%	$1,205	$44.63	$3,369.03	$103.40	$2.32	$0.43
MG5	Parenting	3,825	12	00.31%	$640	$53.33	$1,789.36	$197.31	$3.70	$0.27
OM1	Exploration	778	26	03.34%	$2,535	$97.50	$7,087.54	$15.02	$0.15	$6.49
OM2	Museum of the Region	489	1	00.20%	$100	$100.00	$279.59	$245.48	$2.45	$0.41
OM3	Museum of Art	2,434	53	02.18%	$2,285	$43.11	$6,388.57	$23.05	$0.53	$1.87
OM4	Symphony	1,609	37	02.30%	$2,480	$67.03	$6,933.77	$21.83	$0.33	$3.07
OM5	City Museum	255	6	02.35%	$295	$49.17	$824.78	$21.34	$0.43	$2.30
OM6	World Wildlife Fund	4,148	48	01.16%	$2,640	$55.00	$7,381.11	$53.49	$0.97	$1.03
OM7	Planetarium	533	11	02.06%	$585	$53.18	$1,635.59	$24.32	$0.46	$2.19
	Total	35,000	357	01.02%	$20,980	$58.77	$58,657.46	$57.55	$0.98	$1.02

Table 13–15 Telemarketing Report: Museum of Art, Lapsed Member Telemarketing Campaign Results, Spring 2001

Date	Contacts	Cost*	Credit Cards	% Credit Cards	$ Credit Cards	Pledges	% Pledges	$ Pledges	Total Contacts Yes** Said Yes	% of Total Contacts Said Yes	Total $**	Average Dues	Cost Per $ Pledged	Prospects Completed	Contact Rate
5/9/01	65	$256.75	2	25%	$150	6	75%	$318	8	12%	$468	$58.50	$0.55	148	44%
5/10/01	63	$248.85	5	50%	$299	5	50%	$478	10	16%	$777	$77.70	$0.32	95	66%
5/11/01	22	$86.90	4	67%	$299	2	33%	$84	6	27%	$383	$63.83	$0.23	26	85%
5/14/01	371	$1,465.45	19	44%	$1,398	24	56%	$1,954	43	12%	$3,352	$77.95	$0.44	603	62%
5/15/01	405	$1,599.75	18	42%	$1,048	25	58%	$1,811	43	11%	$2,859	$66.49	$0.56	672	60%
5/16/01	293	$1,157.35	8	30%	$509	19	70%	$1,215	27	09%	$1,724	$63.85	$0.67	445	66%
5/17/01	293	$1,157.35	15	52%	$1,154	14	48%	$899	29	10%	$2,053	$70.79	$0.56	445	66%
5/18/01	270	$1,066.50	4	20%	$210	16	80%	$964	20	07%	$1,174	$58.70	$0.91	482	56%
5/19/01	72	$284.40	5	63%	$305	3	38%	$310	8	11%	$615	$76.88	$0.46	111	65%
5/21/01	358	$1,414.10	16	48%	$1,169	17	52%	$1,060	33	09%	$2,229	$67.55	$0.63	496	72%
5/22/01	293	$1,157.35	20	45%	$1,311	24	55%	$1,984	44	15%	$3,295	$74.89	$0.35	324	90%
5/23/01	165	$651.75	8	35%	$503	15	65%	$994	23	14%	$1,497	$65.09	$0.44	185	89%
5/24/01	291	$1,149.45	13	39%	$999	20	61%	$1,368	33	11%	$2,367	$71.73	$0.49	335	87%
5/25/01	236	$932.20	9	38%	$420	15	63%	$894	24	10%	$1,314	$54.75	$0.71	260	91%
Totals	**3,197**	**$12,628.15**	**146**	**42%**	**$9,774**	**205**	**58%**	**$14,333**	**351**	**11%**	**$24,107**	**$68.68**	**$0.52**	**4,627**	**69%**

*Cost is based on the rate of $3.95 per contact and does not include project management, postage, and telephone append fees.

**Credit card renewals + pledges.

Table 13–16 Lapsed-Member Mailing Report: History Center, Fall 1997 Lapsed Member Direct Mail Campaign, Results Through February 11, 1998

Code	List	Number Mailed	Responses	Response Rate	Revenue	Average Income	5-year Income
DML95	Lapsed members from 1995	2,585	48	1.86%	$4,030	$83.96	$11,267.38
DML96	Lapsed members from 1996	1,446	22	1.52%	$1,845	$83.86	$ 5,158.39
Total		4,031	70	1.74%	$5,875	$83.93	$16,425.77

the creative execution, the lists, the size of the campaign, or the reputation or awareness of the organization. Response rates higher than this are rare, but possible during time of special circumstances at an organization.

Average gift in a direct mail campaign. Average gifts are usually $5 higher than the entry level ask amount or the most popular category, assuming a graduated range of membership opportunities exists.

On-site membership sales. The goal, if sales are pursued aggressively, is to convert 3 to 5 percent of the audience into members. Professional salespeople can sell four to six memberships per hour on high attendance days.

In general, the cost per dollar raised for acquisition is considered successful if it is at $1.00. This would be a break-even proposition for acquisition. In direct mail the cost per dollar raised may be $1.25 to $1.50 and still be in an acceptable range. Overall, if all acquisition sources were combined, the membership marketing program would be considered successful if it operates at that $1.00 cost per dollar raised.

Telemarketing

Telemarketing numbers vary greatly depending on the telemarketing firm and their level of expertise. Response rates in telemarketing, called pledge rates, will vary depending on how firm the "yes" response is. In general, pledge rates vary from 10 to 30 percent in a lapsed-member campaign. Part of the success in a telemarketing campaign is the caller's ability to get the respondent to use a credit card to fulfill the pledge at the time of the call. The percentage using credit cards can vary from 10 to 75 percent. The higher the credit card rate, usually the lower the pledge rate. With a high credit card rate, the pledge rate is lower because the caller is counting fewer "maybe's" as "yes's." Fulfillment rates on pledges other than credit cards usually range from 40 to 80 percent, depending on the type of campaign.

Budget

For a program of 5,000 to 50,000, the membership department's revenues to expenditure ratio will be approximately 2 to 1. Marketing, including the acquisition budget, will be 25 percent, or more, of the membership budget. Staffing may occupy a similar proportion.

Staffing

Staffing levels depend on the number of members. When starting a new program,

Table 13–17 On-site Sales Results: Grand Opening, New Memberships Only

Sales Results	Friday April 7	Saturday April 8	Sunday April 9	Grand Total
Total number of new memberships sold	379	120	89	588
Revenue	$17,380	$5,695	$4,395	$27,470
Average Gift	$45.86	$47.46	$49.38	$46.72
$25 Student Membership				
Number Sold	8	2	0	10
Revenue	$200	$50	$0	$250
$35 Individual Membership				
Number Sold	30	9	2	41
Revenue	$1,050	$315	$70	$1,435
$45 Family Membership				
Number Sold	334	104	85	523
Revenue	$15,030	$4,680	$3,825	$23,535
$100 Discovery Club Membership				
Number Sold	6	4	0	10
Revenue	$600	$400	$0	$1,000
$250 Naturalist Society Membership				
Number Sold	0	1	2	3
Revenue	$0	$250	$500	$750
$500 Explorers Society Membership				
Number Sold	1	0	0	1
Revenue	$500	$0	$0	$500
Total Sales Hours	57	43.5	24	124.5
Average Sales/Hour	6.65	2.76	3.71	4.72
Expenses				
Supervisor, hourly fee	$345.00	$217.50	$120.00	$682.50
Salespersons, hourly fee	$862.50	$543.75	$300.00	$1,706.25
$5.00 bonus	$1,860.00	$575.00	$435.00	$2,870.00
$7.50 bonus	$52.50	$37.50	$15.00	$105.00
Air fare	$627.00	$627.00	$627.00	$1,881.00
Parking	$42.00	$42.00	$42.00	$126.00
Rental car	$94.28	$94.28	$94.28	$282.84
Accommodations	$333.09	$333.09	$333.09	$999.27
Per diem	$300.00	$300.00	$300.00	$900.00
Total Expenses	$4,516.37	$2,770.12	$2,266.37	$9,552.86
Cost Per Dollar Raised	$0.26	$0.49	$0.52	$0.35

one person may be able to handle the program until a level of 2,000 to 2,500 members is achieved. As the program grows, people will be needed to manage program strategy and the data issues. In general, there should be one data entry person for every 7,500 members, and generally, one staff person for every 5,000 members.

Cost Benefit Analysis Methods

A cost benefit analysis of the membership program's benefit offerings should be done annually. This analysis is helpful for evaluating the cost effectiveness of the benefits and should be used when trying to determine if the benefits or dues structure should be changed. It may also be used to determine the tax deductibility of upper-level membership categories.

This analysis requires knowledge of the cost of the benefits and the members' usage of the various benefits. The budget figures should be available from the previous year's budget. Usage may need to be collected from a variety of sources: from membership surveys, from records kept by the gift shop or the admissions desk, or by the finance office of the organization.

There are three methods of evaluating the cost of the benefits program, and each measures the benefits package from a different perspective and can be used for different purposes. The methods are as follows:

1. Market value method. This method measures the market value, or the perceived value, of the membership benefits. Members who are value oriented will consider this dollar amount when asking themselves if they are "getting their money's worth." This dollar amount can also be used to promote membership: "Receive $99 worth of benefits for a $50 membership!" This method attaches the fair market value to a benefit, rather than the actual cost to deliver that benefit.

2. Actual cost method. This method calculates the actual out-of-pocket amount the membership department pays for the benefits. If another department pays for a benefit, there is no "cost" attached to this benefit. Staff costs are not included here. This method is used to evaluate whether a program is spending too much or too little on benefits, and thus, if the organization is offering enough to be attractive to prospective members.

3. Program cost method. This simple calculation simply divides the total membership budget by the number of members. Membership managers find this to be the easiest and, thus, most-used, calculation. It shows the total cost to attract, service, and renew all members. It takes into consideration the entire budget, including staff and all administrative charges (except rent and utilities). This number should be no more than half of the amount of the entry-level membership category. This method is used to evaluate the overall cost of the membership program and to ascertain if the cost of the program is in line with the amount charged for membership.

An illustration of the market value method and the actual cost method is included in Table 13–18. A fictitious membership program is used for illustration.

In this example (Table 13–18), the $50 membership category has an appropriate market value. The higher the market value, the more attractive the membership will be to the prospective member. However, the actual cost of the delivery of the benefits needs to be in proportion to the category price. It is common for the cost of the benefits to be between $13 and $19 for an entry-level membership category in this price range.

The third calculation is the program cost method. This calculation divides the total cost of the program, everything in the membership budget including staffing, by the number of members. The result should be no more than half the amount of the entry level, the most frequently chosen membership category.

If the figure reached by dividing the budget amount by the number of members is more than half the most common entry-level

Table 13–18 Cost Benefit Analysis Methods

Benefits	Market Value Method	Actual Cost Method
Free admission	$24.00	–
$4 admission × 2 people × 3 visits per year		
Free parking	$ 6.00	–
Newsletter	–	$ 8.00
Invitations to previews, events	$16.00	$ 5.00
Attendance at one preview or event per year. The "market value" of attending a preview may be compared to an evening's entertainment such as going to a movie: e.g., $8 × 2 people equals $16.00		
Membership card	$ .50	$ .50
Car decal	$ .50	$ .50
Free reciprocal admission	–	–
Ability to participate in travel program	–	–
Behind the scenes tour	–	–
Membership premium	$10.00	$ 5.00
Total	**$57.00**	**$19.00**

Note: In this example, the $50 membership category has an appropriate market value. The higher the market value, the more attractive the membership will be to the prospective member. However, the actual cost of the delivery of the benefits needs to be in proportion to the category price. It is common for the cost of the benefits to be between $13 and $19 for an entry-level membership category in this price range.

category, then either too much is being spent to administer the entire membership program, or the entry-level category is priced too low.

These calculations should be carried out on an annual basis, so that a historical perspective for the program can be maintained. It is important to know the costs and values attached to the membership benefits and staffing of the program. Such knowledge and understanding will guide decisions on dues increases, levels of staffing, and adding or deleting membership benefits.

TAX ISSUES IN MEMBERSHIP

The market value method of measuring the value of benefits is the method required by the U.S. Internal Revenue Service (IRS) in determining the tax deductibility of various membership categories. In general, as of 1997, the IRS ruled that memberships up to the $75 level are totally tax deductible. Therefore, it is no longer necessary to calculate the market value for the lower levels of membership. For levels of membership over $75, the organization needs to consider calculating only the market value of the benefits given to members that are in addition to the benefits given to the $75 level and below. For instance, if a $150-level member receives all the benefits that the $75 member receives, plus a free hardbound book, the organization needs to determine only the market value of that book. That market value is determined by the sale price of that book if it were sold on the open market. If that item is not sold on the open market, then the cost to produce it may be used.

The exception to the rule that $75-level memberships and below are totally tax deductible is if items are given that cost more than a dollar amount that the IRS determines annually. (For example, as of April 2001, that amount was $7.60.) For this reason, an organization such as the Smithsonian Institute that gives a subscription to its magazine, priced on the open market at $28, must use the market value to determine the tax deductible amount of a given membership category. The market value of the benefit given that exceeds the $7.60 amount must be deducted from the amount charged for membership. For instance, if the Smithsonian charges $70 for its Contributing Membership Program, then it must deduct the $28 from the $70 amount for a tax-deductible amount of $42. However, it can also use the lowest published price for a benefit given. *Smithsonian Magazine* is sometimes available at the price of $14 in the Publisher's Clearinghouse Sweepstakes. Thus, since that is a published cost in the open marketplace, that number could be used as the portion that is nondeductible.

Other benefits at higher levels must be valued at the market value, not the cost of the benefit. For instance, if a black-tie din-

ner is used as a benefit of a $1,000 membership category, and a sponsor donates the cost of the catering, the market value of a fine dinner must be used (e.g., $50 per person) rather than the actual cost to the institution, which is $0. On the other hand, if a person joined an organization without the promise of a benefit, and if that person is invited to that same dinner, and it was not an expectation at the time of the decision to join, then the value of that offering does not have to be included in the calculation of the amount that is tax deductible. In some cases, members may request not to receive benefits. In this case, their requests should be maintained in writing in the files to prove that they wanted their entire donation to be tax deductible. Their request must be made at the time they make their donations, not after the fact.

In most cases, the IRS is looking for an organization to make a good-faith effort to come to the best possible calculation for its membership program. Using the calculation that is described here could serve as that calculation. Thus, the reason to go through the calculations on an annual basis. It is also necessary to inform the members at the time they make the decision to join. Publishing the tax-deductible amount on the response form or on the invitation to join is advisable. See Chapter 14 for more detail.

Ethical and Legal Dimensions:
Right and Wrong and Everything In Between

Patricia Rich and Michael J. Rosen

Always do right. This will gratify some people and astonish the rest.

—Mark Twain

ETHICS

WHAT SHOULD THE MEMBERSHIP marketing professional do when he or she does not know what to do? Choosing right over wrong is easy, but what should the professional do when there is no purely right or wrong course of action? How can you tell the difference between right and wrong when you do not have the experience to know the difference?

The answers to these questions come with the study of ethics. Unfortunately, many membership marketing professionals do not take the time to study the subject. Most professionals consider themselves to be ethical people already and, indeed, most are. For this reason, this chapter is not intended as a "cure" for unethical behavior, nor as a purely academic or philosophical presentation. Instead, it is designed to provide practical help that will empower ethical professionals to act the way they aspire to, while giving them the tools to explain their actions to members, colleagues, senior staff, and boards. By maintaining a finely adjusted ethical compass, professionals will be able to ensure the success of their membership programs, while also guaranteeing themselves a bright career founded on the highest standards.

Public Expectation

The public has a right to hold nonprofit organizations to a high standard. Society grants nonprofit organizations special status and benefits, including exemption from certain taxes. In exchange, the public expects nonprofit organizations to make society better, to fulfill their missions, and to act ethically. When one organization is found guilty of misdeeds, it reflects poorly on all organizations and erodes public trust in the entire sector. Therefore, those who work for nonprofit organizations must take special care to be worthy of the public trust. People will only support or join those organizations in which they can have confidence.

When Conscience Is Not Enough

The first "ethicist" that most people encounter is Walt Disney's Jiminy Cricket, who said, "Let your conscience be your guide." While this is generally sound advice, it is limited. People develop a conscience through the accumulation of life experiences and the development of personal values. Because of this, a person's conscience can be relied upon for sound judgment only when encountering a situation with which he or she has had some experience, or that can be addressed through his or her value system. When encountering new situations or when adapting to an organization's own value system, the membership professional will need to rely upon

tools other than conscience to ensure sound decision making.

Legal Does Not Mean OK

Bruce Hopkins, Esq., a nonprofit law expert, has said that the law and ethics often have nothing to do with one another. He made this remark at a National Society of Fund Raising Executives (now Association of Fundraising Professionals [AFP]) Washington, D.C., conference. His point was this: just because something is legal does not mean it is ethical. Generally, society first reaches a consensus of what is unethical and then codifies that judgment into law. In other words, many things are considered unethical even though laws and regulations have yet to be written on the subject. Society's views change, and then laws and regulations are rewritten or even repealed.

It is naturally a best practice to obey the law. The AFP Statement of Ethical Principles even states, "AFP members aspire to adhere to the spirit as well as the letter of all applicable laws and regulations" (AFP 2001, 4). But, compliance with laws and regulations is not enough.

Codes

To supplement statutes and regulations, many individual nonprofit organizations and professional associations have developed codes of ethics and standards of professional practice that provide professionals with additional guidelines governing behavior.

"Professional and agency codes of ethics play a role in sustaining system trust. A code gives the public a clear indication of what the profession or agency stands for, and what behaviors will not be tolerated," writes Marilyn Fischer, Ph.D., associate professor of philosophy at the University of

Dayton, in her book, *Ethical Decision Making in Fund Raising* (Fischer 2000, 84).

The AFP Statement of Ethical Principles and Standards of Professional Practice (Exhibit 14–1), as well as the Donor Bill of Rights, can be found at www.afpnet.org. The Association of Professional Researchers for Advancement (APRA) Statement of Ethics can be found at www.aprahome.org. The Direct Marketing Association offers a variety of best practices policy statements that can be found at www.the-dma.org. Other professional organizations and individual nonprofits have also developed codes. While many of the points addressed in these codes address fundraising and prospect research, most of the principles are equally valid for membership professionals.

Unfortunately, codes suffer from the same limitation as the law: they cannot be all-inclusive. And, like conscience, the existing laws and codes are only of value when confronting the specific situations they address. For more ambiguous issues, or when the available guidelines are vague, membership professionals must possess a system for sound decision making.

Ethical Decision Making

Making sound ethical decisions is about asking enough of the right questions. While many models exist for making good decisions, Dr. Fischer presents an excellent model in *Ethical Decision Making in Fund Raising*. Her model involves careful consideration of all possible alternative courses of action to deal with an ethical dilemma. Then, the model has the decision maker examine each alternative from various perspectives.

Exhibit 14–1 AFP Ethical Principles and Standards of Professional Practice

ASSOCIATION OF FUNDRAISING PROFESSIONALS STATEMENT OF ETHICAL PRINCIPLES AND STANDARDS OF PROFESSIONAL PRACTICE

The foundation of philanthropy is ethical fundraising, and a key mission of AFP is to advance and foster the highest ethical standards through its Code of Ethical Principles and Standards of Professional Practice.

Statement of Ethical Principles

Adopted 1964; amended October 1999.

The Association of Fundraising Professionals (AFP) exists to foster the development and growth of fundraising professionals and the profession, to promote high ethical standards in the fundraising profession and to preserve and enhance philanthropy and volunteerism.

Members of AFP are motivated by an inner drive to improve the quality of life through the causes they serve. They serve the ideal of philanthropy; are committed to the preservation and enhancement of volunteerism; and hold stewardship of these concepts as the overriding principle of their professional life. They recognize their responsibility to ensure that needed resources are vigorously and ethically sought and that the intent of the donor is honestly fulfilled. To these ends, AFP members embrace certain values that they strive to uphold in performing their responsibilities for generating charitable support.

continues

Exhibit 14–1 continued

AFP members aspire to:

- Practice their profession with integrity, honesty, truthfulness, and adherence to the absolute obligation to safeguard the public trust.
- Act according to the highest standards and visions of their organization, profession, and conscience.
- Put philanthropic mission above personal gain.
- Inspire others through their own sense of dedication and high purpose.
- Improve their professional knowledge and skills, so that their performance will better serve others.
- Demonstrate concern for the interests and well-being of individuals affected by their actions.
- Value the privacy, freedom of choice and interests of all those affected by their actions.
- Foster cultural diversity and pluralistic values, and treat all people with dignity and respect.
- Affirm, through personal giving, a commitment to philanthropy and its role in society.
- Adhere to the spirit as well as the letter of all applicable laws and regulations.
- Advocate within their organizations, adherence to all applicable laws and regulations.
- Avoid even the appearance of any criminal offense or professional misconduct.
- Bring credit to the fundraising profession by their public demeanor.
- Encourage colleagues to embrace and practice these ethical principles and standards of professional practice.
- Be aware of the codes of ethics promulgated by other professional organizations that serve philanthropy.

Standards of Professional Practice

Furthermore, while striving to act according to the above values, AFP members agree to abide by the AFP Standards of Professional Practice, which are adopted and incorporated into the AFP Code of Ethical Principles. Violation of the Standards may subject the member to disciplinary sanctions, including expulsion, as provided in the *AFP Ethics Enforcement Procedures.*

Professional obligations

1. Members shall not engage in activities that harm the members' organization, clients, or profession.
2. Members shall not engage in activities that conflict with their fiduciary, ethical, and legal obligations to their organizations and their clients.
3. Members shall effectively disclose all potential and actual conflicts of interest; such disclosure does not preclude or imply ethical impropriety.
4. Members shall not exploit any relationship with a donor, prospect, volunteer, or employee to the benefit of the members or the members' organizations.
5. Members shall comply with all applicable local, state, provincial, and federal civil and criminal laws.
6. Members recognize their individual boundaries of competence and are forthcoming and truthful about their professional experience and qualifications.

Solicitation and use of charitable funds

7. Members shall take care to ensure that all solicitation materials are accurate and correctly reflect their organization's mission and use of solicited funds.

continues

Exhibit 14–1 continued

8. Members shall take care to ensure that donors receive informed, accurate, and ethical advice about the value and tax implications of potential gifts.
9. Members shall take care to ensure that contributions are used in accordance with donors' intentions.
10. Members shall take care to ensure proper stewardship of charitable contributions, including timely reports on the use and management of funds.
11. Members shall obtain explicit consent by the donor before altering the conditions of a gift.

Presentation of information

12. Members shall not disclose privileged or confidential information to unauthorized parties.
13. Members shall adhere to the principle that all donor and prospect information created by, or on behalf of, an organization is the property of that organization and shall not be transferred or utilized except on behalf of that organization.
14. Members shall give donors the opportunity to have their names removed from lists that are sold to, rented to, or exchanged with other organizations.
15. Members shall, when stating fundraising results, use accurate and consistent accounting methods that conform to the appropriate guidelines adopted by the American Institute of Certified Public Accountants (AICPA)* for the type of organization involved. (*In countries outside of the United States, comparable authority should be utilized.)

Compensation

16. Members shall not accept compensation that is based on a percentage of charitable contributions; nor shall they accept finder's fees.
17. Members may accept performance-based compensation, such as bonuses, provided such bonuses are in accord with prevailing practices within the members' own organizations, and are not based on a percentage of charitable contributions.
18. Members shall not pay finder's fees, commissions or percentage compensation based on charitable contributions and shall take care to discourage their organizations from making such payments.

Source: Copyright AFP (formerly NSFRE). Used with permission. All rights reserved.

First, decision makers consider how each alternative fits with the organization's mission and basic philanthropic values. Second, decision makers consider how each alternative impacts the relationships within the organization and between the organization and its various publics. Finally, decision makers consider how each alternative affects their own sense of personal integrity. By examining all possible alternatives through the eyes of the organization and its various publics, as well as considering one's own perspective, the membership professional can arrive at the best possible decision (Fischer, 2000).

Having a decision-making process in place is helpful when the existing laws and codes do not address an issue. A decision-making model is also helpful when confronting a situation for which no alternative feels perfectly right. By having a decision-making model to rely upon, the best solution can be found, and the decision can be justified more effectively than if the decision were arrived at more haphazardly.

Key Issues

Membership professionals must be prepared to deal with any number of ethical issues on any given day. However, three broad areas in particular affect membership professionals most often: privacy, list ownership, and stewardship.

Privacy

Public concerns over privacy rights continue to increase. Consider the following:

- Sixty-five percent of those surveyed said, "protecting the privacy of consumer information" is "very important" to them, according to the Equifax/Harris Consumer Privacy Survey (1996).
- Seventy-two percent of Internet users want new privacy laws, and 84 percent object to the sale of personal information, according to the Tenth WWW User Survey produced by the Graphic, Visualization, and Usability Center at Georgia Tech University (1998). Proving that the privacy issue extends beyond the Internet, the same survey also found that 80 percent of those surveyed do not want magazines to which they subscribe to have the right to sell their names and addresses to companies they feel will be of interest.
- The Direct Marketing Association (DMA) adopted new guidelines, called the Privacy Promise (see Chapter 6) that went into effect for members on July 1, 1999. In part, the guidelines read, "All members of the DMA will follow certain specific practices to protect consumer privacy"(DMA 1997). Some of the specific measures include requiring the maintenance of in-house suppression lists and giving consumers the opportunity to opt-out of list trades or rentals.

- The U.S. Supreme Court has supported privacy rights over commercial free speech. One such case is the *Los Angeles Police Department v. United Reporting Publishing Corporation* in 1999. In that case, the Court said that the Los Angeles Police Department (LAPD) could restrict the distribution of parolee contact lists to marketers, even though the LAPD made the list available to journalists (Los Angeles Department v. United Reporting Publishing, No. 98-678, 1999).
- At the end of 2000, the U.S. Department of Health and Human Services (2000) issued new regulations governing the use of patient information by health care providers and their related foundations (Standards for Privacy of Individually Identifiable Health Information). The impetus behind the new regulations was increased pressure to protect patient privacy. The new regulations even impact how health care foundations can use patient information for fundraising purposes.

The list goes on. Privacy issues of one type or another are regular news. A simple Web search on February 19, 2002 using Lycos (www.lycos.com) found 41,284,465 Web sites with the word "privacy," this is an 18 percent increase in less than one year. Because of media attention and public pressure, the government will continue to look at developing new consumer protection laws and regulations. For the membership professional, adhering to these new rules is critical. Beyond that, being sensitive to the public mood is likewise important.

Membership files should only contain the information relevant to the membership effort. As a general rule, the membership professional should never feel uncomfortable about showing a member his or her file if asked. If the professional would be uncomfortable doing so, it is a likely sign that the file contains information that should not be included.

Membership files should be kept secure with authorized access granted only to those who need access to perform their jobs. Members should have the opportunity to have their names removed from lists that are sold to, rented to, or exchanged with other organizations. A small-print note, with the organization's phone number or e-mail address, should be included in every newsletter or other regular communication to remind members that they may have their name deleted from any list sale or exchange. The item should be clear about how members go about removing their names.

List Ownership

"Constituent information is the property of the institution for which it was collected....Constituent information for one institution shall not be taken to another institution," states the APRA Statement of Ethics (APRA 1998). In other words, membership lists and files belong to the membership organization, not the membership professional. When the professional moves on, the data remains behind. The AFP Standards of Professional Practice concurs on this point.

When working with direct response agencies, organizations should negotiate contracts that provide the nonprofit organization, rather than the agency, with list ownership rights. Members are establishing a relationship with the organization. Members expect that their personal information will be kept by the organization and not used by a third party for other purposes. However, some direct response agencies may maintain an interest in the list without

asserting rights of ownership. For example, an agency might receive a fee if the nonprofit organization rents its membership list to another party. But this is only if the organization intends for the list to be rented, and it gives its consent. However, a nonprofit organization should always retain control of the list. An organization can decide to put its list on the rental market, legally and legitimately, and it becomes a source of income. Even if the list is "on the market," the organization controls who may rent it. Some national groups make significant income from the rental of their lists.

Stewardship

Through sound stewardship, membership professionals will develop loyalty among the members. Loyalty will lead to long-term relationships and the possibility of additional support through charitable giving in addition to membership dues.

Stewardship means many things. Professionals should make certain that members receive the acknowledgment and the benefits promised on a timely basis. Members should receive updates of how their money is used if there is a charitable gift component to the membership dues. Membership professionals should ensure that the opt-out requests of members are fulfilled. Membership professionals should report to each member how much of his or her membership dues is tax deductible.

LEGAL ISSUES

Ethical situations and issues can provoke discussion. Ethical decisions are sometimes gray, rather than black or white. When it comes to the legal issues involved in nonprofit organizations, however, it behooves everyone to follow Mark Twain's adage: "Always do right." There are rules that must be followed. In membership organizations (e.g., professional associations or participant organizations), it is important for membership staff to make certain that all legal requirements are met. For example, the organization must file Form 990 if gross receipts exceed $25,000. (See discussion of the 990 below.) In a membership program that is part of a larger organization (e.g., museums), most of the legal concerns are addressed by the organization's management. The membership staff, though, along with development, is usually responsible for the legal issues related to fundraising matters.

Nonprofit Status

Many membership groups never become formal organizations. The neighborhood book club, the group devoted to bringing volunteers together to clean a stream, or the social dinner club that convenes over food are very informal, providing something for their members, but having little need for organizational structure or public fundraising.

If a group decides to become a formal one, the first necessity is to become a nonprofit organization. The U.S. Internal Revenue Service (IRS) confers this designation. For groups considering this, it is important to find legal counsel to help with the process. A group that meets the requirements of the 501(c)(3) or other IRS designations (see Exhibit 14–2) will be able to offer tax deductibility for gifts.

Form 990

A "cost" of tax deductibility is submitting the Form 990 to the IRS each year.

Exhibit 14–2 Descriptions and the General Nature of Activities of Tax-exempt Organizations

Section of 1954 Code	Description of Organization	General Nature of Activities	Example of Organization
501(c)(1)*	Corporations organized under Act of Congress (including Federal Credit Unions)	Instrumentalities of the United States	Federal Deposit Insurance Corporation
501(c)(2)	Title holding corporation for exempt organizations	Holding title to property of an exempt organization	Naugatuck Masonic Building Corporation
501(c)(3)*	Religious, educational, charitable, scientific, literary, public safety, certain national or international amateur sports competition, or children or animal organizations; includes private foundations.	Activities of nature implied by description of class or organization	American Heart Association, Inc.
501(c)(4)	Civic leagues, social welfare, and local associations of employees	Promotion of community welfare, charitable, educational, or recreational	Lions Club

continues

Exhibit 14–2 continued

Section of 1954 Code	Description of Organization	General Nature of Activities	Example of Organization
501(c)(5)	Labor, agricultural, and horticultural	Educational or instructive, purpose being to improve work conditions and products	AFL-CIO
501(c)(6)	Business leagues, chambers of commerce, real estate boards	Improvement of business conditions	Chamber of Commerce
501(c)(7)	Social & recreational clubs	Pleasure, recreation, social activities	Ocean Ski club
501(c)(8)	Fraternal beneficiary societies & associations	Lodge providing for payment of life, sickness, accident or other benefits to members	Knights of Columbus
501(c)(9)	Voluntary employees' beneficiary associations	Providing for payment of life, sickness, accident or other benefits to members	Warren Firefighters Fund Association
501(c)(10)	Domestic fraternal societies and associations	Lodge devoting net earnings to charitable, and other specified purposes; no benefits to members.	Knights Templar of the US 33 Natick Commandery
501(c)(11)	Teachers' retirement fund associations	Teachers' association for payment of retirement benefits	
501(c)(12)	Benevolent life insurance associations, mutual ditch or irrigation companies, mutual or cooperative telephone companies	Activities of a nature similar to those implied by the descriptions of class of organization beneficial to members	Salem Rural Water Corporation
501(c)(13)*	Cemetery companies	Burials & incidental activities for members	Williamson Cemetery Association
501(c)(14)	State chartered credit unions, mutual reserve funds	Loans to members	Williamson County Catholic Credit Union

continues

Exhibit 14–2 continued

Section of 1954 Code	Description of Organization	General Nature of Activities	Example of Organization
501(c)(15)	Mutual insurance companies or associations	Providing insurance to members at cost limited to organizations with gross income of $150,000 or less	Sand-Clay Mutual Burial Association
501(c)(16)	Cooperative organizations to finance crop operations	Financing crop operations in conjunction with activities of a marketing or purchasing association unemployment compensation benefits	
501(c)(17)	Supplemental unemployment benefit trust	Payment of supplemental unemployment compensation benefits	Dayton Malleable Iron Company
501(c)(18)	Employee funded pension trust	Payment of benefits under a pension plan funded by employees	
501(c)(19)*	Post or organization of war veterans	Activities implied by nature of organization	American Legion Posts
501(c)(20)	Trusts for prepaid group legal services	Forms part of a qualified group legal service plan or plans	
501(c)(21)	Black Lung Trusts	Satisfies claims for compensation under Black Lung Acts	
501(d)	Religious and apostolic associations	Regular business activities; communal religious community	
501(e)*	Cooperative hospital service organizations	Enumerated cooperative services for hospitals	
501(f)*	Cooperative service organizations of operating educational organizations	Collective investment services for educational organizations	

continues

Exhibit 14–2 continued

Section of 1954 Code	Description of Organization	General Nature of Activities	Example of Organization
521(a)	Farmers' cooperative associations	Cooperative marketing and purchasing for agricultural producers	Land O'Lakes, Inc.

*Generally, contributions under this Code subsection are tax deductible. Other organizations not asterisked could establish trusts under Code subsection 501(c)(3) that may receive tax-deductible contributions.

Note: Examples are not shown for organizations for which there is very little activity.
Source: Reprinted from the Internal Revenue Service.

Organizations with annual gross receipts of more than $25,000 or an average of $25,000 annual gross receipts for the past three years must file a 990. It is due by the fifteenth day of the fifth month after the end of the organization's fiscal year. Some smaller organizations may find it helpful to submit a Form 990 even though it is not required. A tip from Bruce Hopkins, a noted lawyer for nonprofits, notes: "An organization with gross receipts that are normally not more than $25,000 should consider filing with the IRS anyway. This is done by completing the top portion of the return (name, address, and the like) and checking the box on line K. The purpose of this is to be certain that the IRS has the organization's correct address and realizes that the organization is not filing because it is not required to, rather than because it is unaware of or is ignoring the requirement. The IRS also requests that, when an organization of this type receives a Form 990 in the mail, the top portion of the return be filed using the mailing label" (Hopkins 1999, 217).

For all organizations, it is now federal law that an organization's filed Form 990 must be given to anyone who asks for it. If someone asks in person, the Form 990 must be immediately available. If the request is by telephone or mail, the organization has 30 days in which to mail back a copy. The organization may charge $1 for the first page and $.15 for each additional page (IRS Bulletin No. 1999-17, 6). To avoid having to copy the form, the organization may post its Form 990 on its own Web site (IRS Bulletin No. 1999-17, 7). GuideStar® (at www.guidestar.org) is a service of Philanthropic Research, Inc.—it is a Web site, which now contains information on more than 850,000 nonprofits. The IRS sends GuideStar the 990's, which GuideStar then posts on the GuideStar Web site.

While often the membership manager is not responsible for filling out the 990, there is an opportunity to have input. The 990 asks for basic information, which, if viewed from a marketing perspective, is an opportunity to talk about the work of the organization and mention how, if appropriate, members play a role. Considering that many people will be reviewing your 990s on the Internet in the future, do not overlook this opportunity to market the organization and membership.

Tax Deductibility

The one question that is always asked about membership dues is how much is tax deductible? The following is adapted from IRS Publication 526, *Charitable Contributions; Contributions You Can Deduct* (IRS 2000). This information is also shown in Exhibit 14–3.

Membership Fees or Dues

A member may be able to deduct membership fees or dues paid to a qualified organization. However, the member can deduct only the amount that is more than the value of the benefits received. The member cannot deduct dues, fees, or assessments paid to country clubs and other social organizations. They are not qualified organizations. (Refer to Exhibit 14–2.)

Certain membership benefits can be disregarded. The member and the organization can disregard certain membership benefits given in return for an annual payment of *$75 or less* to the qualified organization. The member can pay more than $75 to the organization if the organization does not require a larger payment to get the benefits. The benefits covered under this rule are:

Exhibit 14–3 Charitable Gift Receipt and Disclosure Rules, 2001

Written Statements		
Gifts of $250 or more	**Multiple gifts of <$250 from one donor in same year are not aggregated for purposes of this rule**	**Gift portion, not the entire payment, must be $250 or more**
Content	• Amount of cash, description of non-cash items donated • Statement of whether charity provided any goods or services ("benefits") in exchange (other than those that can be disregarded) • If benefits are provided, a description and good faith estimate of their value	Need not provide value of goods and services provided to employees or partners of donor Need not mention benefits that can be disregarded
Timing	Donor must have statement by earlier of due date for return, or actual filing date; single statement may cover multiple contributions by same donor	
Penalty	Contribution not deductible	
Volunteer expenses	Statement must include description of services provided by volunteer, instead of description of donated cash or other property	Need not specify date of services
Payroll deduction	Charity provides pledge card or other document stating that no benefits are provided in exchange for gift	Amount withheld from each paycheck is separate gift

continues

Exhibit 14–3 continued

CRTs	No substantiation required for gifts to charitable remainder trusts
Pooled income funds	Substantiation required; retained income interest not treated as benefit received in exchange for gift
Gift annuities	Substantiation required; annuity interest not treated as benefit received in exchange for gift
Matching gifts	Benefits are listed on the substantiation provided to the party receiving them, even if attributable to matching gifts made by another party

Quid pro quo gifts over $75		***Entire payment, not gift portion, exceeds $75***

Content	• Statement that the amount deductible for federal tax purposes is limited to the excess of the value of the property contributed over the value of any goods or services provided by the organization • Good faith estimate of value of benefits provided
Timing	In connection with solicitation or receipt of the gift
Penalty	$10 per gift, up to $5,000 per campaign or event, payable by charity

Benefits to be Disregarded

Insubstantial value	Items of insubstantial value, if value of all benefits is < 2 percent of payment and < $76	
Token items	Token items bearing charity's name or logo, if — • Donor's payment is >$38*, and • Only benefits received are bookmarks, calendars, key chains, mugs, posters, T-shirts, etc. bearing the organization's name or logo, and • Aggregate cost of all items for this donor for year is < $7.60*	
Newsletters	Members-only newsletters and program guides not of commercial quality (with primary purpose of informing members about activities)	
Frequently exercisable benefits	Annual membership benefits (other than access to college athletic tickets) that can be exercised frequently. Same benefit must be offered at a membership level of $75 or less.	Ex.: Free or discounted admission, gift shop discounts
Member events	Admission to members-only events with projected cost per person of < $7.60*. Same benefit must be offered at a membership level of $75 or less.	Ex.: "Meet-the-artist" event for membership

continues

Exhibit 14–3 continued

Employees	Benefits provided to employees of a corporate donor or partners of a partnership donor may be disregarded according to the same rules.	Ex.: Open house for employees of corporate donor

Good Faith Estimate of Value

Market value	Fair market value: price at which the property would change hands between a willing buyer and a willing seller, neither being under any compulsion to buy or sell and both having reasonable knowledge of relevant facts.	
Method	May use any reasonable method for valuation	
Unique items	Unique items can be valued based on similar or comparable items, without regard to the unique feature	Ex.: Value of dinner in art museum has same value as comparable dinner in restaurant
Celebrities	Celebrity presence has no additional value	Ex.: Dinner at Tiger Woods' house has same value as dinner at any private home.
Ticket access	Right to purchase college athletic tickets has value equal to 20 percent of the payment	Ex.: Where $200 donors have right to purchase tickets (at full price), value of the access to the tickets is 20 percent of $200.
Auctions	Tip: For auction items, list estimate of value (in addition to "minimum bid") in auction book	

*For 2001 gifts. Adjusted annually for inflation.
Source: J. Hazen Graves, Faegre & Benson LLP. Copyright 2001 Faegre & Benson. All rights reserved.

1. Any rights or privileges that can be used frequently while a member, such as:
   a. free or discounted admission to the organization's facilities or events
   b. free or discounted parking
   c. preferred access to goods or services
   d. discounts on the purchase of goods and services
2. Admission, while a member, to events that are open only to members of the organization if the organization reasonably projects that the cost per per-

son (excluding any allocated overhead) is not more than a specified amount, which may be adjusted annually for inflation. (This is the amount for low-cost articles given in the annual revenue procedure with inflation-adjusted amounts for the current year. This figure is available from the IRS.)

Token Items

You can deduct the entire payment to a qualified organization as a charitable contribution if both of the following are true:

1. There is a small item or other benefit of token value.
2. The qualified organization correctly determines that the value of the item or benefit received is not substantial and informs the members that they can deduct their payment in full.

The organization determines whether the value of an item or benefit is substantial by calling the IRS or an accountant.

Written Statement

A qualified organization must give the member a written statement if he or she makes a payment to it that is **more than $75** and is partly a contribution and partly for goods or services. The statement must tell the member that he or she can deduct only the amount of the payment that is more than the value of the goods or services received. It must also give a good-faith estimate of the value of those goods or services.

The organization can give the statement either when it solicits or when it receives the payment.

Exception. An organization will not have to give the member this statement if one of the following is true:

1. The member receives only items whose value is not substantial as described under "Token Items," earlier.
2. The member receives only membership benefits that can be disregarded, as described earlier.

Athletic Events

For colleges and universities that offer access to tickets to athletic events, follow the IRS rules from Publication 526 (Internal Revenue Service 2000, 3).

For alumni groups, access to athletic tickets can be a very powerful benefit. It needs to be handled in the appropriate manner. If the member makes a payment to, or for the benefit of, a college or university and, as a result, receives the right to buy tickets to an athletic event in the athletic stadium of the college or university, the member can deduct 80 percent of the payment as a charitable contribution. If any part of the payment is for tickets (rather than the right to buy tickets), that part is not deductible. In that case, subtract the price of the tickets from the payment. Eighty percent of the remaining amount is a charitable contribution.

Example 1. The member pays $300 a year for membership in an athletic scholarship program maintained by a university (a qualified organization). The only benefit of membership is that members have the right to buy one season ticket for a seat in a designated area of the stadium at the university's home football games. The member can deduct $240 (80 percent of $300) as a charitable contribution.

Example 2. The facts are the same as in Example 1 except that the $300 payment includes the purchase of one season ticket for the stated ticket price of $120. The member must subtract the usual price of a ticket ($120) from the $300 payment. The result is

$180. The deductible charitable contribution is $144 (80 percent of $180).

More examples are provided in Exhibit 14–3.

Reporting to Members

Members today are very cognizant of the tax-deductibility issue. Many will want receipts that state that their gift is fully tax deductible even if they do not need one. The membership manager needs to be ready to send the appropriate information when it is requested. Actually letting donors know how much of their gift is tax deductible can be done on the membership form itself (see Exhibit 14–4) or included in the information that the donor receives with his or her membership card and packet. Examples of wording that is most helpful to members include:

- For lower level members: "Membership is 100% tax deductible"
- For higher-level members: "$950 tax-deductible" (of a $1,000 membership).

Another way to say this is "All but $50 of your membership is considered to be tax-deductible." At the higher levels, every organization will have a different amount of tax deductibility for each of its levels, depending on the benefits offered. For one organization, it may be $950 of $1,000, for another it may be $890 of $1,000, and for yet another it may be $825 of $1,000. It is the responsibility of the organization to figure out what the tax-deductible amount is for the purposes of informing the members. Giving the amount or percent of tax deductibility is far preferable than saying, "Your membership is tax-deductible to the full extent of the law."

The membership manager may have to send another letter close to tax season when the donor cannot find the original letter.

Keeping copies of these letters or having the ability to generate them quickly is helpful for this reason. Some organizations choose to send a blanket acknowledgment to all donors at the end of the year along with another thank-you (see Exhibit 14–5).

Other Regulations

Closer to home, many states have their own nonprofit statutes. It is important to be up-to-date on what they are. If the state has laws governing fundraising, membership professionals should be aware of any that might have an impact on membership solicitations. A number of states now have registration and annual financial reporting requirements. Many states require specific wording on direct mail solicitations.

Additionally, some states now have rules governing telephone solicitation, which must be followed. These rules must be followed for the nonprofit's home state, and also for any state in which the nonprofit solicits.

Be aware that many states consider membership programs to be fundraising programs while other states recognize that bona fide membership programs are distinct from fundraising. Seeking expert legal advice about compliance issues is recommended.

There are currently attempts underway to deal with multiple registrations and filings for nonprofits that work in more than one state with a unified registration statement. Specific information can be found at the Web site nonprofits.org/library/gov/urs. The National Association of State Charities Officials (NASCO) and the National Association of Attorneys General (NAAG) have organized this Web site. It is also linked to GuideStar,® which says, "…this site attempts to 'consolidate the information and data requirements of all states that require registration of nonprofit organiza-

Exhibit 14–4 Membership Form With Tax Information

Sample Membership Levels and Benefits		
Individual	• Admission for one • Discount in shop • Invitations to events • Newsletter • 100% tax deductible	$40
Dual	• Above benefits for 2 adults and children under 16 • 100% tax deductible	$60
Dual plus	• Above benefits • Plus 4 guest passes • 100% tax deductible	$75
Contributor	• Above benefits • Plus 8 guest passes • Reciprocal admissions to other institutions • $120 is tax deductible	$150
Supporter	• Above benefits • Plus quarterly letter from the director • One-time discount on facility rental • $230 is tax deductible	$300
Patron	• Above benefits • Plus priority registration for member activities • 10 guest passes • Invitation to a behind-the-scenes tour with the director • $660 is tax deductible	$750
Benefactor	• Above benefits • Plus travel opportunities • Invitation to Awards dinner • $1,250 is tax deductible	$1,500

tions performing charitable solicitations within their jurisdictions.' It also lists which states require registration and provides specific details for each state" (www.guidestar.com). In addition, local chapters of AFP often have a government affairs committee that follows the state rules and regulations.

Nonprofits need to be cognizant of what is happening locally and nationally. Membership programs that are nonprofit need to be mindful of those laws that all nonprofits must heed. All membership programs need to be aware of the tax deductibility issues. Keeping up with these topics is not difficult because there is a lot of available informa-

Exhibit 14–5 Opera Theatre 2000 Tax Deduction Index

Please calculate the tax deductibility based upon your use of the following Opera Theatre benefits. Deduct the cost of those benefits you've enjoyed to determine the tax-deductible portion of your gift.

Description of Type of Gift	Non–Tax-Deductible Portion

Annual Fund/Friends of the Festival Membership
Please deduct the cost of those benefits used

Master Classes	$5/class
Parking	$4/performance
Poster	$45 (signed poster)
Libretti	$10/libretto
Tent dinner	$30/person
"Club Box" seats	$55/seat

OPERAtors Wine Tasting and Silent Auction (February 2000)

- For Wine Tasting attendees, non–tax-deductible portion . . . . $30 per person
- Auction purchases are deductible only above the value of purchased item.
- Grab bag purchases are non-deductible.

Guild Fans of the Ensemble (May 2000)

- For Fans attendees, non–tax-deductible portion . . . . $45 per person
- All contributions (non-attending donations) are 100% tax deductible.
- For Ensemble Member Sponsorship ($30), 100% is tax deductible.
- Raffle Ticket Purchases ($10/ticket) are not tax deductible.

Spring Gala (May 2000)

- For Gala attendees, non–tax-deductible portion . . . . $150 per person
- All contributions (non-attending donations) are 100% tax deductible.

Holiday Benefit (December 2000)

- For $200 tickets, non–tax-deductible portion . . . . $75 per person
- All contributions (non-attending donations) are 100% tax deductible.

Guild Autumn in France Event

- For $65 tickets, non–tax-deductible portion . . . . $30 per person
- All contributions (non-attending donations) are 100% tax deductible.

Other Contributions

"Special Projects" Contributions	100% tax deductible
All Endowment Gifts	100% tax deductible
OTSL or Guild Trip Contributions	100% tax deductible
Donated Tickets & Ticket Exchanges . . .	100% tax deductible
Tributes	100% tax deductible
Program Book Advertisements	Non–tax-deductible

Courtesy of Opera Theatre of Saint Louis, St. Louis, MO.

tion. AFP nationally provides legislative updates for members. Reading periodicals that follow the nonprofit sector is another way to stay abreast of changes. As noted above, information is also available on the Internet through Web sites such as GuideStar. In the case of legal and reporting issues that can have an impact on a membership program, ignorance is not bliss.

Conflict of Interest

Another legal issue that a membership manager can face is that of conflict of interest. It is always an ethical question and can become a legal one, depending on the state statutes regulating nonprofits. Conflicts of interest occur sometimes because someone is trying to help and sometimes because people are interested in personal gain. Because a large membership program can spend a significant amount of money for vendors selling items such as printing, direct mail, telemarketing, catering, "goodies"— the token gifts—and market research, it is helpful to have policies in place to avoid these situations.

The conflict occurs when someone active in the program, perhaps a board member or his or her relative, receives personal gain from a transaction. Having a policy that requires three bids on items over a certain amount of money makes certain that transactions are fair to both the vendors and the nonprofit. This does not mean that those who are involved cannot do business with the nonprofit. The issue here is both the appearance and the reality of fairness. It does a program no good in the community if it appears that all business is going in one direction without others having an opportunity to bid on it.

SUMMARY

Obeying the law, learning from various codes of ethics, using a sound ethical decision making model, protecting member privacy, maintaining proper list ownership, and providing effective stewardship will all build trust between the organization and its members. This in turn will help secure the future for the organization and help ensure a successful career for the membership professional.

References

Association of Fundraising Professionals. 2001. *Code of ethical principles and standards of professional practice.* Alexandria, VA.

Association of Professional Researchers for Advancement. *Statement of ethics, September 1998,* www.aprahome.organization, accessed February 19, 2002.

Direct Marketing Association. *Privacy promise member compliance guide,* October 1997, www.dma.org, accessed February 19, 2002.

Equifax/Harris. 1996. 1996 Equifax/Harris *Consumer Privacy Survey.* http://www.mindspring.com/~mdeeb/equifax/cc/parchive/svry96/survy96a.html, accessed February 19, 2002.

Fischer, M. 2000. *Ethical decision making in fund raising.* New York: John Wiley & Sons.

Graphic, Visualization, and Usability Center. Georgia Tech University. 1998. *Tenth WWW User Survey,* www.gvu.gatech.edu/user_surveys/survey_1998, accessed February 19, 2002.

Hopkins, B. 1999. *The second legal answer book for nonprofit organizations.* New York: John Wiley & Sons.

U.S. Department of Health and Human Services. 2000. *Standards for privacy of individually identifiable health information,* www.hhs.gov/ocr/hipaa, accessed February 19, 2002.

U.S. Internal Revenue Service. 2000. Publication 526: *Charitable contributions you can deduct,* www.irs.gov, accessed February 19, 2002.

U.S. Internal Revenue Service. 2002. *The Digital Daily:* Charities and Non-Profits, Filing Requirements, www.irs.gov, accessed February 19, 2002.

Planning Worksheets

Exhibit A–1 Acquisition Planning Worksheet

PLANNING WORKSHEET
ACQUISITION

SELECT A FOCUS _____

_____

OBJECTIVE   1. _____

_____

ACTION PLANS   a._____
                     b._____
                     c._____
                     d._____

OBJECTIVE   2. _____

_____

ACTION PLANS   a._____
                     b._____
                     c._____
                     d._____

OBJECTIVE   3. _____

_____

ACTION PLANS   a._____
                     b._____
                     c._____
                     d._____

Exhibit A–2 Renewal Planning Worksheet

PLANNING WORKSHEET
RENEWALS
CURRENT MEMBERS/LAPSED MEMBERS

SELECT A FOCUS _____

_____

OBJECTIVE   1. _____

_____

ACTION PLANS   a._____
                       b._____
                       c._____
                       d._____

OBJECTIVE   2. _____

_____

ACTION PLANS   a._____
                       b._____
                       c._____
                       d._____

OBJECTIVE   3. _____

_____

ACTION PLANS   a._____
                       b._____
                       c._____
                       d._____

Exhibit A–3 Upgrades Planning Worksheet

PLANNING WORKSHEET
UPGRADES

SELECT A FOCUS _____

_____

OBJECTIVE   1. _____

_____

ACTION PLANS   a._____
                      b._____
                      c._____
                      d._____

OBJECTIVE   2. _____

_____

ACTION PLANS   a._____
                      b._____
                      c._____
                      d._____

OBJECTIVE   3. _____

_____

ACTION PLANS   a._____
                      b._____
                      c._____
                      d._____

Exhibit A–4 Activities Planning Worksheet

**PLANNING WORKSHEET
ACTIVITIES**

SELECT A FOCUS _____

_____

OBJECTIVE 1. _____

_____

ACTION PLANS a._____

b._____

c._____

d._____

OBJECTIVE 2. _____

_____

ACTION PLANS a._____

b._____

c._____

d._____

OBJECTIVE 3. _____

_____

ACTION PLANS a._____

b._____

c._____

d._____

Exhibit A–5 Other Planning Worksheet

PLANNING WORKSHEET
OTHER

SELECT A FOCUS _____

_____

OBJECTIVE 1. _____

_____

ACTION PLANS a._____
b._____
c._____
d._____

OBJECTIVE 2. _____

_____

ACTION PLANS a._____
b._____
c._____
d._____

OBJECTIVE 3. _____

_____

ACTION PLANS a._____
b._____
c._____
d._____

Report Worksheets

Table B–1 Flow of New Members Worksheet

FLOW OF NEW MEMBERS

	JAN	FEB	MAR	APR	MAY	JUN	JUL	AUG	SEP	OCT	NOV	DEC	TOTAL
Direct Mail													
On-site													
Online													
Gifts													
Admissions													
Shop sales													
Miscellaneous													
Total													

Table B–2 Members by Month Worksheet

MEMBERS BY MONTH

	JAN	FEB	MAR	APR	MAY	JUN	JUL	AUG	SEP	OCT	NOV	DEC	TOTAL
New members													
Renewing members													
Total													

Table B–3 Monthly Membership Projections Worksheet

MONTHLY MEMBERSHIP PROJECTIONS

	JAN	FEB	MAR	APR	MAY	JUN	JUL	AUG	SEP	OCT	NOV	DEC	TOTAL
Renewals Due													
Renewal rate for:													
1st notice													
2nd notice													
3rd notice													
Total renewals													
Renewals to date													
New members													
New members to date													
Members by month													
Members to date													

Table B–4 Membership Cash Flow Projections Worksheet

MEMBERSHIP CASH FLOW PROJECTIONS

	JAN	FEB	MAR	APR	MAY	JUN	JUL	AUG	SEP	OCT	NOV	DEC	TOTAL
Members by month													
Member category distribution													
(Dollar amount × percentage × members by month)													
$XX%													
$XX%													
$XX%													
$XX%													
$XX%													
Total Revenue													
Revenue year to date													

APPENDIX C

Budgets and Members

MEMBERSHIP PROGRAMS VARY IN many ways, but the one issue that all programs must work with is budget. The following are suggestions for what a program of a certain size might do. The suggestions and amounts are guidelines, not absolutes; each organization needs to determine what is best for its program. For example, when a program is small, under 2,000 members, the ratio of income to expenses can be as high as 80 percent, or the program may lose money for the first few years while it is starting. Much depends on the size of the organization, whether the program is stand-alone or part of a larger institution. A large institution beginning a membership program may already have an extensive newsletter that is charged to another department; a start-up organization may have board members willing to contribute printing and design work and not have to pay for these services. As said, it all depends.

The budgets shown here for small groups assume that everything is done in a minimal way. A new organization could as easily spend money on direct mail to reach a critical mass quickly (if its leaders believe it can), print beautiful brochures, and immediately hire staff. The organization must decide which way it wants to proceed; there is no one right answer for all organizations. At about 3,000 members, the costs start to be about one-half of the income—income of $150,000 will cost about $75,000 to generate. Again, the program could choose to lose money for the start-up years and consider it an investment in the institution's future. The 2:1 ratio exists until a program reaches about 50,000 members, when economies of scale become significant.

These projections are made on the basis of an average gift of $50. If the actual amount asked for at the first level in a graduated dues structure is $50, the average gift will actually be about $55 because some members will give at higher levels. At institutions with many support members, the income will be far greater than the amounts suggested here.

EXAMPLE 1: BUDGET OF $1,000 TO $2,000; UP TO 500 MEMBERS

The income from a program with 100 members and an average gift of $50 is $5,000; with expenses at $1,000, the net is $4,000, or 80 percent, a high rate of return on investment. A program this size would be new or appeal to a very small prospective membership base. It would be staffed by one or more volunteers and assumes that there is some computer capability, either in a volunteer's home or at the organization's office. As many in-kind donations as possible should be solicited for items such as printing, paper, mailing, incentives for joining, or refreshments for events. The

major costs will be copying/printing and postage. This budget assumes that everything is kept very simple.

Acquisition must be done with personal solicitation, either in person or by personal letter, and with letters sent to names suggested by board members, staff, volunteers, and others close to the organization. Memberships should be solicited at the facility (e.g., museum), if it is a visitation-based institution. Use personal contact for renewal follow-up in addition to the notices. For recordkeeping, the organization should use an off-the-shelf database program or 4"x 6" cards to keep information. Provide an address, regular and/or e-mail, for members' questions and comments and/or provide a telephone number if someone is there to answer it in a timely manner. Recognition for members should be included in the newsletter and at the events.

EXAMPLE 2: BUDGET OF $15,000; 1,000 MEMBERS

With a $50 average gift, the income will be $50,000; net to organization is $35,000. The program is staffed mainly with volunteer help. If paid staff is possible, consider paying a person for a few hours a month to send out renewals and help with mailings. In addition to the above, add one or two small direct mail campaigns of 5,000 to 10,000 names from an exchange with a like organization, if possible. Use an incentive for the direct mail program, such as a mug or a tote bag. Consider adding a members' day or reception and increase the newsletter to six times a year. At this point, the program income to expense ratio is about 2:1 or better—about $35,000 in income is generated for $15,000 in expenses.

Exhibit C–1 Budget of $1,000–$2,000: Up to 500 Members

	100 MEMBERS (New Program)	500 MEMBERS (Small Program)
BUDGET OF $1,000–$2,000 UP TO 500 MEMBERS		
ACQUISITION		
Membership brochure		
Desktop publishing; 1,000 copied	150	150
5 mailings of 200 each, bulk @ $0.15 each	150	150
Computer generated personalized letters on organization's stationery; personal notes included from someone prospect knows	0	0
Membership cards		
Desktop publishing; 1,000 copied or printed	20	20
Mailing membership packet with thank-you letter, card, list of benefits @ $0.50 each	50	250
RENEWALS		
Monthly personalized letters, assume average of two renewal notices per member @ $0.50	100	250
COMMUNICATIONS		
Newsletter 4 times a year		
Desktop publishing; copying; mailing (bulk mail for 500)	175	400
Invitations to two events	100	300
ACTIVITIES		
Two events		
Pro bono speakers, refreshments donated	0	0
Miscellaneous	100	100
Miscellaneous membership supplies	150	200
	$995	**$1,820**

EXAMPLE 3: BUDGET OF $75,000; 3,000 MEMBERS

With a $50 average gift, the income will be $150,000; net to organization is $75,000. If there is a 75 percent renewal rate, the program will need to generate 750 new members per year to remain sta-ble. This will take direct mail, on-site solicitation if possible, and continued personal solicitation of members. The program has now passed the critical mass stage and needs staff. There should be one half-time person, whose main responsibilities would be doing data entry, sending out membership packets, sending out re-

Exhibit C–2 Budget of $15,000: 1,000 Members

<table>
<tr><td colspan="2" align="center">**BUDGET OF $15,000**
1,000 MEMBERS</td></tr>
<tr><td></td><td align="right">**1,000 MEMBERS**</td></tr>
<tr><td colspan="2">**ACQUISITION**</td></tr>
<tr><td>Membership brochure</td><td></td></tr>
<tr><td>　2,000 Designed and printed</td><td></td></tr>
<tr><td>　for use in personal solicitation letters and</td><td></td></tr>
<tr><td>　on-site solicitation to generate 150 members</td><td align="right">1,500</td></tr>
<tr><td>Two direct mail campaigns of 2,500 ($1.00 per piece)</td><td align="right">5,000</td></tr>
<tr><td>　Assumes lists by exchange, no cost</td><td></td></tr>
<tr><td>　to generate 100 new members</td><td></td></tr>
<tr><td>Membership cards</td><td></td></tr>
<tr><td>　Desktop publishing; 2,000 copied or printed</td><td align="right">200</td></tr>
<tr><td>Mailing membership packet with thank-you letter,</td><td></td></tr>
<tr><td>　card, list of benefits @ $0.50 each</td><td align="right">500</td></tr>
<tr><td colspan="2">**RENEWALS**</td></tr>
<tr><td>Monthly personalized letters, assume average of two</td><td></td></tr>
<tr><td>　renewal notices per member @ $0.50</td><td align="right">1,000</td></tr>
<tr><td colspan="2">**COMMUNICATIONS**</td></tr>
<tr><td>Newsletter 4 times a year</td><td></td></tr>
<tr><td>　Desktop publishing; copying</td><td align="right">2,000</td></tr>
<tr><td>Invitations to two events</td><td align="right">1,000</td></tr>
<tr><td colspan="2">**ACTIVITIES**</td></tr>
<tr><td>Two events</td><td></td></tr>
<tr><td>　Pro bono speakers, refreshments donated</td><td align="right">0</td></tr>
<tr><td>　Miscellaneous</td><td align="right">500</td></tr>
<tr><td>**Miscellaneous membership supplies**</td><td align="right">500</td></tr>
<tr><td>**Staffing**</td><td></td></tr>
<tr><td>　20 hours per month @ $10.00 per hour (20 × 12 × 10)</td><td align="right">2,400</td></tr>
<tr><td></td><td align="right">**$14,600**</td></tr>
</table>

newals, and answering any membership questions. This may be half of the time from a full-time staff member who also has other responsibilities; however, the staff person needs to consider the membership program as a major responsibility. With this size program, add volunteer telephoning for renewal follow-up. Add an event.

If there is not enough volunteer time for activities and communications, and the organization has other staff, these will become additional responsibilities of that staff. For example, the development direc-

Exhibit C–3 Budget of $75,000: 3,000 Members

BUDGET OF $75,000
3,000 MEMBERS

	3,000 MEMBERS
ACQUISITION	
Membership brochure	
5,000 Designed and printed	
for use in personal solicitation letters and	
on-site solicitation to generate 350 members	3,000
Two direct mail campaigns of 20,000 ($0.75 per piece)	30,000
to generate 400 new members	
Membership cards	
Letters with card attached 4,000 @ $0.30	1,200
Mailing membership packet with thank-you letter,	
card, list of benefits @ $0.60 each	1,800
RENEWALS	
Monthly personalized letters, assume average	
of two renewal notices per member @ $0.50	3,000
COMMUNICATIONS	
Newsletter 4 times a year	
Designed and Printed	
3,000 members @ $0.75	9,000
Three invitations to events @ $0.75	6,750
ACTIVITIES	
Three events	
• Pro bono speakers, refreshments donated	
One event with cost	1,000
Miscellaneous	500
Miscellaneous membership supplies	1,200
Staffing	
20 hours per week plus benefits	17,000
	$74,450

tor might be responsible for the overall management of the program; the public relations staff person might be responsible for the newsletter and other communications; and events would stay under volunteer management. The budget increase will be spent on the staffing, increasing the direct mail, and using a mail house for all mailings. Also by this time, computer software will be necessary. This budget assumes that the capital expenditure for this equipment and software is taken care of by capital funds,

Exhibit C–4 Budget of $500,000: 20,000 Members

	20,000 MEMBERS
BUDGET OF $500,000 **20,000 MEMBERS**	
ACQUISITION	
Membership brochure	
25,000 Designed and printed	
for use in personal solicitation letters and	
on-site solicitation to generate 1,000 members	12,000
Three direct mail campaigns of 100,000 ($0.50 per piece)	150,000
to generate 3,000 new members	
Membership cards	
Letters with card attached 20,000 @ $0.30	6,000
Mailing membership packet with thank-you letter,	
card, list of benefits @ $0.40 each	8,000
RENEWALS	
Monthly personalized letters, assume an average of	16,000
two renewals per member @ $0.40	
COMMUNICATIONS	
Newsletter 6 times a year @ $1.00	120,000
Invitations to four events @ $0.40	32,000
ACTIVITIES	
Four events	
A mix of lectures, social, networking and interest	
related events	10,000
Miscellaneous membership supplies	5,000
Staffing	
Four full time staff plus benefits	140,000
	$500,000

not the operating budget of the membership program.

EXAMPLE 4: BUDGET OF $500,000; 20,000 MEMBERS

With a $50 average gift, the income will be $1,000,000; net to the organization is about $500,000. If there is a 75 percent renewal rate, the program will need to generate 5,000 new members per year to remain stable. This will take direct mail, on-site solicitation, if possible, and continued personal solicitation. This program needs four staff people: one to manage the program, including planning, activities and communications; and three for data entry, renewals, and

Exhibit C–5 Budget of $1,000,000: 50,000 Members

BUDGET OF $1,000,000
50,000 MEMBERS

	50,000 MEMBERS
ACQUISITION	
Membership brochure	
75,000 Designed and printed	
for use in personal solicitation letters and	
on-site solicitation to generate 1,000 members	20,000
On-site program	30,000
to generate 2,000 new members	
Three direct mail campaigns of 200,000 ($0.50 per piece)	300,000
to generate 6,000 new members	
Membership cards	
Letters with card attached 50,000 @ $0.30	15,000
Mailing membership packet with thank-you letter,	
card, list of benefits @ $0.40 each	20,000
RENEWALS	
Monthly personalized letters, assumes an average of	
two renewal notices per member	22,500
Lapsed member campaign: telemarketing	
(calling 8,000–10,000 names) 1,000 members	35,000
COMMUNICATIONS	
Newsletter 6 times a year @ $0.75	225,000
Invitations to six events @ $0.20	60,000
ACTIVITIES	
Six events	
A mix of lectures, social, networking and interest	
related events	50,000
Miscellaneous membership supplies	10,000
Staffing	
Nine full time staff plus benefits	300,000
	$1,087,500

member service. Additional monies must be spent on direct mail and other acquisition methods, more renewal follow-up, and more activities and communications. Benefits are increased as seems appropriate. Add tele-phoning for renewal follow-up, and add a lapsed-member campaign. Add another event. Volunteers in this program will be helpful in creating and implementing events, telephoning for renewals, and on-site solicitation. If there is not enough volunteer time for these activities, consider outsourcing some projects and including other staff in other projects. For example, the public relations staff person might be responsible for the newsletter and other communications and events.

EXAMPLE 5: BUDGET OF $1,000,000; 50,000 MEMBERS

With a $50 average gift, the income will be $2,500,000 and net to the organization is about $1,350,000. At this point there are economies of scale, which begin to increase the ratio of income to expenses. If there is a 75 percent renewal rate, the program will need to generate 12,500 new members each year to remain stable. This will take direct mail, on-site solicitation, if possible, and continued personal solicitation. This program needs nine staff people: one to manage the program, including planning, activities, and communications; one to help with events and communications; and seven for data entry, renewals, and member service, including one as supervisor. Funds must be spent on direct mail and other acquisition methods, more renewal follow-up, and more activities and communications. If the renewal rate can be raised to 80 percent, new member acquisition can be lowered or growth can come with the acquisition.

Benefits are increased as seems appropriate. Add paid professional telephoning for renewal follow-up, and add several lapsed-member direct mail campaigns yearly. Volunteers in this program will be helpful in creating and implementing events, and on-site and other acquisition solicitations. Direct mail and telemarketing should be outsourced unless the organization has the capability of in-house printing and/or telephoning. A mail house takes care of all mailings, except those for special activities for upper-level (support) members' events, which may be hand addressed by volunteers.

Case Studies

CASE STUDY 1: NATIONAL BASEBALL HALL OF FAME AND MUSEUM— THE BASICS WORK

THIS IS AN EXCELLENT EXAMPLE OF how a program can develop from 3,000 members and net income of $7,000 to one of 13,000 members and net income of $314,000 in three years by doing some very basic things. The National Baseball Hall of Fame and Museum has also incorporated significant use of its Web site.

1980–1997: The Hall of Fame Fan Club

- Single level of membership
- Average of 2,500 to 3,500 members annually
- Limited on-site presence for membership
- Limited direct mail
- One letter renewal, with a renewal rate of 60 percent
- Three-week turnaround for new members and renewals

- Revenue of $102,000
- Net of $6,800

1998: Re-launched as Friends of the Hall of Fame

- Graduated tiers of membership
- Limited on-site presence
- Limited direct mail
- Nonsecure Web presence
- One letter renewal, with a renewal rate of 55 percent
- 3,441 enrolled
- Three-week turnaround for new members and renewals
- Revenue of $189,000
- Net of $112,000

1999: Friends of the Hall of Fame

- Graduated tiers of membership
- Limited on-site presence
- Limited direct mail
- Nonsecure Web presence
- 4,899 enrolled
- Three-week turnaround for new members and renewals
- Revenue of $342,000
- Net of $223,000

2000: Increased Profile

- New marketing materials
- Member activities
- Increased on-site presence
- Direct mail acquisition
- Three-letter renewal sequence
- Secure Web presence
- 13,000 enrolled—increased from 4,899
- Turnaround 48 hours or less
- Revenue of $625,000
- Net of $314,000
- Fulfillment in 48 hours because
  - premiums selected for rapid fulfillment

- welcome letter, membership card, gift message combined and mailed immediately upon processing
- premiums shipped ASAP after welcome package
- print pieces shipped direct from printer
- fulfillment currently in-house
- renewal clerk hired

Increased Online Activity

- Promotions for Hall of Fame now directed toward having people visit the Web site rather than visiting Cooperstown
- April 2000: 150,000 Web visitors, with 110 members enrolled
- April 2001: 191,000 Web visitors, with 110 members enrolled
- May 2001: launch of direct e-mail program
  - knowledge-based e-newsletter
  - content- and mission-driven format
  - opt-out option
  - custom offers
  - full tracking of click through activity

Courtesy of The National Baseball Hall of Fame and Museum, Cooperstown, New York.

CASE STUDY 2: ARIZONA-SONORA DESERT MUSEUM—IMPROVING AN ALREADY SUCCESSFUL PROGRAM

The Arizona-Sonora Desert Museum's membership program is an example of a program that had experienced success in terms of membership size, but still had much potential to continue growing. This program needed tweaking in order to produce more revenue and to improve its renewal rate and renewal strategies.

1999: Membership Status

- 19,915 members
- Approximately $875,985 in membership revenues
- 4,596 new members annually
- On-site membership sales predominant source of new members
- No direct mail since early 1990s
- One letter renewal, with renewal rate of 60 percent
- Three-week turnaround for membership processing
- Two data entry staff, one manager
- Net $601,046

2000: Renewed Emphasis on Membership

- Developed strategic plan for membership.
- Conducted a membership audit of entire program.
- Re-instituted aggressive use of direct mail, with three campaigns per year.
- Mailed 175,000 pieces, attracted 1,843 new direct mail members, with a healthy 1.04 percent response rate, but a low average gift of $43.
- Recaptured 960 lapsed members via a telemarketing campaign with a 75 percent credit card rate.

- Had a Web presence, was able to process memberships online.
- Instituted a four-letter renewal system, with renewal rate of 72 percent.
- Acquired 6,601 new members.
- Increased to 23,500 members, for an 18 percent growth in one year.
- Continued three-week turnaround for membership processing.
- Increased revenue to $1,035,085, for an 18.6 percent increase in one year.
- Had net of $544,558.

2001: After Two Years of a Growth Focus

- New membership marketing materials
- New membership categories, increased dues
- Direct mail acquisition: 225,000 pieces generated 2,100 new members, with a greatly increased average gift of $54
- Four letter renewal sequence, with a renewal rate of 75 percent
- 21,869 members (a decrease in members, but with an increase in revenues. Did not repeat a telemarketing campaign that generated 960 members in previous year; visitation and on-site sales at gate were down)
- Revenue of $1,157,797
- Net of $825,501

Appendix E

Software Options

T HERE ARE MANY SOFTWARE OP-tions for recordkeeping for a membership program. For many programs, adding a membership module to current fundraising software may be the answer. For others, especially small or new groups, using a database program such as FileMaker or Microsoft Access may be a good solution. It is important to do the "homework" before making a software decision.

DOING THE HOMEWORK

If deciding on software for the first time or considering a change, questions to be answered include:

1. What is the plan for growth?
2. How quickly will it grow?
3. Who will be using the program?
   a. Single user?
   b. Multi-users?
4. What will be the computer hardware capabilities?
   a. Windows or Macintosh?
   b. Single computer?

c. Server and network?

d. Power and size?

e. Speed?

5. Will the membership be the donor base? If so, will donor information be kept as well as membership information?

6. Is there a need for other software capabilities, such as event management or ticket sales?

7. Is there technical support available for the software program from the vendor?

8. What are the yearly costs for software support and upgrades (new versions)?

9. How "user friendly" is the software program?

10. What training is available?

a. What is the cost?

b. Is it available locally? Or will there be travel?

c Is it available on video or CD-ROM?

11. Is there a user group in the area, so that there is some local support?

12. Does the membership software program need to interface with an accounting program?

13. If there is an interest in using the Internet for membership, is there a way to use the software with the Internet?

14. If converting from one software program system to another, how does the conversion work?

a. What is the cost?

b. How much time is involved?

15. How much funding is available?

a. Is it possible to find funding for the data needs?

Answer the above questions, and speak to other organizations to find out what they are using and how their software programs work.

Check the vendor Web sites, and ask for information from five or six of the vendors whose products fit the organization's needs. After reading and examining the information (a CD-ROM with a sample will often be included), ask three of the vendors for a proposal. Make the decision. From beginning to end, this process will take as little as a few weeks (if using an off-the-shelf software program) to several months if using a more complicated software program.

At least once a year, nonprofit publications such as the *Chronicle of Philanthropy*, *NonProfit Times*, and *Contributions* have a section devoted to software. At least two Web sites have long lists of vendors: The Nonprofit Software Index at www.npinfotech.org and Charity Village at charityvillage.com/marketplace/software.

The following list is a small sample of the vendors who currently provide software. New vendors appear periodically and current ones disappear. This list does not imply an endorsement, but rather is given here as a service to those who work in membership.

SOFTWARE VENDORS

Ascend

Ascend Technologies

800-756-7483 or 319-626-5490

www.Ascend-tech.com

Convio

888-528-9501 or 512-652-2600

www.convio.com

DonorPerfect

SofterWare, Inc. 800-220-8111 or 215-628-3209

www.donorperfect.com

eTapestry.com

(Runs on the Internet)

888-739-3827 or 317-545-4170
www.eTapestry.com

FileMaker
800-325-2747
www.filemaker.com

GiftMakerPRO
Campagne Associates
800-582-3489
www.campagne.com

iMIS Fund Raising
Advanced Solutions International, Inc.
800-727-8682 or 512-491-0550
www.advsol.com

JSI Paradigm
JSI FundRaising Systems, Inc.
800-521-0132
www.jsi.com/frs

Microsoft Access
800-642-7676
www.microsoft.com/office/access

Paciolan
Paciolan Systems, Inc.
562-595-7900 or 866-722-4652
www.paciolan.com

The Raiser's Edge
Blackbaud, Inc.
800-443-9441
www.blackbaud.com

VISTA Software
2b Technology
800-296-8464 or 804-421-8400
www.tmvista.com

Glossary and Benchmarks

There is much jargon with membership programs. The following are some of the terms that are frequently used. The benchmarks are included where applicable for use as a rule of thumb. Each organization, however, is different, and the benchmarks for any individual institution may vary.

Acquisition: The process of asking prospects to join the organization's membership. Acquisition methods include direct mail, telemarketing, personal solicitation, and many other methods.

Ask: The solicitation of a gift. The ask is the actual "asking" for the gift and sometimes refers to the amount of the gift.

Average gift: The average of all gifts received. It is the calculation of the total amount of revenue generated divided by the number of respondents. For example, if $50,000 is raised from 1,000 members, the average gift is $50. In acquisition campaigns, the average gift is equal to about $5.00 more than the most popular entry-level membership category.

Benefits: The items that are offered in exchange for joining the organization. Benefits may be tangible, such as a newsletter or free admission, or intangible, such as pride and esteem.

BRE: See Business reply envelope.

Business reply envelope (BRE): A business reply envelope (BRE) is often included with a membership solicitation to make it easy for the potential member to return the form. A BRE is printed with postage paid by the organization, though some organizations indicate on the envelope that if the member uses a stamp, it will save the organization money. The organization must collect those BREs with stamps and return them to the post office for a refund.

Cost per dollar raised: The cost to raise $1 in donations. Divide the total cost of the campaign by the total amount raised. For example, a campaign cost of $4,000 divided by $5,000 raised equals $.80 cost per dollar raised. In direct mail, the most expensive acquisition method, it may cost $1.25 to $1.50 to raise $1. "Profits" are realized in year two or year three with membership renewals.

Dedupe: See Deduplication.

Deduplication: The merging of mailing lists for the purpose of eliminating the duplicates. Also known as merge/ purge processing.

Downgrade: A member who chooses to decrease his or her membership level.

Drop: The term used when a campaign mails at the post office; or for a particular mailing. For example, there might be a May drop and a September drop.

Dues: The amount paid for a membership. Sometimes called the donation or contribution for the membership.

First-year member: A new member during his or her first year of membership. The first year renewal rate will be lower than the overall renewal rate. The first year renewal rate should be at least 50 percent.

Five-year income: What a campaign produces financially if the five-year life of a member is taken into consideration. First-, second-, third-, and fourth-year renewal rates must be known and taken into consideration.

Flat dues: A dues structure that offers dues at one level. All members pay the same amount. See Graduated dues.

Fulfillment: The act of generating and distributing the appropriate information and benefits to a member who joins or renews.

Graduated dues: A dues structure that has multilevel dues. A member selects the dues level at which he or she joins. Different benefits are offered at each level. See Flat dues.

Incentive: A gift that is offered to encourage joining or renewing. Examples include a tote bag, mug, and so forth. Used interchangeably with "premium."

Kill file: The file of names of those who do not want to receive direct mail or tele-

marketing from the organization. Also called a suppression file.

Lapsed Member: One who has been a member, but not renewed within a specified renewal cycle, usually about six months.

Lifetime value: The monetary value of a member over the time lifetime of his or her membership. When the organization knows the average length of time of membership (e.g., ten years), it is possible to determine the lifetime value.

Lockbox: A service from a bank or other company that receives the member's enrollment form, receives and opens the members enrollment form, deposits the check, and sends a report to the institution.

Membership: The belonging to an organization or institution that involves receiving benefits and being a part of a membership program.

Merge/purge: The merging of mailing lists for the purpose of purging the duplicates. Also known as "deduplication" or "deduping."

Multi-year member: A member who has renewed at least once. Multi-year renewal rates should range from 80 to 95 percent.

Multis: Names that appear in duplicate when all mailing lists are merged and before duplicates are removed. Multis may be mailed to more than once because they appear on more than one list. A response rate of 50 to 80 percent of the response rate of the first mailing can be expected in a follow-up mailing to multis.

Premium: A gift that is offered to encourage joining or renewing. Examples are items like tote bags and mugs. Used interchangeably with "incentive."

Pull: The productivity of a direct mail campaign; the response a direct mail campaign generates. A campaign that "pulled" a 1 percent response rate produced a response rate of 1 percent.

Renewal: The process of asking members to renew and continue their membership; a member who has renewed.

Renewal rates: The rate at which members renew their membership. Renewal rates for multi-year members should range between 80 and 95 percent. Renewal rates for first-year members should be between 45 and 50 percent, but will be lower than the rate for multi-year members. The overall renewal rate should be between 70 and 80 percent.

Response Rate: The responses received in a direct mail campaign divided by the number mailed. For example, 50 responses divided by 5,000 mailed equals a 1.0 percent response rate. In direct mail acquisition, the response rate should be between 0.5 and 1 percent. In some circumstances (e.g., a new organization, announcing a blockbuster exhibit, a controversial issue), the response rate can be as high as 2 percent.

Retention: The retaining of members. The retention rate is the renewal rate.

Return On Investment (ROI): The return on the money invested in a campaign, or the amount that will be returned to the organization for every dollar spent. For example, $5,000 raised divided by the $4,000 spent equals $1.25 ROI. This campaign produced $1.25 of revenue for every $1.00 spent on the effort.

ROI: See Return on investment.

Roll out: The mailing of a large number of direct mail appeals after testing with a smaller quantity.

SCF: See Sectional center facility.

Sectional center facility (SCF): The first three digits of a ZIP code; a reference to the postal handling facility; used when ordering lists for direct mail.

Stewardship: The actions taken to make certain that the member's gift is properly spent and accounted for.

Support member: A member who elects a dues or donation level that is clearly more than the perceived economic value of the membership. The donation made includes financial support for the institution. In many organizations, support-member levels of membership become donor clubs to recognize this support. See Value member.

Suppression file: The file of names of those who do not want to receive direct mail or telemarketing from the organization. Also called a kill file.

Upgrade: A member who chooses to increase his or her membership level.

Value member: A member who elects a dues or donation level that provides the tangible benefits that are of interest. The perceived value of the membership is equivalent to or more than the dues contributed. The donation made may or may not include financial support for the institution; however, the motivation to join is in the benefits. In an organization with graduated dues, the first several levels will usually be value levels. See Support member.

Index